THE DUBLIN SCUFFLE

THE
DUBLIN
SCUFFLE

John Dunton

With an introduction and notes by
ANDREW CARPENTER

FOUR COURTS PRESS
in association with the
NATIONAL LIBRARY OF IRELAND

Typeset in 11 pt on 14 pt Caslon by
Carrigboy Typesetting Services, County Cork for
FOUR COURTS PRESS LTD
Fumbally Court, Fumbally Lane, Dublin 8, Ireland
e-mail: info@four-courts-press.ie
and in North America for
FOUR COURTS PRESS
c/o ISBS, 5804 N.E. Hassalo Street, Portland, OR 97213.

A catalogue record for this title is available
from the British Library.

ISBN 1–85182–446–4

**This edition is limited to six hundred copies,
one hundred of which are *hors commerce*.**

Printed in England
by MPG Books, Bodmin, Cornwall

Contents

List of Illustrations

Introduction

John Dunton, author of *The Dublin Scuffle*—one of the most curious books ever written about Ireland—was born in 1659, son of the Reverend John Dunton, rector of Grafham, Huntingdonshire. Not only Dunton's father but his grandfather and great-grandfather (all bearing the name John Dunton) had been ordained ministers of the Church of England—a fact which this John Dunton never forgot. His mother died shortly after Dunton's birth and his father went to Ireland for about four years where he acted as chaplain to Sir Henry Ingoldsby, governor of Limerick. The young John Dunton was left in England to be educated. He later vividly described his experience of being at school where mistakes of grammar had often 'steer'd my penitent Buttocks to a Burchen Wood, and made the Butt-end of my Person weep Carnation Tears'.[1]

Despite his father's wish that he should proceed to ordination, Dunton was obviously not suited for a career in the church and he was bound apprentice to the famous London nonconformist bookseller Thomas Parkhurst in December 1674. Eight years later, in 1682, Dunton set up shop as a printer, publisher and bookseller in London. Soon there appeared a stream of books printed by or for John Dunton 'at the Black Raven' (his trade sign) 'in the Poultrey', an old poultry market where several booksellers of similar political and religious views as his own—that is, Whig and strongly Protestant— had their shops. Dunton's early publications were mostly sermons or small devotional works with titles like *Directions and Perswasions to a sound Conversion* (Parks 16) and *A Necessary Companion for a Serious Christian* (Parks 21). Other volumes were for a wider audience and reflected Dunton's own interest in the nature of the world at large. He also favoured flamboyant titles. It is hard to resist seeking out a work such as the following, which Dunton published early in 1684:

---

1 John Dunton, *A Voyage round the World* (London, 1691), i, 60 (quoted in Parks, p. 7).

The Amazement of Future Ages: or, this swaggering world turn'd up-side down. By which means the astonishing curiosities … of the world … are faithfully described, to the satisfaction of every curious palate. Written by T.R. on purpose to make delightful sport and pastime these winter nights.

Not content with merely publishing the works of others, however, Dunton soon began his own career as an author with a book entitled *The Informer's Doom: or an amazing and seasonable letter from Utopia, directed to the man in the Moon …* , which he published in 1683 (Parks 20). Even the title of this work signals an eccentric and original approach to the business of authorship. In fact, Dunton was to put considerable energy into writing over the next few years producing, among many other works, three substantial volumes heavily loaded with autobiography, *A Voyage round the World* (1691), *The Dublin Scuffle* (1699) and *The Life and Errors of John Dunton late citizen of London* (1705) (Parks 138, 293 and 330). He also left two unpublished manuscripts of autobiography containing detailed descriptions of what he saw during his visits to Ireland and New England.[2] Clearly, once he had developed a taste for it, Dunton enjoyed writing, particularly about himself. Parks estimates (p. 44) that he was author or part-author of about two dozen works.

Dunton also, of course, put considerable energy into the business of bookselling; however, despite the fact that some of his titles were very successful, he seems to have been often in debt. In 1685, there was a general down-turn in trade following Monmouth's rebellion and Dunton decided to travel to New England to try and sell some books and to recover some money he was owed. By this course of action, he was able, at a single stroke, to combine bookselling with travelling or 'rambling' as he always described it, something which he greatly enjoyed. He took a quantity of books with him when he sailed for the New World, and set up as bookseller in Boston. He used the opportunity of being in New England to travel as widely as

---

2 The first of these, which Dunton called informally 'A Summer Ramble', is in the Bodleian Library, Oxford (Rawlinson D 71) and the second, 'Letters written from New England', was printed in the fourth volume of the *Publications of the Prince Society* (Boston 1867).

he could and to make useful contacts in the book trade. After his return to Europe, he spent some time in Holland and Germany and in 1688 set up business again as bookseller in London. All these travels were described in his various autobiographical publications.

The next few years were the most successful and profitable of Dunton's life. Not only did his bookselling business go well—partly due to the business abilities of his wife Elizabeth (whom he called 'Iris')—but Dunton had the wit to start a number of periodicals at a moment when such a venture, which had not been tried in England before, caught the public imagination. One of these periodicals, the *Athenian Mercury*, had a remarkable success and is still remembered today.

The *Athenian Mercury* (1691) was a bi-weekly paper distributed mostly in the coffee houses of London. The first issue states that its purpose was 'to satisfy all ingenious and curious Enquirers in to Speculations, Divine, Moral and Natural &c.' The format of the paper was a simple 'questions and answers' one, aimed to arouse the curiosity of the frequenters of the London coffee houses. The questions were purportedly sent in by members of the public and answered by members of a mysterious Athenian Society. In fact, almost the whole thing was written by Dunton with the assistance of his two brothers-in-law, Samuel Wesley (father of John Wesley) and Richard Sault (later the notorious 'methodiser' of *The Second Spira*). It was a journal to appeal to all tastes. The first issue answered questions about the soul, angels, wife-beating and the origin of the spots on the moon, while later issues carried scores of questions from 'Whither the Wind goes after a Storm' to questions of a distinctly more serious nature, such as 'How many years, according to the exactest Computation of Time, must it be before the fall of Antichrist and his Kingdom?' Dunton was fortunate that Wesley was well able to answer questions on religion, history, chronology and literature, while Sault could handle queries on mathematics, surveying, physics and astronomy. Miscellaneous questions on, for instance, courtship, marriage, social behaviour, witchcraft and apparitions seem to have been answered by any of the three editors. Dunton maintained a secrecy about the whole procedure which added to the public's fascination with the journal.

The extraordinary success of the *Athenian Mercury* can be gauged from the fact that, among many learned people who took the project seriously was Swift's famous mentor, Sir William Temple, who submitted a lengthy contribution concerning talismans.[3] Swift himself, having seen all four volumes of the *Athenian Mercury* 'with their Supplements' in Temple's library at Moor Park, and having been given a favourable account of the Athenian Society by '*a very learned Gentleman*' in Oxford, sent Dunton his 'Ode to the Athenian Society' to be printed in the *Mercury* with a long, obsequious letter in which he asked the members of the Athenian Society

> to *descend* so far, as to write two or three lines to me of your Pleasure upon it. Which as I cannot but expect from Gentlemen, who have so well shewn upon so many occasions, that *greatest Character* of Scholars ... [4]

When Swift's Ode appeared in the Fifth Supplement to the *Athenian Mercury*—published on 1 April (All Fools Day) 1692, it was his first printed work. He wrote to his cousin Thomas that the Ode he had sent to the Athenian Society '... was so well thought of that the unknown Gentlemen have printed it before one of their Books ... so that perhaps I was in a good humor all the week ...'[5] The reaction of Swift when he discovered that the 'Athenian Society' was no more than John Dunton and his brothers-in-law is not recorded.[6] However,

---

3 McEwen, p. 33. More work needs to be done on the extent of Temple's actual involvement with the Athenian project, as Elias has noted (A.C. Elias Jr., *Swift at Moor Park* (Philadelphia: University of Pennsylvania Press, 1982), p. 246, n. 48). Dunton himself claimed that the marquis of Halifax, Sir Thomas Pope Blount, Sir Peter Pett, Sir William Hedges (the governor of Bengal) and no less a person than the duke of Ormonde were regular readers of the *Athenian Mercury*. (*Life and Errors*, pp. 191–5.)

4 *The Correspondence of Jonathan Swift DD.*, edited by David Woolley (Frankfurt-am-Main, Peter Lang, 1999), i, 107.

5 Ibid., 109–10. See also Elias, p. 246, n. 48 for a close (and in some ways persuasive) reading of this phrase which differs from mine.

6 Elias asserts (p. 246, n. 46) that Swift probably knew the secret, citing Parks, p. 86, but the quotation Parks is using here (from Elkanah Settle) dates from more than a year after Swift's encounter with the Athenian Society and, in any case, Parks suggests that the secret was 'an open secret among the [book] trade'. Would Swift or Temple have been privy, at this time, to *book trade* secrets and would not Temple

some contemporaries did see through the Athenian Society and Elkanah Settle mocked them effectively in *The New Athenian Comedy* (1693). The modern view is well summed up by Brean Hammond 'This thinly spread and motley crew of self-appointed pundits certainly did not deserve to be arbiters of polite taste.'[7]

Although the *Athenian Mercury* and other periodical publications occupied a lot of Dunton's time in the early 1690s, he continued to publish and sell books of all kinds, 1692 and 1693 being particularly productive and successful years. In 1693, he published *The Second Spira*, a book which was to haunt him for the rest of his professional life. The book purported to be an account of the recent death of an atheist, a 'miserable Gentleman',[8] and to have been made up from notes kept by a clergyman who attended him. In fact it was, as McEwen describes it, 'a pious hoax' (p. 67). Richard Sault, Dunton's brother-in-law, had 'methodised' or adapted a well-known story about the physical and mental tortures endured by a sixteenth-century Italian lawyer named Francis Spira whose religious vacillations caused him to be labelled an atheist. The story of the original Spira first appeared in England in 1637 and was frequently reprinted—a warning to the faithful not to leave the strait and narrow path to salvation. The title page of Sault's *Second Spira* makes its purpose clear. The book is '*a fearful Example of An Atheist, who Had Apostasized from the Christian Religion, and dyed in Despair at Westminster, Decem. 8. 1692 ...*' It contains accounts of his 'dreadful Expressions and Blasphemies when he left the World' and is published 'for an Example to others, and recommended to all young Persons to settle them in their Religion ...' The book itself caused a considerable stir and Dunton was visited by clerical deputations who asked 'embarrassing questions' about the facts of the atheist's case.[9] When it became clear

(who was very concerned with scholarship and good judgement) have dissuaded Swift from contacting the Athenian Society if he had suspected its real status? However that may be, Swift later pilloried Dunton in *A Tale of a Tub*—though for his printing of spurious 'Last Speeches' rather than for the Athenian Society—but Temple continued to regard Dunton with respect and instructed Thomas Swift to send him advice on a project in 1694. (Letter quoted in Parks, p. 60).

7 Brean S. Hammond, *Professional Imaginative Writing in England 1670–1740* (Oxford, Clarendon Press, 1997), p. 158.
8 *Life and Errors* (1705), p. 218.
9 McEwen, p. 71.

that there had been no such death in Westminster and that the book was merely a re-working of the story of the original Spira, Dunton tried to find out more about the manuscript he had published and eventually decided that Richard Sault himself was a closet atheist, writing about himself. 'It is hard to conceive how any Man could write such a DISMAL NARRATIVE, that did not himself feel what he there relates.'[10] Dunton later wished he had never published the book, but he kept returning to the affair in his writings, and it is mentioned several times in *The Dublin Scuffle.*

Dunton published the last number of the *Athenian Mercury* in 1696, which was also the year in which his bookselling and publishing business began to decline. The main reason for this decline was that his wife, who had a far better business sense than did Dunton himself, became ill, and when she died in May 1697, Dunton lost his most important ally.

In December of the same year, Dunton remarried. His new bride, Sarah Nicholas, features frequently in *The Dublin Scuffle* under the name Dunton gave her of 'Valeria'. Despite Dunton's frequent and fervent wishes throughout that book that he and Valeria would be happy together, the marriage proved disastrous in every way. Without his first wife to manage financial matters—and with an intransigent and mistrustful new mother-in-law who was determined that Dunton should not get financial help from her or her daughter—Dunton was to find life increasingly difficult. In particular, he was weighed down by debt and his creditors were seeking payment. One of his few assets was a stock of books in storage and Dunton determined to try and sell them by auction to recoup, at least, some of the money he had laid out on them. He chose to do this in a new country, and set out for Ireland in April 1698.

John Dunton only spent about eight months in Ireland but it was a period of intense activity during which he not only became deeply embroiled with the bookselling fraternity of Dublin but found time to travel, or 'ramble', to many parts of the country. His account of his time in Ireland is preserved in two places, *The Dublin Scuffle*, which

---

10 *Life and Errors* (1705), pp. 218–19.

he wrote towards the end of his time in Ireland and published soon after his return to London, and the long manuscript entitled 'A Summer Ramble',[11] a bowdlerised and incomplete version of which was printed as an appendix to Edward MacLysaght's *Irish Life in the Seventeenth Century* (Cork, 1950, reprinted Shannon, 1969).

'A Summer Ramble' is cast in the form of letters recounting Dunton's travels—from Dublin to Galway and Iar-Connacht as well as to Kildare, Kilkenny and Drogheda—, and provides a fascinating insight into the life and customs of the people of Ireland in the late seventeenth century. Though some passages are borrowed directly from contemporary sources, particularly *A Brief Character of Ireland*,[12] much of the work is clearly first-hand description of events and scenes which Dunton experienced. As elsewhere in his work, the reader is struck by the vividness and energy of his style and the brightness of his descriptions.

The Dublin Scuffle is a much less straightforward piece of writing. It is, in fact, made up of three separate but interconnected books, *The Dublin Scuffle*, *The Billet Doux sent by a Citizens Wife*, and *Some Account of my Conversation in Ireland*. Though each of these has a separate title page, the book was conceived as a single unit, as is made plain in the full wording of the 1699 title page (reproduced in facsimile on p. 1 below).

> The *Dublin Scuffle*: being a Challenge sent by *John Dunton*, Citizen of *London*, to *Patrick Campbel*, Bookseller in Dublin. Together with the small Skirmishes of Bills and Advertisements. // To which is Added, *The Billet Doux*, sent him by a *Citizens Wife* in *Dublin*, Tempting him to Lewdness. With *His Answers to Her*. // Also Some Account of his *Conversation in Ireland*, Intermixt with particular Characters of the most Eminent Persons he Convers'd with in that Kingdom; but more especially in the City of *Dublin* // *In several Letters to the Spectators of this Scuffle; With a Poem on the whole Encounter*. // *I wear my Pen as others do their Sword.*—Oldham. // *London*, (Printed for the Author) and are to be Sold by *A. Baldwin*, near the *Oxford-Arms* in *Warwick-Lane*, and by the Booksellers in *Dublin*. 1699.

11 Bodleian Library, Oxford, ms. Rawlinson D.71.
12 For details of this work, see below, pp. xx–xxi.

This title page alone prepares the reader for the singular work which is to follow—as idiosyncratic in its form, style, language and tone as anything ever written on Ireland. The epigraph taken from the poet John Oldham, 'I wear my Pen as others do their Sword', applies particularly to *The Dublin Scuffle* itself, the first part of the book which is, in places, tediously pugnacious. The second part of the book, with its endless moralising about sexual behaviour, can wear the patience too. However, the third part, Dunton's *Conversation in Ireland*, is full of interest and must rank as an essential text for anyone wishing to understand seventeenth-century Ireland.

Before we proceed to a brief consideration of the various parts of *The Dublin Scuffle*, it might be in order to suggest a way of reading the book. Most of those who have tried to read *The Dublin Scuffle* confess that they find it a confusing book, in places tediously full of apparently unnecessary self-justification. Many become irritated with Dunton himself. However, the purpose and plan of the book become clearer if we realise that, whatever the ostensible subject of the work, its real subject is indeed Dunton himself.

A few pages from the end of the third section, Dunton allows himself an extended and elaborate whimsical fantasy in which he personifies a side of his character which he characterises as 'treacherous' under the name of 'Argus'. It is clear that Dunton believes that, if this aspect of his personality is in charge of his actions, he can be dishonest in various ways. He asserts that he intends to find 'Argus' and deal with him—in other words, to try and master tendencies towards dishonesty which he detects in himself.

In the light of this, the violent reactions of the earlier parts of the book begin to make sense. If Dunton feels he is repressing tendencies towards dishonesty and lechery in his own character, then his overreaction to the dishonesty of Patrick Campbell and the lewd thoughts of the fictitious Dorinda can be seen as projections. His hysterical and repetitious attacks on these two characters only make sense when viewed from this perspective. The letters sent to Dunton by his correspondents are clearly doctored so that those responding to his account of his skirmish with Patrick Campbell praise his honesty and those which comment on his encounter with Dorinda praise his abhorrence of lasciviousness. The fact that Dunton himself was descended from a family of clergymen—and should therefore be purer in thought and deed than other men—clearly exacerbated his problem. One way of making sense of the apparent excesses of Dunton's book is therefore, I suggest, to see it as an elaborate structure of dialogue with the less welcome sides of his own personality.

Like most books of the age, *The Dublin Scuffle* starts with a substantial amount of preliminary matter—an aspect of late seventeenth-century bookmaking which Swift was to satirise in *A Tale of a Tub* a few years later. The sixteen preliminary pages to this book contain a dedication to a patron, a letter to the spectators of the Dublin scuffle, two poems in praise of the book, and appropriate letters before and after the poems. Though several authors are stated to be involved in the writing of these various pieces, it seems clear that Dunton himself adapted, amended or even completely invented most of this material.

The first of the three main sections in the volume, *The Dublin Scuffle*, mixes fact and fiction in a potentially confusing way. The text consists of twelve letters from Dunton to a bookseller friend in London and the bookseller's supposed responses or 'Remarks' on each of Dunton's letters. Dunton's letters describe what was, it seems, a real-life disagreement between Dunton and the Scottish bookseller Patrick Campbell. Dunton's first Irish book auction took place in Dick's Coffee House, the most famous coffee house of the period, situated in a large building on Skinner Row, in the centre of Dublin. He expected to be able to use the same venue for further auctions. However, Patrick Campbell persuaded Dick not to honour his agreement with Dunton but to let the room to him instead, so that he could hold his own book auctions there. Dunton, furious at this sleight-of-hand, was forced to hold his remaining auctions in another coffee house, but vowed to get his own back on Campbell (and to a lesser extent on Dick). The story unfolds in the twelve letters Dunton sends to his London bookseller friend.

The letters which purport to come back to Dunton from the bookseller—a series of twelve 'Remarks' on the original letters—seem to have been written partially or even wholly by Dunton himself. He admits as much in the third section of the book when he asserts that part of his character is base enough to 'suppress letters, merely to carry on a correspondence of his own with the same persons'. In effect, Dunton uses an authorial sleight-of-hand to give his readers a one-sided account of his quarrel with Patrick Campbell and then to bombard us with apparently objective assertions of the probity of his own actions. What, we may ask, is the point of all this?

From one point of view of course, Dunton is engaging in a public relations exercise, and there can be no doubt that his reiterated public statements and hysterical challenges to Campbell raised public interest and increased the numbers of those attending his auctions. In addition, his over-reaction to Patrick Campbell's sharp practice is, in my view, linked to the fact that he detects tendencies towards dishonesty in himself. If we were spectators of a mock-epic (by Dryden, for instance), we could laugh at sharp business practice being described as sin of enormous proportions; but *The Dublin Scuffle* is a personal and moral adventure rather than a literary one and Dunton can not distance himself from the affair to any degree. On the contrary, he is doggedly determined that no reader should miss any detail of the quarrel or any nuance of the positive interpretation put upon it by his 'correspondent'. Thus he prints not only the text of the imaginary correspondence between himself and the London bookseller, but also full supporting documentation including testimonials from historically-verifiable third parties asserting his honesty, copies of his own advertisements and copies of the printed notices issued both by himself and, in one case, by Patrick Campbell. The increasingly bemused reader is assailed with documents of varying levels of authenticity and authority.

We may not be in the presence of a literary genius as we read through this section of *The Dublin Scuffle*, but we are certainly experiencing a remarkably agile and fluid writer, one able to shift register with alacrity and to reproduce on paper the speech of those around him with great skill. Dunton was a born parodist and, when he chose to be, a fine satirist. These skills are abundantly evident in this first part of *The Dublin Scuffle* particularly if, as I believe, almost every word of the text—even the testimonials which purport to come from real-life individuals—is from his own pen. The material said to have been written by Patrick Campbell on page 72 is a fine piece of scurrilous parodic writing.

The extended 'Farewell to Dublin' which rounds off this first part of the book is of more interest than the reiterated paens of self-praise in the earlier letters. Before Dunton returned to London to tend to his ailing bookselling business and to continue justifying the publication of *The Second Spira*, he wanted to put on record the names of the friends who had stood by him in Dublin during his skirmish with Patrick Campbell and to point out his 'worst enemies'—those who had 'snarled at *The Second Spira*' and those who had 'bought what they won't pay for' (p. 78). Though Dunton continues his self-justifications in this section also, we are given a list of the books he says he bought in Dublin (pp. 80–1) and a set of character sketches of his Dublin friends and clients (pp. 96–103)—all of whom he clearly expected to rush out and buy a copy of the book when it appeared. Dunton's comments on the houses, families and physical appearance of these mostly prominent citizens give us a unique insight into seventeenth-century Dublin life. He includes also descriptions of three prominent Dublin printers of the time, John Brent, John Brocas and Stephen Powell. This portion of the book is of considerable interest to students of seventeenth-century Ireland.

Dunton's technique of creating a character with whom to carry on a dialogue lies at the centre of the second part of *The Dublin Scuffle*, though the actual *Billet Doux Sent by a Citizens-Wife in Dublin Tempting Me to Leudness* takes up less than one page of this section. The rest of the 27-page text is made up of Dunton's moralising 'Answers' to 'Dorinda', as he calls the citizen's wife, and the unfailingly laudatory 'Remarks' of the same imaginary London bookseller to whom Dunton had sent letters in the first part of *The Dublin Scuffle*. Dunton's moral position throughout this text echoes that of the authors of the sermons and devotional books he had been printing in London during the previous sixteen years and the tone of self-important moralising is similar to that he had adopted in parts of the *Athenian Mercury*. The use of carefully constructed argument, of regular quotation from scripture and of illustrations and examples of the wicked as well as of the good all reflect the rhetoric of the more Puritan wing of the Church of England—though there are occasional, surprising lapses into the language of other denominations, such as the references to the Virgin Mary sending prayers to God and carrying 'but one soul' to him (p. 142). However, despite all the self-serving rhetoric about his own piety, Dunton seems to have been less than certain of his own denominational affiliation, describing himself (p. 152) as 'a Christian, a follower of Christ … and my own man', and making it clear that he attended as many non-conformist chapels in Dublin as he did churches of the Established Church of Ireland. We only (unfortunately!) hear from the lewd 'Dorinda' once, so the dialogue in this section is between the moralising and self-righteously upright Dunton and his admiring London correspondent. Here we see in action the professional writer who, from the days of the *Athenian Mercury*, had been accustomed to writing letters to himself and to answering them himself, using on at least one side of the correspondence a tone of unctuous moral superiority.

Even by the standards of the day, thirty pages of relentless moralising seems an excessive reaction to one suggestive letter. However, Dunton clearly had difficulties in his relationships with women and, in my opinion, these difficulties lie behind the peculiarities of this section. The descriptions of women in *The Dublin Scuffle* are remarkably excited and sensual and Dunton seems to have considered almost any woman he met as a potential sexual partner. If we suppose this interest in the sensual to be something the virtuous side of Dunton's character wanted to repress, the point of this section of the book becomes clear. 'Dorinda' is being treated as a seductress and a temptress, someone who represents uncontrollable sexual licence. As such, she must be ruthlessly stamped on—one sermon is not enough for her, and Dunton actually sends her three. Strangely though, 'Dorinda' does have enough intimate knowledge of Dunton to address him by his pet name 'Philaret'. There is an air of titillating mystery around her. The reaction of the moralist in Dunton to the sensual temptation of 'Dorinda' is, again, an overreaction. The person being subjected to stern moralising is, as it was in the previous section, Dunton himself—or rather a side of himself he wished he could control. 'Dorinda' may not be a real person, but what she represents in Dunton's mind was real enough for him.

From the point of view of the Irish cultural historian, much the most interesting part of *The Dublin Scuffle* as a whole is its third section,

Some Account of my Conversation in Ireland. Again Dunton uses the form of an exchange of letters between himself and a correspondent, this time 'an Honourable Lady'. As many references throughout this section make clear, Dunton certainly had a real lady in mind as his correspondent. This lady helped Dunton get over his grief at the death of a mysterious female friend known as D—ne, and she shared several other friends in common with him. It seems clear, however, that Dunton himself wrote, or substantially rewrote for publication, the letters which purport to have been sent by her to him. Since the purpose of this part of the book is description rather than self-justification, the presence of the lady is a mere formality and what she purports to write of little consequence. Again, the spotlight is firmly on Dunton himself, on his spiritual state, on his ability to refute atheism (pp. 154–5), on his opinion on a whole variety of matters. But he also gives lively accounts of his travels around Ireland.

Many commentators have quoted from Dunton's descriptions of Ireland assuming that they were accurate, if eccentric and prejudiced. However, Dunton was a practised plagiarist, as was first recognised nearly ninety years ago. In an article in the *Publications of the Colonial Society of Massachusetts*, C.N. Greenough pointed out Dunton's 'unacknowledged indebtedness' in his *Letters from New-England* to Overbury's *Characters*, Fuller's *Holy and Profane State*, Earle's *Microcosmography* and other works for at least eighty-four items, mostly 'characters'.[13] Sir Geoffrey Keynes noticed that Dunton's 1691 imitation of Sir Thomas Browne's *Religio Medici, Religio Bibliopolae* (Parks 134) was full of plagiarism, and this matter has been explored in detail by A.C. Howell.[14]

Dunton's practice of unacknowledged borrowing of material has to be seen in the context of ambiguity about literary property in late seventeenth-century England, a time when it was not at all uncommon

13 C.N. Greenough, 'John Dunton's Letters from New England', *Publications of the Colonial Society of Massachusetts*, vol. iv (March 1912), 213–57. A 'character' is a formal, detailed report of a person's characteristics. Dunton himself always put inverted commas around the 'characters' he wrote to set them apart from the surrounding text.
14 Sir Geoffrey Keynes, *A Bibliography of Sir Thomas Browne Kt, M.D.* (Cambridge, 1924), no. 407 and A.C. Howell, 'John Dunton and the Imitation of the *Religio Medici*', *Studies in Philology* xxix [1932], 442–62.

to use material borrowed from other writers—nor was this necessarily seen as an infringement of their rights.[15] It was generally accepted that those who acquired literary copy had the right to reproduce it as often as they wished, and moves to change this situation ran into difficulty. The 1662 Licensing Act, which had required the licensing of works at Stationers' Hall, lapsed in 1695, and the Copyright Act was not to be enacted until 1709.

Given this state of affairs, and Dunton's own predilection for borrowing material as it suited him, it is not surprising that there are some glaring plagiarisms in *The Dublin Scuffle* as a whole. The most audacious examples are in the third part, Dunton's *Conversation in Ireland*, where he prints—and claims as his own—several verses of a poem by Swift (pp. 215–16). In addition, extensive passages in this section, containing descriptions of the life of the native Irish, were copied verbatim from a rare, anonymous, pugnaciously bigoted anti-Irish work printed in London in 1692 entitled *A Brief Character of Ireland, with some Observations of the Customs &c. of the meaner sort of the National Inhabitants of that Kingdom*. Though he gets its title wrong, Dunton does not hide the fact that he was copying some of his descriptions from another work and he tells the 'Honourable Lady':

> Yet, madam, if you'd see the picture of poor Teague more at large, I'd refer you to a book called *The Description of Ireland*, that ingenious author being the person I so often quote in this character of the Dear Joys.[16]

The passages Dunton copied from *A Brief Character of Ireland*—in places consisting of whole paragraphs—are not marked as quotations but are integrated into his own prose. In places, he has made small editorial amendments to the text he is copying for its new context. No clear pattern in these changes is evident, however. For instance, though Dunton copied his description of keening at a wake (p. 235) almost word for word from *A Brief Character*, he omits a phrase in

---

15 The subtitle of the third chapter of Brean Hammond's *Professional Imaginative Writing in England 1670–1740*, is 'The rhetoric of plagiarism'.
16 p. 236.

which the author of *A Brief Character* had described the tears of the keeners as 'as big as Turnips'—which might suggest that Dunton wished to remove a gratuitous insult to the native Irish. But in the same passage, he also removes a reference to the keening taking place 'when the Melodious Harp, or Bag-pipe is out of the way'—a reference which might be said to be benign.[17] Elsewhere, Dunton changes the welcome given to a passing traveller from 'a Dozen of Eggs' to 'an Egg extraordinary'[18] and where the author of *A Brief Character* writes of the women of Ireland that 'one would think they never had their Faces wash'd, but at their Baptism', Dunton changes the last phrase to 'in their whole Lives'.[19] There seems no clear reason for these changes.

A close examination of Dunton's text, with the knowledge of his plagiarism in mind, does not suggest, however, that Dunton's insertion of particular passages from another source reduces his value as an eye-witness of late seventeenth-century Ireland. He seems to have used *A Brief Character* only for general descriptions of the country and its people, not for specific details. In any case, though the author of *A Brief Character* clearly knew Ireland well, his hatred of both the country and its inhabitants colours every page of the work. Dunton liked being in Ireland and his Protestant bigotry and English chauvinism are both, in comparison, harmless eccentricities—though the effect of copying passages from *A Brief Character* can extend into his own prose so that he sounds uncommonly like the author of that tract in short passages as, for example, at the bottom of page 235. On the whole, however, Dunton enjoyed his rambles around Ireland and he wrote about the country and its people with an infectious enthusiasm which is quite lacking in the other text. It is clear that the great majority of Dunton's *Conversation in Ireland* is his own work and is based on his own observation and experience.

To take two examples: when recounting his visit to Kilkenny, Dunton describes the paintings he saw in the gallery at Kilkenny Castle—and contemporary inventories bear out the accuracy of his

---

17 *The Dublin Scuffle*, p. 402, *A Brief Character*, p. 44.
18 *The Dublin Scuffle*, p. 401, *A Brief Character*, p. 26.
19 *The Dublin Scuffle*, pp. 400–1, *A Brief Character*, p. 14.

list.[20] Secondly, Dunton's description of buildings in Dublin and of the appearance of the areas around Dublin can be corroborated from other contemporary accounts, from maps and from illustrations. There is no reason to doubt that he actually visited Ireland and met the people he says he met. His descriptions of the Smock Alley play-house, of having lunch at an 'ordinary' eating house, of St Stephen's Green, of the bowling green, of Kilkenny, the Curragh and Malahide are not only highly entertaining but historically and culturally valuable. His interaction with the Dublin bookselling community is also of considerable interest and his descriptions of the actual individuals involved in the Dublin print trade are, in almost all cases, the only descriptions we have. In sum, Dunton's account of his Irish under-taking is an important source for our knowledge of Ireland at the end of the seventeenth century.

Dunton had a sharp eye and an excellent descriptive pen so that many of the details of what Ireland actually looked like during his visit—its gardens, vistas, trees, buildings—are vividly presented in his *Conversation of Ireland*. He is also good at describing people but, probably hoping that all those he mentioned in his book would buy a copy of it, gave formal 'characters' of many of the inhabitants of Dublin. These written 'characters' are too laudatory and uncritical to tell us much of interest about the individuals and they are also, too often, written to a formula. Even if he admits he has never seen or met an individual, Dunton is capable of writing a glowing 'character' detailing his or her 'matchless virtue and piety' on the basis of second-hand information. But outside these formal 'characters' are many valuable asides—details of the taverns at which Dunton drank, the people he met by chance in the street, the kindness of a landlord and landlady, the chat in a coach, or the effect of the weather when he was travelling around Ireland on horseback.

Dunton's own character remains something of a puzzle, however. On the surface, he presents himself as an obsessively committed church-going Christian who takes every opportunity to deliver long sermon-like rebukes to anyone around him whose conduct falls below his standards. He seems hypercritical and puritanical. Yet as

20 My thanks to Dr Jane Fenlon for information on this matter.

soon as we find Dunton encountering an attractive woman, he becomes a very different person; his account of what is said and his descriptions of how it is said on these occasions leads one to suspect that he found women a source of irresistible temptation. Priggishness and prurience exist side by side also in his 'Summer Ramble', where he recounts bawdy stories with obvious relish and provides gratuitously suggestive comments on the women he meets. After working with the latter text, Edward MacLysaght described Dunton, in an exasperated passage, as 'that old hypocrite'.[21] My own view, outlined earlier, is that Dunton was aware of various contradictions in his character and hoped, in some measure, to exorcise them in his writing. The eccentricities of *The Dublin Scuffle* can best be explained as manifestations of Dunton's attempt to come to terms with those parts of his own personality which he habitually repressed.

The *Conversation in Ireland* reminds us again how strongly Dunton makes his presence felt throughout this book. Hardly a page passes without whatever is being discussed being linked directly to Dunton's own views or experience; boringly repetitive though Dunton's views on some matters soon become, the reader simply has to put up with it. Brean Hammond has summed up well the effect of Dunton's fierce, energetic writing in another work, *A New Voyage round the World*:

> In its chronic use of digression, rugged indifference towards the reader, constant self-referentiality, interruption, use of different accents and registers of language—in summary its transforming and protean character—this discourse is truly dialogic in the Bakhtinian sense.[22]

Elsewhere Hammond perceptively likens Dunton to a ventriloquist capable 'of representing both the cynosure of urbane counsel and the height of ill-bred churlishness at one and the same time'.[23] We find the same unholy mixture of urbanity and churlishness throughout the three parts of *The Dublin Scuffle*, and it creates the same

21 MacLysaght, p. 320.
22 Hammond, p. 159.
23 Hammond, p. 160.

unsettling effect. In the hands of writers like Swift, Sterne or Joyce—all able to exercise rigid control over techniques of dislocation and discontinuity and able to keep themselves apart from their works— this kind of writing can dramatically extend the possibilities of language and produce texts of enduring value. But Dunton's real-life enthusiasms and eccentricities constantly seem to have deflected his pen from the work in hand back to his need to air, once again, his own personal obsessions. He fails, also, to make the most of the other voices he creates; they are not developed into credible personae but are merely used to echo what had been said by Dunton himself earlier. The digressions throughout the book have no clear artistic purpose—unlike those in Swift, Sterne or Joyce—and remain merely digressions; Dunton's brusque abuse of the reader sometimes seems to have no real point to it. In stark contrast to his contemporary, Jonathan Swift, Dunton simply did not exploit the possibilities he had created for himself in this work.

Despite the fact that Dunton clearly had a lively mind, a quick wit, a ready pen, a sharp power of observation and abundant *joie de vivre*, the reader often feels almost overwhelmed by the weight of his pompous self-importance and his lack of a sense of humour about himself. His determination to drag before his reader every detail in his mind constantly dilutes the power of his writing, and his habit of regularly buttonholing the reader with extended explanations of the virtue of his motives or the significance of his religious devotions arouses irritation rather than sympathy. However entertaining he may be in places—and Dunton can be very entertaining indeed—there are other places where his self-indulgence becomes tedious, where one regrets his lack of tact, and laments his execrable literary judgement.

Had Dunton been a writer of genius—or even someone able to keep life and literature apart and manipulate the reader through his own understanding of that difference—what he wrote would have had a much more powerful effect on the reader. He might now be mentioned in the same breath as Sterne and Joyce, for many of his techniques are precisely those which these two writers later used to such effect.[24]

---

24 The first volume of Dunton's *A Voyage round the World* was reprinted, under a different title and with some alterations, in 1762 to show the world that

To invoke such comparisons is not to detract from what Dunton did achieve in this work; it is simply to regret that he did not make the most of the promising and original format he created for his three-part *Dublin Scuffle*.

When he returned to London from Dublin, Dunton found difficulties in both his business and his personal life. His second wife's mother was determined to protect her daughter from him and Dunton even had to move out of his own house. He found creditors seeking payment on all sides and his health began to fail. Parks sums up this period of Dunton's life graphically.

> During these unhappy years, his attacks of the [kidney] stone … became so frequent and so painful that he had to be attended constantly. Separated from his wife, Dunton was cared for by his landladies and by numerous female friends. When his pain subsided, Dunton exhausted himself composing diatribes against his mother-in-law and by dashing about London in attempts to interest booksellers in his new projects.[25]

Gradually Dunton's writing became more eccentric though, in *The Art of Living Incognito* (1700), he wrote a revealing epitaph on himself: 'Here lies his Dust, who chiefly aimed to know / Himself; and chose to live Incognito …' Dunton returned to the theme of self-knowledge time and again in his writing and it is clear that more work needs to be done on this aspect of his work.

Despite the difficulties of his personal and professional life, Dunton continued to write as energetically as he was able to for a further twenty-eight years. His most important publication was his auto-

'Shandeism, (or something very like it)' was not as new as it seemed. About this time, Sterne himself was charged with plagiarising from Dunton and is reported to have written to a friend that he had met with Dunton's book in a London circulating library and had taken 'many of his ideas' from it. See Parks, pp. 50–1 and the sources cited by Parks, Wilbur Cross, *The Life and Times of Laurence Sterne* (new edition, New Haven, 1925), I, 132–3 and T.M. Hatfield, 'The True Secret of Mr John Dunton', unpublished Ph.D. thesis, Harvard University, 1926, p. 91n.

25 Parks, p. 148.

biography, *The Life and Errors of John Dunton, late Citizen of London*, which appeared in 1705 and which remains an extremely useful book. It not only gives us extensive insights into Dunton and his life but provides important details about the London book trade or the period. Dunton also continued with projects for periodicals and other publications and became a prolific writer of political pamphlets'. At the height of his own career as a political writer, Swift described Dunton's *Neck or Nothing* (1714, Parks 378), an attack on Bolingbroke, as 'the shrewdest piece, and written with the most Spirit of any which have appeared from that Side [the Whig side] since the Change in the Ministry'. Swift called Dunton's work 'a most cutting Satire' and commented that 'having employed his Studies in so great a Variety of other Subjects, he hath, I think, but lately turned his Genius to Politicks'.[26] Swift commended Dunton's 'Keenness of Satire, and Variety of Reading'—praise which, quite rightly, delighted Dunton. In 1715, George I awarded Dunton a gold medal for his services to the Hanoverian succession—a medal which he proudly wore around his neck to the amusement of those who saw him.

On the whole, however, Dunton's career as a writer and as a bookseller was in slow decline after 1700. He was increasingly treated as an eccentric—Narcissus Luttrell described him in 1707 as 'a poor craz'd silly Fellow'[27]—and, despite a few successful publications, was never able to shake off his creditors. He was several times arrested for debt, and even when not in the Fleet prison, seems to have been tenaciously pursued by those to whom he owed money. By 1713, he had become, in Parks' words, a sick old man who was 'the laughing-stock of London'.[28] But his energetic turn of mind and satirical touch never left him and among his publications in the second half of his life were some with striking titles: *The Shortest Way with Whores and Rogues* (1703) in which he returned to the themes of *The Dublin Scuffle*, *Bumography: or A Touch at the Lady's Tails* (1707), *The He-Strumpets* (1707), *The Pulpit Fool* (1707), *Stinking Fish* (1708), *Dunton's Ghost* (1714), and *A Trip to the Mug House at Night to Drink a Health*

---

26 *The Publick Spirit of the Whigs, The Prose Works of Jonathan Swift* (14 volumes) eds. Herbert Davis and others (Oxford, 1939–68), viii, 31–2.
27 Parks, p. 349.
28 Parks, p. 168.

to King George (1716). One of his last publications was *Mr John Dunton's Dying Groans from the Fleet-Prison* (1725). Eventually John Dunton died in 1732 and his remaining books were sold off 'very cheap'.[29]

From an Irish point of view, Dunton's *The Dublin Scuffle* and his manuscript 'Summer Ramble' are his most important works. Though it is clearly a flawed work from a literary perspective, *The Dublin Scuffle* contains material of great interest to Irish cultural historians. Much work still remains to be done on it. It is astonishing that a text of such Irish significance as this one, incorporating valuable first-hand accounts of the people and places of the 1690s, has never been fully reprinted, and it is our hope that this edition will raise interest not only in the book itself and in its author, but also in late seventeenth-century Ireland.

A NOTE ON THE TEXT OF THIS EDITION

The 1699 printing of *The Dublin Scuffle* appears awkward and forbidding to a modern reader. Not only is the text studded with words and passages in italics, bold type, Gothic type and small capitals, but the book as a whole is printed in bewildering variety of font sizes. The look of the text is further complicated by shouldernotes, footnotes, dashes of varying lengths and brackets of different kinds. Even the pagination of the 1699 edition is erratic and inaccurate.

The aim of this edition is to provide the reader with a modernised text which still retains some of the flavour of the 1699 edition. Dunton's seventeenth-century syntax and his complex sentences are reproduced exactly, as is much of his punctuation. Like most late-seventeenth century writers, Dunton punctuated his text rhetorically—a semicolon indicating a longer pause than a comma for instance—and though the 1699 punctuation has been modernised in such matters as direct speech, the main punctuation marks of that edition have only been altered where they make the text hard to understand. One feature which has been left is the question mark after an indirect

29 Parks, p. 178.

question, though this usage is no longer current. Spelling is a more difficult matter; unfamiliar spellings can divert the reader's attention unnecessarily, and it has therefore been decided to modernise most of Dunton's spellings—'chuse' becomes 'choose' for instance, and 'inlarge' becomes 'enlarge'. In a few instances, the 1699 spelling has been retained where it seems not to interrupt the flow of the text, but in general archaic or awkward spellings have been silently amended (here are some more examples: 'publisht' becomes 'published', 'you'l' becomes 'you'll', ''em' becomes 'them', 'leud' becomes 'lewd', 'meager' become 'meagre' and ''scape' becomes 'escape'). The many contractions in the text have been expanded (e.g. 'ben't' becomes 'be not', 'e'n't' becomes 'is not' and 'han't' becomes 'have not'), possessives have been amended to conform with modern usage and place names have been given in their modern forms. Dunton's spelling of proper names is so inconsistent, however, that some of these have been retained in the form that he uses because it is hard to be sure to whom he is referring. Initial capitals for substantives have been removed and words and passages which the 1699 text gives in italics, small capitals or Gothic type are printed here in roman type. Overall, the aim is not to reproduce the 1699 text, which many libraries possess in the original or in the 1974 facsimile reprint by Garland Publishing of New York, but to provide a text which modern readers would find easy to use. It must be stressed, however, that those wishing to quote from Dunton's text are advised to use the 1699 text or the Garland facsimile.

Some of the problems associated with this text are outlined in the introduction, and it must be stressed that much primary work remains to be done before a full scholarly edition of *The Dublin Scuffle* can be produced. The present edition is designed to stimulate interest in the text and to provide sufficient notes for a reader reasonably familiar with late seventeenth-century Ireland to be able to read it with pleasure.

The annotations are designed to assist the modern reader by pointing out unfamiliar allusions and references. Notes are provided for the individuals Dunton meets or mentions except in the case of those merely mentioned in passing or in a list of names. A list of the Irish booksellers mentioned is provided in Appendix A. Some of the more obscure of Dunton's quotations and references are currently untraced.

Readers should note that, despite the fact that it is divided into three sections, *The Dublin Scuffle* is treated as a single book for the purposes of annotation so that only the first appearance of a person or quotation is annotated.

SHORT TITLES FOR BOOKS FREQUENTLY CITED

Bliss	Alan Bliss, *Spoken English in Ireland 1600–1740*. Dublin, Cadenus Press, 1979.
Gilbert	John T. Gilbert, *A History of the City of Dublin*, 3 volumes, Dublin, 1854–59.
Life and Errors	*The Life and Errors of John Dunton ... to which are added Dunton's 'Conversation in Ireland', selections from his other genuine works ...* (2 vols) ed. J.B. Nichols. London 1818, reprinted New York, Burt Franklin, 1969.
McEwen	Gilbert D. McEwen, *The Oracle of the Coffee House: John Dunton's 'Athenian Mercury'*. San Marino, The Huntington Library, 1972.
Parks	Stephen Parks, *John Dunton and the English Book Trade: A Study of his Career with a Checklist of his Publications*. New York, Garland, 1976.
Phillips	James W. Phillips, *Printing and Bookselling in Dublin 1670–1800*. Dublin, Irish Academic Press, 1998.
Pollard	M. Pollard, *Dublin's Trade in Books 1550–1800*. Oxford, Clarendon Press, 1989.
Sweeney	Tony Sweeney, *Ireland and the Printed Word: A Short Descriptive Catalogue of early Books, Pamphlets, Newsletters and Broadsides relating to Ireland. Printed 1475–1700*. Dublin, Edmund Burke, 1997.

ACKNOWLEDGEMENTS

I should like to thank the staff in the National Library of Ireland, the Library of Trinity College Dublin, the Library of University College Dublin and the Gilbert Collection of the Dublin Public Library for their help while I have been working on Dunton. Particular thanks are due to Gerry O'Flaherty who provided many of the notes for this edition and undertook valuable preliminary work on several aspects of the text; to Ray Astbury of University College Dublin who provided translations of Dunton's Latin tags and quotations; and, for assistance of various kinds, to Michael Adams, Charles Benson, Dorothy Carpenter, Arch Elias, Jane Fenlon, Máire Kennedy, Christopher Murray, Mary Pollard and James Woolley.

THE
Dublin Scuffle:
BEING A
CHALLENGE
SENT BY

John Dunton, Citizen of *London*,
TO
Patrick Campbel, Bookseller in *Dublin*.

Together with the small Skirmishes of
Bills and Advertisements.

To which is Added,

The *Billet Doux*, sent him by a Citizens Wife
in *Dublin*, Tempting him to Lewdness.
WITH

His Answers to Her.

ALSO

Some Account of his Conversation in Ireland,
Intermixt with particular Characters of the
most Eminent Persons he Convers'd with in
that Kingdom; but more especially in the
City of *Dublin*.

In several Letters to the Spectators of this Scuffle;
With a Poem on the whole Encounter.

I wear my Pen as others do their Sword.——Oldham.

London, (Printed for the Author) and are to be Sold by
A. Baldwin, near the *Oxford-Arms* in *Warwick-Lane*, and by
the Booksellers in *Dublin*. 1699.

To the Honourable Colonel Butler,
a Member of the House of Commons in Ireland[1]

Honoured and worthy Sir,

The generous encouragement, which you were pleased to give to all my auctions of books, and the extraordinary and unmerited kindnesses I received at your hands, when in Ireland, embolden me to trouble you with this Dedication.

I confess it may justly seem unworthy of the acceptance of a person of so great honour and endowments, as you are known to be: nor can anything less than your own goodness find an excuse for this presumption: but having had such large experience of the excellency of your temper, and of the greatness of your soul, I should be unjust to your character, if I did not publicly own, that you measure the tokens of gratitude by the affection of your friend, and not by the value of the thing presented.

Give me leave then, worthy Sir, to inscribe your name to the following sheets, as a great patron of learning, and a generous friend to an injured stranger, who came to promote the interest of learning in your country.

The kindness you were pleased to vouchsafe unto me, and the concern you expressed for my welfare, persuade me that you will not disdain to be my patron in defending myself in print in England, seeing I could not have the opportunity of doing it in Ireland.

I must indeed own that your character and courage entitles you to be the champion of such as are engaged in a more masculine quarrel than the *Scuffle* between Patrick Campbell[2] and myself. Yet you know, Sir, that the greatest captains, after the campaign is over, do sometimes divert themselves by seeing a mockfight on the stage. This, Sir, has something more in it, as being a real piece of injustice first committed, and then defended by my adversary, who has armed himself with impudence and malice, and manages his attacks by fraud and forgery; as I have made sufficiently clear in the following sheets.

I confess, Sir, the entertainment you will meet with here is not answerable to that hospitable and generous treatment I was honoured with at your house; and that I am not capable of gratifying your curiosity with such excellent pieces of my own drawing, as you were pleased to feast my eyes with, when I beheld with wonder, the effects of your happy pencil![3] Yet, Sir, I dare say that I present you here with an ORIGINAL; which, though drawn by an unskilful hand, has something very surprising in it; such features, such a mixture of hypocrisy and double dealing covered over with a false varnish of religion, that I question much, whether Patrick may not pass for a *Judas Redivivus*?[4] And were my pen able to keep pace with your pencil; or had I the art of tempering my colours, drawing the features to the life, and observing due proportion, I doubt very much, whether Africa could shew any such monster, as I should here present to the public view?

But, worthy Sir, I must beg your pardon for daring to offend the eye of such a curious[5] artist as yourself, with such a deformed piece. It were indeed pardonable, did I not know that by one glance of the eye upon your own perfections and eminent virtues, you will immediately race[6] out those foul ideas which the sight of Patrick may impress upon your imagination. Contraries exposed to the view at one and the same time, do mightily illustrate one another; and therefore when you see his picture, and reflect upon your own, you will find great cause to bless him who has made the distinction. Pardon me, Sir, I don't think your virtues need any such foil to set them off; for they are such, as when compared with those which render the enjoyers of them amiable in the eyes of mankind, will undoubtedly give you the preference amongst thousands; but I must break off, lest my affection should offer violence to your modesty, and lest it should be said, I only commend myself in extolling my patron: I must indeed own that the honour of your friendship is one of those things that I value myself most upon, and esteem myself happy in some measure by Patrick's enmity, which gives me this opportunity of letting the world know that Colonel Butler is my friend: or, if that be a degradation to you, that you are an encourager of learning, and a protector of those that endeavour to promote it.

I shall add no more, but beg your pardon for prefixing your name to such a trifle. You know, Sir, that how meanly soever it be performed, it was absolutely necessary for the defence of my reputation, which Patrick Campbell has so unjustly endeavoured to destroy; and seeing it is usual with authors to atone for their own defects, by choosing an honourable patron, I hope, Sir, you will indulge me the same liberty. May you live long, to be an ornament to your country, and the object of his highest esteem, who is,

Honoured Sir,
Your much obliged, and
most obedient servant,
John Dunton

London, Feb. 20, 1698/9

To the Spectators of the Dublin Scuffle

Gentlemen,

It may be justly expected I should give some account of the reason of this undertaking; which is, in short, to vindicate my reputation from the malice of some of my own profession, who have unjustly endeavoured to bespatter me. I need not say much as to my conversation at home; those who have dealt with me will allow the fairness of my dealing in the way of trade. It's true, some reflections have been thrown upon me about the 2nd Spira,[1] and the multitude of things I have printed; both which are here accounted for; and I think I may make bold to say, that my adversaries are fairly disarmed.

As to my *Scuffle* with Patrick Campbell (a Dublin bookseller) I found myself obliged to publish all the circumstances of it to the world, that I might not be wanting to my own reputation on that head. Here the reader will find I have acted fairly and above board; and that I don't depend either upon my own evidence or judgment in the matter; therefore I have here made it plain, that I have the testimony of persons of the greatest figure in Church and State in Ireland, for my conduct there, which I hope will be sufficient to stop the mouths of all cavillers.

The second part of my book is entitled (what is really was) a *Billet Doux sent to me by a Citizen's Wife in Dublin; with my Answers to her.* And as LUST was her master-sin, so in my First and Second Letter I check her impudence; and then prescribe remedies for her disease: and in my Third Letter I tell her the way how she and her husband (whom she calls Argus) may yet be happy in wedlock.

Gentlemen, by this attempt of Dorinda[2] (at a time when I was scuffling with Campbell) you may see I was condemned to fight with beasts of both sexes; though I am apt to think (as my London correspondent observed) that it was a trap of Patrick's laying; and that he had a mind to try what he could do by women, since he durst not face me himself, or answer my challenge in print: and therefore I publish Dorinda's *Billet* with my *Dublin Scuffle*, as it seems to be part of it.

Had I been caught in the snare (as my ingenious friend further observes) there's no reason to doubt but Patrick would have blazed it on the house-top. It is true, the *Billet* was really sent me (and my answer directed to St Lawrence's Coffee House on Cork-hill, where it lies still for anything I know to the contrary) but would it save my life, I could not tell who sent it, nor could I ever guess at the author; but I know my innocence, and therefore am not afraid or ashamed that the world should see Dorinda's *Billet*, and what an enemy I was to her assignation, which is written as if she were acquainted with me, the better to allure or fright me to her wanton arms.

As to the third part of my Book, which I call my *Conversation in Ireland*, it was necessary to add it to my *Scuffle* with Campbell, and the Irish Dorinda, that the world might see (by my method of living in that country) what little reason I gave Patrick to scuffle with me; or to the Irish Dorinda to tempt me to her lewd embraces.

This *Account of my Conversation* was really sent in a letter to a lady of high birth; and the answer to it is a letter of her own writing, but who she is, I having promised to conceal her name, even racks and gibbets should not squeeze it from me: though would she honour me so far as to let me tell who she is, it would add greatly to the sale of my book, and perhaps occasion several impressions.[3] But this is a favour I can't expect. However, to make my conversation as agreeable as I well could, I've intermixed it with particular characters of the most eminent persons I conversed with in the kingdom of Ireland; but more especially in the city of Dublin: and if in these characters I've been too lavish in anyone's praise, or have described some persons what they should be, rather than what they are, it is excusable sure; for who knows but these, by seeing how charming virtue would make them, may endeavour to practise it?

Gentlemen, if these be not reasons sufficient for publishing my *Conversation in Ireland*, I might add one more; and that is—I publish it to please myself; why may not I have my humour, as well as others? I promised my *Summer Rambles*[4] for the diversion of the gentlemen in Ireland, who encouraged my auctions; and this *Conversation* is a part of them: and, gentlemen, if that honourable lady to whom it is directed (or yourselves) do but cast a favourable eye upon it, I have my end: and, who knows what success I may have? For the world is at present much upon the search after voyages and travels; to which rambles being something akin, they are I hope coming in fashion too;

and I may be allowed to offer at something of that nature, since I have crossed the sea half a dozen times, visited America, and been four months together on the ocean.

Sir William Cornwallis⁵ says of Montaign's *Essays*, that it was the likeliest book to advance wisdom, because the author's own experience is the chiefest argument in it: and indeed, should every man write an history of his life, comprehending as well his vices as virtues, and have them with simplicity related; how useful would this prove to the public! But this may rather be wished for than expected, since men have ever preferred their own private reputation before the real good of themselves or others. But now, if contrary to the mode of such travellers as lose their thoughts in the open air where they were conceived, I have with more diligence registered mine: it was out of no opinion they deserve a longer life, but to prevent idleness. The chief thing I seek in publishing this *Dublin Scuffle* and *Conversation in Ireland* (next to clearing my innocence with respect to Campbell, Dorinda, and other enemies) is by my pen to find employment for a spirit that would break the vessel, had it nothing to work upon. To those that are angry at my frequent digressions, I answer here (with the ingenious Montaign) that constancy is not so absolutely necessary in authors as in husbands; and for my own part, when I have my pen in my hand and subject in my head, I look upon myself as mounted my horse to ride a journey; wherein, although I design to reach such a town by night, yet will I not deny myself the satisfaction of going a mile or two out of the way to gratify my senses with some new and diverting prospect. Now he that is of this rambling humour perhaps will be pleased with my *Conversation* (which is little else than a hasty digression from one thing to another). However, in this I have (as I said before) the honour to imitate the great Montaign, whose umbrage is sufficient to protect me against any one age of critics; and it is well it is so, for, gentlemen, I am very sensible that it is safer to make 50 challenges at sword and buckler, long sword and quarter-staff, than to play one author's prize on the bookseller's stall; for the one draws but blood, but by the other a man is drawn and quartered. To appear in print is worse than hanging; for the torture of the halter is but an hour or so; but he that lies on the rack in print has his flesh torn off by the teeth of envy and calumny, though he meant nobody no harm. Nay, some of my brethren themselves are turned demi-critics, and call everything stuff that has not their own name to it. There's P.C., T.F.[6] and two or three more ill-natured fops, if an angel should send a copy to Phil – – they would call it stuff, except they had a share in it. But I shall meet with them elsewhere; and would have these ill-natured critics take notice, that I wear my pen as others do their sword, and for that same end too; and don't care one rush whether they approve or condemn what I write. It is not their judgment that I value, and therefore think it below my regard, any other wise than to vindicate myself from their calumnies.

Thus, Gentlemen, have I given you a distinct account of the three parts of my *Dublin Scuffle*, with the true reasons for my publishing of it. As to the *Two Letters and Verses* that lead the van, they came to me with no other direction than, For John Dunton; at the Raven in Jewen-street;[7] and I think I can do no less in point of gratitude and civility to their authors, than to print them as an *Introduction* to my *Scuffle*, with this assurance, that you have them in the very dress they came to me in. The *Letters and Verses* will, I presume, speak for themselves; but for my own performance I shall say nothing. I must own you have hitherto used me with much civility, which makes me the less apprehensive of any danger now; but come what will, I'm resolved to stand to your courtesy, and shall always acknowledge the former obligations you have laid upon

Your humble servant
John Dunton

London, February 20. 1698/9

A Poem on the Dublin Scuffle[1]

I hope (Sir) you will not esteem it an uncivil address, if I put you in mind of the *Scuffle* you promised us; I can tell you that we are all in mighty pain for it; and truly, unless you speedily deliver us, shall be apt to conclude you have given up the cause. You can't imagine what advantage the Scotchman[2] makes of the interval; I met him accidentally the other day at your friend Dick's,[3] where his chief business was to traduce and revile you, and, indeed, I believe he had went on with his show, if I had not started the *Scuffle* in your vindication; when I told him we expected it here in a month, I found it stung him to the very soul; he put himself instantly into his natural posture of rubbing and scratching, and in my conscience made as many wry faces as he used to do formerly at the buckling on of his pack;[4] and verily, I was not wanting to give him now and then a lift.

But after all, you must send it away with the utmost expedition; all your friends, nay, the whole town, earnestly expect it from you, and truly in my judgment you cannot come off of it now, without a manifest injury both to your interest and reputation.

And here's poor Dorinda, too; what can you imagine she thinks of the matter? I'll warrant you her pulse beats very high upon the point? Who she is, we cannot learn. But most people that understand Dublin, believe her to be a dependant upon the Order of St Patrick.[5] Let her be who she will, I can tell her that our city dames resent the thing so very ill, that if they should once find her out, I would not be in her coat for his whole pack; and for Niff Naff[6] himself too, if after all they should find that he had any finger in the contrivance, he had best be sure to keep a strong padlock upon his trouses.[7]

Well, but I have sent you a few Irish rhymes too, which you may either commit to the flames, or some empty place in your book, as you shall think them worthy. You know Ireland's but a barren country for such sort of commodities; however, sign-post painting may serve to put you in mind of your friends, as well as the best; and if it does but that it will be a sufficient satisfaction to

Yours, Farewell,

Dublin Feb. 6. 1698/9   T.B.

To Mr John Dunton
upon his Dublin Scuffle

My friend, could I but let thee see
How much I love and value thee,
I'm sure thou'dst reckon this offence
At worst, a kind impertinence.
I know thy learning and thy parts,
Thy knowledge in the noblest arts;
Thy CONVERSATION and thy wit,
Speak thee for my advice unfit;
But what of that, true friendship still
Atones for every other ill.

    Believe me then, in this hard Scuffle,
Poor John, thou seem'st confined to ruffle
Not only with the Scotch man's pride,
But other knaves and fools beside.
He that is forced to draw his pen,
Must fight with beasts in shapes of men.
They'll pointed censures at him dart,
Which though they cannot reach his heart,
Will reach his better part, his fame,
And wound him deep in his good name.
Thou'll find too late, this paper war
Is worse, even than intestine jar.[8]
But be it so, or be it not,
You must go on, this scurvy Scot
Has broke the peace, and the proud loon
Insults, unless you take him down.
Besides, thou hast a safe defence,
I mean thy truth and innocence.
Thy honesty will be thy guard,
And thy fair dealing thy reward.
'Tis true, the wretch of Skinner Row[9]
Is for thy pen too base and low;

And so is false Dorinda too,
A subject far too mean for you:
And so is Dick, but what of that,
Here's Wilde and I, and honest Pat,[10]
Nay, all the town, but two or three,
Speak well, and justly value thee:
So thou'rt engag'd for different ends,
To right thy self, and please thy friends.

T.B.

The Second Letter to Mr John Dunton, upon his Dublin Scuffle

Why John, here's Niff Naff
Would make a man laugh,
To see how he sets up his back.[11]
I'll tell thee by th' by,
'Tis mounted as high
As when formerly guirded to th' pack.[12]

I protest he's half mad,
Is not that very sad?
And swears by his namesake, St Patrick,
When thy *Scuffle* come's o're
He'll meet it a shore,
And in spite of them all play it a trick.

You know he's a SCOT,
And then what is he not?
Why every thing now but a pedler.
But he's got into th' Row,[13]
How he came there we know,
Yet I hate the repute of a medler.

Then prithee good John,
With thy *Scuffle* go on,
'Tis you that must humble the loon;
What the De'el, would he have
All Dublin his slave,
And encroach all the business o' the town.

No, no, Mr SCOT,
Excuse us in that,
We know you too well for the future.
Is this your pretence
Of conscience and sense
To use honest John like a Jew, Sir?

And DICK too I'll tell thee,
What e're bad befell thee,
Thou had'st better have kept to thy word;
And for Mrs Dorinda,
Whom we cannot find a —
John values her not of a T —

No! he's too well weigh'd
To be fool'd or betray'd
By a knave, or a jilt in disguise.
I'll tell thee but that,
'Twill be better for PAT,
And make thee hereafter more wise.

To let his room o're his head,[14]
I'd have first wanted bread
Before I'd have pleasured the loon.
The more (Dick) I think on't,
The more you still stink on't,
And grow nauseous all over the town.

To conclude, honest Dunton,[15]
Ne're value't a button,
Thy candor, fair-dealing, and sense,
Have placed you too high,
For such insects to fly,
And will still be thy guard and defence.

Here's Wilde's thy true friend,
Whom even interest can't bend
To forfeit thy love or thy trust.
He'll tell thee the town
Does in general own
That all thy proposals were just.

Though the pedler and whore
And one or two more,
Attempt to surprise and trapan[16] thee,
The rest are all thine,
Both the lay and divine,
With all the true friendship that can be.

Sir,

I presume you will not believe I am so much an ape, to be fond of the deformed brat I here send you;[17] you see I have not set my name to it; which perhaps may occasion Campbell, &c. to make reflections. To be plain with him, I have no manner of apprehension of him, or any of his party; my only concern is, that when you come to peruse it, you will think it unworthy of the meanest place in your book; and then I'm confident, both in point of wisdom and interest, I ought to keep myself concealed. In short, I am one of those that by your fair and genteel dealing, you have solemnly engaged to your friendship; and one of those too, that earnestly expect your SCUFFLE. As for my name, &c. if the Scotchman insists upon it, when you think fit, he shall know it: and withal, be further satisfied with what sincerity I am,

Yours

Dublin Feb 10. 1698/9   S.M.[18]

The Dublin Scuffle. Letter I

Sir,

In the history of my Irish travels, I am come so far as to speak of the auction I made in Dublin, which I fear will end in a sort of scuffle (something like your counter-scuffle in London).[1] But that you may have the better idea of this rambling project, and of Patrick Campbell, the chief adversary I have yet met with, I here send it in the words it was published.

> *An Account of the Three Auctions to be held in the City of Dublin: in a Letter to the Wise, Learned, and Studious Gentlemen of the Kingdom of Ireland, but more especially to those in the City of Dublin.*

Gentlemen,

Though the summer be a time for rambling, and the season of the year invite all men abroad that love to see foreign countries, yet it was not this alone, but the good acceptance the way of sale by auction has met with from all lovers of books, that encouraged me to bring to this Kingdom of Ireland, a general collection of the most valuable pieces in Divinity, History, Philosophy, Law, Physic, Mathematics, Horsemanship, Merchandise, Limning,[2] Military Discipline, Heraldry, Music, Fortification, Fireworks, Husbandry, Gardening, romances, novels, poems, plays, bibles and school-books, that have been printed in England since the dreadful fire in London in 1666, to this present time.

In this general collection you'll find that many a good book has lain asleep, as not being known, and when a book is not published, it cannot be nourished by the favourable acceptance of the world: I might instance in Mr Turner's *History of the Remarkable Providences which have happened in this Age*,[3] of which there is near a thousand disposed of in London, and scarce twenty of them sold in Ireland, though by viewing the contents of this work (which are given *gratis* at Dick's Coffee-House in Skinner Row) it will evidently appear there is not a more useful book.

Now, Gentlemen, as books are the best furniture in a house, so I see no reason why others with myself, should not think their variety the most excusable prodigality; and therefore as the good success auctions have met, with my natural love of travelling (as appears by my venture of this nature to New-England, Holland, and other parts, in the year 1686) put me upon this undertaking, so I hope you will give it encouragement in some proportion to my great expense in purchasing and bringing over so large a collection; and indeed, Gentlemen, as this sale is designed for your profit, as well as my own, so it seems of right to challenge your protection, which if it receives, I shall not value what some little prejudiced people can do to discourage it: I design by this no reflection on my brethren in this city, for to do them justice, they acted generously, and gave me all the countenance I could expect (all save Patrick Campbell, who grins at my undertaking). Though had they not, learning and knowledge are such real things, they need no other props to support them but what is cut out of themselves; and a better medium to effect it, than by reading books, I know not. And though there be a complaint that the world seems oppressed with books, yet do we daily want them; if it were not so, what is the reason that many of great estates can hardly make their minds or thoughts stretch to a geometrical measuring of their own lands? But surely he that has money in his pockets and will starve his brains (when so many new and valuable pieces are brought to his door) deserves to be posted;[4] for what can a man's rusty bags afford him, to the profits and treasures of books? Plato was accounted a wise man, and we find it recorded of him[a] that he thought it a rich purchase when he bought three books of philosophy belonging to Philolaus,[5] a Pythagorean in Sicily, though at an incredible rate; and that Atlas of learning, that orthodox scholar,[b] Archbish. Ussher[6] (whose name makes Ireland famous, as it was the birth-place of so great a man), he it was that sent to Samaria for sundry copies of the Samaritan Pentateuch;[7] and with a dear purchase it was also he that brought the Syriac Bible with other books from Syria. It's recorded that Solomon's library was the feather in the plume of his glorious enjoyments, a part whereof he thought was the choicest present he could make to the Queen of Sheba,[8] for the recompense of her great pains in travelling to profit herself, and honour him; and seeing the

a. See Mr Stanley's *Philosophy*.[9]   b. See Mr Leigh, *Of Religion and Learning*.[10]

variety of books (says the ingenious Burton[11]) he must needs be a block that's affected with none. King James the First, when he saw the Oxford Library, wished that if it ever happened that he should be a prisoner, that there he might be kept, and that those chained books might be his fellows, and the chains his fetters: and who will not say that good books and good company are the very epitome of heaven? In a word, there's nothing comparable to the purchase of knowledge, and whenever men begin to taste it, they will say I speak truth with a witness.

Gentlemen, having said thus much of auctions, learning, and the collection of books I have brought into this kingdom, I would have no man displeased if he finds not all he expected in my first catalogue, for if he has patience, his expectation will be fully answered: but the great variety of books I have brought over, have rendered it impossible to have them all bound time enough for my first sale. I have therefore divided them into three auctions: the first of which will begin July 7th, 1698. Neither can I exceed that time, my design being to take Scotland, France and Italy, &c. in my way home, and to be in London by next Christmas.

There will be a distinct catalogue for every auction, and when printed (of which public notice shall be given) will be delivered *gratis* at Dick's Coffee-House (the place of sale) and at the coffee-houses in Limerick, Cork, Kilkenny, Clonmel, Wexford, Galway, and other places so that those that live at a distance may send their commissions to their relations in Dublin, or to my friend Mr Richard Wilde, and they shall have their orders faithfully executed; for as this country is obliged to his universal knowledge in books, for the goodness of this collection, so to his care and fidelity (my health calling me to Wexford to drink the waters) is committed the charge of the whole undertaking. And I think I need add no more, for though it has been customary to usher in undertakings of this nature with insignificant and tedious commendations, which served only to tire the reader's patience and stagger his belief, and may perhaps be expected now upon a collection which might justly challenge the precedence of what has ever been exposed to sale in Ireland; yet being resolved to proceed in quite contrary methods to what has been formerly used, I'll manage the whole with that candour and sincerity, as shall leave no room for exception: for as gentlemen come here supposing to buy a penny-worth,[12] so I do assure them I think it unjust to advance the rate upon them by any underhand bidding: and for every penny I get that way, I will restore a pound; neither did I suffer any of my scarce and valuable pieces to be culled out from the rest (though importuned thereto by several gentlemen, and booksellers) that all might have equal treatment, and the greater reason to attend my auctions. And I am very willing that the ingenious and learned should be their own judges in this matter, not doubting but upon an impartial view of my three catalogues (of which this is the first) they will find not only such variety of new books as were never before in Ireland (and scarce ones nowhere else to be purchased) but such curiosities in manu-scripts and pamphlets (of all sorts) as will be sufficient to invite them to exert a generosity, as may further encourage

Your humble servant
John Dunton

Dublin June 24. 1698

Sir,

If you'll give me your thoughts upon this auction, the conditions of sale, and the *Scuffle* I'm like to be engaged in, on the account of this undertaking, I shall own it as a mark of your friendship: write as supposing me still on the road; I am yet on my *Summer's Ramble*, and to-morrow (having met with agreeable company) shall set out for the Boyne, Kilkenny, Galway, &c. in order to view the cabins, customs, and manners of the wild Irish[13]—direct your answer to be left with my worthy friend Dr Wood,[14] at his house in Kilkenny, for I design to make him a visit when I leave Dublin. Pray, Sir, write by the first post, for I intend your answer shall come into my *Summer-Ramble*, for my method, different from other travellers, is to get remarks upon all I see, but sixpence once, twice,[a] and the next word is to assure you, that I am

Your very humble servant,
John Dunton

a. This is the second letter I sent you, since I came to Ireland.

Remarks on my First Letter

Sir,

I have received the kindness of yours, by which I perceive that neither distance of place, multiplicity of business, nor variety of diversions, and sometimes distractions, are able to divert the stream of solid friendship, but that you have still a minute to spare in remembrance of your old acquaintance.

I am glad to find you have encouragement to go on with your generous undertaking of imparting to Ireland so many valuable pieces of learning. I don't know why some of them may not be accounted phœnixes, as being revived since the fire of London, or rather sprung up from its ashes.

Time was when Ireland was famous for learning, and hence it came to be said of a certain great man, whose name does not now occur to me,

> *Ivit ad Hibernos Sophia mirabile claros.*[15]

But I am afraid the case is much altered since. Slavery and popery have had so long and universal a possession of that country, that the spirits of the native (or wild Irish at least) are much degenerated, so that we may now apply to them as a proper reverse,

> *Vervecam in Patria crassoque sub aere Nati.*[16]

If your design may be any way subservient to restore learning among them, you will have cause to value yourself upon it while you live.

But, my friend, I perceive by your fears of a SCUFFLE, that you will find it more difficult to conquer their prejudices, at least of some of them, than Richard Strongbow found it to make a conquest of their nation;[17] but I hope you are so much a philosopher as to prepare yourself beforehand for cross emergents, that you don't lose courage on their approach.

Never was there that great or good design yet in the world which did not meet with opposition, and if yours happen to be singular in this respect, it will be as remarkable a passage as many that are recorded in the Irish story.

You know I am no pretender to the spirit of prophecy, but methinks I foresee a storm coming upon you. My reason is this, whatever the honesty of your design, and the fairness of your way of dealing may be, and which I persuade myself the Irish climate will never be able to alter; yet you must expect that those of your own calling will look upon you as an interloper, or perhaps a forestaller and engrosser:[18] if you can convey learning to Ireland through their channels, so as there may be some gold-dust left for themselves at the bottom, you may perhaps escape pretty well; but if otherwise, I am much mistaken if you don't experimentally find the falsehood of that old saying, that Ireland entertains no venomous creature.[19]

I cannot but applaud your honesty in promising not to advance the prices upon gentlemen that come to buy, by underhand bidding. To do otherwise, is not only to act two different parts with the satyr in the fable, but according to the northern proverb, to play both the thief and the merchant, and I wish you had left more of that sort of honesty amongst some of your brethren at home.[20] We have not so much of it ourselves, as to send such a cargo of it at once to our neighbours; the worst I shall wish those gentlemen, who practise the contrary method, is, that they may never have any other buyers but their own underhand bidders, for that is the likeliest way to reform them.

But though I am confident you will be as good as your promise in this matter, yet all your honesty will not be armour of proof against a weapon you have put into the hands of your enemies, which is, that you promise a pennyworth to those that will buy at your auction.

The proposal is indeed as charitable as that of selling below the market price to the starving poor, but you know those who practise this method, have as many curses from the engrossers of corn, as blessings from the starvlings whom they save from death.

Learning, I do verily believe, runs low in Ireland, generally speaking; and no wonder it should, when they have not books at moderate rates, and therefore your bountiful design to the public will not be able to atone for the injury which some persons will be ready to apprehend from you in their private affairs. If you sell a better pennyworth than they, you must expect their envy; and the consequence of that is all that's unjust and mischievous.

But let none of these things discourage you; go on with your good design of dispersing those books in Ireland that are fitted for their introduction and diversion; profit and pleasure ought to go hand in hand.

I would not frighten you by representing only the black side of the cloud. I hope you will meet with some fair weather; try if you can invite the Muses in your *Summer's Ramble* to make a visit once more to the Irish Parnassus[21] and to disperse the liberal arts amongst the kerns.[22] What pity is it, that a people who are generally so fair of body should not have better means to cultivate their souls.

You are very well furnished with proper materials for so good a work, if they fall into charitable hands.

You are accustomed to rambling, to use your own term, though some would have the ambition to call it travelling; and if as other travellers do generally drop money in those countries which they visit, you drop learning too, it will be a double advantage.

I must take leave to dissent from one of your propositions, that books are the best furniture in a house, and I believe you will be of my mind too, when you know what it is; and I will tell it you frankly, that I think a good wife is better; but both of them do well together. I could the more readily have pardoned your mistake, if you had not known the truth of what I say, by both sides of experience, but of this enough. It would seem by you that Solomon thought them equal, seeing he presented the Queen of Sheba with part of his library, for if we may believe Prester John,[23] she was one of his concubines, that passed for a sort of wife in those days, and from their bed it is he pretends to derive his own original. This must needs enhance the value of books (and the stationers' trade) seeing they were the noblest present that the wisest of princes could think on, to make to the wisest of queens.

Had that prince happened to live when printing was invented, he had certainly been a great encourager of the booksellers' trade—he who knew the sweets of wisdom and understanding, and pressed others so earnestly to the pursuit of it, would have thought himself very happy in such a proper and easy method of acquiring and diffusing it.

Yet such is the unhappy genius of too many in this age, that they care not how empty their brains be, so they can but stuff their bags, or their bellies—covetousness and sensuality are equally enemies to learning. The miser laughs at those who spend their time and strength in search of the philosopher's stone, the grand elixir, and *Aurum potabile*,[24] whilst he has the *Aurum potabile* under a sure guard of locks and bars. The sensualist does in the same manner ridicule those who abridge themselves of sleep and other conveniences, in the pursuit of knowledge. He thinks the best ornament for the head is a fine hat and a slanting wig; a good complexion owing to the bottle, is preferable in his sense, to a pale face, the usual reward of study. He had rather be taught how to cut capers with his heels,[25] than enabled to judge between truth and error with his head.

These are some of the principal reasons why learning makes so little progress amongst many, who by Providence and Nature are furnished with opportunity and ability to acquire it.

Your instances of the value put upon books, by Plato, Archbishop Ussher, and King James I, are pertinently brought in, and may they be as perfectly copied. Knowledge is, without doubt, the most valuable of all sublunary treasures. Solomon was certainly of that opinion, when he said that a poor and wise child was better than an old and a foolish king. Wisdom had something more charming in his eyes than any thing the crown and scepter could afford; whence we may rationally infer, that Solomon would have preferred the industry of those that should have brought him a cargo of good books, to the industry of his richest merchants that brought him gold and silver from the Indies, which some modern authors understand by Ophir.

The thoughts of this may be enough to support you against the cavils of those who may happen to oppose you. Seeing the native result of your voyage to Ireland is to make good books common there at a moderate rate, for which others would exact upon their customers.[26]

I shall conclude this long letter with this one remark, that your fancy soars too high, and your mind is too nimble for your body. To talk of completing your ramble in Ireland, to visit Scotland, France, and Italy, and to be in London by Christmas next, is somewhat too much for Pegasus[27] himself; for you have known him sometimes play the jade. I find you are already obliged to go to Wexford for your health, whence I am afraid you will be induced to alter your project.

For if your body won't keep pace with your mind, you must send your thoughts upon the ramble, and spare the carcass: however, I approve of your return to London by Christmas, for at that time we have generally as good cheer in England as you will find anywhere else.

Give me leave to add one word, as to your conditions of sale. If the conditions of your chapmen[28] be as fair, you have reason to expect all possible encouragement; but I am afraid you will find Solomon's observation hold as true in Ireland as in other kingdoms, where the buyers do usually say of the merchandise, it is naught, it is naught, but when they have once got it into their possession, they will be sure to boast of their pennyworth. I have no more to add, but pray you to make haste home and in the meantime fortify yourself against the distemper of the country, by its own natural product, I mean a good frieze[29] coat, lined with usquebaugh;[30] but don't linger too long, least[31] our minced pies be all eat[32] before you get over, for I look upon them to be a more proper cordial for a true English stomach. But I shall exceed the bounds of a letter, and therefore without any further ceremony, subscribe myself,

Your friend and servant, &c.

The Second Letter

My worthy friend,

I have received yours, with your thoughts of my Dublin auction and of the conditions of sale, for which I return you hearty thanks. I have already found that your conjectures of envy's attending my design were too well grounded, and have reaped some benefit by your advice. Therefore I have here sent you an account of an unhappy *Scuffle* between me and a Dublin bookseller. That you may the better be possessed of the whole matter I have here sent you the copies of the letters and proceedings that have yet passed on this occasion, and hope you will oblige me with the favour of your thoughts upon this, as you did upon my former. This *Scuffle* was first occasioned by his taking my auction room over my head, which obliged me to publish the following Reasons for my Removal to another, directed to the gentlemen of Dublin.

The Reasons for my Removal to Pat's Coffee-House

Gentlemen,

I have drawn up some reasons for my removal to Pat's Coffee-House, which I had sent to the press, where they were composed and the letters set,[1] but the printer, being overawed by Mr Campbell, refused to print them. But, Gentlemen, if money will purchase the printing of them elsewhere, you shall have them in print tomorrow morning, or otherwise in writing at Pat's Coffee-House in High Street.

John Dunton

Gentlemen,

The above lines were printed before my catalogue for November the seventh, and owned as a truth by my printer in Dublin (in the presence of Mr George Larkin and Mr Richard Wilde) who then declared that Mr Campbell threatened to arrest him, and his partner, and to take away all his work then in the house, if he went on with the printing of my reasons for removing to Pat's. Gentlemen, Patrick's frighting printers with actions (and by this way locking up the press) is, I confess, a pretty way of answering my charge against him, and sufficiently shews his guilt; but I am so far from being frighted with bugbears of that nature, having a just cause to defend, that at the same hour he enters one action, I'll enter two, and pursue it further than he is aware of; and though my printer had not soul brave enough to work off at the press what was composed in his house (for my letter annexed was directed to him), yet other printers in Dublin, being satisfied with the truth of my charge, assured me in the presence of Mr Larkin, that they would have printed it with all their hearts, had they done my former work; however, Gentlemen, I here present you in writing with what I design to publish, with this promise to the printers of Dublin that were afraid to print the following paper; that whatever they shall print against me, I will take no advantage against them for it, provided they'll declare the author; and if I cannot have the liberty of the press here, as I can in London (though for every sheet printed in this *Scuffle*, I'll give a double price), I'll answer what my adversary shall print every day in manuscript with my name to it, and leave it at Pat's Coffee-House.

An Account of my Third Auction in Dublin, to be held at Pat's Coffee-House, over against St Michael's Church in High-street, on Monday November 7th, 1698, with my Reasons for removing thither.

In a second Letter to those Gentlemen, who have bought books at my two former Auctions.

Gentlemen,

This present Monday being November the seventh, at three of the clock in the afternoon, will begin my third auction at Pat's Coffee-House in High-street. It is true, I fully designed that this third auction, as well as my first and second, should have been sold at Dick's Coffee-House in Skinner Row, for I had agreed with Dick for his back room as long as my sale lasted, and though I never released the bargain (as Dick himself has owned at the Ram[2] in the presence of divers persons) any further, than by telling him, that I did not doubt to have done in a few days, which I only said, to shew my readiness to quit his room as soon as possible I could; but Dick catching at these words, and one Patrick Campbell designing himself to keep an auction of books there, and thinking that the room where gentlemen had found such fair usage in my auction would give a reputation to his, takes it over my head (and Mr Wilde's[3] too, as he had the promise on it, when my sale was done) pressing Dick to the bargain by those moving arguments of a double price, or going to another place, and easy Dick (though otherwise, I hope, honest) finding that it was the law of auctions that he who bids most is the buyer, even lets the room to Patrick, at the time when it was actually mine, without being so fair as to cry ten shillings once,[a] ten shillings twice, either to myself, or to Mr Wilde, to whom he promised the refusal. Gentlemen, this was odd treatment, but because my stay in Dublin won't permit me to do myself justice, I chose rather to quit my right, than contend for it; but had Dick considered how far the rules of civility to me, and gratitude to Mr Wilde, should have swayed with him (Mr Wilde not only being the proprietor of the shelves, that stood in the room, but also the first that brought an

a. Note, ten shillings a week was as much more as I had agreed with Dick for.

auction thither, that had kept several there, and was the means of bringing Mr Thornton's formerly, and mine now), I say had Dick reflected on these things, his eyes had been proof against the double price (that Dick in his letter tells me, Patrick had agreed to give him) and the Scot might have ganged with his pack of bewks to another place.[4]

I shall be glad to see Patrick acquit himself, but I much doubt it, when I consider the dark usage I had in Turner[5] (of which more thereafter) and the forty shillings I had of him, was a second part to the same tune: you must know, Gentlemen, he bragged of lending me forty shillings, when I first came to Dublin, thinking, I suppose, to lessen my credit with printers, stationers, and binders, not knowing how forward they were to serve me that so my venture might sleep in quiet, till this geud man[6] had culled out my best books, which I judge he thought (if the binders were made infidels) he should have for a song, and the rest, Gentlemen, you know might have been serviceable to your ladies under minced pies;[7] in this you see the very soul of Patrick; for he could not but know, that I had not a drop of mechanic blood in my whole body (myself being the fourth John Dunton in a lineal descent from the tribe of Levi)[8] that I could bow low, but could never creep to anything; that I was born to a good estate in land, and had made it treble by a late marriage; that I had brought a venture of books to Dublin (of near ten ton) which could not yield less then 1500*l.*, and 290*l.* more could I approve of setters;[9] and he as well knew that if I wanted an 100*l.* (for the King's customs, and other charges, &c.) that I could have it at a word's speaking, from Mr Lum, a Parliament man:[10] but for all this, he talked so loud of his forty shillings (though then he owed me a greater sum, and to this hour is not out of my debt) that the sound of it reached to England, and Mr Wilde, who was then in London, sent me word, he admired[11] I should want forty shillings, when a bill had been sent me of forty pounds.

Gentlemen, by what I have mentioned, you see what the Scotchman itched to be at; and to add to his favours, he now takes my room over my head; which I must tell him, resembles a man I once met in my travels, who sold the same book with two different titles, turning Hodder into Cocker, Cumpstey into Whaley, &c.[12]

(according as his customer wanted) with as much dexterity as the sutler in King James's camp, who drew ale out of one end of the barrel, and beer at the other. Nothing that's said here is designed as a reflection on any other of my brethren in this city, for to do them justice (as I said in my first letter) they acted generously, and gave me all the countenance I could expect; all save Niff-Naff (the proud loon of Skinner Row) who formerly grinned and now barks at my undertaking. But when I came to Ireland, I expected to fight with beasts at Ephesus;[13] and if he proceeds as he has begun, we shall *scuffle* in earnest; but if we do (as good luck is) such is the impenetrability of innocence, and my just undertaking, that he can do me no harm: for I bless God, my name and reputation stands much above him, but he labours (though it is yet in private) to bespatter me all he can; nay, Gentlemen, so foul and nauseous is the venom he spits at me, that it is easy to think that Nature spoiled him in the making, and set his mouth at the wrong end; certainly, there must be a corrupted and putrified soul within, whence (as my friends tell me) there daily steams out so much odious and stinking breath. It is true, Gentlemen, he calls himself the een mon of coonshence;[14] but I am afraid to tell you what persuasion[15] he is of, seeing he has so very little either of justice or humanity, but at present he's the chief, if not the only, enemy I have; his private slanders (the more impudent, as given at a time when he owed me money) are too notorious to need my answer, but may teach us this, that we should judge of all men's religion by their charity, and that to believe one report in twenty is to give a very large allowance.

I might next ask Patrick a few questions (for modern Athens[a] owes its rise to my doubts and fears) about Campbell (alias Ure) and a certain organist (his tenant for one night).[16] I should next drag Patrick to Waterford, and shew him Mr Hart's house, and here I could ask very odd questions; and now my hand's in at asking of questions, I'll ask Patrick how he rested on Sunday night? For he was visiting the press by seven on Monday morning, sent his spies by eight, and his honest drudges were on the stool of repentance by nine, and by ten (with cap in hand) were at down-right asking my pardon for composing Reasons they durst not print; this again makes me ask, whether Campbell did not privately see my Reasons before

a. As you will find in the *History of the Athenian Society*, printed for Jam. Dowley.[17]

they went to the press, and a printed copy of them after it was told me the title was distributed? and whether they did not pay the printers for composing them, they being so willing, if I'd suppress this paper, to excuse me in that matter? And if so, upon the whole, whether the two printers, and Patrick, be not three?

Gentlemen, being fallen amongst printers, I shall ask a question or two about the Dublin booksellers; as, are they a forgiving company? (for they are so in London) and can they pardon a kneeling Patrick, for some little lie in way of trade? and which he has owned to them; sure they may, when he's a saint of their own country; I have more questions to ask, and from thence could descend to other particulars; but I'll spare Patrick for his late justice, in detecting the thieves that robbed my warehouse; and if I knew of one more virtue he had, I'd proclaim it on the house-top, and to make it the more observed, I would afterwards blaze it in the *London Gazette*:[18] for, Gentlemen, as I'm a true friend where I take a fancy, so Patrick shall find me as fair an enemy; sure I am, did gentlemen know my great charge in removing to Pat's, the folios, and buyers, which I lost upon that occasion, they'd say I treat Patrick with a world of tenderness; all that I've said yet is but self-defence; and though this feud should end with a bloody nose (for Dick suspects it began with one) yet I'll still be so just to Patrick, as not to belie the devil. Gentlemen, to convince you of this I'll venture at no buts nor hints of things (buts and hints, when they are no more, are the worst sort of murdering a man) but what I can (and will when he answers this) prove at length, on which I'll bestow a few annotations, as a key to the darker passages.

Thus, Gentlemen, have I given you the reasons for my removal to Pat's, wherein I have advanced nothing relating to Dick, or the een, alias only, mon of coonshence (as the geud man at the Bible has called himself)[19] but what I'll prove, and reply to every day, if there be occasion.

Gentlemen, though I have been thus thrust out of my room to make way for St Patrick and his auction; I hope you will allow me to say something of my own, though your general acknowledgment of the fair dealing you had in it seems to render this work unnecessary; for you all know, I began my sale on a just foundation, did not interfere with any man's auction (there was none mentioned in

Dublin till I came) nor did I take any man's room over his head; or had I innocently done such a thing as that, upon notice given by the injured person (such as Patrick has had over and over) I'd have flung up the bargain at first word: and I may speak the freer in this matter, as it is a thing I have done in London; and as I began my auction on a just foundation in Dublin, so the books I sold were as fairly bought in London; I took advantage of no man's ignorance, as Mr Wilde knows, in getting in the whole venture; of this he can give you several instances, but that of Mr Sh—n might suffice for all; and as my books were honestly bought, and the sale begun on a right foundation, so I have had a blessing on the undertaking; and though I fight with beasts at Ephesus, whilst I've a cordial in my own breast I shall fear nothing; the truth is, I was ever more afraid of myself than of all the world; a man cannot fly from himself (every man carries an executioner in his own breast), so that a man's conscience (in some sense) is the only friend or enemy he has in the world.

Gentlemen, had I begun my auctions (or carried them on) by other means than is here mentioned, I should own it a piece of impudence to desire your company a third time; or had I pretended conscience to you, and yet played the knave with Dick (for I did not take his room from week to week, as he falsely asserts, but for as long as my sale lasted, as several witnesses will depose upon oath), it would have shown you at first glance what candour you were to have in my three auctions; but to rob Peter to pay Paul, is a doctrine I never practised, and scarce know what it is called; and would you have a name for it, you must send to the een mon of coonshence;[20] but though I am able to stand the test with the same allowance that every man would wish for himself under the like circumstance, as to my auctions here, and the whole trading part of my life, yet I have enemies as well as other men (two of a trade can never agree) and you would wonder if I had not, for I have printed six hundred books, written by authors of different judgments, and it is strange if in drawing upon one another, the bookseller (a sort of second in such duels) should always escape without any wound; but though I have enemies, they are only those that never knew me, or never heard what I had to say for myself, or else such narrow souls as are wholly guided by self-interest.

Of all that have traded with me (though for many thousands) I know not of one enemy I have in the whole world, save Patrick Campbell at the Bible in Skinner-Row, and a piece of trash that I smell beyond the herring pond: and to the immortal glory of the Stationers' Company, I know but two more such in London, and not one of them lives in St Paul's Church-Yard, or at the Bible and Three Crowns;[21] but, Gentlemen, if I find out more, you shall know the names their godfathers gave them; but it will be time enough to descend to particulars when I leave Ireland, and then I'll surely do it, in a Farewell Letter to those gentlemen that buy what they won't pay for.

Now Gentlemen, if my friend Campbell thinks himself injured by these reflections, the press is open, to him I mean, but not to me (as he has ordered it). But if I have a clear stage, I desire no quarter from him, for I have yet so much by me which will keep cold, as would make a pedlar sweat, or as stout a man as the great Campbell. But, Gentlemen, conscience makes cowards of us all, and for that reason Campbell will scarce give you the diversion of a paper war. No, Patrick is a great man, and to scorn my charge (as in yesterday's *Flying Post*)[22] is the easiest way to answer it; the truly valiant dare face their danger, but I doubt my enemy won't meet me with any weapon but his old one of Niff-Naff, for fear his defence in print should move me to new discoveries, or to fall to writing of ears;[23] but if he hangs out his flag of defiance, and dares answer this, let him do it while I'm here, and subscribe it with his right name, as I will my reply with John Dunton; for it is a pitiful cowardice that strikes a man in the dark, or like T.W.[24] bites a man by the heel, and then like a serpent creeps into his hole again, for want of courage to abet his actions. I never in my whole life was the first aggressor in any quarrel, but when I am justly provoked, I wear my pen as others do their sword; and if Campbell replies to this, I'll answer his charge, *de die in diem*,[25] till I have worn my pen to the stumps.

> What though I lose the day, yet I aim high;
> And to dare something, is some victory.[26]

Though Patrick can fright the printers that live by him, yet I do assure him (as I tell Dorinda in my Answer to her Billet Doux) till he's virtuous I can't love him, and it is not in my nature to fear anything; neither will I forget him, nor the Brass in Copper-Alley,[27] in the history of my *Summer's Ramble*, which will be a crown bound,[28] and shall be sent to Dublin in few weeks. When we have thus boxed it out, we'll kiss (as the gentlemen of Ireland do), wash ourselves, shake hands and part.

But whither does my just resentment carry me? Yet, Gentlemen, I hope you'll pardon it, for when at any time I go out of the way, it is rather upon the account of licence than oversight; there be pieces in Plutarch,[29] as well as in Dunton, where he forgets his theme; besides I'm the more excusable, as I told you I loved rambling, and should visit Scotland on my way home, and you see I'm as good as my word.

Gentlemen, I shall only add, that the candid treatment you have found in my two auctions, I hope will invite you this afternoon to visit my third; and to engage you to it, you will find daily in my printed bills that I have yet divers good books, as Doctor Barrow's *Works*, Josephus *History* in English, Rawleigh the best edition, Milton's *Political Works*, and many others I have not time to mention.[30]

You will also find, I have several excellent law books in all volumes, such as the Irish Statutes in folio, and the year books of the best edition, &c.

I have also, in this third auction, a collection of scarce pamphlets on most subjects, and when my catalogue of manuscripts is published (it containing a great variety of curious subjects never yet in print) I shan't doubt the company of ingenuous persons, but this being my last sale for the year, 1698, and my time of embarking for London being very soon, I can allow but two days after the auction is ended, for the taking away what you buy in it.

To conclude, I told you in my first letter that I thought it unjust to advance the rate upon you by any underhand bidding, and for every penny I got that way, I'd restore a pound; which was not said to serve a turn, for I have been true to my word, as a worthy member of the House of Commons (who has been a great encourager of my auction) has done me the honour to declare; and as honest Dobbs, a considerable buyer, and all the servants attending my auction, can testify; but surely, Gentlemen, the buyer should be just as well as the seller, and if you consider the vast charge I am at to serve you (with such an auction of new books as never was sold in Ireland) you will be as forward to pay me, as I am to subscribe myself

Your very humble servant,

Dublin, Nov. 5th. 1698   John Dunton

To the end the foregoing letter might be forthwith printed, I sent it to the person, who printed my auction-bills, with this letter (viz.)

To the Printer

Sir,

Finding a necessity of vindicating myself, against the ill usage of Mr Patrick Campbell, and Mr Richard Pue,[31] I send this second letter (giving an account of my third auction) for you to print; you see I have subscribed my name to it, and will own it in the face of the sun; and if Mr Campbell be a generous enemy, he will be no more angry at your printing this, than I shall be if you print his answer; nor will I ever give you any trouble upon that account, how scandalous and false soever the things may be that you shall print against me, provided you will be ready to testify who is the author; but if you have not soul brave enough to assist a stranger in a just cause, especially one who has been so great a benefactor to your art both in England and Ireland, in the last of which, I have been none of the worst of customers to you; I shall then be obliged to take other measures to right myself: but hoping you won't give me that unnecessary trouble, I shall only add, that I am

Your hearty friend,
John Dunton

Sir,

Thus I have given you a true and impartial account of my *Dublin Scuffle*, on which I desire such remarks as you were pleased to oblige me with on my former. I know you will deal freely with me, and therefore shall accept your reproof, for anything wherein you think I am faulty, as kindly as your approbation when you think I have right on my side; for you know I was never a slave to my own judgment, but have always desired the opinion of those whose thoughts I valued. I am

Yours to command,
John Dunton

Remarks upon the Second Letter

Sir,

I am sorry that I have happened to be too true a prophet. I told you in my last, that I foresaw you would meet with opposition, and that too from those of your own way of business, but I could scarcely have thought that any man who calls himself a Christian would have attempted it in such a mean and scandalous method.

Your adversary may perhaps have read the Ten Commandments; but it would seem he has altogether forgot the last, or at least to put it in practice; seeing he had so little conscience as fraudulently to take your auction-room over your head. Perhaps he may think it was but a just reprisal to over-bid you, on pretence that you had under-sold him, which though it had been so, is contrary to the law of Christianity, which forbids rewarding evil for evil. But I don't see the least pretence he had for it. You were not the first that set up an auction in Dublin, and it seems Patrick Campbell resolved you should not be the last, seeing he followed your example, and slyly bought you out of your room, but had that been disposed of by way of auction too, I am apt to think you would have been able to cope with him either for purse,[32] or in offering a fair price.

By what I can perceive, your adversary's courage and Christianity are both of a piece. He was resolved to fight you, but that he might assure himself of the victory, he would first disarm you, or at least make sure of the longest weapon. Like another Guy Fawks, he undermined your auction-house; and then, like an Almanzor, he huffs and braves you.[33]

Truth did never yet of its own accord affect a lurking-hole, but has always courage enough to stand the test. Had Patrick's practice been open and fair, he would never have hindered its being published in print. There were other methods to be taken for vindicating his fame than threatening your printers, and out-bidding you there too: had you advanced any falsehoods, the law was open; but Patrick thought it safer to silence the press. Every cock is stout on his own dunghill Patrick claims a privilege to crow at Dublin, but he cannot hinder you to answer him at London, so as you may be heard beyond St George's Channel; and I am apt to think he will take no great pleasure in hearing the story related.

I am glad to find you retain your courage, and are not to be frighted into anything that's sneaking by your adversary's big looks or words. Your natural temper affords you strength enough to bear up against greater attacks than those; and if it want a support, you know it is to be found in him who always patronizes a just cause. Though you be now at a distance from your well-furnished closet, there's no want of proper helps in your present auction-room. Brook's *Remedies against Satan's Devices*[34] may be a proper book for you to consult on this occasion. I am glad to hear that my former [letter] has contributed anything to fortify you against this encounter. I am of opinion, your adversary will have no occasion to triumph, when he casts up his accounts, either with his own conscience (if it be his custom to keep a fair reckoning there) or when he comes to count his gains by his envious auction, which fastens the brand of foul guilt upon him. But it seems Patrick has a mind to be the sole bookseller and auctioneer in Dublin, at what rate soever.

I am much surprised at the meanness of his temper in talking of lending you forty shillings, which to be sure he knew you could not want, when you brought such a cargo of books with you, though you had not had a good estate in England to depend upon. I question very much whether Patrick's estate be able to balance yours, and I am satisfied he cannot be a better husband than you are known to be, nor more industrious in his calling; but malice and covetousness in one man (and indeed they are seldom to be found asunder) are enough to transform him into a monster, and by your character of Patrick, I can form no other idea of him but that he is one of the worst sort. His pretensions to conscience on the one hand, and making no conscience of depriving you of your auction-room, and bespattering your reputation on the other, are very becoming a man who can sell one book for two, under different titles. So that Patrick it seems is a saint on one side, and a devil on the other, and can shew himself in various shapes, as occasion requires: I am glad you were aware of his tricks, and did not suffer him to cull your library, though there's no doubt his disappointment in that is one of the chief causes of the base treatment you meet with at his hands.

I am very well pleased that the other Dublin booksellers behaved themselves with more candour and generosity towards you, and that the whole mass was not corrupted by Patrick's envy.

The questions you propose to him, and the odd hints you give of his practice, I hope are founded upon good information; otherwise, I would not advise you to publish them; lest they be thought envious, and may detract from your own reputation, instead of painting him in his true colours; but if the things be known, and that the divulging of them is necessary for your own vindication, I have the less to say against it. It is fit an hypocrite should be discovered to the world, that he may be rendered incapable of deceiving more.

I cannot however approve of your national reflections, for you know there are good and bad in all countries; and it may perhaps be ill resented, if ever you should attempt an auction at Edinburgh, as you seem to design.

It's true, you have provocation enough from Patrick to display his personal faults, for I perceive he is not so open hearted as you are, but works like a mole underground, and undermines you with very much art. Were his industry and management rightly applied, he would deserve a commendation but as it is otherwise, the more industrious and dexterous he is, the more he discovers[35] his wickedness. Your commending him when he does well, gives an air of ingenuity and truth to the whole of your accusation; and I am verily persuaded, that if any part of it be a lie, it's none of your making—and seeing you offer to prove the truth of everything, if Patrick dares to contradict it, I must needs say, it's a fair offer, but inauspicious for Patrick; for go which way it will, he's like to come off with the loss. If he does not answer you, he seems to own the truth of your charge; so that were he of my temper, he would rather venture to try it out with you, for he can but come off with loss at last.

I am glad you have so many witnesses to prove the fairness of your proceedings, for they are as many to fasten the guilt upon Patrick and

Dick; and therefore I plainly see through the reason of Patrick's unwillingness to engage you in print; he is better at the short dagger of calumny and reproach behind your back, than at fair weapons face to face; he's for underhand buying, and underhand fighting: yet he may remember, that Guy Fawks was at last blown up by his own dark lanthorn.[36]

I must confess, that your having printed so many books as you mention, is very extraordinary; and it had been a miracle if you could have escaped without reflections from one or other upon that very account; and therefore you have reason to bear with the common fate of those of your trade, who print for authors of different judgments; wherein you have scarcely had a common share, for I dare venture to say it, that there are few of the calling, but have more enemies than yourself. I never heard of any you had before, and therefore you have reasons to boast, if you have but one or two in three kingdoms.

I must needs approve your design of printing your defence when you come to England, since Patrick it seems has the sole privilege of the press in Ireland; but if you do, be sure to keep within due bounds, and don't make use of all the advantage, which the goodness of your cause puts in your hand, though I think you have little need of this caution; you have promised your adversary generous treatment, and I never yet knew you worse than your word.

If Patrick does not reply, it must be because he cannot, for that advertisement which you mention of his in the *Flying Post*, is sufficient to shew that he would if he could; and if that be the issue, then you have reason to crow over him in England, as he insulted you in Ireland. But one thing I would advise you against, be not too voluminous. There are but few, who will be at the pains to read a large relation of a particular quarrel; and therefore, I would advise you to set bounds to your fancy. Your credit is well enough established in England, and I don't find that you have done anything to lessen it in Ireland, so that a short defence will serve. Nay, I am of opinion that a plain narrative of matter of fact will be apology enough for yourself, and punishment enough for Patrick Campbell.

The copy of your letter to the printer is so fair and generous that nothing can be said more to prove that your adversary has neither candour nor courage, if he does not allow the printer to accept your offer; but by what I can guess of the man's temper you are neither to expect that, nor anything else that is fair from him; and therefore a victory over such an adversary is scarce worth the contending for.

I am, Sir, Yours, &c.

The Third Letter

Sir,

Your remarks upon my *Dublin Scuffle* hitherto have been so impartial, that it encourages me to proceed in my giving you the remaining part of this encounter; I have proceeded so far as to give you a hint of our first scuffle at Dick's Coffee-House, and my reasons for removing to Pat's: I shall now proceed to tell you, that the next day after I went to Pat's, I printed the following advertisement, that so the citizens of Dublin might know of my removal, and my reasons for it: the advertisement was this, viz.

> Gentlemen,
> The Reasons for Removing my Third Auction to Pat's Coffee-House had been published yesterday, had not Mr Patrick Campbell over-awed the printer, by threatening to take away his work, and arrest him into the bargain, in case he proceeded to print off what was composed at his house. The said Reasons, fairly written on a sheet of royal paper,[1] may be seen by any gentleman that pleases, with my name subscribed to it, at Pat's Coffee-House, this afternoon at three of the clock.
>
> John Dunton.

This Advertisement was no sooner published, but the English packet[2] arrived; and that day, in the *Flying Post*, my adversary published the following reflections, which I shall insert here, that the world may see he has a fair enemy, and that I do him all the justice I can.

His reflections were these, viz.

> Whereas it is published by Mr Richard Wilde in Mr John Dunton's Advertisement of the second of November, that the auction-room was taken over his head. — This is to inform all

persons, that the said report is false and malicious; for Mr Wilde was not the person that did take the house; and Mr Dunton, who took it, had it only from week to week, and gave me notice, in the beginning of October, that he would have done within the said month; and I can certify that Mr Campbell, who has now taken the said room, was very cautious and well informed, that he did not take it over another man's head: and now says he scorns Mr Dunton's reflections, and shall neither give him, nor Mr Wilde, any other answer.

Richard Pue

Sir,

I was no sooner made acquainted that my enemy had published the above mentioned reflections, but I went to Pat's Coffee-House, and there wrote the following answer.

A Brief Answer to some Lying and Scandalous Reflections, published by Richard Pue, in the reprinted Flying Post, *November 7, 1698.*

Whereas in the *Flying Post* reprinted at Dublin, and published November the 7th, 1698, there is a lying advertisement, subscribed by Rich. Pue (who is made the cat's foot by Patrick Cambell) without either sense or coherence, which runs thus: Whereas it is published by Mr Richard Wilde, in Mr John Dunton's advertisement of the second of November, that the auction-room was taken over his head, &c. This indeed Mr Wilde has not only published, but is ready to prove by several witnesses, as he has already done to Mr Pue's face: to this Mr Pue (according to his usual modesty) answers, that the report is false and malicious, for Mr Wilde is not the person that did take the house: Mr Wilde never said he did; nor had Dick wronged me (if he had also added when his hand was in) nor Mr Dunton neither; for I took only the auction-room. But this is either according to Dick's understanding; or else one of Patrick's jesuitical equivocations to creep out at: the sense of which is, that the auction-room was not taken over Mr Wilde's head, because he is not the person that took the house: now where the coherence of this is, he that knows can tell. But though Mr Wilde did not take the house, yet Mr Pue promised him the refusal of the auction-room, when my auction was done, which Dick has not only owned, but told Mr Campbell as much. To this Dick very wisely says nothing, because he has nothing to the purpose to say. As to myself, he tells two notorious untruths: one is, that I took his auction-room only from week to week; whereas I took it during the whole time of the sale of my three auctions, paying 5s. per week while I kept it. This I can prove by two witnesses upon oath. The other untruth is, that I gave him notice the beginning of October, that I should have done by the end of that month; whereas he himself, not long since, confessed before several witnesses, that I took it during the whole sale of my auctions, and that I never released him. This he did so lately, he can't forget it: and he that will put his name to so notorious a lie, and know it to be so (which is Dick's case), may well be supposed to scruple nothing. As to what he says of Patrick's being so cautious of taking the room over my head, it is like a man's asking his fellow whether he be a thief. And for his saying, that Campbell scorns my reflections; I believe it is the wisest course he can take; for I am sure it is far easier to scorn them, than answer them. But though he scorns them, understanding men will see what weight, as well as what truth, there is in them: to whose impartial judgment I submit them. But I shall add no more here, but refer all gentlemen to Pat's Coffee-House in High-street, where my Reasons (for removing thither) are to be seen fairly writ in two sheets of royal paper.

John Dunton

Sir,
After I had published this answer to Mr Pue's reflections, Mr Wilde, being therein abused as well as myself, thought it proper to publish the following lines, viz.

Whereas R. Pue hath yesterday, by the instigation of his neighbour Mr Campbell, published in the re-printed *Flying*

Post, a notorious false advertisement, that the auction-room at Dick's was not taken over my head, I do by these certify, that I can prove by several witnesses that I had Dick's solemn promises of the refusal of the said room as soon as Mr Dunton had done with it: and the reasons for such his promises were, for that I was the proprietor of the shelves then standing in his room, and that I had kept several of my own auctions, and brought Mr Thornton's and Mr Dunton's thither.

Richard Wilde

Thus, Sir, have I fairly stated the controversy between Patrick Campbell (his tool Dick) and myself, but least you should think me too partial in my own cause, as you have heard what myself and Mr Wilde have to say for ourselves (for engaging in this *Scuffle*), so I'll next insert the testimony of three persons (and you know, Sir, a threefold cord is[a] not easily broken) further confirming the truth of what I have said.

Nov. 24, 1698

We, the persons whose names are hereunto subscribed, do hereby attest and declare, that about the beginning of this month of November, Richard Pue did publicly own in our hearing, that Mr Dunton never released him of the agreement he first made with him, which agreement was, that Mr Dunton should have the auction-room as long as he had occasion for it, paying 5s. per week.

Subscribed in the presence of:

Math. Gunne	Heneage Price
Samuel Lucas	George Larkin
Patrick Tracy	William Robinson

---

a. Eccles. 4.11.

Thus, Sir, have I given you a further account of my *Scuffle* with
Patrick Campbell, on which your impartial thoughts are desired by

Your obliged friend and servant,

John Dunton

Remarks on my Third Letter

Sir,

I am glad if my remarks be any way pleasing or useful to you, and
shall answer your desire in sending you my thoughts upon your further
scuffling with Patrick and Dick. Your advertisement upon your removal
to Pat's Coffee-House was necessary and just, and Patrick's preventing
your publishing your reasons in print, according to his usual sly
manner, is argument enough to prove that he durst not refer his cause
to the determination of the public; and indeed I do not wonder at it,
for injustice may well be ashamed to show its face. Besides, it seems
it's Patrick's character, to work like a mole underground; for though
he loves to act unjustly, he does not love to appear so. It's the nature
of a hypocrite to wear a rough garment to deceive.

It was the next and only course left you, to publish your advertisement, that Patrick might a little appear in his colours; and in the
meantime to publish your reasons in writing, was an argument of true
English courage, to face your adversary with such weapons as you could
come at, when your cowardly adversary had deprived you of any other,
because he knew he durst not engage you on equal terms.

His publishing a reflection upon you in the reprinted *Flying Post*
was another effect of his dastardly temper, seeing he would not allow
you the same liberty; and therefore Mr Wilde's advertisement against
Campbell and Dick was very proper and necessary; nothing could
more effectually vindicate your honesty, and prove your adversary's
falsehood, and unfair way of dealing; and I doubt not, but the public
would take it as a sufficient proof of it.

Your own answer too was highly necessary, and in my opinion very
pertinent: you therein expose Patrick's and Dick's hypocritical
equivocations to the life, and seeing Mr Wilde seconded the truth of
your assertions, by his advertisement, and that you so boldly offer to

prove the truth of what you assert in yours, it's next to proving Patrick a liar on record.

I am far from questioning the truth of what you have from time to time informed me of as to the *Dublin Scuffle*, and should have believed it on your own assertion. I have not known you so long, but that I am very well satisfied you were never taken for a liar at home, and I have no reason to think you have changed your temper by going to Ireland. However, your prudence and caution are commendable to have your proceedings well attested, for that is certainly the best way to stop the mouths of your cavilling adversaries. I am, Sir,

Your assured friend and servant

The Fourth Letter

Sir,

I have now proceeded to give you the history of the *Dublin Scuffle*, so far as the small skirmishes of bills and advertisements. I am next to tell you, what the learned gentlemen of Ireland (who were spectators of this *Scuffle*) thought of the encounter: and to set this matter in the truer light, I shall here insert the letter I sent by Mr Wilde, to the Right Reverend the Lord Bishop of Clogher;[1] with the answer his Lordship was pleased to send me. I had not presumed to have published the Bishop's answer, but his lordship is a person of very great honour, and strict justice (as I hint in my Farewell Letter) and will be the sooner inclined to pardon a presumption, which is so absolutely necessary to the vindication of my innocence.

My Letter to the Right Reverend the Lord Bishop of Clogher, in Dublin, December the 17th 1698

May it please your lordship!

I am sorry I had not the honour to be in my auction-room this morning, when your lordship was there, that I might have returned my humble thanks for that great encouragement your lordship has given to my book-adventure, as Mr Wilde informs me: had I met with none but such generous buyers as your lord-ship and the rest of the clergy of Ireland, my undertaking had been more fortunate: for, my lord, I have had great injustice from some persons who have bought what they won't pay for; and, in particular, from one Campbell, who attempted to murder my reputation; and not contented with that piece of revenge (for my endeavouring to serve this country with books) he afterwards takes my auction-room over mine and Mr Wilde's head; and whilst I was in it, declares, I had setters;[2] though I assured the buyer, that for every penny I got that unlawful way, I'd restore a pound: my lord, I own it my duty, to forgive injuries; but Campbell justifies this vile treatment; and therefore, my lord, I am obliged to publish this *Dublin Scuffle*, to justify my own innocence; and to bring him, if possible (according to the Scotch phrase) to the stool of repentance.[3] I am pleased to hear your lordship is not angry at my intention herein; and as the Speaker of the House of Commons[4] has done me the honour, to desire a sight of my first draft, in manuscript; so your lordship has likewise been pleased to honour me, by desiring a sight of the same, in print; which as it obliges me to publish nothing but real truth, so it encourages me to hope, that the publishing my *Dublin Scuffle*, will bring Campbell to a sense of his error. I have only to beg your lordship's pardon for this presumption, and to assure your lordship, that I am,

Your lordship's most obliged and very humble servant,
John Dunton

The Bishop of Clogher's Answer to the Foregoing Letter
December 17th 1698

Mr Dunton!
I received your letter, and am extremely well satisfied of your justice and fair dealing in your late auction, and of the fidelity of Mr Wilde, whom you employed: you shall always have this testimony, from

Your humble servant,
St. Geo: Clogher

Sir,
Your remarks upon this honourable testimony of the Bishop of Clogher relating to my SCUFFLE with Patrick Campbell, will further oblige,

Your humble servant
John Dunton

Remarks on my Fourth Letter

Sir,
I was sufficiently satisfied by your last, that your justice, in relation to the controversy between Patrick Campbell and yourself, was undeniable; and therefore the further testimonies which you have now sent me of it, are *ex superabundanti*;[5] but I confess, the quality of them is such, that you ought not to have omitted them; especially when you had seemingly transgressed the rules of good breeding so far as to trouble such an eminent person as the Lord Bishop of Clogher with a letter on that subject.

It was indeed a necessary piece of gratitude, and an acknowledgment due to the bishop's character and personal merit, to return his lordship thanks for the encouragement he had given to your auction, and it was no less than justice to the clergy of Ireland, to own their generous deportment, and the countenance they gave to your undertaking; but I cannot altogether approve of your troubling that great prelate, who has the charge of so many weighty affairs upon his shoulders, with such a minute affair as your *Scuffle* with Patrick Campbell.

But seeing his lordship was so kind as to take your presumption in good part, and has been so condescending as to give you such a generous testimony of the fairness of your dealing in your auction: I cannot but admire the excellency of his lordship's temper, and applaud your successful boldness.

You and your friend Mr Wilde have reason to value yourselves upon the testimony of a person of so great worth, which to be sure will give a reputation to your management with all men of sense and honour; for I cannot but think, that the testimony of a bishop and privy counsellor will infinitely outweigh the calumnies of a pedlar turned bookseller, and his tool a coffee-man. Besides, the reputation

46

which his lordship has for his learning and piety makes it evident, that he looked upon your design as very subservient to the interest of learning in that kingdom; seeing he gave so much encouragement to it.

What you say of bringing Patrick to the stool of repentance has something of an impropriety in it, except you suppose him to have been cock-baud[6] to your Dorinda, for that penance is not (as I am informed) enjoined in his country upon any but those who are guilty of uncleanness. But perhaps, because Patrick may have a Dorinda, which he may love as himself, you may think that he ought to mount the stool of repentance for her billet douxes. If this be your meaning, I wish you had let it alone, for I am afraid if that custom should take place, it might bring a great many of your acquaintance in England to stand in a white sheet for the faults of their she-friends; and I know you are so good-natured, that you would not willingly wish them so much harm.

It's true, that you for your own part have been happier than many. Your first wife's virtue put her beyond the reach of suspicion, and that of your second is unattackable; but though you and they have been mutually happy in one another, so that you had no occasion for a she-friend, yet you ought to consider that there are many of your acquaintance that have not had so good a fate.

However, as to your adversary Patrick, whether he deserves the stool of repentance for his own personal crimes or not, I know not; but this I am sure of, that if the character given of him be true, he deserves an advancement of as public a nature,[7] and something like the other too; for as the stool of repentance in his country is raised so high, that the criminal who is placed upon it may be seen by all that are in the church; he seems to deserve to be elevated above his brethren in a public market-place, with a hole for his head, and one for each hand, and to have the title page of Hodder transformed into Cocker, &c.[8] nailed over his head.

But to return to your *Scuffle*. Your imparting that affair to the Lord Bishop of Clogher, and the Speaker of the House of Commons, seems to be a very good *Imprimatur*;[9] but at the same time, it is incumbent upon you to take care, that there be nothing in it too mean to deserve such a licence, and that may be unfit for one of your business and reputation to divulge; for though, I doubt not, but you will keep religiously to truth; yet you know that all the truth is not to be spoken at all times, and some things may be too trifling to deserve the view of the public; therefore peruse everything carefully before it be printed off. You see I make use of my wonted freedom with you, as becomes one who is

Sir, Your cordial friend

The Fifth Letter

Sir,

I am still scuffling with Patrick Campbell; but such is the advantage of a just cause, that my auction prospers maugre[1] all the malice and venom he spits at that and me. The first auction I made (after my removal to Pat's Coffee-House) was still crowded with generous buyers; and notwithstanding the opposition I meet from Campbell, I have now proceeded so far in the disposing my whole venture, as to come to what I call (the word auction being worn thread-bare) my Farewell Sale. That I may give you the better idea of these proceedings, and set the *Dublin-Scuffle* in a yet clearer light, I here send you the account of this Farewell Sale, with the attestation concerning myself, and my three auctions, which are now ended. This further account of the *Dublin-Scuffle*, you'll find in my Third Letter, to those worthy gentlemen that were encouragers of my undertaking; which letter was entitled,

The Farewell Sale at Pat's Coffee-House

[And is as follows, viz.]

Gentlemen,

Though my three auctions are now ended, I have yet variety of books left, so I design to try your generous bidding a fourth time, which I'll call my Farewell Sale. I shall begin the following Monday at three in the afternoon at Pat's Coffee-House in High-Street, and shall end December the first; neither will I exceed that, resolving (God willing) to embark for London December 5th. It is true I have books enough to continue the sale much longer, but native country has charms in it, and I am very desirous to be at home: and therefore December 5th, I shall bid you all farewell: for though when my fourth sale is over, I shall still have quantities left, yet all that is then remaining I'll lump to the booksellers of Dublin (to whom you must give higher rates, of which the sale of the *French Book of Martyrs*[2] is a late instance) or if we can't agree, the same ship that brought them hither will be able to carry them back.

The conditions of this last sale are: that whatever is bought till Thursday night, be all paid the following Friday; and for what has been bought in my three past auctions, it is expected they should be all fetched away by Saturday the 26th instant: in order to which, constant attendance shall be given at Pat's Coffee-House, from eight in the morning till eight at night.

Gentlemen, I promised you in my last catalogue, the *Dublin Scuffle*—and the *History of my Summer's Ramble*, and I'll be as good as my word (for I'll print them as soon as I get to London) and send them to Pat's Coffee-House in High-Street, except[3] Patrick will publicly own the public injury he did me, and then I will even forgive Patrick Campbell, and forget his taking my room over my head (though it is thought I'm a hundred pounds the worse for it, considering the goods and buyers I lost on that occasion) but if he has not the grace to ask my pardon (for the notorious injuries he did me) I pray God forgive him and Dick too, and in return I hope they'll wish me a bon-voyage, in regard they'll be rid of one durst tell them the truth, and afterwards send it to Pat's Coffee-House in red-letters.[4] And seeing they dare not answer my broadside whilst I am in Dublin (and whenever they do, I'll reply to them, though as far as Rome), that they might not wrong me after I am gone, some of my friends, that best know me, have voluntarily subscribed the following attestation.

The Attestation

'We whose names are hereunto subscribed, being all of us present at Mr John Dunton's three auctions in Dublin, and having seen the management thereof every day; do hereby attest, that as all was carried on and managed with the greatest candour and sincerity imaginable, by Mr Dunton, so the generality of those gentlemen that bought his books have acknowledged in our hearing, that they had all the fair dealing that they could desire: and we can more particularly affirm, that Mr Dunton's demeanour during his whole auctions has been such, as has given content to all gentlemen there: for whereas in other auctions it is common to have setters to raise the value of the books, in Mr Dunton's auction we are sure there was none, from the beginning to the end: Mr Dunton having absolutely declared against it, as not fair nor honest. And we do further attest, to our certain knowledge, that in all his concernments, with the printers, stationers, binders, and others (which was very considerable) he paid everyone, not only to a penny, but even to a single half-penny, so very exact and scrupulous he was of wronging them. And as to the several places where the said Mr Dunton lodged, he not only paid his quarters according to agreement, but likewise gratified them for any trouble that was extraordinary, by sickness, or otherwise. And that in all his said lodgings, his way of living was so inoffensive and blameless, that he was (as Caesar would have had his wife) not only free from blame, but from all suspicion of it. And as to the controversy he has had with Mr Patrick Campbell, we do hereby attest, that Mr Campbell was altogether the aggressor; for though Mr Campbell had used Mr Dunton very barbarously at his first coming over, yet Mr Dunton took no notice of it, till Campbell had taken his auction-room over his head, by offering a double price (as Dick the coffee-man alleged in our hearing) and yet even then Mr Dunton was so fair, as to offer to close his auctions in one week's time more, provided he might tarry in it so long, though he had then two hundred pounds worth of books to sell, and that he would lump the remainder; which Campbell absolutely refused. And notwithstanding such his refusal, yet we do attest, that Mr Dunton has been so favourable to the said Campbell, that he has not related those ill things of him which he might have done, and which he was urged by several persons to do. Nor is there anything Mr Dunton has said of him, but what to our knowledge he has divers witnesses to prove it, if there be occasion.'

Dublin, Nov. 23. 1698

Subscribed in the presence of:

Fra. Lee,	Richard Wilde
Matth. Gunne	Heneage Price
Matthew Read	George Larkin
Samuel Lucas	William Robinson

Gentlemen

The foregoing attestation is printed word for word as my friends brought it to me, and is subscribed by four persons of known integrity, and signed in the presence of four more; which I hope will fully convince you that I am (as I said in my last catalogue)

Your very faithful, and very humble servant,

John Dunton

Dublin, Nov. 23. 1698

Thus (Sir) you find I am come to the conclusion of my three auctions, wherein I have related my *Scuffle* with Patrick Campbell, with as much sincerity and candour as I would have done were I now leaving the world; but whether I have done so or no, is left to your remarks, which I desire by the first post, by which you'll further oblige

Your hearty friend and servant

John Dunton

Remarks on my Fifth Letter

Sir,

I am sorry to find that Patrick is not yet reduced to reason, though I think there's no great cause to wonder at it, for I am apt to think his reason and religion are much of a piece. I am glad, however, that his malice proves toothless, or that at best it is worn to the stumps. It is but just, that dishonesty should be unsuccessful, though many times we see the all-wise Providence order it otherwise, for a while at least.

Your Farewell Sale demonstrates your courage and honesty, in that you durst appeal to the public, and Patrick's own conscience, for the justice of your cause. The offer you made him of suppressing your designed narrative or character of him, if he would publicly own the injury he did you, is highly generous; considering how much you had been a loser by it. There are few men, but would have demanded restitution as well as repentance, but I don't find that Patrick is so good a Christian as to offer you either; and, therefore, I think no man can justly blame you for exposing him in his own colours to the view of the world, according to your promise: but be sure to keep a steady hand; for though I am of opinion you can scarcely miss such ugly and coarse features; yet you know the proverb *Give the Devil his due*,[5] includes a good lesson of morality in it, and, therefore, I hope you will represent him no worse than he really is. I must needs also tell you, that unless you be satisfied in your own conscience, that it is necessary to do this for the defence of your own reputation, you will run a great hazard of breaking the ninth commandment.

The proposals you make to your buyers in your Farewell Sale are just and reasonable, and a proof at the same time that you designed no injury to your brethren the booksellers by your auction, seeing you are willing to let them have lumping pennyworths at last, that they may be sharers in the profit of your book-adventure, as well as others.

As to the attestation of your friends, it was kind in them to offer it, and necessary for you to have it. I question much whether Patrick can produce the like behaviour in any respect.

Your precaution in this matter is very commendable, for you have thereby in my opinion stopped the mouths of all cavillers, as to every part of your conversation, since you arrived in Dublin; and in London, your just and scrupulous way of dealing sets you above detraction: or, at worst, a generous mastiff minds not the yelping of every little cur. I am glad to find, that the ill treatment you have met with from others has not inspired you with the same unjust sentiments towards them. And that it is fully proved by this attestation, that Patrick was the first aggressor, and took your room over your head; and, therefore, I think that the publishing of this, and some other of the most remarkable passages of Patrick's injustice, were enough to blacken him, and to vindicate you in the eyes of all honest men, without your putting yourself to the trouble and expense of a voluminous detail of particulars, which few can purchase; besides, Patrick is not a man of that character, that his life will be much regarded, though it had been written by Plutarch himself; and therefore, it will be your wisdom and interest to be brief. I am, Sir,

Your friend and servant

The Sixth Letter

Sir,

In the history of the *Dublin Scuffle*, I am come so far as to acquaint you (in spite of all the opposition made against me by Patrick Campbell) that I was got to the conclusion of my three auctions and Farewell Sale. I have had many a weary step (as well as the impudence of Campbell, to cope with) in the disposing of this venture; but (through God's blessing on my undertaking) I am now come near the winding up of my bottom[1] in this country; for yesterday I published a paper which I called *The Packing Penny*[2] (a new phrase to invite company). Sir, as this paper has some relation to Patrick Campbell, it is fit I should send you a copy of it, that nothing relating to my *Scuffle* with him might escape your censure. This paper was my Fifth Letter to those gentlemen that attended my auctions, and was entitled,

The Packing Penny

[And is as follows, viz.]

Gentlemen,

Though my three auctions and Farewell Sale are now ended, yet I have still quantities of books left, which (for a Packing-Penny) I'll sell at very reasonable rates (the sale to begin Tuesday December the 13th in the morning, and to end the same evening). Gentlemen, I shan't sell these remaining books by way of auction, but at such easy rates as shall be agreed upon between Mr Wilde and the buyer. It is true, when I consider I had no setter in any of my four sales, I could not have thought that any would have been so unjust as to buy what they won't pay for; but I was mistaken! But (to the honour of the tribe of Levi) no clergyman in Ireland has treated me in this manner: I mention this, that the world may see I designed no reflection on those learned gentlemen, in my advertisements of July the 9th, for though the enemies of my undertaking wrested my words to that purpose, yet nothing was ever further from my thoughts; for besides that I myself have the honour to be the son of a clergyman (who, as a poet[a] says, *Do all breathe something more than common air*) I dare boldly assert, that no man in this kingdom has an higher esteem of that sacred order than myself. But as in this I have done justice to the clergy of Ireland, so I resolve to do some to myself; and whatever notions some YOUNG CASUISTS may have of refusing to fetch what others (whom they outbid) would have honestly paid for; yet they shall find I dare call a spade a spade, if they live to read the *History of my Summer's Ramble*, &c. or, the *Dublin-Scuffle*, which I finished in this country (at the barbarous provocation of Patrick Campbell) and will publish as soon as I get to London.

And here, Gentlemen, I can't forbear telling you (a second time) that notwithstanding I have with an excessive charge brought over the best collection of valuable books that ever was exposed in this kingdom, and have treated, both in my catalogues and otherwise, my brethren in this city, and the rest of mankind, with the greatest respect and civility; and been so just to them, as not in the least to employ any setter (in any of my four sales) but wholly to submit my large venture to the mercy, candour, and generosity of the bidders: yet after all this fair play for their money, I understand such has been the

---

a. See the Poem dedicated to the Sons of the Clergy on their Annual Feast in 1682.[3] All gentlemen are desired to take notice, that what is bought at this sale is to be delivered and paid for at the same time.

practice of some persons (from some of whom better usage might be expected, considering their character in the world) as maliciously and ignorantly to discourage those worthy gentlemen and clergymen that were disposed to furnish themselves with good books. Gentlemen, this usage is unbecoming anything of a Christian, especially, &c.[4] who by his setting up for a banterer, contrary to Christianity, spoils his neighbour's fair market; making good what Solomon so long ago observed, *It is naught, it is naught, saith the buyer, but when he is gone, he boasteth.*[5] This is therefore to give notice to the world, that as I act upon the fairest and justest bottom[6] that can be, in this last sale, which I call the Packing Penny, so I am resolved to vindicate my proceedings; and in order thereunto, if I can have but good proof, that either without doors, but more especially at my sale, of any persons that shall take the liberty to spoil my market; I am resolved to bring actions of damage against those persons that shall be guilty of such notorious actions.

Gentlemen, I shall only add, that as I never reflected on Patrick Campbell, or any man in my whole life, without a just provocation (as I am ready to prove whilst I am in Dublin), so I must acquit all the persons concerned in my auctions, of having any hand in anything I published here, it being (as the *Scuffle* is) written with my own hand, and subscribed by

Gentlemen,

Your most obliged and humble servant
John Dunton

Dublin, Decem. 12th. 1698

Sir,

This packing penny was no sooner taken, and the remaining books sold in the lump to Honest Gun[7] (for about an hundred pounds) but Mr Wilde published the following advertisement, further proving my charge against Dick and Campbell. It also gives an account of an auction, he [Wilde] designs on his own account, as soon as I leave Ireland.

Mr Wilde's Advertisement was this, viz.

> My friend Mr Dunton's three Auctions, Farewell Sale, and
> Packing Penny, ending this night, I thought fit to give notice to
> all the lovers of learning, that I design (God willing) within a
> few days after Mr Dunton's departure, to expose by auction a
> considerable parcel of good books of my own, at Pat's Coffee-
> House in High-Street, where I now am, by reason of Dick the
> coffee-man's (contrary to solemn promises before witnesses, as
> well as all the bonds of gratitude) letting the room I had, to Mr
> Campbell over my head; and though Mr Campbell thinks to
> excuse himself by laying the sole fault upon Dick; yet casuists
> will inform him, that he who either by his threats of taking the
> great room at the Duke's-Head tavern, or by the mighty allure-
> ment of a double rate, as Dick has under his hand asserted, shall
> tempt or corrupt a person that is not proof against a base temp-
> tation, is as much, if not more to blame, than the person so
> corrupted.
>
> R. Wilde

Thus, Sir, have I sent you an account of the Packing Penny (it
relating to the *Dublin Scuffle*) and also Mr Wilde's opinion of
Campbell and Pue (on which I desire your thoughts) I formerly sent
you those other papers, wherein the *Scuffle* between John Dunton
and Patrick Campbell is any ways hinted at; all which papers (save
my Reasons for removing to Pat's) were printed in Dublin; but what
I have further to send you relating to this *Scuffle* is what the printers
of Dublin durst not meddle with; but I suppose, when I get to
London, the printers there (at three hundred miles distance) will be
no more afraid of Patrick than I am, though now on the spot with
him. I have only to add, that I am

Your very humble servant
John Dunton

Remarks on my Sixth Letter

Sir,

I have received yours with the account of your Packing Penny, and the continuance of the *Scuffle* between Patrick and you. I perceive you are a couple of good game-cocks, and know no[t] when to give over; it's a pity you are not both in England: the gown-men that frequent Westminster Hall[8] would find a way to make a penny of you, and for anything I know, might sell you by auction too; for I am apt to think you would weary them at last, if money did not make them proof against the fatigue.

I perceive Patrick's malice is very keen, and your resentments are not without a tolerable edge, and therefore would advise you to beware of cutting your own fingers. Be sure to summon up all your patience, for I perceive you have need of it; don't let Patrick's injustice provoke you to indecencies of passion, for that may be a snare laid to gain an advantage against you, either by an action at law, or blemishing your reputation.

I approve your diligence and ingenuity in promoting the sale of your books, but am sorry you have met with such as buy and don't pay. I am glad to find, however, that though you had so much unfair dealing from others, you have found the clergy just in their bargains, and that you vindicate yourself from having reflected upon them in your advertisement of July 9th. This is a time when every man that has any value for the Christian religion should be very tender in his reflections on the clergy, and indeed rather conceal their real faults, than proclaim them on the house-tops; and much less utter ground-less suspicions against them. You are obliged particularly both by parentage, and the profession of religion you make, to be very careful in this matter; and therefore, I am glad to find you so sensible of your duty in this respect—The old barbarous verse of *Presbyteri nati raro solent esse Beati*[9] is as far from truth as good Latin; though those who are enemies to the order may please themselves with the reflection, the common experience of mankind demonstrates the falsehood of it; for if the number of clergymen's children be compared with those of others, and their morals, religion, and success in the world laid in the balance with those of the children of other ranks of men, it will appear to have been a mere forgery of those who were against the marriage of priests of old; and licked up and improved by such who, if not professed, are at least crafty underhand enemies to the Christian religion.

I wish from my heart that all clergymen themselves took more care to obviate this reflection, by a careful looking after their own practice, and their children's education; and then the injustice of it would be more apparent. And I am sorry to find, that though the Irish clergy have been just to their bargains, that yet any one of them should have taken indirect measures to injure you in your auctions, but they are earthen vessels as well as others. Therefore I would advise you not to be sharp in your resentments upon them. Some of your books might perhaps be disrelishing to them, but that was their fault. Your design was to serve the interest of learning in general, and not to please every man's humour, which you knew was impossible.

Your vindication of those concerned in your auctions from having any share in what you printed against Campbell, is generous and just —and no less can be said of Mr Wilde's advertisement concerning the design of an auction of his own, and publicly avowing Patrick's injustice to you, which makes it so notorious, that I think there is the less need of your printing much more about it. I am,

Sir, Your humble servant

The Seventh Letter

Well, Sir, I'll tell you news; my adversary Campbell has now sent a trumpeter (a few equivocating lines) with a parley, or rather with articles of peace; but I fear his message is rather to sham off a debt he owes me, than any design to be reconciled. However, I here send you a copy of his letter (for I'll keep the original) that you may the better judge of the proposals he makes—[His letter is as follows, viz.]

December 9th, 1698

Mr Dunton,

Ye have begun to dun me,[1] though I find you to be in my debt, and easily able to make it appear; as for any letters ye have under my hand, I will not give you one farthing to burn it: for I will own what is just and right, though not under my hand; I have no mind either to write or print myself a liar, as some men has done. But I shall be pleased very well to meet you, either before a magistrate, or any other creditable citizen; and what is thought just, I will perform on my part; I do not intend to render railing for railing, and am sure have rendered you good for evil, and shall continue to be just to every man; and for your justice, yourself may boast of it, as much as ye will, but other men must believe as they find: I shall only add, Evil to them that evil thinks.[2]

Pa. Campbell

My Answer to Campbell's Proposal

Dublin, December 10th, 1698

Mr Campbell,

I received yours, which is still the second part to the same tune; for instead of being penitent for the great injuries you did me, you do but justify yourself; so that you are the railer, and not I; neither have I written or printed anything against you but plain matter of fact, and dressed in softer terms than you deserve: and as to my being in your debt, it is all Patrick Campbell, I mean a piece of nonsense; for you are certainly in mine, if four pounds be more than forty shillings. However, I'll meet you if you please before a magistrate (for I'm so much for strict justice, I would talk with you there about Hodder)[3] or where else you please—I shall name Thursday night, at seven of the clock at the Keys in High-Street, and shall bring a friend with me, and I am willing you should do the like; but I tell you beforehand, you must resolve upon a printed confession of the public injuries you have done me, or you'll dearly repent your abusing

John Dunton

Sir,

Thus have I sent (what must needs surprise ye) Patrick's proposals about a peace, with my answer to him; I shall send you more of his ill practices by next post; but, at present, your thoughts upon the parley is what is desired by

Yours to command,
John Dunton

Remarks on my Seventh Letter

Sir,

I have received yours with the copy of Mr Campbell's letter, proposing a meeting and reference.

Sir, this proposal of Campbell's is cunning and piquant enough, and demonstrates what I always thought, that he is a crafty intriguing man. It carries an air of religion and ingenuity at first view; but by the railing mixed throughout, and the reflecting conclusion, he does not seem ever to have designed any meeting with you; for if he had, there's reason to think he would have proposed it in fairer terms, and not have aggravated matters to incense you, if he had designed an amicable accommodation.

This may partly justify the sharpness of your reply, and serving him in his own coin, by proposing such terms of agreement as you might reasonably think he would never comply with: for I find nothing less would serve your turn than public repentance; and he tells you plainly, that he was not willing either to print or write himself a liar. So that it was impossible to reconcile you. This, if Patrick be conscious of his guilt, argues an obstinacy inconsistent with Christianity. Yet I cannot wholly approve your conduct, nor policy in your reply. Had you accepted of a meeting without anything of ripping up sores, or telling him the preliminaries, you might possibly have had either an opportunity of bringing him to a sense of his fault, or of having further evidence against him; and indeed I see nothing that can excuse your oversight in this matter, but that letter to Mr Wilde giving an account of Patrick's further ill practices against you, which you promise to send me. I am

Your hearty friend, &c.

The Eighth Letter

Sir,

I am now to acquaint ye, that Campbell's proposal (about a treaty of peace) was all trick and delusion; for nothwithstanding his seeming desire of meeting before a magistrate, or any other creditable citizen, and my readiness to comply with his motion herein, yet he never once came to the Keys in High-Street, the place appointed to meet at, but I was there myself, according to promise, as Mr Servant (his own binder) and several others, can testify; so that our *Dublin Scuffle* continues still, and if Campbell remains as obstinate as he is at present, for anything I can yet see, it will be left to our posterity to fight it out. And that as I formerly sent you the sentiments of the clergy of Ireland upon this encounter; so I shall now send you an account of what the citizens of Dublin (the daily spectators of this *Scuffle*) think of it, and of Campbell's proposal to me about a peace, and this can't be better done than by inserting here a letter directed

To Mr Richard Wilde at Pat's Coffee-House in High-Street

Which letter was this following, viz.

December 16th

Sir,

Now Campbell finds Mr Dunton's reputation above his reach, like himself he would fain put to reference the ruin he intended; but if Mr Dunton does not compel him to public acknowledgement, he will hereafter repent it; for in the first place, he did not only incense all that he had opportunity against him, but forbid all his auction, telling that he employed Foster and others as setters, which he would prove by Weir, and in the next place he made a faction against him, because he was an Englishman; and he took all Mr Dunton's papers to council[1] and advised on them with intention to prosecute him at law, and getting no encouragement, he proceeds this way, which I hope Mr Dunton does not take to proceed from—a prick of— nor from friendship, but merely for want of—[2] I will say no more, that gentleman having justice to vindicate himself, as well as sense to know Campbell, whose best word was, You were all rogues; I shall say no more, but assure you that I have been a good customer, and have given all encouragement to you, and am Mr Dunton's and your real friend.

Sir,

Though you see by this letter (directed to Mr Wilde) what opinion the citizens of Dublin have of the treatment I have from Campbell, and of his proposal of his being friends with me; yet seeing peace is a desirable thing (if to be had upon honourable terms) I desire your sentiments upon this letter to Mr Wilde; and how you'd advise me to act in this critical juncture; your speedy answer will greatly oblige,

Your very humble servant,
John Dunton

Remarks on my Eighth Letter

Sir,

I have received (by the last post) the further account you promised me of Patrick's ill practices, his deceitful dealing with you about a peace, and the letter to Mr Wilde, giving the sentiments of the citizens of Dublin upon this *Scuffle*: I must say, the writer of this letter is much your friend, and if you be sure of the credibility of the informer, I see no reason why you should not publish it, but you ought to be exactly careful in enquiring, whether the writer of it can be relied upon; and if you be satisfied in that, publish it with all the corroborating evidence you can, for there's nothing can be more effectual to prove the justice of your cause, and the baseness of your adversary.

I am the rather indeed inclined to believe it, because it corresponds with the preceding part of your own information, and is confirmed by his declining to meet you according to appointment; for truth is always bold, and never seeks corners, as it is evident Patrick has done all along. I add no more, but referring you to the direction of the Almighty, who knows the justice of your cause, I am

Sir, Yours.

The Ninth Letter

Sir,

I formerly told you of Patrick's sending a trumpeter, with proposals of peace, and how he served me on that account, you have also had the sentiments of the citizens of Dublin, with respect to my *Scuffle* with him, and his seeming willingness to make an end of it; but though I met at the place appointed, he never appeared (as I formerly sent you word) yet he has the impudence to give out that I refuse to meet him, which I no sooner heard of, but I sent the following letters, the one directed

To Mr Thomas Servant, a Binder in Golden Lane,

and the other directed,

To Mr Patrick Campbell, at the Bible in Skinner-Row.

My letter to Mr Servant was in these words, viz.

December 20th. 1698

Honest Thomas,

I wrote the following letter, with a design to send it to Patrick Campbell, just as I was going to embark; but hearing he reports I refused to meet him (which he durst not do but that he thinks I am shipped off) I desire that you would read the following lines, that you may see his baseness, for yourself were present where he refused to meet me, and can testify to what I write. As soon as you have read my letter, deliver it with your own hand; for if Patrick should still fly me, it is designed as my farewell to him. You know, Sir (though you are his chief binder, and would favour his cause as much as possible), that I offered to make you the sole judge of the debt he owes me; but for the slander, and taking the room over my head, it was a public injury; and (though I forgive it myself), the world expects a public acknowledgment of the injuries he has done to

Your hearty friend and servant,
John Dunton

63

My Farewell Letter to Patrick Campbell

Mr Campbell

Though I have one foot in the boat, in order to embark for England, yet I here send a messenger to tell you, I'll wait an hour (to shake hands with you) if you'll confess the wrongs you did, or there were any hopes of your penitence: and isn't it strange, that Patrick Campbell, who is so religious as to say grace over a dish of coffee, should have no qualms after slandering his neighbour, or refusing to pay his debts? I say debts, for I sent your account fairly stated (and proved you owe me a round sum) without receiving your answer to it. Then with what face (but you supposed I was shipped off) could you tell Bently[1] I was your debter, and refused to meet you before a magistrate, or at the Keys in High-Street, where I waited for you above an hour? But though you durst not appear then, I'm now waiting in the boat for you, in hopes you'll appear at last, and to engage you to it (if you'll ask pardon) I'll even here receive you with open arms. It is true, you have given great provocation, and had I not been tender of you, I had long since sent you the length of my sword or, as you're beneath my notice, some porter to have broke your pate.[2] Sir, put on your sword (if it be not in trouble) and let me see your face; for your private slandering is very sordid, and I am sure deserves to be soundly drubbed; for by backbiting of me you still sneak your head out of the collar, and I am hurt by I don't know who. It is true, it was Palmer's saying, the Martyr, that no man ought to be counted valiant, but such as contemn injuries:[3] I confess, I am not so humble as this comes to, yet I forgive Patrick with all my heart; but, Sir, I think it my duty to print the *Scuffle* you engaged me in; for you justify your barbarous treatment, so that to forget and forgive you too, will but encourage you to abuse others, or perhaps myself again, for such tenderness: for save a — from the gallows, and he'll cut your throat.[4] But for all this, I'll burn the *Scuffle*, if you'll come hither, and shake hands, and tell the world (when I am gone) that you did abuse me, but are sorry for it. It is reported of St Katherine, that she sucked the invenomed wounds of a fellow who had impudently wronged her:[5] I don't pretend to such flights as these; but if you'll come to the boat (and remember it is the last offer) and own your errors, I'll be more your friend than ever I was your enemy: and though Pickance (the master of the *Diamond*) waits for his ship's crew, yet if you'll do me justice, I'll return to Dublin a second time, to drink your health (in the first place) and another to honest Gun, Servant, Bently, and the rest of our learned brethren; and by coming thus to confession, you'll cease being a trouble to your friends, and a scandal to yourself: but if you will not repent, as a wounded Roman said upon a set challenge, the *Scuffle* must appear, and shall be followed (if you dare answer it) with the *History of your Life*, from the hour the parson christened you, to (mark you me that) the very hour you christened yourself; and pray remember that one blot many times stains a whole generation: but my *Scuffle* is just, and without your public repentance, I resolve to publish it; for truly, St Patrick, I have a greater regard to my honour than my life: and though my arms should fail me to fight (they are the words of this noble Roman) yet my heart still encourages me to die in vindication of a good name.

And so Patrick, farewell; for you don't appear, and our ship is under sail; but if you repent at last (and I'll press you to it in the *Dublin Scuffle*) I hope we shall meet in heaven, but scarce in Ireland, whilst you are afraid of

Dublin, Decemb. 20th. 1698.   John Dunton

Sir,
About three hours after I had sent the aforegoing message to Honest Thomas,[6] and my farewell letter to Patrick, he sends me (by order from Campbell) the following letter.

Sir,

I was with Mr Campbell last night, and told him (as you desired) that you would meet him when, and where he pleased, &c. His answer was, that he was ready to meet you at any time or place, and that if you bring one citizen with you, he will bring another; therefore, if you please, you may let him know your mind, as to time, place, and person; and if this will any way contribute toward your peace and friendship, it will be very satisfactory to.

Your humble servant

Decem. 20th. 1698   Tho. Servant

I no sooner received this letter from Mr Servant, but I sent Mr Robinson[7] to him with the following answer,

Mr Servant,

Since my writing a note to you, and my farewell letter to Campbell, I received yours, intimating Mr Campbell will now meet me; I am glad to hear it with all my heart, and I do again resolve to meet him at the Keys in High-Street, at five in the afternoon (though he disappointed me once at this very place) and will only bring one citizen with me, for that's enough with a good cause; but as for Patrick, if he will, he may bring forty or, if he pleases, the whole city.

Sir, could you have thought that Campbell would now have bantered me a second time, but so it was (for having a bad cause, he durst not appear, as Mr Fisher, the Earl of Meath's chaplain, and Mr Thornton, the King's stationer)[8] can testify. However, I thought it proper (whilst on the spot) to send him the following note, viz.

Mr Campbell,

I am now at the Keys, and you send word you will not come, though I came hither by your own appointment, and this is the second time you had notice I was willing to treat with you. Sir, I have given you liberty of bringing forty men, or a whole city, against myself, and but one more, and he too of your own trade; but I have other business to do, than to wait long for an enemy that dares not face me. However, I have several to witness, I came to meet you (as you desired) this night, and you refuse coming, so that now I shall put my debt into a lawyer's hands, and for your other treatment, the world shall know it; for I'll dance no more after ye, but will wait here an hour longer to prove my charge; and to give you time to match Mr Thornton. I am

Your abused friend,
John Dunton

Decem. 20th. 1698

Sir,

Your thoughts upon this new parley, Mr Servant's mediation, my farewell letter to Campbell, and his refusing to meet this second time (though it was an appointment of his own making) is earnestly desired by

Your humble servant,
John Dunton

Remarks on my Ninth Letter

Sir,

I have received yours, with the account of a new parley offered by Patrick, Mr Servant's mediation, your farewell letter to him, and of his disappointing you again, though the appointment was of his own making. I must needs tell you, that were you as much surfeited with the *Scuffle*, as I am with hearing of it, you would have given over long before now. I don't think it worth your while to buy Patrick's confession at so dear a rate, as to take so much pains for it. If he were truly sensible of his fault, you need not dun him to repentance, and how great soever his hypocrisy may be in other instances, I don't find he has a mind to play the hypocrite in this, that is, so much as to feign a repentance.

You have, I think, over-done it, in soliciting him so much; nor do I think this public confession, considering how you have characterized him, would be much for your advantage. To be commended or slandered by a false tongue, is much the same thing, for they that know a liar will believe him in neither. You have done well however to follow peace as much as you could, and it was prudent to have so many witnesses of your having kept your appointment, and made such fair proffers of reconciliation; but I perceive Patrick's resentments are become downright rancour, and that the sore is so much festered, that there's no hopes of cure. Take care that you yourself don't learn to be froward,[9] by conversing with the froward. Be sure to keep a calm and even temper within your own breast, that you have not raging waves to deal with, within as well as without, when you cross the main. You have sufficiently proved him to be an ill man, and his declining to meet you, and to offer what he could say in his own defence, seems to be a tacit acknowledgement of the guilt—nay, I may say a direct proclaiming it on the house-tops, seeing he durst not refer the trial of his debt to his own friend—and refused to come to a hearing, though so often and so publicly invited to it. All I have more to add is, that you have come off conqueror, have choked Patrick with one lie upon the back of another, and that if he were not case-hardened, he must needs have had qualms of conscience before now, but those I am afraid are reserved to another time, and for his greater punishment. In the meantime, let me again advise you to make a discreet use of your victory, don't discover your own weakness in triumphing over a conquered enemy, and publish no minute-circumstances, but such only as tend to vindicate your own reputation; which may be reduced to a narrow compass, and the shorter the better.

I am, Sir, Yours.

The Tenth Letter

You had in my last an account of the pains Mr Servant took to reconcile Patrick and I. I also sent ye my farewell-letter to Campbell occasioned by his false report that I durst not meet him. I next told ye of a second parley I had with him, and his reason for not coming to the Keys in High-Street, though it was a place of his own appointment. I likewise sent you a letter Mr Wilde received; wherein, as I formerly gave you the sentiments of some clergymen upon my *Scuffle* with Patrick; so you there saw the opinion of the citizens of Dublin upon this encounter: having proceeded thus far in the history of the Dublin wrangle, this letter is to conclude the *Scuffle* so far as I was concerned with Patrick. But the *Dublin-Scuffle* did not end here, for I had no sooner silenced the Scotch loon, but I was attacked by other enemies (perhaps some that were set on by Patrick; for being foiled himself, he was willing still to be gnashing his teeth); who these new enemies were, you shall know in my next letter, and when you have answered that, I'll send ye a copy of my Last-Farewell to my friends in Dublin that stood by me in every skirmish, and in this (as I formerly promised) I shall point at my worst enemies; I mean those that snarled at the Second Spira, have been very zealous to cut my throat (for private slandering is of that nature) or, which is worse, have bought what they won't pay for: and with this farewell (to both friends and enemies) I design to conclude my *Scuffle*; and you'll say it is time, for Patrick is now sick of it, and calls out for help; I mean having done me what mischief he can himself, he is now setting the lawyers a-scuffling too, and next term John Dunton and Patrick Campbell are to be the *Grand Scuffle* (in the Four Courts) amongst the lawyers. But Sir, I as little fear his law, as he minds the Gospel; and to convince ye of this, I no sooner heard that Patrick had a warrant for me, and was resolved to turn our paper-war into a lawsuit, but I sent to his printer the following letter,

[It was directed thus, viz.]

To Mr Brent,[1] Printer, in Skinner-Row

Sir,
If you find Patrick Campbell has a mind still to continue our *Scuffle* by going to law, print the following advertisement in my next catalogue; but if he's sensible of the damage he did me, you may (if you please) commit it to the flames; but as for the printed *Scuffle* he has forced me to, it can be suppressed on no

other terms but his owning in print the public injury he did me, and if he'll own this in the *Flying Post*, I'll be as forward to forgive him as he was to do me all the mischief he could; but a public injury must have a public repentance—I have only to add, that I am

Your friend and servant,

Nov. 26. 1698 John Dunton

The advertisement I desired the printer to publish, was this following, viz.

> Whereas a report was spread about town, as if Patrick Campbell had a design to expose himself by prosecuting me, for publishing several papers, shewing the injuries done me by his taking my auction-room over my head, &c. — This is to give notice (to condescend to the words of Dick the coffee-man) that the same seems false and malicious; for I no sooner heard that Patrick had a mind to continue scuffling, but I went myself to his printer (Mr Brent) to desire him to tell Patrick that if he had anything to say to me, I was come to his house on purpose to answer him; but Campbell never appeared, but sent word he knew my lodgings, and would send to me when he thought convenient; so that I believe he has a better stomach to print Cocker and Whalely,[2] than to run the hazard of two indictments, and besides that, an action of five hundred pound damage for defaming myself and auction, and another action for the monies he yet owes me,
>
> John Dunton

Sir,
I sent the foregoing letter and advertisement to Mr Brent, by my friend Mr George Larkin, who was present with me when I sent Mr Campbell word; I was then at Mr Powel's, ready to obey his warrant (for hearing he had a warrant, I was zealous to have it executed) and to make good my charge against him; but Campbell durst not appear; but notwithstanding that, and the frequent overtures I made

of meeting him at other places (as Mr Servant and others are able to testify) he tells Dick (as thinking I was now embarked) that at the arrival of next post he intended to write against me; hearing by chance of this, I sent him (though under sail) the following letter.

Dated from on board the *Diamond*, owner Pickance, Master, Monday Decem. 26th. 1698 at ten in the morning.

Mr Campbell,
I am told you received my farewell letter, inviting you to give me a meeting to the last minute I stayed in Ireland; but you never appeared, and I not going at the time I expected, to shew I had no malice against Dick, I went to bid him farewell; and he generously tells me, that at the arrival of the next post (that is, when I am gone, and you think I shan't hear your abuses) you design to write against me, not considering that all the town will fling dirt in your eyes (to use the words of a gentleman who heard of it) for slandering an innocent person, who, when he was present, you durst not look in the face. Sir, if you abuse me in this sneaking manner, though your clandestine way of scribbling shews the badness of your cause, and what little regard will be given to it: yet for all that, least my silence should make you wise in your own conceit; I will take Solomon's counsel, and answer you according to your folly,[3] and that before I publish the *Scuffle* you have engaged me in. Sir, in the *Dublin Scuffle*, if I am treated in this cowardly manner, shall be printed a key to explain what is meant by Cocker, Cumpstey,[4] and the darker passages: to which shall be added a true copy (which I have by me) of what the booksellers of Dublin charge you with: and if you have courage to answer this, you may expect a rejoinder, including the ludicrous passages of your whole life (for I have materials enough for that purpose): neither is the account you sent in answer to the debt you owe me less false or ridiculous than your other actions; for you make yourself debtor but for three Turners,[5] when I can produce a letter under your hand, declaring you owe for seven; does my great civility (ungrateful man as you are) of taking two of them back again, discharge you of the other two?

Thus have I fairly told you what I will do, and what the world will say, if you belie[6] me after I am gone: and have as fairly anwered the account you sent me: wherein my lawyer shall prove (since you durst not meet me whilst I was here) that you are still about forty shillings in my debt. When your cowardly reflections appear, I have ordered this to be printed; but have yet to tell you, that I can still forgive you (when I see you penitent). And so farewell, though I am

Your abused friend,
John Dunton

Sir,
Campbell was no sooner informed that I was certainly gone for England, but he had the impudence (according to what he told Dick) to print the following advertisement, notwithstanding my sending the foregoing letter, and his constant refusing to meet me —

The advertisement Campbell printed, as soon as I left Ireland, was this following, viz.

Mr John Dunton having Publish'd several scurrilous Lybels against me this 2 moneth past; I hav taken no notic of them, till last Week I sent both by Writ and a Friend, that I was ready and willing to meet him, either before a Magistrat, or any honest Gent. or creditable Citizen; and if after a fair hearing of both Parties, it should apear that I did him wrong, I wold submit: And if it apear that I hav not wronged him, it must necessarily follow, that he hes don me mach wrong: First, in averring that I took the *Auction-Room* over his Head, which I affirm to be a fals impudent Lie: And nixt, in setting upe in his long Lybel in the *Cofee-House*, that I owe him several Pounds, whereas it shall easily apear, that he is in my Debt. The desired Meeting he refused, and I declare myself readie to give said Meeting upon the Terms abav; that is, either before a Magistrat, or any creditable Gentleman or Citizen; but I do not think the crew that Mr. *Dunton* ordinarily Converses with, fit to bring any such into their Company.

Patrick Campbell

Sir,

By this advertisement (published after I left Ireland) you may observe three things.

First, Patrick's noble education, how finely he writes and spells, for I have not altered a letter from the copy my friend sent me.

Secondly, his great cowardice, in not daring to publish this till I left Dublin.

And thirdly, his great honesty in handing privately to the world a paper, filled with nothing but lies (as I have proved already, so need not do it again); but as base as he was in printing such notorious lies, when I wasn't on the spot to disprove them, yet I must own to his honour (for he has not a virtue, but I blaze it abroad with greater pleasure than I do his vices) that he did not publish them openly, but only caused three of them to be printed off, to shew to some particular friends, or perhaps (as my friend observes) to his beautiful wife, to convince her she had married a wit.

Thus Sir, having sent you the remaining part of the *Scuffle* between Patrick and I (and all I shall send ye about Campbell) your thoughts as formerly are desired by

Your obliged friend and servant,
John Dunton

Remarks on my Tenth Letter

Sir,

I am sorry that you are still haunted with serpents in Ireland, where the world has always thought there were none. It seems Patrick is a man of interest as well as intrigue, when you are no sooner rid of one of his familiar spirits, but you are straightways attacked by another; Patrick has gnashed his teeth, as you word it, so long, that I wonder his grinders are not worn to the stumps by this time. You tell you design speedily to conclude your *Scuffle*, which is very well, but I am sure it had been much better you had never begun it, or at least that you had given it over sooner. You say, that he now threatens you with the law, which, if he does, you are like to be a good booty to the gentlemen of the long robe,[7] and I dare say, they will not turn you out for wranglers so long as the cash holds; and therefore I hope Patrick

73

and you will be both better advised. I do believe it is only a copy of his countenance, for he will be as unwilling to be exposed before the Bench, as to come to the stool of repentance, and in that sense I doubt not but it's true, that you fear his law as little as he minds the Gospel. It's unhappy for Patrick, that he fell upon such an adversary as is ready to answer him at all weapons. I must needs commend your courage, though perhaps it had been more prudent, and some will say more Christian too, if you had rather put up the wrong, for there's a great deal of truth in that North-Country saying, that It's the second blow makes the fray. However, your own conscience is the best judge of your circumstances, and to that I leave you, as to this matter; but thus far I think I may venture to say, that it is no ill policy in you to make Patrick sensible of the advantages you have against him, that way too, if he have a mind to change the scene. It was both generous and Christian to offer a personal conference, and to stand the test of his warrant with which he threatened you, and his declining it is an argument of his being highly defective in both respects.

Your letter to him from on board, I think (all things considered), was needful enough, and I perceive your pen was nothing blunted, notwithstanding you had wrote so much; your threats are terrible, like those of an Almanzor,[8] and I perceive you had a mind to convince Patrick of the truth of what you have formerly asserted, that you wear your pen as others do their sword; all that I can say to you further on the matter is this, that seeing you are engaged, be sure either to give over, or else let your thrusts be home, and your blows keen; for boxing and caning is porters' way of fighting, and I would not have booksellers do anything that may forfeit their right to the title of gentlemen.

Thus have I sent remarks upon Patrick's pretended warrant, your answer to it, and the letter you sent him whilst under sail; I shall next add (for I now answer two of your letters together) that I perceive by yours on the road, that you have left a correspondent behind you in Dublin to observe Patrick's motions; by the account you give me of his printing, and not publishing his advertisement, I perceive your letter from on board had some, though not all, the desired effect upon him. His printing after you were gone is a clear proof of his cowardice, his uttering such manifest untruths is the like of his falsehood, and his forbearing to publish them seems to argue his being conscious of his own guilt. Whatever proof it might be to convince his beautiful wife she had married a wit, it could be none that she had married either a wise or an honest man. As to your remark on his education, that might have been spared; perhaps it was none of his fault that it was not better and therefore he ought not to be upbraided with it, except it proceeded from his own neglect. His malice is indeed very remarkable, in designing to publish such a false libel against you, and particularly in reflecting upon those you ordinarily conversed with, for it appears plain enough by what I have heard from you before, that you had the honour to converse with those that were far above Patrick's merit, as being some of the greatest note in Church and State, but any excuse is better than none. I am glad, however, that your *Scuffle* with Patrick is ended at last, both for your sake and my own, for to be plain with you I have enough of it, and I am sure, whether you think so or not, you have too much. I am

Sir, Yours

The Eleventh Letter

Sir,

I told ye in my last from Chester, I had done scuffling with Patrick Campbell; but sure enough I am still fighting with beasts at Ephesus: for no sooner was my *Scuffle* with Patrick a little over, but I was surrounded on every side.

First, F — [1] (a meagre sort of animal) threatens a token (in English, a warrant) to fright me to a compliance with unreasonable rates for binding; but F — saw he was in the wrong box, and found it his interest to be friends with me.

I was no sooner delivered from this impertinence, but a young stripling[2] summons me before the Lord Mayor of Dublin; he could not but think he was too rash, and therefore had no stomach to argue before a magistrate; so honest Servant[3] (a true lover of peace) gets us both to the Bull in Nicholas-Street, where the lad saw his error, and we parted friends; and I'll say that for TOM— 'That though he is a little hasty, yet he's a very honest fellow, was very faithful in the post I set him, and (writing an extraordinary hand) is fit for a good place, which he can't miss of in Dublin, for he might be trusted with untold gold.'

But I must leave Nelson to speak of the Brass[4] in Copper-Alley, who is another beast I am yet to fight with; this fellow serves me with a token (I told ye the English of it before) and before the Lord Mayor I must go; I was more ready to go than he was to have me, for there needed nothing to plead for me but the bare stating my case; when his lordship heard my defence, he did me the honour to say (Mr Wilde being then present) that I had made my adversary a very just proposal. My proposal was, that one of his own trade, and one concerned in the same agreement, should end the controversy; so that all that Brass got by his token was to be hissed at by honest men, and to be thought (if it could be) a little more impudent than heretofore; Sir, you'll find his picture in the following letters; but more at large (excepts he repents) in my *Summer-Ramble* ——

I next encountred a female devil (a woman, a thing in petticoats) her contrivance was to c——d[5] her husband; and to tempt me to this wickedness, she sends me a billet doux (a copy of which you shall have hereafter) and calls herself Dorinda; had her billet taken effect, her smiles had been more fatal than Patrick's frowns; but God preserved me in this temptation.

I was no sooner delivered from this siren but a grave ancient don lays claim to a quarto manuscript that I purchased of Mr Daniel,[6] but this *scuffle* was very short, for I no sooner discoursed him, but he honestly owns before Mr A —— (a giddy, talking, bauling fellow) my just right to the copy, and so we parted (friends) over a dish of coffee.

There were other beasts I contended with, as the M —— of H —— the K —— of, and the D —— of,[7] but I pass them by, 'till I hear how they carry themselves.

Thus, Sir, have I given ye a further account of my Dublin enemies, and the scuffles I had with them; in my next expect a copy of my Last Farewell to Ireland, and with that farewell I'll conclude scuffling in this country. In the meantime I desire your thoughts on these new encounters, by which you'll further oblige.

Your humble servant,
John Dunton

Remarks on my Eleventh Letter

Sir,

I was in hopes that when your *Scuffle* with Patrick was over, you should have had nobody else to scuffle with, but either your own shadow or Don Quixote's windmill, but it seems your adversaries are of Hydra's breed; no sooner is one head cut off, but two spring up in its stead.[8] Had Richard Strongbow met with such obstinate and unwearied opposition from the Irish, for anything I know Ireland had remained unconquered to this day. I perceive, however, that Patrick was the giant with the hundred hands[9] and, having foiled him, it was scarcely worth your while to draw upon the rest; the grumbling of a mastiff is enough to quell snarling curs at any time; if he do but turn his head, they will be sure to turn their tail, and so I perceive it fared with your other little adversaries, and therefore they deserve no further regard neither from you nor me. Nor were they worth your mentioning, but that you had thereby an opportunity of my Lord Mayor of Dublin's approving the fairness of your proceedings, and perhaps Patrick foresaw the like as to the controversy between you and him, and therefore he would never appear with you before a magistrate.

I had almost forgot the dangerous assault made upon you by the siren, which to a man of a knight-errant-like-temper is the hardest thing in the world to resist; and therefore, I never admired the heroes so much for spurning up oaks with their feet, and blowing down castles with their breath, as for resisting the attacks of the Phyllis's and Dorinda's. It's well you're married, else such a character as this might perhaps give the fair sex a bad impression of you as a hard hearted man, the consequences of which would be that you were not likely to find theirs very soft. But you are out of the power of such a temptation, and therefore there's now no danger on that head; or if there were, you have a golden shower at command, which would conquer a Danae herself;[10] though you had no personal merit. Thus, Sir, I leave you to glory in your conquest, and Dorinda to fret at her disappointment; when I see her billet doux, I shall be more able to judge whether she were a formidable enemy or not. But don't publish your conquest all at a time, lest your name be made use of in future ages to frighten peevish bantlings[11] into a better humour, for it's too much for one man thus to triumph over the Irish men, women, and children all at once. I am

Sir, Yours

The Twelfth Letter

Sir,

I sent you word (by the last post) how Campbell and I parted when I left Ireland; I have also told ye of other enemies, who continued scuffling after Patrick had done his worst. I shall now (as I promised) send ye a copy of my — *Last Farewell to my Friends in Dublin*, that stood by me in every skirmish, and here (likewise) I shall point at my worst enemies; I mean those that have snarled at the second Spira, have been very zealous to cut my throat (for private-slandering is of that nature) or which is worse, have bought what they won't pay for, and with this Farewell (to both friends and enemies) I shall conclude the *Dublin Scuffle*. I don't doubt, but in this Farewell I shall say something that will vex the guilty, yet I find it necessary for my reputation, and (Sir, you'll find) I fear nothing in defence of that: it is true I can't fight my way in tropes and figures;[1] but truth needs no varnish (it shines brightest in its native dress) and therefore in this retreat (which is the most difficult part of war) I face all my enemies at once; and, if I could not spell my name, I'd venture at them; for I'd rather be thought a poor scribe than a coward, as you'll find by the following lines; which I call

My Last Farewell
to my Acquaintance in Dublin whether Friends, or Enemies

[And is as follows, viz.]

Gentlemen,

Having now sold the venture of books I brought into this country (maugre all the opposition I met with from Patrick Campbell and

108   *My Farewel to Dublin.*

my Name, I'd venture at 'em; for I'd rather be thought *a poor Scribe then a Coward,* as you'll find by the following Lines; which *I* call

MY

Laſt Farewel

To my Acquaintance in

DUBLIN

Whether Friends, or Enemies.

[*And is as follows,* viz.]

Gentlemen,

HAving now Sold the *Venture of Books I* brought into this Countrey (maugre all the Oppoſition *I* met with from *Patrick Campbel* and other Enemies) and being to Embark an Hour hence for *England, I* ſend this as my *Laſt Farewel to my Acquaintance in* Ireland (whether Friends or Enemies) and with this ſhall conclude the *Dublin Scuffle.*

Gentlemen !

I Told you in my *Firſt Letter,* That I had brought into this Kingdom, *A General Collection of the moſt Valuable Books, Printed in* England, *ſince the Fire in* London *in* 66. *to this very time ;* to which, I told you, *was added,* —— *Great*
Va-

other enemies) and being to embark an hour hence for England, I send this as my Last Farewell to my Acquaintance in Ireland (whether friends or enemies) and with this shall conclude the *Dublin Scuffle*.

Gentlemen!
I told you in my first letter, that I had brought into this kingdom a general collection of the most valuable books, printed in England, since the fire in London in '66, to this very time; to which, I told you, was added,—great variety of scarce books—a collection of pamphlets, in all volumes:[2]—and a parcel of manuscripts, never yet in print; and that I have made good my word is acknowledged by all that have seen my catalogues, and printed bills of evedays sale,[3] for near six months. Neither can it be thought that the gentlemen of Ireland, who are owned to be very ingenious, would give one thousand five hundred pounds for a parcel of trash (as my venture was called by some selfish people, of which more anon) except—Bibles—Common-Prayer Books—Pool's *Annotations*—Clark's Bible—Hammond on the *New Testament*—*Book of Martyrs* the best edition—Duty of Man's Works—Dupin's *Ecclesiastical History*—Josephus the best—Rawleigh's *History of the World*—Heylin's *Cosmography* in folio—Eusebius' the best edition—Baker's *Chronicle*—Stanley's *Lives*—Cambden's *Brittania*—Terryl's *History*—Lock on *Human Understanding*—L'Estrange's *Æsop*—Seneca's *Morals*—Cambridge *Concordance*—*The Great Historical Dictionary*—Greoad's *Dictionary*—Littleton's *Dictionary*—Gouldman's *Dictionary*—Cole's *Dictionary*—Screvelius' *Lexicon*—Speed's Maps—Morden's *Geography*—*The Irish Statutes*—Cook upon Littleton—Wingate's *Abridgment*—Ben Johnson's Works—Shakespeare's Works—Beaumont and Fletcher's Works—Cowley's Works—Oldham's Works—Dryden's Works—Congreve's Works—Wesley's *Life of Christ*—*Prince Arthur*—Judge Hale's Works—Mr Boil's Works—and the Works of Archbishop Ussher—Archbishop Tillotson—Bishop Taylor—Bishop Patrick—Bishop Sprat—Bishop Barlow—Bishop Fowler—Bishop Wilkins—Bishop Stillingfleet—Bishop Burnet—Bishop Kidder—Dr Barrow—Dr Sherlock—Dr Scot—Dr Horneck —Dr South—Dr Wake—Dr Lucas—Dr Claget—Mr Norris—Mr Edwards—Mr Dorington

—Dr Annesley—Dr Bates—Dr Manson—Mr Charnock—
Mr Howe—Mr Alsop—Mr Clarkson—Mr Williams—Mr Mead—
Mr Baxter—Mr Flavel—Mr Boyce—Mr Showers—Mr Rogers
—Mr Calamy—and such like, may be reckoned into that number.[4]

And, Gentlemen, as I have fully answered your expectations as to
the goodness and variety of the books that I brought over, so I find
you are all pleased with the candour you had in the sale; you may
remember I told you I thought it a sort of picking your pocket (as
you came to my auctions supposing to buy a pennyworth) to advance
the rate upon you by any underhand bidding; and to shew this was
not to serve a turn: I again declare (though I'm leaving Ireland) that
for every penny I got that way I'll restore a pound. But the dignity of
truth is lost by much protesting, so I'll say no more to prove my
innocence, for it is what you all believe.

And, Gentlemen, as you have been all satisfied with the part I
acted in this matter; so I hope you have been all pleased with the
genteel treatment you had from Mr Wilde throughout the whole
sale. The truth is, he has shewn a matchless command over his
passions under very great provocations, and therefore it is (my design
in these adventures being to please the buyer and myself too) that I
have engaged him in a second auction I design for Scotland, and
were I to make a third as far as Rome (as who knows but I may, for I
design[5] to see his Holiness) Mr Richard Wilde should be the sole
manager, not only as his universal knowledge in books renders him
fit for it, but as I have found his candour and diligence to be as great
as his knowledge – and, Gentlemen, as Mr Wilde has treated you
with the greatest respect imaginable, so I hope he has done you as
much justice as he has me, in the whole management.

And I hope you have been as much pleased with my book-keeper
Mr Price, as to his great fidelity in prizing[6] what you bought, as I
have been with his accounting with me for all the moneys received;
or if you can prove any mistake (for no man's infallible) I shall be
forward to have it rectified, though ne're so much to my loss.

And as Mr Wilde, Mr Price, and myself have laboured to give you
content, so I hope so much as honest Robinson—trusty James—and
my very porter Bacon (who brought the bill of every day's sale to
your doors) have not been wanting in their respective place. In a

word, I suppose you are all content, for we all endeavoured to make you so, but, for all my care in these particulars, I find I have some enemies; but (Gentlemen) my comfort is[a] that I have no enemy that's acquainted with me, or has bought a book in my three auctions; it was said of a bookseller lately dead, that he had no enemies but those that knew him; but I thank God, if I have any friends, they are chiefly those that have dealt with me. But I find it is impossible to please all, for though Mr Wilde and myself managed the whole affair (from the first minute I proposed it to him, to the last book he sold in Dublin) with that sincerity as we thought had left no room for exception; not so much as a penny was paid in the auction (if any doubt arose from whom it was received) but I gave it to the poor, for fear I had received more than my due. But for all this scrupulous care, there was a certain person beyond the herring-pond,[7] and in Dublin too (for they echoed to one another), that whispered about, that I had brought you nothing but a parcel of trash. And that the auctioneer was a grand sharper. Gentlemen, it is a pitiful cowardice (as I told Campbell) that strikes a man in the dark, but I suppose you know who I mean by the littleness of his soul, for all such books that he has not a hand in, he calls not fit to wipe his B — ch,[8] and a copy from heaven would be a foolish paper with him, if T.F.[9] were not the bookseller.—Strange how far ignorance, self-interest and pride will carry men, especially men that rise from nothing, or come of mechanic parents.[10]—It is true, I could take a singular pleasure in forgiving this sneaking fellow, there is such a noble pride attends this generous conquest of an enemy as far surpasses the celebrated sweetness of revenge. And this made Judge Hales[11] say, he thanked God, he had learnt to forget injuries; and I wish I could say the same (for I hate to gratify my passion the common way and because T.F. has acted the part of a mean spirit, I must do so or worse by giving scope to my rage) but though I had rather suffer a thousand wrongs than offer one, yet for all that, when a man persists in a base practice, he ought to be jerked in hopes of a reformation, and T.F. the most of any I know in London; for how often has he called—*The Heads of*

a. As I told you in my Second Letter

Agreement (assented to by the United Ministers)—*The Morning Exercises* (published by my reverend father in law, Dr Annesley)—*The French Book of Martyrs* (published by order of Queen Mary, and was the only book she ever gave her royal hand to)—Malbranche's *Search after Truth* (so much commended by the learned Mr Norris, in his *Advice to his Children*—Mr Coke's *Detection of the Court and State of England* (of which large work there is three editions)—*The Works of the Lord Delamere* (published by consent of the now Earl of Warrington)—Dr Burthogg's *Essay on Reason, and the Nature of Spirits* (dedicated to Mr Lock)—*The Tigurine Liturgy* (published by the approbation of six learned prelates)—Bp Barlow's *Remains* (published from his Lordship's original papers) by Sir Peter Pett, Kt. Advocate General for the Kingdom of Ireland—Mr Baxter's *Life*, in folio (written with his own hand)—*The Life of that charitable divine Mr Thomas Brand*—*The Life and Death of Mr John Elliot*, the first preacher of the Gospel to the Indians in America (of which there is three editions)—*The Bloody Assizes*, containing the trials and dying speeches of those that died in the West (of which there is four editions)—*Sermons on the whole Parable of Dives and Lazarus*, by Joseph Stevens, late lecturer of Cripplegate and Lothbury churches—*The Tragedies of Sin*, by Mr Jay, rector of Chinner—Mr William's *Gospel Truth* (of which there is three editions)—Mackenzye's *Narrative of the Seige of Derry*—Mr Boyse's *Answer to Bishop King* (first printed in Dublin, and then in London)—Mr Shower's *Mourners' Companion*—Mr Rogers' *Practical Discourses*—*The Poems* writ by the Pindarick Lady—and the *Athenian Gazette* (which has been continued to 20 volumes, and is so much valued in Dublin, that the sale of that book alone has come to an hundred pounds).[12]

Gentlemen, I should prove tedious, or I would enlarge, for these be not the fifth part of those valuable pieces I print; and to which to show his parts (or rather his envy) he gives the title of—mere stuff, perfect trash: sweet rhetoric! (Gentlemen) which, with something will keep cold, has made his conscience as black as his sign.

I was likewise treated in this manner, by another critic, near Hatton-Garden, who, though he struts like a turkey-cock at a red petticoat, wipes his mouth in London, and is very saucy to every book that he don't print himself;[13] yet his sin has found him out in Dublin; and it is very remarkable that I myself should first discover it, whom he has most abused of any man in London; but he's quiet enough at present, and if he repents, I can forgive; but if he stir hand or foot against this small revenge, the world shall know (as proud as he is) who has abused the name of a late peer, by a notorious sham-title—Gentlemen, such, and only such as these, are my enemies, and this is the undermining treatment I have had from them.

But though there be little souls in the world that have great dealings; yet, I find the gentlemen of Ireland have more honour than to belie their senses, or to call that stuff or trash, which they find to be solid diet—I am sure, in proportion to the great number of books I have printed, no man has printed less trash than myself: I am sure, T.F. has not, if you take in his black lists, his false titles, his printing other men's copies, and new vamping of old books. But, Gentlemen, it is losing time to speak in praise of my bookish venture (or to talk more of my enemy's trash) seeing[a] a worthy member of the House of Commons did me the honour to say, that I had been (by this undertaking) a great benefactor to this country; and no longer than yesterday, a clergyman told Mr Penny (an English gentleman) that I had done more service to learning, by my three auctions, than any one single man that had come into Ireland these hundred years.—I speak not this out of ostentation, but to rectify their opinions, who judge men by what they hear from the scandalous tongues of their selfish prejudiced enemies: but, though boasting is none of my talent, yet I must say, that my venture has been serviceable to this country is not only the sentiment of one or two, but of all I meet with; and therefore it is I am desired, by some of the best quality, to make an annual auction of books in Dublin; but my ramble to Scotland will hinder this; or if it don't, I'll still promise, you shall have no setter in my auctions, and as good books as now.—Not that I pretend to be more infallible than other people; and of six hundred books I have printed (as I said in my Second Letter) it would be strange if all should be alike good: but though in my unthinking age, I have printed something I wish I had never seen (though of 600, I know

a. As is hinted in the *Account of my Conversation, in Ireland.*

but of six I am angry at) yet where I have erred, it is from heaven, and not from man, that I heartily ask forgiveness: I confess it was a noble saying of the great Mountaigne,[14] after he had finished his rambles, that were he to live over his life again, he would live exactly as he had done: I neither, says he, complain of the past, nor do I fear the future. I can't say so, for though I am but turned of my 30th year, and have always devoted my time and rambles to the knowledge of countries, books, and men; yet were I to correct the erratas of my short life, I would quite alter the press.—Would time unweave my age again to the first thread, what another man would I be? but as willing as I am to confess this, yet where I have erred with respect to printing, I must cast the fault into the great heap of human error; for seeing we digress in all the ways of our lives, yea, seeing the life of man is nothing else but digression, I may the better be excused, and the rather, as I am truly grieved when any good man is displeased; not that I ever printed a book in my whole life, but what I had a just end in the publication. But if others won't think so, I can't help it; not but I must own, that having printed a great many books (and not reading through the twentieth part of what I print) some errors have escaped my hand; but this is my misfortune, and not my crime; and ill success ruins the merit of a good meaning; however the way to amendment is never out of date.—Repentance is a plank we (book-merchants) have still left, on which we may swim to shore; and having erred, the noblest thing we can do is to own it. He that repents, is well near innocent.—Diogenes, seeing a lad sneaking out of a bawdy house, bid him hold up his head, for he need not be ashamed of coming out, but of going in.[15] I could even forgive Patrick Campbell, if I saw him a true penitent; such a penitent, as the thief who robbed me in Dublin, who begging my pardon, I scarce suffered him to kneel for it, but as readily gave it, as he was to ask it.

Thus, Gentlemen, you see (at our last parting) that though I am no more perfect than other folks, yet that I don't deserve that ill usage I had from T.F. in London, or Patrick Campbell in Dublin, and (by the grace of God) for the future will deserve it less; for as I grow in years, I alter my opinion of things; when I now print a book, I put on my graver spectacles, and consult as well with my judgment as interest: when I first began to print, I had then seen but the outside of the world and men, and conceived them according to their appearing glister.

You know, Gentlemen, youth is rash and heedless, green heads are very ill judges of the productions of the mind: the first glance is apt to deceive and surprise; novelties have charms that are very taking, but a little leisure and consideration discovers the imposture; these false lights are dispelled upon a serious review, and second thoughts are wiser than the first, and this is my very case. But though I am no more infallible than other people, yet I have ever had that regard to justice, that I never printed any man's copy, or stole his author by private slanders; and though I have printed six hundred books, I never printed a new title to an old book, nor never damned any man's book because I must buy it with ready money; and I ever thought it as base injustice to run upon another's project, neither did I ever murder any man's name (with saying he printed this or that) the more cunningly to praise myself, and whoever will prove one single instance of this in all the books I have printed (a jolly company for the small time I have traded) I'll own myself of as poor a spirit as those are (be they who they will) that practise what I here condemn —and I as little like underselling others to get chapmen.[16] I believe T.F. will own (though a great offender in this kind) that I keep my copies as punctual as any man; Mr Wilde knows in all the notes[17] I made for Dublin, that I put the same price to every man, and would any bookseller be at the pains to compare all my notes together (though I exchanged with all the trade) for every penny he finds charged more to himself than to other men, he shall have five pound reward, and a thousand thanks into the bargain for rectifying a mistake I never designed. Then pray, Gentlemen (for I am now speaking to the booksellers of Dublin) no more reflections (as if I injured the trade by auctions) for is it not your own case? There's few eminent booksellers but have traded this wholesale way; is that a crime in me, which is seen in your daily practice?—If I have a fancy to travel a year or so, and after that to live a studious and retired life (as I have done several years) what harm do I do in selling my stock, and making of auctions without setters? For my own part, I have enough to bear my charge to the grave (for thither, Gentlemen, we are all going) and am contriving now to live for myself, as well as for other people—I would have business, but exempt from strife[a]—and therefore, it is I have done with shops, the hurry of them is apt to engross our thoughts, and I'm loth to venture eternity upon my last breath; to what purpose should I covet much?

I really pity those that (like the dog in a wheel) toil to roast meat for others' eating.[18] Abraham, see how he beginneth to possess the world! by no land, pasture, or arable lordship, the first thing is a grave. The Reverend Mr Stevens (author of the *Sermons on Dives and Lazarus*) gave orders for the making his coffin[b] in perfect health: I desire to follow such examples as these; and therefore, instead of losing time in a shop, I'd now, in a quiet retreat from the world, be studying what good I may do to my friends with what I have, and how little a time I may live to enjoy it; being troubled with the [c]distemper my father died of. I take my last leave (as I now do of Dublin) of every place I depart from?

And that's the reason I now follow the world with such indifference, as if it was no matter whether I overtook it or not. But though I'm come from behind the counter, yet methinks a man out of business, like a rotten tree, only encumbers the ground, so I won't altogether desert printing, or that learned trade, which my father so much approved of, whilst there's an author in London, or a pen in the world; but (with submission to better judgments) I think it is a great madness to be laying new foundations of life, when I am half way through it.

> And they methinks deserve my Pity,
> Who for it can indure the Stings,
> The Crowd, and Buz, and Murmurings,
> Of this great Hive, the City.[19]   *Cowley*

So that being tired with galloping after the world, I'll walk now with a horse in my hand, and who ever sees my house (and green prospects before and behind it) will own it is suited to this purpose. And here, Gentlemen, don't let us mistake one another (at parting) or think I prescribe my method of living as a rule for others to walk

a. Cowley.[20]   b. I had it from his own mouth.[21]   c. The stone.[22]

by. No! He that takes me for a guide in this (or in anything else) may perhaps fall[a] into the ditch, for I must confess that if he alone is a wise man, who has a clear and certain knowledge of things, then I am excluded, for I mistake everything. I feel a mountain of ignorance on my understanding which I struggle under, but cannot remove. I dwell in the outside of things; do what I can, circumstances do always so uneven the scales, that I cannot balance things aright; when I weigh the conditions of men (whether friends, or enemies) if I come near them, I am within a circle, and am strait-ways as if conjured from giving a true verdict; these things are best seen at a distance, when I have sometimes given a right sentence, a new relation, or some other event, has stept in, and violently blindfolded me. Again, when I have beheld a worldling as full of earth as a worm, one that loads himself with thick clay, that walks in the sunshine daily, and never enquires who has lighted him that glorious candle; as goes rooting as if he were a mole in human shape, and cannibal-like devours poor men's flesh; when I had clearly seen, I confidently affirmed his gold to be dross, and himself, beautified with all his pomp, to be but a jade in trappings; when I had made use of him, as an occasion of admiring divine Providence for sparing such a monstrous hog; yea, when I had outlawed him, as one altogether unworthy of protection; yet how has the tender of some few courtesies (or a bare pretence to a reconciliation, as in the case of Campbell) been ready to make me reverse it, has not only stopped my mouth, but muddied my sounder judgment of him, so that now I have had enough to do to see the fault, through my friend, my very judging faculty has been somewhat bribed to spare the sin, least I should fall too foul upon the subject of it; and how have I found out a weak brain, a strong temptation, or something or other to extenuate the offence. Yea, an intent of assaying[23] the world myself has disposed me to the pondering, yea, almost to the entertainment of his principles, and a resolution of returning again to the hurries of a shop; and some possibility of arriving at his height has been such a powdermine, that I have been well nigh blown up in my own trenches; and my affections have been like a navy in a storm at sea, hardly kept together. I therefore thought the

a. Mat. 15:11

best prospective to see the world in its genuine and proper state, was a great distance from it. A man must play the cunning astronomer, who, when he would gaze at a star, gets not on the top of a pyramid, but descends some deep pit, for so the visual spirits are kept together; thus a man should look, as a wise man, just before him. Earthly things are a very mist; before a man comes at it, he may see the dimensions of a fog, and perhaps look over it, but when once enveloped and clouded within it, his sight is limited to a small extent. Gentlemen, such thoughts as these made me retreat to that country-like seat where (after *scuffling* a while in Dublin) I'm now going to live again; which being still and private, and suited to a studious life, is (next to my wife) the only thing on earth I love—.

Gentlemen, having (largely) shewn you, why I leave the hurries of Dublin, and given my reasons for a private life when I return home; having also told ye my thoughts of shopkeeping, and of the several copies I printed, perhaps my enemies will expect here (being fallen amongst books) that I say something of the second Spira,[24] for though it is a book quite forgot, yet my innocence is such (with respect to the printing of it) that I dare bring it again on the stage; and the rather still, as my Dublin enemies (and some in London) have snarled at it with so much fury.

As to this second Spira, which my enemies so nibble at, perhaps the publishing of that relation was one of the most innocent actions of my whole life: Gentlemen, to prove this, I'll lead you step by step into this affair, so far as I was concerned in it—This narrative was put into my hands about Decem. 26. 1692. by the methodizer of it,[25] who assured me, that he received the memoirs that composed it, from a divine of the Church of England, and as a confirmation of this, he delivered into my hands a letter and preface, which are printed in the said book (both of which he said were sent to him by the divine that visited the sick man) wherein the divine says, 'That having examined the piece now it is perfected, with the original notes and papers which he drew himself, he finds the substance and material part very faithfully done'; he further adds, 'I dare affirm, that there's nothing material left out, nor is there any interpollations which are not genuine'—And in his letter to the methodizer, he begins thus, 'Sir, I had yours with the manuscript, and having compared it with the memoires

I took, I think you have done me, and the case of that miserable gentleman, a rigid justice'. My way being made thus plain by these attestations given me by a gentleman I had long known to be a person of integrity, I procured Mr Bohun's[26] licence to the book (which I have still by me). After the book was published, several clergymen and others inquiring of me the truth of the relation, I went with them myself to the methodizer of it (for so he had ordered me to do, if anyone enquired about the truth of it) who gave them all (as he owns in his preface to this book) the very same account he had given me, and they thereupon did me that justice as to acquit me of any unfair dealing in the case, and the same thing has been also done by the methodizer himself in the third, fourth, fifth, and sixth editions of this book; so that I need add no more on my own account, for what can appear fairer? But that no doubt may remain as to my innocence in this matter, I further (and solemnly) declare in the presence of God the searcher of all hearts that I never thought of the second Spira till it was brought to me, and that it was all (every page, line and syllable of it) delivered to me as a true narrative. And it is worth remark (as it shews the generosity of the London booksellers) that but three of them quarrelled with this book, and the first was that very person who (as I can prove) offered to be partner in it; and that too, after his going with me to the methodizer, by which he could know no more of Spira than I did, so that it is clear if I have printed a false Spira (as I hope not) that it is no more than an older man would have done, upon the same informations which I received.

But to do this bookseller justice, there were several divines (as well as he and I) that believed the truth of the second Spira (from the account the methodizer gave of it). I could name two that (from the pulpit) advised their hearers to read it.—It is true, this bookseller tells you, he afterwards altered his mind (what the divines did, I can't say), but what of that? This no way affects me, for he would fain have been concerned at first (and to tempt me to it, promises a preface to recommend the book) and I could see no more into futurity than he, and therefore I fell ablushing (for his sake, not my own) to hear him rail at the book.—Gentlemen, I really thought if second Spira had wanted a champion, this had been the very man, he was so zealous for a share in it; but I rejecting the offers he made, instead of being the last (as I might expect) he was the first public enemy it met with.

And the next to him was a man who leers under his hat, and may now see his sins in his punishment, in those lashes Mr Mather gives him, in p. 68.[27] But I won't name the book or passage, for (when I remember how abusive he was) I think it revenge enough to forgive him.

A third slanderer of second Spira (and is all I met with amongst booksellers) was a gentleman-stationer, who had no grudge against me or the book, yet had the conscience to send it to — to serve a turn, I would explain myself (for here we are about-ship, as we shall cry by and by at sea) but that, he's below himself, that is not above an injury, or at least the ingratitude of a little fellow. I am thus particular in telling the enemies to second Spira, and in the defending of my printing of it, that the world may see what a vile thing slandering is (especially the private slanderer). 'The thing is true, but pray say nothing you had it from me,' is a wound can never be cured.—It is stabbing a man behind, and is the worst sort of murder, as it leaves no room for defence.

And this has been my fate, for I verily think, were all the lies that were told about second Spira printed in one book, it would scarce be printed in two years.—But I am willing now (for I have bore long) to be out of the slanderer's debt, and I hope what I here affirm will give satisfaction to all the world.

For, Gentlemen, you see my innocence as to this book, and how much I suffered (when formerly railed at for publishing of it) by the malice of some, and ignorance of others; and therefore I thought it proper now to set Spira in a true light, for I can't run everywhere to answer slanderers, especially my Dublin enemies (for I'm now leaving them) and these have treated (both Spira and) me without the least mixture of candour, though Archbishop Tillotson tells them, in p. 515 in his works,[28] That if there were any need that a man should be evil spoken of, it is but fair and equal that his good and bad qualities should be mentioned together, otherwise he may be strangely misrepresented, and an indifferent man may be made a monster.—They (continues this great prelate) that will observe nothing in a good man but his failings and infirmities, may make a shift to render a very wise and good man (and I never pretended to be either) very despicable.—If one should heap together all the passionate speeches, all the froward[29] and imprudent actions of the best man, all that he had said or done amiss in his whole life, and present it all at one view, concealing his wisdom and virtues, the man in this disguise would look like a mad-man or a fury; and yet if his life were fairly represented, and just in the same manner it was led; and his many and great virtues set over against his failings and infirmities, he would appear to all the world to be an admirable and excellent person. But (adds this learned author) how many and great soever any man's ill qualities are, it is but just, that with all this heavy load of faults, he should have the due praise of the few real virtues that are in him.—Herbert says,

> He that will but one side hear,
> Though he judge right, is no good Justicer.[30]

One would have thought this distich, with the foregoing passage of Archbishop Tillotson, were enough to cure censuring, and to have inclined the readers of the second Spira, to have been more charitable to the publisher of it, for if I had not one good quality to mention with my bad (as Bishop Tillotson advises) yet they were wholly ignorant of me, and could not tell (did they give me a hearing) but I might clear my innocence, and having now done it, I expect they recant their old reflections, and revive that opinion they had of me before the publishing of this book.—The reason why I expect this generous treatment (and am thus positive in the account I give of the second Spira) is because I write this, as if I made an affidavit before a master in chancery. For Livy, the famous historian, says that he that writes a lie for truth is the greatest of perjured persons, and his reason is, because he imposes upon generations to come; and this makes me yet think that the second Spira is a true narrative: for hadn't there been as strange concealments (who'd have thought that Overbury's murder would have come to light 5 years after it was done)[31] and I believe the methodizer, a man of that honour and virtue, that had he the least suspicion, that I.S. (the divine which he says gave him the notes)[32] had imposed upon him, he'd soon publish the same to the world and, as a Christian ought, own his error in being imposed upon.—This is what I believe of the methodizer; and as for my own share, my innocence is such (as I have here shewn by running through all the steps of the publication) that if I find second Spira a lie (though it were ten years hence) I'd be the first should tell it; and be as zealous for printing the methodizer's recantation. But till such discovery is made, I shall still believe it as much the true Spira, as his in Newgate-Street, who, to shew the honesty of his little soul, calls his book the True Spira,[33] that mine might be thought a false one, or as is the relation of Francis Spira, whence this second Spira has its name.—Now, Gentlemen, what I have here said of the second Spira, being what I am able to swear to, upon all the Bibles in the King's dominions, and if my credit appears hitherto unspotted and free, and not stained with base little and dishonourable actions, I hope (to use the words of the methodizer) I shall have that common charity in this affair, which everyone would be unwilling to be denied, were he in my circumstances; and you can't go to a binder, printer, or stationer, in Dublin, or London either (for I owe not one of them a brass farthing) but you may have full satisfaction upon this last head. But if after all I have here said, there is anyone yet so base, as to reflect upon the methodizer of the second Spira, or upon myself, for printing that dismal narrative, I have only to tell them, that I as little matter, as I deserve, their uncharitable censures:—Gentlemen, I shall only add, (as to second Spira) that the methodizer never saw this apology for printing of it; for truth is ever the same: and having said nothing but what I can prove at large, I thought it a greater proof of my innocence, to publish it without his knowledge: neither could I have consulted him, if I would, for he lives 300 miles from Dublin; and I do declare, in the presence of God, angels and men, that I wrote this defence of Spira and Farewell Letter, with my own hand, whilst I lived with Mr Cawley in that city, and that in the presence of Mr Larkin, who is now going for England with me, and I hope you'll wish us a *bon voyage*.—And I think, Gentlemen, my not consulting with the methodizer in this matter, is enough of itself (had I omitted all that I said before) to shew my innocence as to second Spira, concerning which, I have said nothing but what I would say, were I now taking my last leave of the world, and the Irish voyage, on which I am just entering, is near akin to that long and awful journey.—But so much for the second Spira, of which I sold about 20000, and when the gentleman is known, I believe I shall treble the number.

Thus, Gentlemen, having in this Farewell further accounted for the *Dublin Scuffle*—for the venture I brought to Ireland—for the auctions I made in it—for the candour you had from me with respect to setters—for Mr Wilde's generous management—for my book-keeper's great fidelity—for my servants of an inferior station—for the notes I made with the London booksellers—for the hurries of Dublin—for my private living in Jewen-Street—for my aversion to shop-keeping—for the several copies I printed (and in particular for the second Spira)—and for an annual auction in Dublin (which I told ye was proposed to me) and, Gentlemen, I must tell ye, if anything put me upon it, it is my great desire to bring Patrick to a sense of his error, and the fair dealing I had from others. And here I'll take my leave (a while) of the generous buyers, to give

A Farewell

to those that have BOUGHT,
what they won't PAY for

And truly, Gentlemen (for it is of the non-paymasters I'm now taking my leave) if you won't be just, I'll persuade you to it, and to that purpose I've agreed in the lump[34] (for I'm now leaving Ireland, and shall relapse into no more duns) with an honest lawyer (yes, an honest lawyer) and two bailiffs, who will fear nothing in the just execution of their office—Gentlemen, could I stay in Dublin, I'd give as much time as you would desire, but I have been long from my native country, have a house and servants to look after, and which is more, am daily expected by a young and obliging wife; and, Gentlemen, were it your own case, a day under such a circumstance would seem an age. Then pray be honest in a few days, that even lawyers and bailiffs may be kind to ye. I suppose none have been so unjust to buy what they could not pay for. And pray let me ask you a sober question, Is it reasonable I should have justice? Make my case your own, and you'll say, It is; for my venture was bought and sold at a great expense (and without setters too) and which is yet heavier upon me, you have bought what others would have honestly paid for; neither do I serve your city of Dublin as you have served me, for of 400*l*. &c. I have expended in it, with printers, stationers, binders, and the servants concerned in my three auctions, &c. I have receipts from all I have dealt with, to a very half penny; or if any binder (or other person) has injured himself, by forgetting anything, or by mistakes, in summing up his bill (though it be but the worth of a farthing) if he discovers it ten years hence, I'll pay it myself, if I am then living, or in case of my death, my heir shall do it, or forfeit my whole estate.—

And as I have been just to *meum* and *tuum*[35] in this city, so I was ever as true to another's reputation as to my own: I never struck at any man's fame in Dublin (or in any part of the world) till he fell to murdering mine; even Patrick Campbell (though the most barbarous fellow I ever met with) did not hear from me till he took my room over my head.

And now, Gentlemen (I mean you that are still in my debt), I leave you to think upon these things, whilst I return again to the generous buyers: and here, Gentlemen, it is my duty to tell you, that as I ill resent the bad usage I have from the non-paymasters, so I can never enough acknowledge your honest dealings; you have strictly observed the golden rule, of doing as you would be done by, and I doubt not but the books you have fairly bought will be a blessing to you and your children after you.—When some came to my auction with Naught, Naught,[a] you never sided with them, or belied your conscience to have six pence. You never bid, but in same proportion to the worth of a book: you knew I had no setters, and therefore acted a nobler justice than to bid as if a book were stolen.

In a word, you all acted so honourably, both in your bidding and paying for books (especially the noble colonel)[36] as if, like mere conquerors over covetousness, and such mean beggarly vices, you had a mind to shame the other buyers into gratitude, for the charge I was at to serve them. Gentlemen, by this treatment, I have been able to see, how much of heaven can live upon earth; and surely men of such

a. Pro. 20.24.[37]

just principles, as I found you of, need but die to be in that blessed place. Men of so great a soul seem only lent to the city of Dublin, as a universal pattern for others to imitate.

Gentlemen, if in my next ramble I meet with such men as you, men so refined from all mixture to our grosser elements, men so spiritualized before their time, I shall ramble to Scotland to good purpose, and despise the proverb of a rolling-stone.[38]

I would here (this being my Last Farewell) descend to particular characters of some of the chief encouragers of my three auctions.—

And here I should first acknowledge, my great obligations to the Right Reverend the Bishop of Clogher (who was mentioned before, in pp. 44–5); this learned prelate was a generous encourager of my undertaking; he is a person of great worth, knowledge and humility, and by his hard study and travels has to so great a degree improved his own extraordinary parts, that soon after the thirtieth year of his age (which is the year of qualification for that office) he was made Provost of Trinity College in Dublin, a place of great honour and trust; where he so well acquitted himself, that in a little time he was constituted Bishop of Clogher, and soon after that, for his great accomplishments, was made one of His Majesty's Privy Councillors for the kingdom of Ireland. I might mention his great knowledge of the tongues and most sciences, but the bare relating the public stations he is in, are sufficient demonstrations of the reasons of his deserved promotions, and of the great honour he did me by personally encouraging my undertaking, and therefore I hope his Lordship will pardon me for presuming to mention him in this Farewell; for I should think myself very ungrateful should I leave Ireland without making this public acknowledgement of the favours I received from him. His Lordship's name is St George Ashe.

I should likewise in this Farewell take my leave of the Reverend Mr John Jones,[39] the most eminent schoolmaster in all Ireland; he has sent many scholars to the University of Dublin, and I don't wonder he's so accomplished; for he's a man of so great a soul, that I found he was seldom out-bid in my auction for any book he had a mind to. He's a very studious person, and does not (like some authors) lose his time by being busy about nothing; nor make so poor a use of the world, as to hug and embrace it: I shall ever acknowledge the generous encouragement he gave my auctions. In the short conference I had with him, I found him to be a person of great piety, and of a most sweet disposition; he is free from vice, if ever any man was, because he has no occasion to use it, and is above those ends that make men wicked. In a word, Mr Jones is a person of great worth, learning, and humility; lives universally beloved, and his conversation is coveted by all that have the happiness to know him.

But I take leave of the Reverend Mr Jones, that I may next shed a few tears on the grave of the most ingenious Mr Davis;[40] for though he is dead and gone, the service he did my auction shall live as long as I can write or read; he was famous for a schoolmaster, and so eminent for preaching, that his death was lamented by all that knew him; and I may truly say of him, *Vixit post funera virtues*[41]—I had not the happiness of once hearing this extraordinary preacher, and I can't say I ever saw him; but I am told (by one that knew him well) that if I have erred in his character, it is that I have said too little—but though I can't do justice to his personal merits (being wholly a stranger to him) yet Mr Wilde tells me, he was a true friend to my undertaking, and therefore at leaving Dublin I ought to strew some flowers on his hearse, and to thank his very ashes for the kindness he did his unknown admirer.

Leaving this good man asleep in his grave, I shall next take leave of the reverend and truly pious Dr John Stearn,[42] minister of St Nicholas-Church; he is a most excellent preacher, and as good a liver; this worthy divine was my friend, not only in buying diverse books for his own use, but also in buying for others, and so far was he from that ungenerous temper (not to call it worse) of depriving me of reasonable rates, that he would assure the bidders such and such books were good, and a pennyworth at such and such rates, as he informed them of; neither was his generous-bidding for books all the favour I received from him: I would go on with this gentleman's character, but that he's too humble to hear it mentioned; besides it is very improper to tire my friends at a parting visit. I shall therefore here take leave of this reverend doctor, and next step to the College, where I have so many farewells to make, that I don't know where to begin, nor where to end; for I should here pay my acknowledgments to the Reverend Dr Lloyd, Dr Hall, Mr Gilbert, Mr Baldwin, Mr

Young, &c. These and several other Fellows of the College of Dublin did, as their occasions served, generously encourage my auction, as did divers others of inferior rank in the College, to whom I here give my parting thanks.

I might, had I time, take my leave of many more worthy clergymen that were encouragers of my auction, such as the Reverend Dean Trench, Dean Synge, Archdeacon Handcock, Dr Bolton, Mr Marsh, Mr Hemsworth, Mr Burridge, Mr Lucas, Mr Aspin, Mr Moulins, Mr Drury, Mr Vivian.

And here I would in a particular manner take my leave of Dean Francis;[43] for I wanted (till now) an opportunity to thank him for the encouragement he gave my auctions: he makes an eminent figure in the Church of Ireland, and is too great for me to attempt his character, but if any man does not know him, let him go every Sunday morning to St Michael's in High-Street, where he'll hear, as Mr Larkin and I did upon that text,[a] *And Foelix trembled*, as much clear reason, scripture, and divinity, as ever was yet delivered in a pulpit. And those that go to this church in the afternoon will find the same entertainment by my learned friend the Reverend Mr Searl, the present lecturer.[44] But to proceed to the character of Dean Francis: his piety is as remarkable as his preaching, and his charity as remarkable as either. Mr Feltham says, A good tongue never wanted ears to hear it; for my own share, I must say, that morning Mr Larkin and I heard the Dean, he preached in so refined a manner, that I could have heard him with pleasure till night, and my friend (as I found by the remarks he made on the sermon) could gladly have heard him as long as I. I would enlarge on the Dean's character, but that he was a generous buyer, and (as the case stands) I think it proper to say little of the great benefactors; so I shall leave the Dean (with humble thanks for the favours he did me) to pay a visit and farewell to my true friend, and great benefactor, the Reverend Mr Searl; he was a frequent buyer at my auction, which I did not forget to acknowledge both at my auction, and afterwards at the Curragh, where (in my ramble to Kilkenny) I had the good luck to meet him. I had now and then the happiness of spending a few agreeable minutes in this gentleman's

a. Acts 24.25.

company, which I thought no ordinary blessing, as he was a person of a truly humble and affable carriage—As to his preaching, it is plain, pure, and edifying, and generally without-book: the last sermon I heard in Ireland was preached by the Reverend Mr Searle, upon these words,[a] *For unto you is born this day in the city of David a Saviour, which is Christ the Lord*, and I thought it the most practical and awakening discourse I ever heard in my life. He succeeded Mr Davis (whose death I mentioned before) and is no way inferior to him, either for good preaching or virtuous living. In a word, I have such an idea of the piety and moderation of this eminent divine, that I could dwell on his character for ever; but (I must remember) Pickance is ready to sail, and I have other visits to make, and so, worthy Sir, Adieu.

For I am now going to take my leave of the Reverend Mr Rowe, a country minister, a pious humble man, and a great encourager of my book-adventure. I haven't the happiness to be known to this generous buyer, so I'll take my leave with this short acknowledgment—

And my next farewell shall be to the Reverend Mr Fisher[45] (chaplain to the Right Honourable the Earl of Meath): this gentleman was a great encourager of my auction, by which means I had the happiness of enjoying his company often; we were together that very time when Patrick Campbell refused to meet me at the Keys in High Street. The satisfaction I received in Mr Fisher's company obliges me to attempt his character. He is all that's delightful in conversation, so easy company, and so far from all constraint, that it is a real pleasure to talk with him; he's a person of a sweet natural temper, one that's never out of humour and, I must say, I found his friendship to be ever equal and the same—in a word, it is a virtue to know him, and a glimpse of heaven to hear him preach: but, dear Sir, Adieu, for the wind is fair, and I must be gone; but I leave your company with as much regret as ever I did any earthly blessing.

Having taken my leave of the clergy, my next visits must be to the laity; and these must be very short, for fear the ship should sail before I finish my letter.

a. Luke 2.11

And here I shall first take my leave of the honourable Colonel Butler,[46] a Member of Parliament; he is a great lover of books, and was a constant and generous encourager of all my auctions. His affability, candour, and extraordinary sense, but more especially his ingenuity in painting to the life, is beyond what I ever saw (in my whole life) but at his house, and in his person. It is to this honourable gentleman I dedicate my *Dublin Scuffle*, where (and in my visit to him) you have his character more at large, so with a short farewell to the noble colonel,

I shall next pass on to own my great obligations to Mr Lum, — Gradon Esq, Counsellor Reading, and diverse other Members of the honourable House of Commons, who were great encouragers of my undertaking, and in this farewell I return them my humble thanks.[47]

Neither can I in this place forget the many favours I received from that worthy gentleman, Christopher Ussher Esq.[48] (a relation of that famous prelate Archbishop Ussher). He's a person of true piety, solid judgment, and great estate, and God has given him a heart to do good with it in his lifetime, for he is very eminent for his great charity, and a vast encourager of learning; he laid out several pounds at my auction, and almost daily honoured me with his presence at my sale. I could write a folio on this gentleman's praise, but he's as humble as he's rich; so I shan't enlarge, lest I offend his modesty: but this hint is enough to shew how worthy he is of that great name he bears; and therefore however he may resent this public farewell (considering his great humility) yet I could not think of leaving Ireland without paying my thanks to him, not only as he was my friend, but one of my chief benefactors.

I should also (before I embark) pay my acknowledgements to Sir Henry Tichbourn, Robert Stopford Esq; Captain Aughmuty, Mr Recorder of Dublin (an eminent counsellor), Stephen Ludlow Esq;[49] one of the six clerks to Mr Justice Coot of the King's Bench, a person of great piety, lives universally beloved, and justly merits the honour he enjoys: he was pleased to cause several books to be bought for him at my sale. And here I cannot omit to add to the rest of my benefactors (in this farewell) Mr Baron Ecling,[50] a person of great honour, and of a greatness of soul beyond most that I ever heard of: he is such a universal lover of books, that very few, if any, shall escape him, whatever they cost: he has a very large and curious library, yet as inquisitive still after rarities, as if he had none: he is a most noble encourager of the book-selling-trade, and whenever he dies, the stationers of England and Ireland will have a great loss, besides what the public will sustain thereby.

I fear if I write on, I shall lose my passage, but, Gentlemen, you see by my unwillingness to leave Ireland how I resent your generous treatment. But should I take my leave of all my friends of the laity that were kind to me and my auction, I should swell this farewell beyond bounds. However, though I scribble till the ship is gone, I won't forget, at parting, to give my thanks to my true and generous friend Mr Robert Fey:[51] he was one of those that gave me a farewell treat in Essex Street, and was my true friend from first to last, and the chief person I advised with in Dublin, under any difficulty: he is a real lover of learning, as appeared by what he bought at my auction, extremely civil and obliging in his conversation; and a man of great integrity (and of such quick despatch in business) that had I a thousand causes, they should all be entrusted in his hands. I would enlarge in his character, but that I shall meet him again in the account I design to give of my *Conversation in Ireland*.

I have also many thanks to return to Captain Simon Annion, Mr Rath. Jones, Mr Sholdham, Mr Cuppage, Mr John Smith, Mr Moss, Mr Williamson, Mr George Osborn, Mr Bonny, Mr Samuel Martin, and diverse other eminent attorneys, who were great encouragers of my undertaking.[52]

Neither can I think of leaving Dublin, before I have taken my leave of my three printers, Mr Brent, Mr Powel, and Mr Brocas,[53] for they come into the number of my benefactors and, I'm told, bought several books in my auction; besides, to forget these, would be a little unkind, not only as they served me (once) at a pinch, but as they printed my daily catalogues: and it was only by their presses, that I could now and then thunder at Patrick Campbell, and defy all my enemies; so that, at shaking hands, sheer gratitude obliges me to give each of these printers a particular character.

And I shall first begin with Mr Brent, who, I think, is the oldest partner, he's a scrupulous honest, conscientious man, and I do think, a true Nathaniel,[54] he's perfect innocence, yet a man of letters; he knows no harm, and therefore contrives none: and by his frequent attempts to make Campbell and I friends, it is clear, he never promoted the *Dublin-Scuffle*, though the printing of it would have furnished him with daily work; so that he's what we may truly call a religious printer (and I was going to say) he hates vice, almost as much by nature as grace; and this I think is his true character.

As to Mr Powel (the second partner) his person is handsome (I don't know whether he knows it or no) and his mind has as many charms: he's the very life and spirit of the company where he comes, and it is impossible to be sad if he sets upon it: he's a man of a great deal of wit and sense (and I hope of as much honesty) and his repartees are so quaint, apposite and genteel, it is a pleasure to observe how handsomely he acquits himself; in the meantime, he's neither scurrilous nor profane, but a good man, and a good printer, as well as a good companion.

I come next to honest Brocas, the third partner, and with him (if he's returned from Holland) take leave of my three printers.

Mr Brocas is much of a gentleman; he gave me a noble welcome to Dublin, and never grew less obliging: he's one that loves his friend as his life (nay, he values Mr Wilde beyond it) and I may say, without offence to the printers of Dublin, that no man in the universe better understands the noble art and mystery of printing than John Brocas in Skinner Row; and as a threefold cord is not easily broken, so Mr Brent, Mr Powel, Mr Brocas, it is my advice tee yee all (at parting) that you never divide your interests: for what would you have? Your house is a mere Paradise: Oh spacious dwelling!

> A Garden in a Paradise, would be
> But a too mean periphrasis of thee.[55]

And, Gentlemen, as your house is airy, great and noble (and the top printing-house in all Dublin) so if you keep together, copies so crowd in (from Patrick Campbell, &c.) you'll soon be aldermen of Dublin, and in time arrive to the honour of Lord Mayor; and what a charming figure will the beautiful Powel make, when attended with sword and mace, surrounded with aldermen, bedecked with jewels, and glittering with a gold chain.—

But I don't know when to have done, I see, so, gentlemen printers, farewell tee yee all three; but when I come to Dublin with another cargo of books, it will be in company with Mr Larkin, and then expect my custom again, and to find us both at the Dolphin.[56]

And this (though he's going with me) brings me, in the last place, to own my great obligations to my most ingenious friend, Mr George Larkin, whose noble treatment at his own house, and great readiness to serve me at all hours, and upon all occasions, from the first minute I saw Dublin, to the last hour I stayed in it, shall be kindly acknowledged to my dying day.—But I can't enlarge, for Mr Larkin is come to tell me, the ship is going to sail, which makes me tremble, for though I've crossed the ocean often, yet I still dread the Irish Sea; but my comfort is, Mr Larkin (like a true friend) still ventures his life with me, and I can never die in better company.

Thus have I paid my thanks where I think it due, and given a farewell to all my friends, and as I took my leave, have characterized my benefactors, concerning whom I have said nothing but the real truth; and, Gentlemen, I have often wished, there were no such thing as a compliment in the world, and therefore I flatter no man in these characters; I have no occasion to do it (for my auction is ended, and I'm leaving Ireland); besides I was not born to creep, neither is it agreeable to my temper of mind; but a man may be grateful sure, without being of a mean spirit.

But perhaps my enemies will say, I'm thus large in praising my friends, that my *Scuffle* may sell the better. I do declare, this is all as false as what they said about second Spira, &c. for I don't write this farewell, or the *Dublin-Scuffle*, to get a penny; my circumstances set me above it (the Athenians long since told you, my raven was gone to roost),[57] neither do I publish it out of vainglory, to be talked of when I'm gone; for as Cowley says, I'd live unthought of, and unheard of die: and my aversion to shops (and private dwelling in Jewin-Street) proves I'm of this humour; but I publish it purely to do justice to myself (in the first place) and then to my Dublin enemies; and (lastly) that the world may see how generous my friends were; and who knows, but my enemies, by seeing other men's virtue (and how charming it makes them look) may endeavour to practise it; but whether they do or no, I must declare the honest dealings I had from them, is that alone which has put me i' th' head of a second auction, so that as soon as I get to London, I shall fall to printing several copies in order to furnish out a new venture, with which I shall march directly for Scotland, and when I return from thence, having cleared with all the world (for as to my[a] morals I am, or should be, an honest man) I'll embark for France, Italy, &c. but more of this in my *Summer Ramble*, or *History of my Travels through Ten Kingdoms*, &c. (of which I have seen four) Scotland, France and Italy make it seven, and when I have crossed the Hellespont (where poor Leander was drowned),[58] Greece, China and the Holy Land are the other three I am bound to, and perhaps (when my hand's in) I may step thence to the Indies; for I'm a true lover of travels, and when I am once mounted, care not whether I meet the sun at his rising or going down, provided only I may but ramble: but as much as I love travelling, I love pleasing my wife better, and were I now entered the city of Rome (as far as it is, and as much as I desire to see it) her least impatience to see me should hurry me back before I had seen anything; or if she's so obliging as to let me gratify my curiosity, ten months will be the longest time I can live from her, and having seen the foresaid places in that time, I'll return to the Raven in Jewin-Street; for though it is good to travel abroad, it is best to die in the arms of a kind wife: but shops are small account (as I formerly hinted) and I hope to get more by travelling abroad than by staying at home. Then if Valeria[59] consents (for without that I'll not stir an inch) I'll soon be on this grand ramble; and when I return, for I go for profit, as well as pleasure (I mean for subject matter to write on), will fall to printing as much as ever.

Gentlemen, this long ramble will be ten volumes, of a crown each; the first of which will be pubished in few weeks, and will contain my American travels. — The second, *My Trip to the Low Countries*. — The third, *My Ramble to Ireland*, wherein you'll find the history of my sea voyage, the conversation on the road, at the inns and towns I stayed at, with particular characters of men and women, and almost everything I saw or conversed with, but more especially in the city of

---

a. As is hinted in the account of my *Conversation*.

Dublin, where two hundred[a] persons will see their pictures, that at present little expect it. The non-paymasters, too, shall have a share in the history; neither will I forget the extortion of Copper-Ally, nor my geud friend at the Bible in Skinner-Row.

This Ramble (through ten kingdoms) will contain about a thousand letters, which I'll write in my travels, and send them to my friends in England; I shall intermix them with characters of men and women, &c. (according to the method in my ramble to Ireland) and hope I shall receive remarks upon what I see by those to whom I direct my letters, and I desire they'll treat me with the same freedom as my correspondent does in the *Dublin-Scuffle*.[60]—

Gentlemen, this rambling project owes its rise to something I found in the *Athenian Mercury*,[61] which being an invention of my own that has pleased the age (for it was continued to twenty volumes) I hope the same by this, for it will be as pleasant a maggot,[62] and I'll endeavour to make it as useful.—

Gentlemen, if you ask me, how I can think of rambling thus, having lately married a second wife? To this I answer, I am married indeed,—but it is to one (to use the words of my first wife)[63] who knows it her prudence and duty, to study my humour, in everything (I mean everything that isn't sinful) and finding I am for travelling (to shew the height of her love) is as willing I should see Europe, as Eliza was I should see America; so that, you see, Gentlemen, neither my first nor my second wife, have been she-clogs,[b] as St Austin called his spouse; they were both pleased as it pleases me, with my rambling humour, then to be sure (this temper is so obliging) as soon as my eye is satisfied with seeing, I'll hasten home to the dear Valeria, run to meet her with devouring arms; and then live, and (if possible) die together.—It is true, the man in the Gospel had married a wife, and he could not leave her, but he was not born to ramble, or he must have pursued his destiny: sure I am, if anything could keep me at home, it is a tender wife, such a one as I NOW enjoy; for there is such a union between us, that we seem but as two souls transformed into one; and I must say, were her mighty tenderness known to the world,

a. See more of this, in the Account of my *Conversation*.
b. See Austin's *Confessions*.[64]

it would once more bring into fashion women's loving and trusting their husbands. But though love is strong as death, and every good man loves his wife as himself, yet I can't think of being confined in a narrower study than the whole world. He is truly a scholar who is versed in the volume of the universe, who does not so much read of Nature, as study Nature herself. Who'd have thought I could ever have left Eliza? For there was an even thread of endearment run through all we said or did: I may truly say, for the fifteen years we lived together, there never passed an angry look: but (as kind as she was) I could not think of growing old in the confines of one city, and therefore in eighty-six[65] I embarked for America, Holland, and other parts: but though we parted a while, it was by free consent of FATHER and WIFE, as my coming now to Ireland was by consent of mother and daughter: I found then that the arms of love were long enough to reach from London to the West-Indies; and to encourage me to ramble now, they are as long as ever: what though Scotland, France and Italy, &c. part our bodies, yet we have souls to be sure, and while they can meet and caress, we may enjoy each other, were we the length of the map asunder: so, that you see, Gentlemen, though I have married a second wife, yet that I love her never the less for rambling, but (were it possible) a great deal more, for distance endears love, and absence makes it thrive.[66]

If a wife does not give me some proof of her love (for fine words are but painted babies to play with), how shall I know she loves me at all? and can she give me a greater test, than by telling of me, in a thousand endearing letters, that to be out of her sight, is to be still the more in her mind? When I was in New-England, I sent Eliza sixty letters by one ship, as you'll find in my ramble thither.

Were Valeria and I always together, these (sort of) endearments were wholly lost, and we to seek (for want of a touchstone) whether we loved in earnest. So that I think to ramble is the best way to endear a wife, and to try her love, if she has any, which is so rare a thing (since women have married for money) that for my own share, I'd ramble as far as China, to be convinced of the least scruple. It is true, for a wife to say, as Eliza did, My dear, I rejoice I am able to serve thee, and as long as I have it, it is all thine (and we had been still happy, had we lost all, but one another), this indeed is very

obliging, and shews she loves me in earnest; but still there is something in rambling beyond this; for this is no more (if her husband be
sober) than richer for poorer,[67] obliges her to; but for a spouse to cry,
Travel as far as you please, and stay as long as you will, for absence
shall never divide us; is a higher flight abundantly, as it shews she can
part with her very husband (ten times dearer to a good wife than her
money) when it tends to his satisfaction—since to ramble then from
my second wife is the best way to express my love, and endears like
anything, I say, considering this, I'll soon be on my Scotch Ramble;
and if I return rich in Valeria's opinion, though St Andrew frown as
much as St Patrick, I shall think I make a good voyage of it.

Thus, Gentlemen, have I fairly proved, that absence endears a
wife, if she's good for anything, and that rambling becomes a duty to
him that's well married. A duty? Ay! sure enough! For Valeria and I
improve our separation to better use than if we had been together; for
by absence, we better fill, and farther extend the possession of our
lives, in being parted; she lives, rejoices and sees for me, and I for her,
as plainly (for we are still but two souls in the same body) as if I had
myself been there.—And I must say that of Eliza too, we did not
pretend affection, and carry on two interests; her sympathy with me
in all the distresses of my life (both at sea and land) make her virtues
shine with the greater lustre, as stars in the darkest night; and assure
the world, she loved me, not my fortunes; like the glow-worm (that
emblem of true friendship) she shined to me, even in the dark: she
has been almost ready to wish us unfortunate, that she might give me
the greater test of her love. My head, no sooner asked, but her heart
felt it; and had I fallen sick (in her dying hour) she'd even then have
crawled upstairs to have seen me; and to requite her love (for a kind
wife makes a kind husband) I'd have parted with garment after
garment; stripped myself to my very skin; yea, mortgaged my very
flesh, to have served her.—And indeed all our distresses of body and
mind were so equally divided, that all hers were mine, and all mine
were hers; we remembered we were one flesh, and therefore were no
more offended with the words, failings or wants of each other, than
we would have been, had they been our own; had we loved at a less
rate, our pretences to love had been mere banter: true conjugal love is
a step above house or land! Neither durst I have married, had I loved

Eliza less than myself. But as true and great as our endearments were, I found I could love as well absent as present; and therefore I as little scrupled the leaving Eliza, as I now do the kind Valeria.—

Gentlemen, I had not troubled you with such soft tender things, but to let you see my rambling now (as well as formerly) is the effect of choice and not disgust. If you doubt this, read the Character[a] of my first wife, and you'll find it confirmed with her last breath.

Then, Gentlemen, cease wondering that I can talk of rambling so soon after marrying a second wife. For you see (by the happiness I enjoy in her) that he that is born under a rambling planet, all that he does to fix him at home does but hasten his travels abroad.—I found it thus when Eliza lived, and the case is the same now: for though I am married again, and that to a wife of whom I may say, 'That she fully understands and practises all the duties of a tender wife, so that she seems to be Eliza still in a new edition, more correct and enlarged; or rather my first wife in a new frame: for I have only changed the person, but not the virtues.'—But for all this present happiness, being born to travel, I am ever and anon talking of ships, the mariner's compass, and going to sea, and can't be easy an hour together, without thinking of some far country. If it were not thus, I had never left mother, daughter, house and home, to ramble I knew not whither, and to see I know not what. Surely in the winding chambers of Nature, I even then lay forming ideas of long voyages and new worlds: for ever since I came into being, to ramble has been as natural to me as eating.—

Thus (at parting) have I set myself in a true light; have thanked my friends for their many favours, and am pretty even with all my enemies; but more especially with P. Campbell, T.F. and the foes to the second Spira, &c. And now if T.F. or anyone else thinks himself injured in this *Scuffle*, I must tell him, as I did Patrick, that the press is open. Gentlemen, if you'd know who I mean by this T.F. I shall answer this, by asking, Who do you mean by I *N.* take thee *M.* in the form of matrimony?[68] I mean nobody but he that shews his guilt by wincing; and whoever that person be, I'll reply to him (as I told Campbell) *de die in diem*,[69] till I wear my pen to the stumps. It is true,

a. Printed for J. Harris at the Harrow in Little Britain.[70]

My Farewel to Dublin.   147

meer Banter : *True Conjugal Love, is a step above Houfe or Land !* Neither durft I ha' marry'd, had I lov'd *Eliza* lefs than my Self. But as True and Great as our Endearments were, I found I cou'd love as well *Abfent* as *Prefent* ; and therefore I as little fcrupl'd the Leaving *Eliza,* as I now do the *Kind Valeria.*————

Gentlemen, I had not troubled you with fuch *foft Tender Things,* but to let you fee my *Rambling Now,* *(*as well as Formerly*)* is the Effect of *Choice* and not *Difguft.* If you doubt this, Read the Character *(a)* of my Firft Wife, and you'll find it confirm'd with her laft Breath.

(a) *Printed for* J. Harris *at the Harrow in* Little Britain

Then, *Gentlemen,* ceafe wondering that I can Talk of Rambling fo foon after Marrying a *Second Wife.* For you fee (by the Happinefs I enjoy in her) that he that is born under a Rambling Planet, all that he does to Fix him at Home, does but Haften his Travels Abroad.—— *I* found it thus when *Eliza,* liv'd, and the cafe is the fame now : For tho *I* am married again, and that to a Wife of whom *I* may fay, " *That She fully Underftands and Practices all* " *the Duties of a Tender Wife,* fo that *fhe feems to* " *be* Eliza *ftill in a New Edition,* more *Correct and* " *Enlarged*; or *rather my Firft Wife in a New* " *Frame : For I have only chang'd the Perfon, but* " not *the Vertues.*————But for all this prefent Happinefs, being born to Travel, *I* am e'er and anon Talking of *Ships, The Mariner's Compafs, and Going to Sea,* and cann't be eafie an hour together, without thinking of fome *far Country.* If 'twere not thus, *I* had never left Mother, Daughter, Houfe and Home, to Ramble I knew not whither, and to fee I know not what. Surely in the *Winding Chambers of Nature,* I even then

L 2

lay

Patrick refused to answer my broadside (I mean my second letter in the *Dublin-Scuffle*) as knowing his own guilt. And I suppose Brass will have more wit than to have his life exposed: but if he has more courage than Patrick had, and will answer this with his name to it, I shall treat him as a generous enemy. But if Brass (or anyone else) offers to murder my reputation in a private manner, I shall smell (as I did before) whence the malice springs, and will do myself justice on Patrick Campbell, and the wanton fop of Copper-Alley, and on a certain person who boasts (for it is only such are my enemies) he has lain with several lewd women: Gentlemen, the hints I have by me on these heads are large enough for a second part of the *Dublin-Scuffle*; which I resolve to publish, if they slander me when I am gone, or offer to cleanse their hands by laying their vile practices at my door, which I am clear of, so much as in thought: neither could they brand me with an ill thing, for the 9 months I lived in Dublin; for I dared them to it again and again, and they durst not say black was my eye:[71] but when I am shipped off, and gone too far to disprove their lies, then to invalidate my charge against them, they'll perhaps call me drunkard, swearer, sheep-stealer, whore-master, murderer, and what not? For how far will revenge carry men? But my comfort is, they may as well call me rhinoceros, as any one of the foresaid monsters; for they can no more prove me one than the other. And therefore whatever lies they spread, or lewd wretches may be tempted to swear; and some evidence[72] (especially Irish) will swear through an inch board, as was seen in the case of the Earl of Shaftsbury, and other trials, yet I defy the worst their revenge can utter, provided I have a fair hearing; but that I shall never have, for they durst not (but in private) slander me whilst I stayed, and when, Gentlemen, I'm gone, rather than want something to charge me with, they'll make that exact justice I did ye all, pass for a piece of hypocrisy. But if that be white and innocent too, then will they go near to indict my very care and my caution, and make my very flying temptations to be (though but superficially) criminal. But if my *Conversation* be fair and honest (the account of which shall be added to the *Dublin-Scuffle*), then will they venture to dive into the very recesses of my soul, for it may be there may skulk some naughty thought, which Patrick's people will not fail to produce as evidence against me.

Gentlemen, of this temper I found my enemies in the *Dublin-Scuffle*, and this is the treatment I expect from them as soon as I am under sail, but they know Mr Wilde is an honest man, and ready on the spot to defend my innocence, and therefore they'll scarce abuse me, but behind the curtain. But if my reputation is murdered by a person who conceals himself, I shall value it as little as I do Patrick's malice, for let the world judge of abuses which the authors are not able to prove, and are ashamed to own. However, Gentlemen, though I'm leaving Ireland, I still dare these sneaking badgers to do their worst, and to prove I'm in good earnest, I do in this last farewell offer 5*l.* to any that will and can honestly swear to anything my enemies say that will bear an action; for if it touches my good name, the law is open, and though it cost me 500*l.* the lawyers shall pursue the slanderer with the utmost rigour; for though an honest reputation is preferable to all the world, yet I ought to own myself guilty of every thing that wounds my name, though[73] I dare not prosecute.

Thus (Gentlemen) you see I am prepared, for the worst that Patrick (and all his scoundrels) can say against me, but having told them the truth, I must expect as abusive dirt as their foul hands are able to fling, but the most false and ridiculous things they can say or invent won't at all surprise me; for I know it is easy to dress up even an apostle in a fool's coat, and to laugh at him: I don't presume to have better luck than the great Sherlock,[74] and several eminent divines who are yet living, who, though men of great piety and learning, could not pass through the world without a slander, or a weasel nibbling at their reputation, and therefore, Gentlemen, had I not known my innocence, (except what I do pennance for in these sheets) I should not have *scuffled* with them; but if they'll let me have fair play, when I am gone, say nothing but what they found—put their names to what they write, and publish nothing but what they'll prove (for accusations make no man a criminal) I defy all my enemies, from the Man in Buff, down to the Black Rose,[75] which (though the best flower in all the garden, yet) when it spreads its leaf, and begins to swell with conceit and pride, it loses its fragrancy, and shall be respected accordingly—thus as I began, so I end my farewell with a defiance to all my enemies.—

But, Gentlemen, I have tired ye all; so I come now to (the last becken[76] of farewell). Then honest Wilde, dear Wainright, generous

Dell, handsome Powel, easy Dick, friend Dobbs (and all my other friends) farewell, farewell for ever, for the wind is fair (Geo. Larkin and Price are already in the boat) and I have but time to tell you that I am (as you found me all along)

Dublin, Dec. 26. 1698
being Monday 8
in the morning

Your very faithful and
very humble servant,
John Dunton

The Answer to my Twelfth Letter, being Remarks on my Farewell to Dublin

Sir,

I have received so many of your letters concerning your Irish adventures, that one more will make them up a baker's dozen:[1] by your last, I perceive you are like a true game cock: being once engaged, there is no disengaging you again.[2] You are so much flushed with your victories in Ireland, that I perceive you breathe nothing but dreadful threats against your enemies in England, enough to make them either run away, or meet you on the road with terms of submission; which (you look so big) I am afraid must be no less than to submit to the will of the conqueror, and surrender on discretion. And to be free with you, I think it will be their best way, and if I knew them, would send them penny-post letters apiece to persuade them to it. You need not make any apology for not fighting your way in tropes and figures, for your flights are so extraordinary, that I do believe they can be reduced under any of the rules of our common rhetoric. To make a handsome retreat is one of the best accomplishments in a good captain; but I don't perceive yours to be anything of that nature: to me, it looks more like the sounding of a new charge; and by your way of marching to the field, I can almost assure you of the victory, without giving myself the trouble of consulting the entrails of birds or beasts.[3]

But now to your *Last Farewell* to your acquaintance in Dublin, whether friends or enemies. Your very first line is a cordial to the former and a corrosive to the latter. You have sold your venture of books; then Patrick, I perceive, has scuffled with you to little purpose. If this be the first note of your retreat, I can scarcely imagine what other you make use of for a triumph; but this I impute to your modesty.

As to the catalogue of your books, which you think fit to exhibit, to shew the world they were not trash, as your enemies maliciously alleged them to be, I am of opinion you might have saved yourself the labour. Those that bought them did not think them so; else they reflected upon themselves, more than your enemies did upon you: and as for booksellers who called them by that name, it would have passed well enough under the notion of the no less true, than common saying, viz. that two of a trade can never agree:—and as to others, your catalogue is no vindication: for there are men in the world who will call the first and best book in your catalogue, trash; I mean the Bible: and therefore well may others be so called: nor indeed is there anything more usual amongst depraved men, than to undervalue what does not agree with their own private sentiments, or what they have not an interest in themselves.

But admitting that in your venture there might be some trash, I would fain know what bookseller there is who has none in his shop; yea, or what gentleman or divine is without it in his closet. If authors have trash in their heads, the world must endure the penance to have it in their houses and hands, so that the reflection is general; and I question very much, whether any, or all of your enemies, are masters of so many good books as were in your venture? And whether there be not more trash, in the best of their shops, than you carried to Ireland?

For the fairness of your dealing, in not employing setters, and making use of trusty servants, it is proper that you make your appeal to the public in your *Last Farewell*: but I am afraid, you have been too particular in that matter, which can scarcely admit of any excuse, but that it shews the goodness of your nature, that not so much as an honest porter shall miss his due praise from you. As to Mr Wilde, I perceive, according to your character, he is a second Millington;[4] so that if you were happy in his assistance, he was happy in your justice. Your design of going to Scotland, I cannot say much to; that country has laboured under discouragements, as to learning, for many years, though it does not want its proportion of learned men; and some of them you know, as the Lord Bishop of Salisbury,[5] to name no more, make a great figure in the world, on that account. But as I am informed, by the constant intercourse they have with London and Holland, they are pretty well furnished with books; and what they buy is generally of the best sort; so that if you go thither, you must have an auction well picked, for those that buy books there are either the chief of the gentry, who are generally men of good breeding, or the richest of their clergy, with whom everything will not go down that is greedily coveted by the wits here.—And besides, there are so many of their own booksellers that come hither yearly, that I question if you will find your account in going thither, except you can afford extraordinary pennyworths.

You talk, I perceive, of going to Rome; I hope you don't design to carry English books there; if you do, you are likely to find a very discouraging market; and for Latin books, such as they value, the Continent can furnish them cheaper than our island: but if you will go, reserve all the trash and stuff you can get, for that auction; the worst that the London booksellers' shops contain is good enough for the Whore of Rome.[6]

Having done with Patrick, and the rest of the scufflers in Dublin, I perceive you now whet your pen against T.F. and others of the same kidney in London; it's but just that you should make reprisals upon one to his face, who has been so cowardly as to attack you behind your back. Envy they say looks pale, and that seems to be so much of T.F.'s quality, that I am afraid all your rhetoric won't be able to make him blush—yet I am confident that upon reading what you say of him, he must needs have some stings within,[7] or else his case is worse than was that of either the first or second Spira.

The great number of books you have printed may very well be allowed in part of an apology for some trash, and I question whether any of your adversaries have printed as many good books, in proportion, as you have done. Your ingenious confession, that you don't approve of all you have printed, ought also to be allowed as another part of your defence, and I think the practice of some of the trade (to print what they can get a penny by) may very well be allowed to complete it, as far as the case will admit of a defence; and therefore whatever rigid casuists may do, it ill becomes booksellers to hit any such thing in your teeth: let him that is without guilt in that respect, throw the first stone at you. But I find T.F. is not the man that must begin; you have by a just Providence hit a blot in his escutchion,[8] by which, I suppose, you have him at command, and can charge him with a downright cheat upon the world, if he be not so wise as (with Merry-Andrew[9] on the stage) to eat his pudding and hold his tongue. What you say as to your general practice in the way of dealing, I conceive, to be so universally known, that few will offer to contradict you; nor can any man in justice upbraid, or be angry with you, for disposing [of] your stock to the best advantage, by auction or otherwise: these are but snarles, and the ordinary effects of envy in ill men, who grudge to see others thrive better than themselves.

I come now to your second Spira, whereof you have given such a full and satisfactory account, that I am of opinion, no thinking man can henceforward entertain an ill thought of you upon that head. If it be a forgery, it's none of your making, or contrivance, nor is there a bookseller in town would have refused the copy upon the like information. As to that person who dealt so basely with you, and exclaimed against the book, though he was so eager to be a sharer in it; your reproof is so sharp and pungent, and yet so true and just, that if he has any resentments within his breast, or were ever accustomed to reflect upon his own ways, I should not much wonder that he became a true subject for a second Spira himself, if he allowed his own conscience a free parley; all that I can say further is this, that you have laid it fairly at the methodizer's door, and that of I.S.[10] the divine, who gave him the information, if they won't vindicate themselves, you were not in that obliged to bear them company. The defence of yourself on this head was certainly necessary, and you have performed it so well, that were any friend of mine engaged in a combat of the like nature, I could not tell where to recommend him to a better second than yourself: you needed not have been at the trouble of such an asseveration, that this defence is the product of your own pen, for I am satisfied everybody that knows you will be ready enough to believe it.

Sir,

I am sorry that to the ill treatment you have met with from Patrick Campbell, you should have that of other unjust men added, who have bought what they won't pay for; it is but just the bums[11] and they should reckon when you are gone, seeing they would not come to an account with yourself: I am glad however that they cannot plead your own example as a precedent, and that no man can charge you with anything you have not paid for: honesty is always uniform, and the same in Ireland as in England, and therefore it is that the provocations you have met with have not been able to make any change upon you, or to influence you to return evil for evil.

Your grateful remembrance of your friends that encouraged your auctions does, in my opinion, bespeak more of the justice of your temper than of your digestedness[12] of thought. It had been sufficient to have named some of the most eminent, and to have included the rest with an &c. Neither do I know how some of them may take it, to have their characters published in this method; modesty is a tender quality, and will soon be offended: the kindness of your heart must be your best apology, and to such as know you, it will be excuse enough; but you ought to have remembered, that there's something else in the old proverb of killing with kindness, than a mere pleasing: it cannot however be supposed, that you have any sordid design in these encomiums, now that your auctions are over, and that your next ramble is designed elsewhere, and therefore all that can be said for it is this, that whereas some men are troubled with an overflowing of the gall, you are troubled with the contrary distemper, if the saying be true, that *jecore amamus*.[13] It may, perhaps, be ill taken by those of the higher sort of your friends, that you should join so many of an inferior rank, as sharers with them in your valedictory elogiums;[14] but I see no great reason for it: no man can live without the services of the meanest vulgar, and therefore justice obliges us to owe no man anything but love. But it seems, you have a mind to supererrogate,[15] and to owe none of that neither, but to pay it all beforehand, or on sight: I must confess, that for my own share, I never could think there was anything of barbarity or want of cultivation in that good nature of some of the Indians, which travellers ridicule them for, viz. that they will not only enquire after the welfare of their friends and their families, but very kindly ask, how their horses and their dogs do; which, in my opinion, includes this principle of natural justice in it, that we ought to be grateful to all sorts of creatures, that yield us lawful profit or pleasure: And thus I bid *farewell*, to your Farewell to all your Dublin friends.

I come next to your project of rambling, as to which I must tell you, that you have rambled more with your head in one year than you will be able to do with your heels in seven; therefore would advise you to make use of the curb a little, and not to be altogether on the spur. You say, your raven[16] was gone to roost, a pretty while ago; and I know no reason why his master should ramble. But if the sight of four kingdoms, and the marrying of two wives, be not enough to qualify this rambling humour, you must rectify your geography a little better, and not talk of crossing the Hellespont to see Greece, for you must either sail by Greece, or travel through it, before you can come at the Hellespont, except you design to take a round, and to repay the Czar his visit; or if you be for a nearer cut, sail down the Danube, and fall into the Black-Sea.

Methinks, the good entertainment you boast of at home should entice you to stay there; if Valeria's arms be so charming, she shall, if she take my advice, transform them into chains, and hold you so fast, that you shall not have leave to stir; if love won't oblige her to it, I am resolved that fear shall; and therefore, Valeria, for it's to you that I now address myself: don't trust the raven too often abroad; you know that Noah's when once sent out, never came in again;[17] and for anything I perceive, yours has a great mind to be following his; it was beyond the Hellespont where that was let loose, and I don't know, if yours once pass the Dardanelles, but they may meet, and so ramble on, and never think of returning to their roost again; Noah's has none to return to, except it be an old rotten piece of the Ark on the mountains of Arrarat, or as some say, of Armenia; and I am satisfied, the Raven in Jewin-Street has better quarters: if nothing else will prevail with him to stay and roost there, tell him, that Noah's raven feeds upon carrion; and you know very well, by his rejecting Dorinda's billet doux, that he hates such entertainment.

But now I return again to your husband, & must tell him, he exposes your virtue too much, first, by rambling from you; and then by giving such a high commendation of you, as were enough, but that you are beyond the reach of temptation, to endanger you, or at least, to make you run Lucretia's fate.[18]—Wherefore, Sir, let me tell you, that as some will charge you with impertinence in troubling the world with an account of your happiness in two wives successfully, when there are so many thousands that, to their grief, can never say, they were happy in one; if any misfortune should befall you on that account, you must blame your own imprudence for it.—Had Tarquin never heard anything of Lucretia's virtue and beauty, he would never have tempted her; and therefore my advice to you is, to stay at home and guard your treasure, and don't both fare well, and cry roast meat too.[19] Remember the old saying,

Sed tacitus pasci si posset Corvus Haberet,
Plus dapis et vixce multo minus invidiaque.[20]

I am, Sir,
Your faithful friend, &c.*

---

* [Here, on p. 160 of the 1699 edition, appeared an 'Advertisment' to this effect: 'The Three following Letters in the Billet Doux, which are called the Eleventh, Twelfth and Thirteenth Letters, are Mis-Printed, and ought to have been Printed the Thirteenth, Fourteenth and Fifteenth Letters.' In the present edition these misprints have been silently corrected.]

meer Banter : *True Conjugal Love, is a ſtep above*
Houſe or Land ! Neither durſt I ha' marry'd, had
I lov'd *Eliza* lefs than my Self. But as True and
Great as our Endearments were, I found I cou'd
love as well *Abſent* as *Preſent* ; and therefore I as
little ſcrupl'd the Leaving *Eliza*, as I now do the
Kind Valeria. ——

Gentlemen, I had not troubled you with ſueh
ſoft Tender Things, but to let you fee my *Rambling*
Now, (as well as Formerly *)* is the Effeᴅ of *Choice*
and not *Diſguſt*. If you doubt this,
Read the Charaᴅer *(a)* of my Firſt   *(a) Printed*
Wife, and you'll find it confirm'd   *for* J. Harris
with her laſt Breath.   *at the Har-*
    Then, *Gentlemen*, ceaſe wondering   *row in* Lit-
that I can Talk of Rambling ſo ſoon   tle Britain
after Marrying a *Second Wife.* For
you fee (by the Happineſs I enjoy in her) that he
that is born under a Rambling Planet, all that
he does to Fix him at Home, does but Haſten his
Travels Abroad. —— *I* found it thus when *Eliza*,
liv'd, and the caſe is the ſame now : For tho *I* am
married again, and that to a Wife of whom *I* may
ſay, " *That She fully Underſtands and Praᴅices all*
" *the Duties of a Tender Wife, ſo that ſhe ſeems to*
" *be* Eliza *ſtill in a New Edition , more Correᴅ and*
" *Enlarged ; or rather my Firſt Wife in a New*
" *Frame : For I have only chang'd the Perſon, but*
" *not the Vertues.* —— —— But for all this preſent
Happineſs, being born to Travel, *I* am e'er
and anon Talking of *Ships, The Mariner's Com-*
paſs, and Going to Sea, and cann't be eaſie an hour
together, without thinking of ſome *far Countrey.*
If 'twere not thus, *I* had never left Mother,
Daughter, Houſe and Home, to Ramble I knew
not whither, and to fee I know not what. Surely in the *Winding Chambers of Nature*, I even then
                       lay

The Thirteenth Letter

Sir,

I formerly gave you an account of my *Scuffle* with Patrick Campbell, who is none of the best of men; and now shall entertain you with a surprising adventure that has befallen me with a lewd woman. It was a billet doux sent me by a citizen's wife in Dublin (as I judge by a passage in it) both enticing and threatening me to her wanton embraces. Your remarks on this, as on my former letters, will add to all the obligations which you have already laid upon,

Sir,

Your very much obliged servant,

John Dunton

The billet was directed thus,

To Mr John Dunton at the Auction-House at Dick's Coffee-House in Skinner-Row

[And is as follows, viz.]

Sure Philaret,[1] you are not always guilty of disrespect to your friends; can't you be more punctual to an assignation; I can assure you, I was punctual both to place and time, and waited more than two hours in hopes of your happy arrival; but when I found my expectations frustrated, and myself only bantered and abused, and forced to retreat without so much as the bare aspect of what I so longed for, none but one of my circumstance is able to imagine the various passions that moved me: fear, hope, love, revenge, all acted their several parts, and so passed off the stage; only love remained to plead excuses for you. Some of them so frivolous, that I am ashamed to mention them, only to tell you (that senseless as they were) they had power enough to prevail with one willing to believe (though against sense or reason) anything that pleads in Philaret's favour; home I went, where I attend² your answer, and am longing with impatience, till I see what excuses (the false) Philaret can frame for himself, for so the present passion styles him; though that sentiment too was over before I had finished the sentence; and I could almost find in my heart to burn my letter; but that I should not have time to write another, before the watchful Argus³ would inspect into my privacies; then I was about to blot it out, only that I feared would spoil the phiz of my billet;⁴ so I resolved to let it stand as a mark of my courage, that I dare at sometimes adventure to think Philaret false; yea, and that I was once bold enough to let you know it; — well, Philaret, I shall one day be even with you, and it may be, you may repent when it may be too late to retrieve the slight value you have had for the most sincere and cordial friendship laid at your feet, by

Your ever faithful,

Sept. 2. 1698. Dorinda.

POST-SCRIPT

Direct your answer to me, to be left at that which was St Lawrence's Coffee-House on Cork-hill, under the borrowed name of Captain John Seamore, and I will order it to be called for by one that will safely deliver it to,

Your own (Dorinda) if you please.

The First Answer to the Citizen's-Wife

Sept. 5th. 1698.—I received a letter subscribed Dorinda, but am wholly a stranger both to your person and meaning—your two hours —your time and place—are Arabic to me, who approve of no assignations but what are just; and therefore it is very certain your letter was wrong directed, and should have gone to some of your lewd companions, who in your drink (for there are such monsters as drunken women) or by the likeness of garb, you mistook for me—or perhaps you're some suburb impudence, who would abuse an honest man in hopes of getting a penny to conceal your slanders. If this is your design (as I am told it is usual with common strumpets) you are as much mistaken in my humour, as you are in my person, and therefore go about your business; for till you're virtuous I can't love ye, and it is not in my nature to fear anything. But you say you'll be even with me, if I fly your lewd embraces, and that (if I won't meet you) I shall repent when it will be too late, the slight value I have for you; but (I thank God) my virtue is proof against all your charms, and my innocence such, as I challenge you to do your worst. But though the repentance you threaten no ways affects me, yet if you do carry on your jest farther, it will be fatal to Mr S———,[5] as he's the only person in Dublin that knows me by the name of Philaret, and must expect (upon the least occasion) to bear the scandal of being your friend. As to your care in concealing your lewdness (for you say you're afraid of your watchful Argus) it no ways obliges me I should more rejoice to hear that such a wanton (as your billet shews you to be) had broke the Devil's fetters, and was kneeling to her husband for pardon; though if he denies it you have no reason to pout; for if citizens' wives will c———d[6] their husbands, and invent new fashions (and frisking strains) of disobedience, which their holy ancestors (and for ought we find in the word) even the worst of women abhorred; why should not their husbands, either send them to the house of correction, or suit them with new forms of disciplines. To what end else are they to dwell with them as men of knowledge? Does this knowledge, think ye, import nothing but pusillanimity and patience? Is the husband God's vicegerent for nothing? And can he not be a saint, unless a fool too? But though the cold water your lewdness has flung upon Argus' affection is enough to extinguish it, yet the way to amendment is never out of date; and who knows, if you prove as kind a wife as you have been to the contrary, but Argus may be yet happy. But he is flesh and blood as well as you, and therefore, except of a wanton you become chaste, he were better travel than live with a w———r;[7] if you think of amendment, fling yourself at your husband's feet; tears in your eyes may carry the cause, where a husband is judge? Without this, you do but dissemble with God and man; neither can Argus think you repent, till you discover[8] your lewd haunts, and the names of those that have defiled his bed; to act thus, is to shake hands with your master sin (which I find is lust) and in some measure to repair the damage you have done to religion by your whorish intrigues. As this will prove your sincerity, so it will make Argus forget your former lewdness, and if he's a generous husband, never to mention them more. And Argus, if she thus repents, prithee receive her again—for what knowest thou, O husband, whether thou shalt save thy wife?[a] Neither are these ungrateful reflections (my own Dorinda, as you call yourself) for there is no faith in sin, and I ought to slight a friendship which can't be true, and would end in the ruin of soul and body; then go and sin no more,[b] be not dilatory in these matters (it is ill venturing eternity upon your last breath) nor suffer your aversion to Argus to spread abroad, for a quarrel concealed is half cured—I have only to add, that I wish you chaste, and better eyes for the future, and then Argus and you will fall a-loving again; and remember at parting, it is your penitence, and nothing else, can set you right in the opinion of, &c.

Thus, Sir, I have given you a faithful account of this new temptation, with which I have been assaulted; and of my reply to this female aggressor; I desire you to use your accustomed freedom with me in your remarks, which shall always be taken in good part, by

Sir, Your very humble servant,
John Dunton

Remarks on the Billet Doux, and J.D.'s Letter in Answer to It

My good friend,
Your last, with the billet doux, is more surprising to me, than anything that happened in your encounter with Patrick Campbell. I cannot but bewail the hardness of your fate, that you should be condemned to fight with beasts of both sexes: I find Ireland cannot boast of her being free from the seed of the serpent, whatever she may say as to her having none of those creatures in specie;[9] and were I to choose, I should rather desire to inhabit amongst adders, than lewd women: happy would it be for Ireland, if she could make an

a. 1 Cor. 7.16.   b. John 8.11.

exchange of the one for the other; but so long as the popish clergy are suffered to nestle in such numbers there, it is in vain to hope for it: Rome may well be called the mother of harlots, when it is the practice of her sons to make as many such as ever they can.

I did not think, however, that the art of writing billet douxes had been so well understood in Ireland: your Dorinda seems to be so very expert in her trade, that I fancy (if there be anything of reality in it, that is to say, if there be not masculine knavery and malice at the bottom of it), she must be some abdicated retainer to our London play-houses; or perhaps, the offcast of some dead or reformed officer, who, having no pay himself, is not able to retain her: nay, for any-thing that I know, she may be the captain of Kirk's troop of twenty five,[10] that they say he had in that country, when so many of the late King James's atheists were sent to fight against their brethren the papists; for I can hardly think, a She-Cit[11] of Dublin, so well versed in Ovid's *De Arte Amandi*,[12] as your Dorinda seems to be.

It's true I might fancy, it were some green-sickness[13] nun, that had gone a catter-wawling from her nunnery, but then, it comes into my mind, that they are sufficiently provided by the monks and friars; for you have heard, it was an observation of Henry the 4th of France, many years ago, that the nunnery was the barn, and the monks the thrashers.

Then give me leave to add one conjecture more: perhaps it might have been a trap of Patrick's laying, and that he had a mind to try what he could do by women, since he was not able to deal with you by wit.

Had you been caught in the snare, there would have been subject of triumph, and there's no reason to doubt but he would have trumpeted your fame. This cannot be accounted uncharitable, if I understand the true character of the man, for he that makes so bold with the last of the Ten Commandments (as it appears Patrick has done) cannot be supposed to have any great value for the other nine: but be that how it will, I applaud your conduct, and think you acted the part of an honest man, in returning such a sharp and pertinent answer; and the part of a prudent man, in doing it with those precautions: you know I never preach up merit, and therefore you will not be offended if I tell you, that it was but your duty: I am not unsensible, what many men in your circumstances would have pleaded in excuse of complying with such a proffer; but you knew the danger of yielding to the passion either of revenge or lust; none but weak men and fools are slaves to those tyrannical masters. Besides the reward of a good conscience, your courage in this affair will enhance your value to your family at home, or at least, it ought to do so, if they be not condemned to perpetual ingratitude.

I am the more confirmed in my thoughts, that it was a snare laid for your reputation, when I consider your way of carrying yourself, the plainness of your habit, and the influence which your illness and late *Scuffle* must needs have had upon your outside; and especially, that the letter was directed to your auction-room, for if the design had taken, then there would have been ground for Patrick to have libelled you in the Irish *Flying Post*, and to have called it an assignation-room for strumpets, instead of an auction-room for books; which would have effectually hindered any man's frequenting it, who had but the least value for his reputation. This is all I shall say at present, and conclude with my hearty wishes, that you may still continue a conqueror over your own passions, as well as over your unjust enemies. I am

Sir,
Your sincere friend and well-wisher.

The Fourteenth Letter

Sir,
You are so very obliging and happy in your remarks and advice, that I make bold to trouble you again with my Second Letter to the Irish Dorinda. I thought it my duty not to let her pass without a severer reproof, the copy of which I here send you, to satisfy you how abominable such crimes are in my eyes, and that I took the most effectual method I could to prevent a second attempt of that nature upon me. I am what I always was,

Sir,
Your very humble and much obliged servant,
John Dunton

To Dorinda

I hope you received my first, which because I think not severe enough, I send you a second. You see I reject your courtship, as I would shake off a toad, or a snake that should crawl upon me; for I look upon your poison to be worse than theirs. Yet because I would not be altogether ungrateful, for that which you proffered me under the notion of a kindness, I send you, as a suitable present, a *Treatise of Fornication*, and a book called *God's Judgments against Whoredom*, both which were printed for me.[1] I recommend them to your serious perusal, they may through God's assistance be instrumental to reform you, and at the same time to satisfy you that you mistook your man, when you directed your billet doux to me. Yet I know not but there may be a providence in it, for you see my auction affords proper remedies for your distemper; and I am so generous as to send you them *gratis*. You must pardon me however, if in my applications I do something resemble the quack; that is to say, if I prescribe physic without seeing the patient; because I remember Solomon says, Go not by the door of the harlot, lest she entice thee; that none but fools follow such, and that the way to her house is the way to hell and death. That the mouth of a strange woman is a deep pit, and that none but those who are abhorred of the Lord shall fall into it.[2]

I wish you would be at the pains to read the fifth and seventh chapters of the Proverbs. You who are ladies of pleasure use to converse much with your looking-glass, and I will assure you, that there is the best mirror you can make use of; it will exactly shew you all your spots and patches.

I doubt not, but you are troubled with all the infectious distempers that attend those of your trade; and seeing the best way to cure ulcers is to lance them well, read this *Treatise of Fornication*; it may prove of sovereign use; or if you find it makes your wounds smart too much, apply the softer remedy of the *Book of God's Judgments against Whoredom*, which being historical may please you better perhaps, and be no less effectual for working your cure. To make the packet complete, I likewise send you another medicine, called *Concubinage and Polygamy Displayed*,[3] which is an answer to a parson, one Mr Butler, who fell out with his wife, and in with his maid, and therefore mustered up all the arguments he could in defence of the more genteel practice of keeping misses. Which you will here find solidly answered and condemned, but much more your own abominable practice, which seems by your letter to be that of a common prostitute, or next a kin to it.

I would offer a few arguments, if it were possible to reclaim you, and therefore would pray you to consider that uncleanness dishonours your body, makes you despicable in the eyes of all men, nay even of those that haunt you, so that your usual reward is an infamous name, loathsome diseases, extreme poverty, and an end suitable to such a vile way of living.

Then it damns your soul, makes you incapable of receiving any good advice, destroys the peace of your family, if you have any, brings a scandal and disgrace upon your children, reflects shame upon your relations, and makes you to be abhorred by all civil company.

It is against reason, for it destroys all property, brings a spurious issue into families, hinders the propagation of mankind, debases human nature, makes you more vile than the brute beasts.

It is against charity, not only, because of the discord it occasions in families, but also because the children of whoredom are many times murdered, and continually neglected, either in their maintenance or education, which is destructive both to their souls and bodies, and upon this account it was as severely punished by the canon law as murder.

It is against all the rules of Christianity—there being nothing more severely censured in the Scriptures than fornication and adultery; persons who continue in those practices, being therein declared unfit for the communion of the Church here, and of the saints hereafter; and liable to everlasting damnation: this is so plain, that I shall not trouble you with quoting texts, for you can turn your eye nowhere, but you will find what I say to be true, that the Holy Ghost threatens God's judgments upon whoremongers and adulterers, and that they shall not inherit the kingdom of heaven.

We see by experience, that they who give themselves up to this sin are very seldom, if ever, reclaimed; but go on in their wickedness till they become vile in the eyes of all the world, hateful to heaven and earth, and fit only to be fuel for hell.

God in his just judgment gives such persons up for the most part to hardness of heart, a reprobate mind, vile affections, and to work all

the Citizens-Wife. 215

debafes Humane Nature, makes you more Vile than the Brute Beafts.

It is againft Charity, not only, becaufe of the Difcord it occafions in Families, but alfo becaufe the Children of Whoredom are many Times murder'd, and continually neglected, either in their Maintenance or Education, which is deftructive both to their Souls and Bodies, and upon this Account it was as feverely punifh'd by the Canon-Law as Murder.

It is againft all the Rules of Chriftianity — There being nothing more feverely Cenfur'd in the Scriptures than Fornication and Adultery; Perfons who continue in thofe Practifes, being therein declar'd unfit for the Communion of the Church here, and of the Saints hereafter; and liable to Everlafting Damnation : This is fo plain, that I fhall not trouble you with quoting Texts, for you can turn your Eye no where, but you will find what I fay to be true, that the Holy Ghoft Threatens *Gods Judgments upon Whoremongers and Adulterers, and that they fhall not inherit the Kingdom of Heaven.*

We fee by Experience, that they who give themfelves up to this Sin are very feldom, if *ever, reclaim'd* ; but go on in their Wickednefs till they become Vile in the Eyes of all the World, hateful to Heaven and Earth, and fit only to be Fewel for Hell.

B b   God

uncleanness with greediness; so that instead of being fit temples for the Holy Ghost to dwell in, they become dens for legions of unclean spirits; and how often does it appear upon the trials of shoplifts, thieves, and murderers, that their falling into this sin of uncleanness has been the first occasion of their committing those other crimes, which bring them to fatal ends.

It were easy to fill a volume with topics against this crying and reigning sin; but your temper is such, that I can scarcely believe you will have patience to read those short hints I here send you. Yet charity obliges me to give you this reproof, though it be no other than to cast pearls before swine.[4]

I have cleared my own conscience by improving this opportunity, and if you do not reform upon this fair warning, remember that it will be a dreadful witness against you at the last day, however slight you may make of it now.

If you have a husband, your guilt is still the greater, as being aggravated with perjury, and the odious crime of ingratitude: nay, perhaps may be attended in time with murder of yourself, husband or children; you entail a disgrace upon your posterity, and fill your relations with shame: the very name of a strumpet, being as offensive to the ears of every modest person, as the sight of a dead carcass, though of the dearest and nearest kindred, is to our eyes, or the scent of it to our nose.

But for all these known consequences of a whorish life, yet there's more wantons in Dublin, besides Dorinda; nay, how common and bare-faced (as I hinted elsewhere) is this vice grown?—'For there's my Lord — L — declares, he could love his wife above all women in the world, if she were not his wife.[5] The Duke of — is of the same mind; and the George and Garter little better. Sir Charles — follows his example; and most have a tang of this rambling fancy. — Where is the man (except myself) that's not a c—d? Or, the woman that so tempers herself in her behaviour with men, as if virtue had settled herself in her looks and eyes? I profess (when I have excepted three or four persons) I know not where to find her. We were wont to say, It was a wise child that knew his own father, but now we may say, It is a wise father that knows his own child. Men and women as familiarly go into a chamber, to damn one another on a feather-bed, as into a tavern, to be merry with wine. She that does not dance so lofty, that you may see her silken garters, and learn to forget shame, is nobody. Who would think to find Hercules, the only worthy of his time, stooping to the meanness of being a servant to Omphale, and in the quality of a wench working at the rock and spindle?[6] Or to see Mark Anthony lose the world for a Cleopatra, a woman, a thing in petticoats?[7] But would flesh and blood listen to Prov. 22:14[8] and remember, that the child often proves the picture of the lover, and discovers it (blessed conclusion of stolen sweets), they'd never invade the right of another.' This vice was formerly punished with death: Abimelech made it death to the men of Gerar, to meddle with the wife of Isaac; and Judah condemned Thamar for her adulterous conception; the Egyptian law was to cut off the nose of the adulteress, and the offending part of the adulterer. The Locrians put out both the adulterer's eyes. The Sermai (as Tacitus reports) placed the adulteress amidst her kindred naked, and caused her husband to beat her with clubs through the city; and the Cumani caused the woman to ride upon an ass naked, and hooted at, and for ever after called her (in scorn) a rider upon the ass:[9] and here in England (which Argus must needs know, and therefore (Dorinda) make no more assignations) it is common for whores to be whipped, or to do penance in a white sheet; and in Scotland they are put into (what they call) the stool of repentance—but, Dorinda, besides the shame that attends whoring, you'll find (if you dare read the *Duty of Man*,[10] p. 218) 'That to accept your offer, is to do Argus many and high injustices, for it is first the robbing him of that which of all other things he should count most precious, the love and fidelity of his wife; nor is this all, but it is further engulfing him (if ever he come to discern it) in that most tormenting passion of jealousy, which is called the rage of a man.' It is yet further bringing upon him the name of a c———d,[11] and though (as this author observes) 'it is very unjust, he should fall under reproach only because he is injured; yet unless the world could be new moulded, it will certainly be his lot.' Besides Dorinda, if you c———d Argus, it is a robbery (as this author further observes) 'in the usual sense of the word; for perhaps, it may be the thrusting in the child of the adulterer into his family, to share both in the maintenance and portions of his own children; and this is an errant theft. First, in respect of the man, who surely intends not the providing for another man's child; and then in respect of the children, who are by that means defrauded of so much as that goes away with. And therefore, whosoever has this circumstance of the sin to repent of, cannot do it effectually without restoring to the family, as much as he has by that means robbed it of.'

Thus (Dorinda) having briefly shewn the shame and many ill consequences that attend the gratifying your wanton appetite: I would next give you directions (would you listen to them) how to mortise[12] your carnal desires, for lust (as I said in my first letter) seems to be your master-sin—it is true, there are persons that seek to justify their commission of this sin, by the impossibility of their abstaining from its commission; but sure, the Apostle Paul would not enjoin the Corinthians to flee fornication, if it were a thing persons cannot flee;[13] the plea of cannot is a mere pretence; the most passionately amorous can contain for a time, upon promise of enjoying the woman he desires; and cannot he then, if he will, contain for always, when better pleasures and enjoyments are assured to him, upon his continency, unto all eternity.

And now (Dorinda), having answered the pretence of impossibility of your being chaste, I shall next proceed to such directions which, if minded, will keep you honest.

I own directions of this nature are so common a theme, that it is impossible to avoid treading in the steps of other writers, but I judge you ladies of pleasure don't love long harangues; I shall therefore say in little, what others have more largely insisted upon.

First, then, in order to the flying adultery, suppress the first desires of uncleanness that do arise in your heart. It is easier (Dorinda) to deal with a spark than with a flame; to crush an egg than kill a cockatrice: the beginning of a temptation is the time to show your greatest valour and vigilance in.

Secondly, hold no dispute against any temptations to uncleanness: to dispute with it, is the way to be overcome by it; hear the temptation but speak for itself, and before you are aware, it insinuates itself into the bosom of you, and it is in your heart before you can think it got into your head; with an unseen fire and insensible power, it melts you into softness, and dissolves you into yielding: I say (Dorinda) give it no consideration, but run away from it, as Joseph did from his tempting mistress.[14] Had our great grandmother Eve done so at first with the Devil's temptation, had she given no ear to his words, set no eye upon the fruit, held no dispute with him, but turned herself, and gone away from him; she had not been the mother of so much sin and misery, as she has been to her posterity.

Thirdly, avoid all things that may externally provoke to lust, as conversation with men that are lewd, &c. Dorinda, if you touch pitch you will be defiled; men's arts to seduce are powerful and prevailing, their blandishments delicate and melting, their words are charming, their looks enchanting, their kisses killing, and their glances are darts to destroy; there's pitch and birdlime in their lips and fingers, and itch of amorousness of skin all over; you may (Dorinda) as well hug a flame without being burnt, as to admit a lewd man within your embraces and not be all on fire with the heat of lust.

To put many things together for brevity sake, avoid the speaking of any wanton words, and if possible the hearing of any spoken; and be sure write no more billet douxes, also the reading of any lascivious books or verses, also the beholding of any impure sights, either of shameful parts or actions themselves, or the pictures of them: avoid also the being a spectator of any wanton plays or shows, balls, or dances, or other lascivious revels, which by the garish dresses, amorous words, and wanton gestures used therein, do not only instruct but stir up to uncleanness. These things (Dorinda) are the great and common bane of modesty.

Fourthly, fly those vices and subdue those passions which incline you to lust, such as drunkenness (for alas it is now become a feminine vice), gluttony, covetousness, idleness, and curiosity.

In the first place shun drunkenness, for though the eye stirs up lust, it is drunkenness sets it on fire; there is but one step (Dorinda) from excessive wine to unlawful lust. Lot's daughters made their father drunk with wine, and the next news you hear of him is that in his drunkenness he lay with his own daughters.[15]

Again, Dorinda, if you'd live a chaste, modest life, you must not eat to excess; Jesurun[16] waxed fat and kicked, that is, waxed wanton upon his high feeding; so Jer. 5:8. They were as fed horses, in the morning every one neighed after his neighbour's wife—it is very difficult to feed high, and live chastely; then (Dorinda) avoid not only the use of all lustful food, but all extravagant feeding on any meat.

Thirdly, don't be too much in love with money, it is the root of all evil (1 Tim. 6.10). There's a huge power in riches to corrupt chastity; few women (if but a little amorous) are proof against the blaze of gold—how many women in Dublin (and in London too) prostitute their bodies to all comers, perhaps for a beggarly 2s. 6d. Yea (and which is a shame to speak) how many men are there, that for the love of money do as it were let themselves out to hire for stallions to satisfy the lust of some women; I suppose ye have heard of G——n;[17] if therefore you're willing to reform, and to live chastely, you must fly covetousness.

Again, I'd advise you to avoid idleness, for lust (as Bishop Taylor[18] observes) usually creeps in at those emptinesses where the soul is un-employed, and the body at ease; and above all idleness, the idleness of the bed and couch is most hurtful; the soft bed is the mother of wanton thoughts—the time when David fell a lusting after Bathsheba was in the evening, after he had been lolling on his bed (1 Sam. 11.2). And therefore (Dorinda) if you'd live honest, you must avoid idleness.

In the next place, I would advise ye (if you'd live chastely) to make a covenant with your eyes; have a chaste eye and a hand, for it is all one (says Bishop Taylor) with what part of the body we commit adultery; what though I have rejected to c——d Argus, yet if I let my eye loose, and enjoy the lust of that, I am an adulterer; for our Saviour says—Look not upon a woman to lust after her; the eye is a great inflamer of lust; we read of eyes full of adultery (2 Pet. 2.14) Joseph's mistress first cast her eye upon Joseph, and then she said, Lie with me (Gen. 39.7). Beauty is a dangerous thing; therefore when you see a handsome man (especially at church, if you ever go there) take heed of eyeing him too much, stare not upon him; you may as well face a basilisk[19] as a pretty face.

Now Dorinda, these depictions, if carefully heeded, will be a means to keep you chaste and honest, but if you find them ineffectual (for I'd fain have you a true penitent) then,

Fifthly, mortify your body, in order to the subduing of your flesh; and to this purpose fast often, and that a considerable time; take away diet and drink, the fuel of lust, and the heat of it will abate, and the fire of it goes out: in the fasts we read of kept by the saints in Scripture, they did neither eat nor drink, that is, not until night, and that which they took then, was very little, and of mean quality, a bit of bread and a draught of water. In this case take meat like medicines, no more than needs must, to keep you alive and preserve you in health. Thus (Dorinda) by often forbearing to eat at all, and a mean diet when you do eat, you'll have little mind to be writing of billet douxes, for thin ordinary food will starve your lust, and bring the flesh (that enemy of yours) (like a town pined out[20] with a long siege) to your own terms. But (Dorinda) if the rebel lust still haunts your mind, then use some sharpness to him, cause him to smart either by praying in painful postures (as on hard stones with bare knees) or else by wearing sackcloth, or hair s–cks upon your flesh, or by scourging your body with the rod or whip. This is a course Saint Paul took with himself (1 Cor. 9.27): I keep under my body, and bring [it] into subjection. One[a] for this end tumbled himself among thorns; another burned his face and hands; a third run sharp prickles up his fingers between the flesh and the nails; and (Dorinda) it is much better to afflict yourself for a while, than be lashed by Satan forever in hell.

Sixthly, meditate on those things, as may by poring on them curb your lust; and here, Dorinda, first, consider the falls of those who have miscarried in this way, as of Jane Shore, Creswel, Nel G—n, &c.,[21] women famous in their generations for wit and beauty; and yet see (Dorinda) to what weakness of body and poorness of spirit they were brought to by this sin.

Secondly, consider the constancy of others that have continued chaste, notwithstanding their temptations to uncleanness; the most remarkable one that I can think of, is that of Joseph, recorded in Gen. 39.7 to 13. He was tempted to it by his mistress, who had some power to command him, and many ways to oblige him, yet he consented not. He was tempted to it, not by looks and glances, hints and intimations (any of which were enough with too many in these our days, to draw them to it) but with downright words, she plainly and boldly said to him, Lie with me; and yet he consented not. He was tempted to it by her, not once or twice only (for trial of him, as might be thought) but many times, to shew she was in earnest; she was often at it with him, tempting him; she spoke to Joseph day by

a. St Bernard.

day, and yet he consented not. He was tempted to it by her, not at unseasonable times only, while company was at home, whereby they might be discovered and descried, but at a time of greatest season- ableness and opportunity, when he might act the thing with greatest secrecy and security, when he had business to do within the house, and there was none of the men of the house there within; and yet he consented not. He was tempted to it by her, not only by winning speech, but by enforcing action; she not only used speech to him, but laid hands on him; she caught him by his garment, saying, *Lie with me*, and yet he consented not. Here (Dorinda) is an example of constancy and chastity worthy of your imitation. Not much unlike was that which St Hierome[22] reports of a son of a king of Nicomedia, who being tempted upon flowers, and a perfumed bed whereon he was tied, by an impure courtesan with all the arts and circumstances of luxury, lest the ease of his posture should abuse him to a yielding to her temptations, bit off his tongue, and spit it in her face. Dorinda, if such chaste examples as these be made familiar to your mind by frequent meditation on them, they will help you toward the victory over uncleanness.

Thirdly, bethink with thyself a while (Dorinda) when thou art under temptation to uncleanness, what a business that face is, which thou so doatest upon, and the consideration therefore will very much allay thy heat, and cool thy desire, and even dash thee out of coun- tenance. For there is nothing certainly that so much masters the desire of the flesh, as to think what that which one loves, is, after once it be dead. And the experience hereof, we have in the hermit, who understanding that a woman, whom he was too too much enamoured on, was dead, went by night to her grave, and having opened it, with the lap of his mantle wiped away some of the filth of the dead corpse, being half rotten, and when afterwards he found himself possessed with any unlawful desires, he laid abroad his foul and stinking mantle, and said thus to himself, Go to now, see what it is that thou dost desire, and take thy fill of it. By which means his heat was cooled and his lust quenched.

Then, seventhly, Dorinda, consider that you cannot act this sin, but there will be eyes upon you.

First, the eye of God is upon you, The eyes of the Lord are in every place, as Solomon tells us (Prov. 15:3), beholding the evil and the good; no possibility of escaping his sight, if ye should attempt the committing of any such fact. And who that has seriously considered of this, could ever have the confidence to do any such thing?

In a fury, or for some politic purpose, such a like thing as this may be acted in the presence of a man; as it once happened in Alexandria, where a Tarlaquin, transported with beastly fury, ran at a woman as she came out of the stove, threw her on the ground and, notwithstanding all the resistance she made, had carnal knowledge of her in the presence of many spectators.[23] And so we read in 2 Sam. 16.22. how to make the breach irreparable between Absalom and his father David, Absalom spread a tent upon the top of the house, and went in unto his father's concubines in the sight of all Israel.

Yet generally in men that have not utterly defaced all the common notices of God, which Nature's hand has written in the heart of man, secrecy for time, and for place, is sought out for the acting of this sin. Nay, Dorinda herself (as lewd as she is) would scarce commit adultery in the view, even of those pimps and bullies who are the most instrumental to her debaucheries.

Now surely, Dorinda, if the eye of man be not to be endured in the commission of this sin, much less should you be able to endure the eye of God upon you. This consideration was effectual to preserve Paphnutius, who being wearied with the solicitations of a tempting Dalilah,[24] at last consented to the act, provided it might be committed where they might not be seen. Whereupon being brought into one room, he alleged they might be seen from this place, and in another, that they might be seen in that place; and still found some exception upon that account; but at last being brought into such a place where could be no reason for such a plea, yet he alleged, that it was not so secret, but that the eye of God would be upon them even there, and that unless his eye too, as well as all others, could be shut out, he durst not do it; by which means he not only preserved his integrity, but converted a harlot.

Secondly, beside the eye of God upon you, who is to be your judge, you have the Devil with you, who does mean to be your accuser. The Devil is pimp-general to the world; not a piece of filthiness Dorinda ever commits, but he is as one at it by his enticements to it. He finds and furnishes with fuel for lust. And as he knows all ye do now, so he will tell all ye have done hereafter; where, and when, and with whom you have played the whore.

Thirdly, besides the eyes of all without you, there is (Dorinda) the eye of your conscience within you, which will also be one day a thousand witnesses against you. In consideration whereof, doubtless it was that Pythagoras[25] gave that good and wise counsel of his, that no man should commit any filthiness either with another, or alone by himself (which self-pollution is a sort of potential murder) and that above all others, he should stand in awe of himself; that is, dread and fear his own conscience (as I formerly hinted to Patrick Campbell).

Now Dorinda, if the following these directions, don't cure your raging lust; then in the eighth place, when you are tempted to uncleanness, seriously think on what is behind, viz. death, judgment, heaven, and hell; and the serious thought of any one of these is enough to extinguish the flames of lust. Dorinda, death is behind thee. Thou canst not live for ever here, thou must die; and you know not how soon; perhaps it may be in the very act of thy uncleanness; and how dismal, Dorinda, would your condition be, if that should befall you? What can befall a person more dreadful, than to be catched, and cut off by death, in the very act of sin?

But, secondly, not death only, but judgment also is behind. Dorinda, thou must not only die, but be judged too for thy uncleanness after death: for whoremongers and adulterers God will judge, Heb. 13.4.

Then again, there is heaven behind, a state of pleasure, joy and happiness, beyond all that the world has or ever had.—Then (Dorinda) if at any time you are tempted to uncleanness, say, shall I, for a brutish pleasure, lose my heaven? lose my happiness? Can the company of all the men in the world (had I the enjoyment of them all) countervail the loss of heaven.

And lastly, Dorinda, there is hell behind. And who are to be turned into this burning lake? Why, the wicked, and amongst the rest, adulterers, and such-like defilers of the image of God, and members of Christ, and temples of the Holy Ghost.[26]

Then (Dorinda) argue with thyself, and say, What, shall I go to hell for a billet doux? Have I a mind to be damned for an assignation? Shall I plunge myself into fire and brimstone, there to lie and roar to all eternity, for the little short nasty pleasure, which is had in the embraces of a lewd person? Thus (Dorinda) at any time, when you come under the temptations of lust, call to mind death, judgment, heaven, and hell, and you will (by God's grace) be so wrought on in that meditation, that you will both fly the acts and detest the thought of uncleanness.

And now, Dorinda, you may perhaps upbraid all this as a sermon, as is usual for the libertines of the age to do. I shall not be much concerned at it, if it happen to be so. I think no shame to own that I am descended from the tribe of Levi by four successive generations, and was likewise allied to it by my first marriage, wherein never was any man more happy.[27] They that honour God will honour his ambassadors; and they that despise them despise him, as they do his message; but at the last hour you will change your mind, and wish to die the death of the righteous, though you never cared to imitate their life.

Break off then from your sins in time, by a true repentance and cordial reformation; learn to entertain pure and chaste flames of devotion in your soul, and they will quickly extinguish those brutish lusts that hurry you head-long to perdition; which if the Almighty grant you grace to do, you will be sensible that you were not mistaken in making application to me as your friend; though you were very much out in the method and as much disappointed in the manner. I add no more, but that I do as earnestly wish your conversion as I hate your vice, and if this may be any way conducive towards it, I shall think myself happy in a good improvement of the first billet doux that ever was put into my hand; and that though you were wicked, that you were not unhappy in sending it. Farewell, Dorinda.

Remarks on J.D.'s Second Letter to the Citizen's-Wife

Sir,

I have perused your second letter to the Irish Dorinda, and am of opinion she never met with such returns to her courtship before. It's not probable, that she will trouble Philaret any more with her billet douxes, and it were to be wished she never troubled anybody else with them. You have done your part to cure her distemper, but that disease in the soul is too often like the gout in the body: *Opprobrium medicorum.*[28]

You have however discharged your duty, be the event what it will. I cannot well tell what you could have said more, for you have touched on most of the ordinary topics; if what you have said does but reach a conviction, she will not grudge to read the treatises you have recommended to her; to which I wish you had added Mr Carr's *Antidote against Lust*;[29] it is also a book of your own printing, and will further inform her judgment, and convince her of the vileness of her practice.

I am glad that you have left behind you in Dublin such proofs of your fair way of dealing, and of your justice to the marriage-bed; had all who have gone hence shewed the Irish such good example, it would have rendered the English conquest of that country more universal and effectual, than ever our arms have yet done.

I have nothing else to say, but that perhaps, when this billet doux comes to see the public, the reality of it may be questioned; not that your person and purse might not have been as tempting as those of others, who have frequent adventures of this sort; but because of ill natured suspicion amongst those of your own trade, and the too frequent abuses of that kind, which some few of them have put upon the public; and indeed had I not seen the original, and been satisfied from the probability of the circumstances as the place to which it was directed, the credible witnesses, who saw you send your answer, and your own affirmation, I should have suspected the truth of it myself.

Your design of putting it in print, I cannot disapprove; it (shews your innocence and) will not only prevent those wanton ladies from making you any more their confidant, but may deter others from the like practices, lest they should have the same fate, and it must needs be a piquant rebuke to the loose Dorinda, to see her billet doux exposed to public view. For though she lives under covert, it may happen some way or other to point her out, as it's but just it should. I am, Sir,

Your very humble servant

The Fifteenth Letter

Sir,

Having troubled you with Dorinda's billet doux, and my former two letters to her, and received your remarks upon them, which were very much to my satisfaction; I give you the trouble of one more, which you will oblige me to peruse, and to give me your thoughts upon it with your usual freedom.

[The letter is as follows, viz.]

Dorinda,

In my first letter, I checked your impudence for contriving to c—d Argus.—In my second letter, I sent you rules for chastity; and having received no answer to either of these letters: I conclude you are ashamed of your billet doux, and are willing to be reformed. If these conjectures are right, it will be proper in the next place to say what I can to set Argus and you a-loving again; and here I shall write nothing but my own experience, to which I'll add rules for Dorinda and Argus to live by, which may (if Dorinda's a true penitent) make them yet a happy pair.

    I shall begin these rules, with telling Dorinda, we are taught from Scripture, that marriage is honourable in all men; so is not a single life; in some it is a snare, and a trouble in the flesh, a prison of unruly desires, which is attempted daily to be broken; a single life is never commanded, but in some cases marriage is; for he that (like Dorinda) cannot contain, must marry; and he that can contain, is not tied to a single life, but may marry very lawfully: marriage was ordained by God, instituted in Paradise; was the relief of a natural necessity, and the first blessing from God himself: he gave to man not a friend, but a wife, that is a friend and a wife too. It is the seminary of the Church, and daily brings forth sons and daughters unto God. Our Blessed Lord, though he was born of a maiden, yet she was veiled under the cover of marriage, and she was married to—A WIDOWER —for Joseph, the supposed father of our Lord, had children by a former wife. The first miracle that ever Jesus did, was to do honour to a wedding. Marriage was in the world before sin, and has been in all ages of the world the greatest antidote against it, and although sin has soured marriage, and stuck the man's head with cares, and the woman's bed with sorrow in the production of children, yet these are but throws[1] of life and glory; and she shall be saved in child-bearing, if she be found in faith and righteousness.—So that marriage is the proper scene of piety and patience, of the duty of parents, and the charity of relatives; here kindness is expanded, and love is united, and made firm as a centre. Marriage is the nursery of heaven; the virgin sends prayers to God, but she carries but one soul to him; but the state of marriage fills up the numbers of the elect, and has in it the labour of love, the delicacies of friendship, the blessing of society, and the union of hands and hearts.

And as marriage is the nursery of heaven, so it is the mother of the world; it preserves kingdoms, fills cities, churches, and heaven itself. —Thus (Dorinda) have I shewn that the state you are entered into, is divine in its institution—sacred in its union—holy in the mystery— honourable in its appellative—religious in its employments. It is advantage to the societies of men, and holiness to the Lord, and is certainly preferable to a single life.

But, Dorinda, as happy a state as marriage is, Argus and you will be ever disappointed in it, if it be not entirely conducted and over-ruled by religion: none are happy in marriage, but those that invite Christ to the wedding; this you did not do, as is clear by your billet doux; but I write to you now, as supposing you a true penitent, so shall adventure to give ye rules, for your happy living in a married state. The rules I shall name, shall be only those that relate to Argus and you, in conjunction; I am not so foolish to think, that all the duty lies on the weaker-vessel,[a] or so barbarous to expect the wife should prove obliging, except the husband be so too—the obligation is mutual—and therefore prescribe nothing (in the following rules) that I think too bitter for Argus's swallow.

Before I give any rules, I premise this, that it is the duty of all that intend to marry, seriously to read the form of matrimony, least when they come to the church, they answer there to what they had not considered beforehand, and then no wonder if they don't practise a

a. 1 Pet. 3.7.

duty of a larger extent than they apprehended. But to proceed to the rules, that Argus and you must walk by, if you'd be yet happy in your married state.

And the first is, that once a week you read and digest the 5th of the Ephesians, from the 22nd verse to the end of the chapter—all Scripture is given for your instruction; and sure I am, all that marry before they love at the rate here described, commit a very great sin, and can't expect the blessing of God on their marriage.—It is the blessing of God crowns the wedding, and they that marry without it (be they never so rich) are but two tied together to make one another miserable. All that intend to wed, would do well to consider, that they who enter into the state of marriage cast a die of the greatest contingency, and yet of the greatest interest in the world, next to the last throw for eternity—life or death, felicity or a lasting sorrow, are the power of marriage.—A woman indeed ventures most, for she has no sanctuary to retire to from an evil husband; she must dwell upon her sorrow, and hatch the eggs which her own folly or infelicity has produced; and she is more under it, because her tormentor has a warrant of prerogative;[2] and the woman may complain to God as subjects do of tyrant princes; but otherwise she has no appeal in the causes of unkindness. And though the man (who marries a shrew, or such a wanton as Dorinda was) can run from many hours of his sadness, yet he must return to it again, and when he sits among his neighbours, he remembers the viper that lies in his bosom, and he sighs deeply, as well he may.

It is the unhappy chance of many men, finding great inconveniences in a single life, to rush into marriage, in hopes to remove their troubles, and there they enter into fetters, as the stags in the Greek epigram,[3] and are bound to sorrow by the cords of a man's, or woman's peevishness; and the worst of the evil is, they are to thank their own follies, for they fell into the snare by entering an improper way; Christ and the Church were no ingredients in their choice; but as the Indian women enter into folly for the price of an elephant, and think their crime warrantable,[4] so many choose for a rich fortune (like Eriphyle the Argive,[5] prefer gold before a good man) and shew themselves to be less than money by over-valuing that, to all the content and happiness of life; but I bless God, I am not of this sordid temper, for I don't (nor never did) think, that the happiness of a man's life consists in the abundance of what he possesses; but in God's giving him a heart to make a sober use of what he lends him (I say lends him) for we are all stewards to the great Lord of heaven and earth.

And Dorinda, as he, or she, deserve to be disappointed that marry for money, so as very a fool is he that chooses for beauty; who chooses for one (as a wit expressed it) whose eyes are witty, and her soul sensual. It is an ill band of affections to tie two hearts together, by a little thread of red and white. These Dorinda will love no longer but till the next ague comes, and are fond of each other but at the chance of fancy, or the small-pox, or child-bearing, or care, or time, or anything that can destroy a pretty flower.

But it is the basest of all, when lust is the paranymph[6] and solicits the suit, makes the contract, and joins the hands. This, Dorinda, was your own case, and is commonly the effect of the former folly; according to the proverb—At first for his fair cheeks and comely beard, the beast is taken for a lion, but at last he is turned to a dragon, or a leopard, or a swine.[7] That which at first is beauty on the face, may prove lust in the manners. He, or she, that looks too curiously upon the beauty of the body, looks too low, has flesh and corruption in his heart, and is judged sensual and earthly in his desires. Sure I am, no marriage will prove happy, that is not blessed with religious affections.

Another thing in which I conceive Dorinda and Argus to be equally concerned (if they'd be happy in wedlock) is, to avoid as much as possible all offences of each other in the beginning of their new honeymoon (for so I may call it, Dorinda having run astray); every little thing can blast an infant-blossom, and an unkind word or careless carriage is apt to give the alarm at the beginning of this union. People generally at first are watchful, and observant, careful and inquisitive, and even the smaller failures of chance or weakness are then interpreted as want of love, and usually affright the inexperienced man, or woman, who make unequal conjectures and fancy mighty sorrows by the proportions of any new and early unkindness. Plutarch[8] compares a new marriage to a vessel: before the hoops are on, every little thing dissolves the union of its parts, but when the joints are stiffened, and the whole tied together by a firm compliance, and proportionate bending, it is then hardly dissolved without violence or burning: in like manner (Dorinda) when once the hearts of a man and wife are endeared and hardened by a mutual confidence, compliance and experience (longer than artifice or pretence can last) (I word it so, for infirmities do not manifest themselves in the first scenes, but in the succession of a long society), there is then no great danger; and there are many things past, and some things present, which will dash all little unkindnesses in pieces.

And therefore (Dorinda) in the next place, I think Argus and you should be very careful (at your first reconciliation especially) to stifle all little differences, and to cut them down as fast as they spring up; for if they are suffered to grow, they render the society troublesome by their numbers, and the affections become loose by an habitual uneasiness. Some people are more vexed with a fly, than with a wound; nor can reason be always upon the guard, in the frequent little accidents of a family; but trifling troubles, if often repeated, will be apt to render you restless, and betray you to passion; and at last to beget an indifferency, if not a disgust and aversation.

Lastly, Dorinda, if you'd (be happy in marriage and would) have Argus love ye again, be extremely watchful against all curious distinctions of mine and thine—for this has caused all the laws, suits, and wars in the world. Let them who have but one person, have also but one interest; for when either of them begins to impropriate, it is like a swelling in the flesh which draws more than its share, and what it feeds on turns to a bile, and a sore. Dorinda, you shine by your husband's honour, and will certainly be darkened if he suffer an eclipse; and therefore it is your interest as well as duty (if Argus be kind and loving) to contribute to his ease and welfare; the use and employment of what man and wife possess should be common to both their necessities, and in this there is no other difference of right, but that the man has the dispensation of all, and may (as a late author expresses it) keep it from his wife, as a governor of a town may keep it from the right owner; he has the power, but not right to do so.

But (Dorinda) you have nothing to fear here, for if Argus be a kind husband, you may do with him what ye list; or if Argus rules, it is because you would obey, and in so obeying you rule as much as he; for my own share, I have been married twice, and was ever so much for a mutual endearment and against the vile distinctions of mine and thine, that I could never approve (except there were reason for it) of keeping of two purses: No! she that keeps my heart, shall keep my purse—two keys to a till supposes a distrust on one side or other; and sure I am, distrust is the bane of love: and Dorinda, when it once appears (but I hope you'll never more give occasion for it) farewell to the comforts of matrimony. It was such a trust as this I reposed in my first wife; and therefore she loved me to that degree, that I judged it my duty to settle her presently in all I had (for it was she, and not her fortune I married) that I might give at the rate I loved her; nay, I was so desirous to requite her tenderness, that I was scarce contented with giving all, but grudged (as I once told her) my funeral expenses, my very shroud and grave, that I might add to her future store.—Dorinda, I need not press ye to believe this, for men in their last-wills appear just as they are, they here grow open and plain hearted, and dare not depart with their hands to a lie; and as this was my carriage to my first wife, so it is no more than I owe to this or, if possible, a greater tenderness.

Thus, Dorinda, have I shewn ye (from my own experience) how Argus and you may fall a-loving again, and be yet happy in a married state; and if ye follow the rules I have sent ye, I shall think my labour very well bestowed.

And now, Dorinda, having brought ye to Argus, I leave ye in his tender arms, where (and not in the arms of other men) you should desire to live and die.

I shall only add, I don't desire your answer, either to this or my other letters, for you see by my way of writing, it is your reformation is all that's desired by

> Your faithful adviser, &c.
> And so farewell.

Thus, Sir, I have entertained Dorinda, which I hope may have some good effect upon her; if not, I have discharged myself of what I thought was incumbent upon me in this case. I am

> Sir, Yours, &c.
> John Dunton

Remarks on J. D.'s Third Letter to the Citizen's-Wife

Sir,

I have received your third to Dorinda, who I suppose will scarcely thank you for your good advice; if she bestows the perusal upon it; which I much doubt. In my opinion you have overdone the matter; your first was enough, your second by consequence too much, and your third must needs be superfluous. I am satisfied Dorinda is of my mind, so that there's two to one against you. As many men, and as few reproofs as can be, suit women of her temper best. Did her husband know you, I am certain he would think you deserved a pair of gloves,⁹ and a wedding dinner, better than the parson that joined him and his unfaithful Dorinda in the bands of matrimony; for I am satisfied he did not read her a lecture so long by one half; and if I say, not half so much to the purpose neither, there are people in the world will vouch for the truth of it.

I think the method you took with Dorinda very genuine and natural, first to lay before her the wickedness of defiling the marriage-bed, and then to endeavour to possess her with honourable thoughts of it. But I am of the mind, she will give an equal ear to both, that is to say, she will not hear one word of either. If her husband had been an Argus as you suppose, I can't see how she could have found out a place, secret enough to write her billet doux in; and I am verily of opinion, except he be one of those whom Juvenal calls *Ductus spectare Lacunar*,¹⁰ he must needs think the peacock's tail a much finer ornament than the ram's head; but perhaps he finds it to be true, what Aesop says, that it is easier to take a bag of fleas, set them a-grazing all day, and gather them into their bag at night again, than to keep guard over an unchaste woman; and being over-watched, his hundred eyes fell asleep all at once, and so Dorinda took the opportunity of making a sally.

If your third letter has so much influence, as to create in her a better opinion of her husband, and make her more faithful to his bed; then he may sleep securely with two hundred eyes, if he had them, and I am sure it is no fault of yours, if it does not.

I shall not trouble you with long remarks upon your letter, only your hint of Joseph's having been a widower, when he was espoused to the Virgin, puts me in the head to ask you this question, whether his hose which they shew at Aix la Chappelle, be of the first or second wife's making? And in which of their times it was he gave the hem,[11] when playing the carpenter, which the Church of Rome has got pent up in a bottle, as a precious relic?

I congratulate the happiness of your wife in so chaste an husband; nor do I see how she can be quits with you by less than an ocean of love and respect. She had best spit[12] in her hand and take fast hold,[13] for if she should drop, you have magnified widowers so much in the person of Joseph, that all the virgins in the town can do no less than proffer themselves to you to cull out one of their number for your third. Yet I am not willing to think that anything of this is at the bottom of your plot; I hope you are no such designing man. I shall take my leave of you, and heartily wish that every Dorinda may meet with such a Philaret. And that all the good women in the city, had such husbands as yourself.

I am
Sir, Yours

SOME
ACCOUNT
OF MY
Conversation
IN
IRELAND.
In a LETTER
TO AN
Honourable Lady.
WITH
Her Anſwer to it.

LONDON:

Printed (for the Author,) and are to be Sold by
A. Baldwin, near the *Oxford-Arms* in *Warwick-Lane,* and by the Bookſellers in *Dublin.*
1699.

Some Account of my Conversation in Ireland: in a Letter to an Honourable Lady, &c.[1]

Madam,

I an extremely satisfied to have the honour of knowing you so well, as to know that you hate to be flattered; and to hope you will not think me guilty of that crime, when I profess to you, that I esteem the favour of having a correspondence with you, to be one of the chiefest blessings of my life. And therefore I ought to take all opportunities to shew myself worthy of it: which I could not be, should I suffer my reputation to be attacked without defending it: and having met with some unhandsome treatment, from a person in Dublin, to whom I never offered the least injury (unless he thinks telling him the truth to be such) I am willing to have my cause tryed at your bar; who, as you will not favour the guilty, so neither will you condemn the innocent. And whether I am such or not, the preceding SCUFFLE will give you the clearest idea. But since no man's profession will justify him, without a correspondent practice, I have designed this letter to give you some account of my *Conversation* (or method of living) whilst I was in Ireland.

The occasion of my first going into this kingdom, is so well known, and manifestly lawful, that I shall not so much as hint at it in this place: but how my *Conversation* has been, while I resided there, is the task that lies now upon me to set forth in a true light; which I will do with such sincerity, that I will even dissect my breast to you; and at the same time make (not only your ladyship, but) the WHOLE WORLD my confessor: but still, with this restriction, as far as my frail nature and weak memory will permit me; and where that's defective, if anywhere invention has supplied it, I hope you'll excuse it. For, Madam, you'll find (at least they will that are touched in the following pages) that

Whatsoe'er of fiction I bring in,
It is so like truth, it seems at least a kin.[2]

Madam, this ACCOUNT OF MY CONVERSATION was all written in haste; and most of it at Pat's Coffee-house in Dublin, as people were

151

dinning my ears with news, or some queries about my auction; so that if neither method nor style is what might be expected from me (when I address to you) I hope to make some amends in my *Summer Ramble*, which I shall dedicate to your ladyship, as an acknowledgement of the honour you did me, in corresponding with me whilst in Ireland; and for your attempts since to quiet my mind upon the loss of one of my best friends (for I may call D——e[3] so, if high birth, virtue, wit, and constancy can entitle to that character). But to proceed to the ACCOUNT OF MY CONVERSATION.

This, madam (for method's sake) will best be comprehended under two general heads; viz. the discharge of my duty towards God, and towards man: these two contain the whole of a Christian: and if I take the great Apostle of the Gentiles[4] for my guide, I hope I shall not wander out of my way: for he has declared, this was his care, to keep a conscience void of offence both towards God, and towards man.

The first of these heads, which respects God, comprehends all the duties of religion; which is a thing in this age admits of so many several modes and forms, that without some further explanation, it is difficult to know what is meant by it. For a man can now no sooner speak of religion, but the next question is, Pray what religion are you of? I need not tell you, Madam, that religion in general is a sense of our duty to God, and the worship we owe to him, according to the best of our understanding, in order to the obtaining of a blessed immortality: and this likewise consists in two parts; first, in its principles; and secondly, in putting those principles in practice; for principles without practice teach men to be hypocrites, but never make them Christians. They may indeed, by a profession of religion, deceive others; but without the practice of it, they more fatally deceive themselves. I will therefore, Madam, in the first place, shew you what my principles are, and then give you an account of what my practice was in Dublin.

If then you ask me (Madam) what persuasion I am of? My answer is, I am that which the disciples were called at Antioch; that is, I am a Christian; a follower of Christ, a servant of God, the world's Master, and my own man. I do not think religion to conflict so much in names as things: Christ's church is not limited to any nation or party; but extends to all places, is propagated in all ages, and contains all saving truth; and in this sense is universal or catholic; and therefore I love a good man of whatever profession; or by what name or title soever he's distinguished. A good navigator can sail with any wind; and why should not a Christian be as dextrous to improve all opportunities that may facilitate his passage to the heavenly Canaan?[5] The various lines that are made from different parts of the circumference may all tend to one and the same centre. I have a large charity, and exercise it to all in whom I see goodness and virtue shew itself, whatever their particular persuasions are, and conformable to this opinion was my practice in Dublin. One Sunday I heard Dr Stern, another Mr Sinclare, a third Mr Searl, a fourth Mr Boyse, a fifth Mr Weld, a sixth the Anabaptist in Francis street.[6] And when William Penn[7] came thither, I went with the crowd to hear him: for when I think of George Keith in London, and William Dobbs in Dublin (two persons of great sense, and as strict justice) I must think that some Quakers are Christians; and, for ought I know, we contend with them about words, while we think the same thing: sure I am, their celebrated light within is what we call the dictates of conscience; and if we could but get them to Baptism and the Lord's Supper, we should begin to call them brethren. And thus you see, by my going one Sunday to one persuasion, and a second to another, that I can go to heaven with any wind, and with any name; and shall think it an happiness to go into Canaan, though it were through a Red Sea.

(Madam) It is true I was born to travel, and am now pursuing my destiny: but if I wander the length of the map, and never see you here, yet I hope we shall meet in heaven at last: what though we differ in our way thither? (I hope we pardon one another.) Men go to China both by the Straits and by the Cape.[8] The good men of Ireland (such as Bishop King, and Mr Boyse)[9] perhaps contend about words, when they heartily think the same thing. But whatever the opinions of others are in polemical matters, yet as to myself, I dare boldly say, I am, or should be, an honest man; for virtue is my business; my writing is my recreation (which made Iris say, she'd bury me with a pen in my hand). God is my father, the church my mother (I need not say this or that church, if I am sound in the main points), the saints my brethren, and all that need me, my friends; and I am likewise too, a friend to myself, for shall I have it, and want necessaries? What though I am now in a far country, yet I have in myself (as Randolph says) an household-government; and wherever I go, do intend to live,

> Lord of myself, accountable to none,
> But to my conscience, and my God alone.[10]

Now, Madam, give me leave to say, however romantic some may think this to be, that I have found (notwithstanding my many infirmities) more peace and satisfaction in the discharge of a good conscience, than in all the pleasures this world can give.

In the next place, Madam, I shall give you a short diary of my practice in Ireland, with respect to religion; but I will first give you a relation of an encounter I had with a sort of atheist I met in Dublin.

I need not tell ye, Madam, that atheism and irreligion abound everywhere (for your last letter suggested as much) and the cause is apparent; for when men have given themselves up so long to the conduct of their own lusts, that they have reason to fear the justice of God due to them for their sins, they would fain hope to secure themselves by denying his being: I can't say this lewd fellow I met in Dublin absolutely denied the being of a God (and I much question whether there be a professed atheist in the world); yet I may say his discourses (as well as his manner of living) had so much of atheism in them, as they made me tremble; I won't insert his atheistical discourses, for they are better forgot than published; but I'll send you some of the arguments I used to refute his atheistical notions: whether they satisfied him or not, I can't say, for he made little reply: I am sure my design was good; but whether I argued as I ought, I leave you, Madam, to judge; what I advanced, was to this effect, viz.

> There are two ways for us to attain to the knowledge of God (or a first principle) by whom the world was made; the one is natural, the other supernatural: that which I call supernatural, is what God has revealed in his word, wherein he has given us the clearest idea of himself, as he by whom all things were made: but because they who deny the being of a God, do generally make a scoff at his word, I will only insist upon that

which is natural. Nature informs us that there was a sovereign being, the author and preserver of all things: this truth I can see with my eyes; when I either behold the earth, view the heavens, or reflect upon myself: when I see such things as are not made but by a superior cause, I am obliged to acknowledge and adore a being which cannot be made, and which made all things else. When I consider myself, I am sure that I could not be without a beginning; therefore it follows, that a person like me could not give me to be; and, by consequence, this puts me upon seeking out a first being; who having had no beginning must be the original of all other things. When my reason conducts me to this first principle, I conclude evidently that this being cannot be limited, because limits suppose a necessity of production and dependance: and if unlimited, it must be a sovereign and incomprehensible being: and this prevents all curious enquirers from comprehending what God is; for who can define that which is unlimited or comprehend that which is incomprehensible? One must be blind indeed, to be ignorant of a first principle; but one must be infinite, like him, to be able to speak exactly of him: for the most that can be said by us, though it may perhaps content the curious, yet it can never satisfy the rational soul.

This, Madam, was the substance of what I spoke on that occasion; which, as I said before, I leave to your censure. And to be yet more free with you, I have those awful thoughts of the Divine Being, that I would never think of him, but with the most profound veneration; and therefore always choose to think of him rather in the abstract, than the concrete; for if I think him good, my finite thought is ready to terminate that good in a conceived subject; and if I conceive him great, my bounded conceit is apt to cast him into a comprehensible figure; I would therefore conceive him a diffused goodness without quality, and represent him an incomprehensible greatness without quantity. . . . And therefore I choose (as Mr Ellis[11] advises) to shun all gross representations of God, or likening him so much as in my thought, to any creature; I am not to worship him after my own conceit or fancy, but according to the rules he has given in his word.

—And to speak my thoughts of religion in a few words, I look upon that to be the best religion, which is pure and peaceable, and takes no pleasure in the expense of blood; whose principles are consonant to the word of God; and which takes most from the creature, and gives most to the Creator: this is that religion which I assure myself is the right, which I will endeavour to practise while I live and rely on when I die.

And this brings me to (what I promised) an account of my practice in Dublin; which I will give you in the form of a diary.

I freely acknowledge, Madam, that the sacred oracles of the Old and New Testaments do sufficiently instruct us in the performance of all those duties which God requires of us. But though the scriptures of the Old and New Testaments are the very word of God, which holy men of God spoke and wrote as they were moved by the Holy Ghost, and contain all things necessary to salvation, and are the standing sealed rule of faith and life; yet I believe that everyone has some particular mode of his own, by which he steers the course of his devotions; especially as to what he performs in his closet.

But to proceed to my diary: and here I shall first acquaint you how I spend Saturday.

Saturday is usually a day of hurry and business with the generality of men; and as the same winds up the week, so do people their affairs: but for my own part, I confess, I never affect multiplicity of business on that day; but on the contrary, have frequently shunned it, though I have observed it has often fallen to my share upon these days to have a great deal; for last Saturday I was so taken up with adjusting some controversies that did arise concerning the affairs of my auction, that I had hardly leisure to take my dinner; however, they were terminated so much the more to my satisfaction, by how much all parties were brought to acquiesce in my determination. By this you see, Madam, I am no Sabbatarian;[12] but for those that are, I am so far from having any hard thoughts of them, that I both pity and respect them; for I can never believe it is an error of wilfulness, but of ignorance only in them: and whereas I do understand divers of them, at least, make a conscience of keeping both days, because they would be sure to be right, I think I have just reason to honour them for it, and cannot choose but think much better of them, than those who totally deny the morality of the Sabbath day.

I confess, Madam, I do not remember to have read anything material concerning the controversy about the said days, and that I am as much at a loss to know certainly when our Christian Sabbath begins, when there is such a variation in the site of places and countries; and that now we experimentally find, where it is day in one place, it is night in another. And, Madam, as I know of no person living, with whom I can so well satisfy my scruples, and inform my understanding than yourself, who are so well skilled both in polemical and practical divinity, so I humbly request your sentiments in this case, promising to make your practice my own.

But, Madam, having told you how I spend Saturday, I am next to inform you how I spend the Sabbath: for in the practice of religion, I look upon the sanctifying of the Lord's day, to be a principal part. Judge Hales[13] recommends to his children a very strict observation of the Lord's day; and tells them, that he had always found that his worldly affairs thrived either more or less (the following week) as he had kept the Sabbath. And therefore on Sunday I usually took leave of my bed sooner than on other days, and strive to dismiss as much as I can, all worldly affairs out of my thoughts; though I have found them, I acknowledge (like the flies that spoil the apothecary's ointment) then most unseasonably thrusting themselves in.

The public worship of God, being the principal duty of this day, I made it my practice to bow my knees before my Maker in private before I went thither, and there beg his blessing on the public ordinances;[14] and previous thereto, have used to read some portion of the Holy Scriptures; being told therein, that everything is sanctified by the word of God, and prayer; which is so much the advantage of a Christian, that I always thought, never prayer rightly made, was made unheard, or heard ungranted: and I believe that prayer is rightly made which is made to God in the name of Christ, in faith, and offered up with humility.

When I come to the house of God (I mean the place of his worship, whether it be a church, or a meeting house) I always keep myself uncovered[15] whilst I continue there: for as holiness becomes his house, so does a behaviour mixed with reverence and godly fear, in all that wait upon him. And therefore during the time of prayer, I either kneel or stand up (believing the humblest posture to be best, when I am invocating the majesty of heaven) and fixing my eyes upwards, I endeavour to apply every part of God's worship to my own conscience, and the present state of my own soul.

I love those sermons best, that check my conscience for sin, and cheer it with applying God's mercy; beginning with the law, and ending with the gospel; searching the wound first, and pouring in the oil of consolation afterwards: and those I reckon the worst preachers, that sooth men up in their sins; persuading men they are good Christians, when they don't know what it is to be born again.

Yet I don't love to be pragmatical, in censuring of ministers; I endeavour, like the industrious bee, to suck honey from the flowers of devotion; and not like the spider, to convert what was intended for nourishment, into poison. If anything drops from the pulpit, which I think not so pertinent, I cover it with the mantle of love, and strive to remember that which is better: for as the divine Herbert[16] observes, if the parson be dull, God preaches to the hearers a lecture of patience.

In the singing of psalms, I labour more to have my soul inflamed with love and zeal, than to have my spirits cheered either by the harmony of voices, or sound of the organ; and could heartily wish that Sternhold and Hopkins's psalms (though well enough 150 years ago) were now removed, and Mr Tate's translation put in their place.[17] As to the receiving the holy sacrament, it has ever been my opinion, that whoever participates of that solemn ordinance (lest he eats and drinks damnation) should retire himself from the world for a day at least, and by a strict recollection of his actions, and serious examination of his own life (attended with fasting and prayer) endeavour so to prepare himself that he may come as a worthy receiver to the table of the Lord, that so by the strength he receives by that spiritual viaticum,[18] he may be enabled to run with patience the race that is set before him: and therein (through the assistance of divine grace) so to run as to obtain the prize.

After the public duties of the day are over, I return to my chamber, and enter into my closet, spending some time therein, in meditating on what I have heard, and in reiterated addresses to the throne of grace, to follow it with his blessing: well knowing, that though Paul may plant, and Apollo water, yet it is God that teaches me to profit.[19] And if in the evening (as sometimes there does) a friend comes to visit me; I spend my time with him in discoursing on divine things; whereby our hearts are warmed, and our affections stirred up to praise God for his goodness; and hereby find the benefit of the communion of saints, which is too much neglected, though an Article of the Creed. Sure I am all the members of the mystical body of Christ have fellowship with the Father and Son, by one Holy Spirit; with angels in their love, care and ministries, with the saints in heaven in their love and prayers, and with one another in the same faith, hope, word and sacrament; and therefore should often confer about heavenly things, holding the unity of the Spirit in the bond of peace.

The operations of the mind being in their own nature much more fatiguing than the labours of the body; it's my usual custom on Sunday night, to go somewhat sooner to bed than ordinary: however, I durst not adventure to go and compose myself to such a rest as so much resembles death itself (and from which many have awakened in eternity) without recommending myself to the care and protection of the Almighty; and to this I have endeavoured always to have the greater regard, since besides the divine authority, which plainly enjoins it, it's a duty so clearly manifested even by the light of Nature, that it is a wonder almost that any should neglect it. I hope you do not, Madam, take this as either dictating or reproving, when it is never meant so by me, who have justly entertained quite other conceptions of you, and am so far from supposing myself a pattern in any respect for your imitation, that I should think myself in danger of running into the notion of a perfectionist, if I could but come near you.

This, Madam, is the method in which I would spend the Sabbath, and is what I have endeavoured to practise; though I must own, to my shame, with so much weakness, and so many infirmities, that it seems rather an account of what I ought to do, than of what I have done: for though it is my duty to watch narrowly over my heart, affections, and thoughts, and all my outward actions, and in a more particular manner should look upon the sanctifying of the Lord's day to be a principal part of religion, yet I must own I have not being so careful as I ought, to satisfy the Lord in my heart on that day, or perform some duties that were incumbent upon me. I have not made

Jehovah my fear and my dread, as I ought; but have indulged myself in sloth, spoken my own words, and thought my own thoughts, contrary to God's holy will and commandment.

I must also accuse myself of being too negligent in preparing myself to attend upon God in his solemn and public appointments, rushing often into his presence without that due preparation which he requires.

Neither have I behaved myself in his house with that fear and reverence as I ought, nor heard God's word with that attention, which so awful a message called for, nor improved it to my spiritual nourishment, as I ought to have done.

I am also sensible, that I have been more ready to find fault with the minister, than to obey the message he has brought; and have not spoken of other men and their affairs, with that care, charity, and affection, as I should have done, but rather have discovered their defects.

I likewise acknowledge, that in singing of psalms, I have not sung with that grace in my heart which God's word requires; and have had my ears more tickled with the harmony of the music, than my soul inflamed with zeal to sing the praises of God.

I do also confess, I have not had such sorrow and repentance for my sins past as I ought; nor have used such diligence in the daily examining of my conscience, and amendment of my life, as I should have done.

I have also reason to be humbled, that I hadn't offered up my prayers unto God, with alacrity and fervour of spirit as I should have done, but have been often distracted, slothful, and cold in my devotions.

I also acknowledge I have been proud and vainglorious in my words and actions.

I have not thought so humbly of myself, as I should have done; nor kept my senses in the house of God, with that care as became a Christian, especially my eyes and my ears.

For all which, and many more errors of my life, which through neglect and inadvertency may have escaped my cognisance, I humbly beg pardon and forgiveness of the Father of Mercies.

Thus (Madam) with the pelican,[20] have I dissected my heart, to shew you where the defects of humanity reside.

I have here (as I told you before) made the whole world (but principally yourself) my confessor: I will only add as to this point, that if my tongue and heart agree not in this confession, my confession will be of no value; he that confesses with his tongue, and wants confession in his heart, is either a vain man, or an hypocrite; and he that confesses with his heart, and wants it in his tongue, is either proud or timorous.

Madam, having given you some account how I endeavoured to spend the Sabbath in Dublin, I shall next inform ye how I spent my time on the weekdays.

I have told you (in the account I gave you of spending Sunday) that it was my practice to go to bed sooner on those nights than at other times. I shall further add, that I'm no sooner lain down on Sunday night, but I compose myself to rest, being so far from being terrified with apparitions, spectrums,[21] and the like, as I have heard some have been: who for that very reason, durst never lie alone; that I humbly adore the majesty of heaven for it, I fear nothing but God and sin.

When I awake, I am transported to find myself so sprightly every way; which made me often wonder what an excellent thing sleep was; considering it as an inestimable jewel; for an hour of which, if a tyrant laid down his crown, he should not be able to purchase it; that it was that golden chain which tied health and our bodies together; and that while sleeping, none complained of pains, wants, cares, or captivities. And that though the story of Endymion's nap for three-score and fifteen years,[22] and then awaking as lively as if he had slept but six hours, be in itself but a mere fable, yet the moral is good, and plainly indicates the necessity and usefulness of rest to our natures, as instituted by the God of Nature himself.

But to proceed in my journal. In the morning, as soon as the cinque-ports[23] are open, I send up some private ejaculations to heaven, giving God thanks that my eyes are open to see the light of another day. After this I get up, and make my most solemn addresses to the divine majesty; remembring Randolph's words.

> First worship God; he that forgets to pray,
> Bids not himself good morrow, nor good day.[24]

In these sorts of duties it has been my constant practice to be rather short and fervent, than long and indifferent: and as we ought to make use of every just and proper motive to excite us to our duty, I will humbly say, I have been the more constant in my practice of this morning-duty, as principally out of a sense of my bounden duty towards God, so also from a consideration of the example of a person of honour (I mean the late Lord Delamere)[25] who has left it upon record to his children, that whenever he happened, which was very seldom, to omit his duty in this kind, though upon never so urgent an occasion, he always found some cross interruptions and disappointments in the business of that day.

Being now, Madam, to sally out into the city, under a necessity of making myself more particularly known, in respect to the affairs I went about, I will presume to suppose you might be inquisitive to understand what sort of figure was proper for me to make. As to my clothes, I confess I was never over-curious, affecting always to appear more plain and cleanly, than gay and finical.[26] The first suit of apparel that ever mortal man wore, came neither from the mercer's shop, nor the merchant's warehouse; and yet Adam's bill would have been sooner taken, than a knight's bond now. The silk-worms had something else to do in those days, than to set up looms, to become free of the weavers. Our old grandsire's breeches were not worth near the value of K. Stephen's hose,[27] that cost but a poor noble; Adam's holy-day suit being made of no better stuff than plain fig-leaves sowed together, and Eve's best gown of the same piece. However, it was best necessary and convenient I should rather appear above than below my quality; and as such I adventured to visit my auction-room.

In the various emergencies of each day, I send up ejaculatory prayers to the God of all my mercies, for his direction, blessing, and conduct, as the matter does require, and as God has commanded, who has bid me in all my ways acknowledge him, and has graciously promised to direct my paths.

In the summer-time, I rose early in the morning and walked abroad into the fields, finding those occasional meditations (that such a walk presented me with subjects for) proper to raise my devotion to a greater fervour; the beauty of the creation, leading me by insensible steps to the adoration of the great Creator, the source and fountain of all excellencies. My walking along the strand (a mile from Dublin) gave me a pleasant prospect of the sea, whose rolling waves put me in

Conversation in Ireland. 317

nient I fhould rather appear above than below my Quality; and as fuch I adventured to vifit my *Au-ction-Room.*

In the *various Emergencies* of each day, I fend up Ejaculatory Prayers to the God of all my Mercies, for his *Direction, Bleffing, and Conduct,* as the matter does require. and as God has Commanded, who has bid me *in all my Ways acknowledge him, and has gra-cioufly promis'd to direct my Paths.*

In the *Summer-time,* I rofe early in the Morning, and walk'd abroad into the Fields, finding thofe oc-cafional *Medi ations* (that fuch a walk prefented me with Subjects for) proper to raife my Devotion to a greater Fervour; *the Beauty of the Creation,* lead-ing me by infenfible fteps to the Adoration of the Great Creator, the Source and Fountain of all Ex-cellencies. My walking along the *Strand* (a Mile from *Dublin*) gave me *a pleafant profpect of the Sea,* whofe rowling Waves put me in mind of the Power of Omnipotence, who commands both the Winds and the Sea, faying, *hitherto fhalt thou come, but no further.*

Leaving the *Strand,* I walk'd up a Hill into the Fields, by the fide of *Ballibaugh-Lane* (which I thought one of the beft Profpects about *Dublin*) ha-ving *Heaven, Earth, and Sea, in view* at the fame Moment, it reprefented to my thoughts the exceed-ing fwiftnefs of fpiritual Bodies, which (though far from Infinite, yet) have a motion quicker than the Eye, and fwifter than our Thoughts. *Thus by the things I have feen, I have been led into the Contem-plation of unfeen things.*

After about *an hours Meditations* in this Nature, my ufual way was to return to my Chamber, unlefs a previous Appointment to meet any one about Bufi-nefs, hinder'd me. For though I had given the *Con-duct* of my *Auctions* to Mr. *Wilde* (who faithfully difcharg'd the Truft I repos'd in him) yet was I not fo freed from Bufinefs my felf, as not to have Ap-plications made to me, both by the Binders, and other Perfons.

B b b   Aft**er**

mind of the power of Omnipotence, who commands both the winds and the sea, saying, Hitherto shalt thou come, but no further.

Leaving the strand, I walked up a hill into the fields, by the side of Ballibaugh-lane[28] (which I thought one of the best prospects about Dublin); having heaven, earth, and sea in view at the same moment, it represented to my thoughts the exceeding swiftness of spiritual bodies, which (though far from infinite, yet) have a motion quicker than the eye, and swifter than our thoughts. Thus by the things I have seen, I have been led into the contemplation of unseen things.

After about an hour's meditations in this nature, my usual way was to return to my chamber, unless a previous appointment to meet anyone about business hindered me. For though I had given the conduct of my auctions to Mr Wilde (who faithfully discharged the trust I reposed in him) yet was I not so freed from business myself, as not to have applications made to me, both by the binders, and other persons.

After some time being in my chamber, and having taken some refreshment, I went to Dick's in Skinner Row; where, after calling for a dish of coffee, my questions were, Where's Darby? (he's Dick's servant, but as honest a lad as lives in Dublin). Is there a packet come from England? And that which prompted me to that enquiry, was, that I then had hopes of hearing from my wife; distance and absence having so endeared her to me, that I was never well but when I was writing to her, or hearing from her. But if a packet came, and there was no letter for me, it struck me into such a melancholy (for fear Valeria was ill) that I could hardly reconcile myself to a good humour all that day.

Madam, perhaps this will make you ask how long I have been absent from her? Why, Madam, not above a month, but am fallen already to telling the minutes, and can scarce live at this cruel distance.

Methinks, Madam, I could pass through an army of beauties untouched for one glimpse of the dear Valeria (for so I design to call her); it is she I love (for why shouldn't I) above beauty, wealth, and those gaudy trifles that dazzle the eyes of others: 'Neither can S— nor the worst of her enemies lessen my opinion of her. Might I talk of her piety (for she's too modest to hear it mentioned) I'd affirm she's so great a scripturist that her memory is a sort of concordance, and the only one I have occasion for: and for the rest of her life, it is nothing else but devotion—.'[29] And, which yet enhances her value, she puts me not off with a common friendship. It is true, an indifferent love would have been good enough for the man that would court her with the blaze of gold; to the fop that has nothing but honour or beauty (that very jest when found in a man) to plead for him; I loved her for better reasons, and therefore ask for a nearer intimacy, a more lasting happiness;

> Sense is enough; where senses only woo;
> But reasoning lovers must have reason too:
> No wonder if the body quickly cloy,
> But minds are infinite, and like themselves enjoy.[30]

A woman of sense (and such I find Valeria) is a noble prize, had she nothing but the treasure of her mind. All the world is pictured in a soul; I'm sure it is so, and that she acts new charms in everything. Then, Madam, if you ever marry (and would be happy in wedlock) marry for pure love, for Valeria and I shall then be upon the square with ye, for we can love more in one day, than others do in all their lives. She that marries a husband on this foundation, will be still finding new charm either in his words or looks; for my own share, I do assert, whilst dignified sparks seek diversion from their misses, and devote their lives to the idle pursuit of a hound or a hawk, I thank God my fancy is not so rambling, but I can confine it to one dear charmer, to whom (if she loves like me) I'll prove the most kind and tender thing in the world. In a word, I bend all the faculties and powers of my body and mind, to please and serve her; all I have, or can command, shall lie at her feet; neither do I love at so cold a rate, as to desire any of the goods of fortune, but for her sake; and this loving humour (as Iris found in the like case) will not only last for a day, or a year, but to the end of her life: then what shall I do for a sight of Valeria? But it can't be had, so that I am now constrained to have recourse to philosophy, though it can supply me with no other remedies but patience; and the thoughts of this made me still duller than I was before: but as dull as it made me, before I left the coffee-house, for (though love has led me out of the way) I don't forget I am still at Dick's. I looked upon the bill[31] I published for that morning:

then read what public papers came from England in the last packet; and from thence, my stomach (the most infallible sort of clock) having chimed all in, I went to dinner; which was usually at a cook's shop, a widow's in Crane-lane, whom I always found very ready to please me, and reasonable in her demands; a thing which few of the Dublin cooks are guilty of; for though both flesh and fish are sold cheap in their markets, yet a man may dine cheaper at a cook's in London. I perceive in these ordinaries,[32] if a man makes a noise, laughs in fashion, and has a grim face to promise quarrelling, he shall be much observed; but though this was none of my talent, yet when I was set down to dinner, I looked as big, and eat as confidently as any of them all. When we had filled our bellies, we all began to talk, and made as great a noise as Dover Court,[33] for every man was willing to say something, though it was nothing to the purpose, rather than be thought to have nothing to say. I had but very bad sauce to my dinner this day; but that, Madam, mistake me not, did not arise from the fault of the cook where I was, but the company; there being in a manner nothing that was serious among them; one's talk was so lewd, as if he had lived in a brothel-house; another was profaneness all over, nothing could be heard from him but railleries (if I may call them so) against serious godliness, one while in jest, then again in earnest, and sometimes, to shew his wit (as I may well suppose) with an inter-mixture of both. Others there were, who seemingly little believed either heaven or hell, to reward or punish; or a supreme and righteous God and judge of all; yet made no bones of calling the dreadful and omnipotent Being for a witness to every frivolous, and I may say, many a false thing; for he that makes no conscience of swearing, will, in my opinion, make less of lying; and it may well (if yet it be not) be made a proverb, A common swearer a common liar. Of all the vices that are but too too rife among the children of men, this of profane swearing is certainly the most unaccountable one of any; something may be said for lying, as that it's profitable; for drinking, that it is for the good company; of whoring, that it is natural for kind to propa-gate its kind, &c. but for swearing, what can any man say? even nothing at all. Upon a mild expostulation with one of the sparks[34] about the usefulness of it, all he could say for it was, that it adorned his discourse. Good God! to what a pass is the world come, and where will these things terminate? But this conversation (which consisted chiefly in noise and nonsense) was quickly at an end. For dinner being ended, away went everyone, according as his business or his humour led him: some to the college, some to the play-house, others to Court, a few to their shops, and Dunton to his auction. When I came there, my first word usually was, Where's Wilde?[35] What sale last night? Call Price. Sir, here's your account ready cast up; thirty pounds received, and here's the discharge[36] on it. Call Nelson, call Robinson, call James, call Bacon. Are the bills[37] printed? And were they dispersed at the coffee houses, College, and Tholsel?[38] Thus, Madam, you see I was a man of business; and that my province was to have a general inspection over all my servants; and to stir them up to their duty with the utmost application.

When I had spent about an hour's time at my auction, and had seen everyone in their proper post, I either went to visit a friend, with whom sometimes I walked into the fields; or else went home to my lodging, and spent my time in my chamber, either in reading Montaign's essays (for it is a book I value at a great rate) or else in writing to my friends in England. And after the shadows of the evening have put a period to the day, I used to make a trip to my auction, and crowd myself among the gentlemen that went thither to buy pennyworths; and so could, unobserved, observe how things went. And here, to do them justice, I observed that several gentlemen bid like themselves, and as those that understood the worth and value of the books they bid for. And others as much betrayed their ignorance, and took no other measures for their bidding, but from the bulk of the book; if it was large (whatever the worth on it was) they bid accordingly. And yet to do these right, if they had but paid for what they had so bought, I have no reason to complain of them. Others there were, that in their bidding took their measures from what they heard another bid before them; and two of these happening to meet together, would strive so to out-bid each other, that they would sometimes raise but an indifferent book to a good price: and these (provided still they paid for them) were very honest chapmen,[39] and helped out those that went too often at an under rate. But whatsoever any bid, it was their own act and deed; for I must do myself that justice, to assert that I had none of those unworthy ways that have been used in some other auctions. I had not one setter (to advance the price, and draw on unwary bidders) in any of my five sales. For howsoever I may have been aspersed in that particular, by Patrick Campbell, I have that satisfaction in myself of my sincerity and innocence herein, as is beyond the testimony of a thousand witnesses.

Having diverted myself a while, with seeing of the various humours of the bidders in my auction, I went away as unperceived as I came thither, and thence retired into my chamber; where, having spent some time in meditation, I make it my endeavour to recollect the actions of the day, and make a scrutiny into my heart, to see what peccant humours[40] have exerted themselves there (being jealous of myself, that I have not been so much upon my watch as I ought to have been) and having thus examined how things stand, I strive by an humble confession of what I find myself guilty of, and a hearty sorrow for it, to reconcile myself to my offended Maker, and so strike a tally in the exchequer of heaven[41] (as an ingenious author expresses it) for my *quietus est*,[42] before I close my eyes, that I may leave no burthen on my conscience. And after my addresses to heaven, by way of confession, &c. my bed is the next place, where I know no more of myself till seven next morning (so strange is the nature of sound sleep) than if I had never been; at which hour I usually digest the future business of the day: yet, Madam, as sound as I sleep, I dream often. You know, Madam, thought must be active, but I take little heed in the morning, what the visions of the night have been (unless that night when I dream of D—ne's[43] appearing to me) and much less care to remember them; but my experience teaches me, that the overnight thoughts come fresh upon me the next day; and how to digest and settle them, was the morning business; the main whereof, next after my morning's devotion, was to answer those letters I had received from England. My custom always is, to begin with that of my wife's, and then to proceed to D—ne's, and then to my other relations and friends, as near as I can, in due order of place and affection. I seal them in the same manner, only I retain that of my wife's to be the first perused, and last closed.

Thus, Madam, I have given you a brief, but true account of my general method of living: and by such steps as these (through the help of divine grace) I strive to climb to heaven; and sometimes find my soul upon the wing thither, before I am aware. There is, methinks, no object in the world that is more delightful than when, in a star-light-night, I survey the spangled canopy of heaven; for if my mind happen to be overcast with melancholy, when I look up and view the glittering firmament, and hope in a short time to soar those starry regions, methinks I breath already the air of a new world; and all those black vapours that overwhelmed my soul are fled in an instant: I then scorn this transitory world, and all its fading pleasures, considering the vanity of the one, and the emptiness of the other.

Thus still my soul moves upwards, as all the heavenly bodies do: but yet, as those bodies are often snatched away to the west, by the rapid motion of the *primum mobile*;[44] so by those epidemical infirmities incident to human nature, I am often turned a clean contrary course; though my soul still persists in her proper motion. And I have oft occasion to be angry with myself, when I consider, that whereas my bountiful Creator intended my body (though a lump of clay) should be a temple of his Holy Spirit, my corrupt affections should turn it so often to a bedlam, and my excesses to a hospital. But as my sin troubles me, so my trouble for sin comforts me: and I believe there is less danger in committing the sin I delight in, than in delighting in the sin I have committed. In a word, Madam, I have experienced that the way to God is by my own corruptions: if I baulk this way, I err; if I travel by the creatures, I wander: for the motion of the heavens will give my soul no rest, nor will the virtue of herbs increase mine; the height of all philosophy, both natural and moral, being to know myself; and the end of this knowledge is to know God, the knowledge of whom is the perfection of love; God being our chiefest good, and the enjoyment of him our highest happiness.

And now, Madam, having given you a specimen of my way of living in Dublin, both on the Sabbath, and on the week days, I come in the next place to give you a journal of my conversation, with respect to the occurrences I met with here; by which you may see what little occasion I gave for the *Dublin Scuffle*; or to the false Dorinda to tempt me to her lewd embraces.

It was in April when I came to Dublin, and near eleven a clock at night when I landed; so that it was with some difficulty that I got a lodging for that night; for which I own myself beholden to Mrs Lisle

(the widow) at the Dukes-head Tavern in Castle-street, the first place
I drank at in Ireland. I have always the unhappiness of being sick at
sea, which, though it be very irksome to bear, yet I find this good in
it, that it endears the sense of God's goodness to me when I come to
land, and makes me the more thankful for my preservation. Which
having performed as well as the fatigue I had been under would
permit, I betook myself to my chamber, and slept that night without
rocking; though in the morning both my bed and chamber seemed
to me to have the same motion that my fluctuating cabin had, the
day before. Being got up the next morning, I again renewed my
thanks to God, for my preservation at sea, and safe arrival at Dublin.
And now being dressed as it were in print[45] (for my business now was
to see and be seen) I marched very methodically out of my lodgings
with two (I can't say a pair of) gloves in one hand and a cane in the
other; and it is not long since I had done sowing my wild oats; and
now I am earnestly hunting after camp-feed.[46] You would smile,
Madam, if you had the picture of your quondam friend at the Black
Raven,[47] like an over-grown oaf newly come to town, staring and
gazing at all the signs, and everything else in the streets; pacing out
their length, and enquiring ever and anon. What call ye this street?
Who dwells in yon great house? Whose fine coach is that? For thus
I rambled through every street, alley, and corner of this spacious
town, as you'll find at large in my *Summer Travels*, where 200 persons
will see their pictures, that at present little expect it; but I leave them
here, to tell ye the first visit I made in Dublin, was to Nat. Gun, a
bookseller in Essex-street to whom I was directed by my friend, Mr
Richard Wilde (whom I had left behind me in London): 'This son of
a gun gave me a hearty welcome; and, to do him justice, he's as
honest a man as the world affords; and is so esteemed by all that
know him. He is a firm adherer to the established government, and a
declared enemy to popery and slavery: so far from dissembling, that
he knows not how to go about it; and will speak his mind, how much
soever it may be to his prejudice. He understands stenography as well
as bookbinding; and he himself is a sort of a short-hand character;
for he is a little fellow, but one that contains a great deal. And as he
is a most incomparable writer of shorthand, so he speaks it as well as
writes it; and to complete his character, he is a constant shopkeeper,

without earnest business calls him to the Drumcondra. This Gun was a constant and generous bidder at my auctions, where he bought a great quantity of books, which he as honestly paid for.'[48]

At Mr Gun's shop, I met with Mr Bently, another bookseller, but his principal business is binding; whom I afterwards employed considerably: 'He is a very honest man, but has met with misfortunes in the world, by thinking some others as honest as himself, who did not prove so.' I asked Mr Bently, whether there was not some eminence in the city, from whence I might survey it? He told me there was; and that from the top of the Tholsel the whole city might be seen; so we went to the Tholsel, where we ascended about half a score stairs from the street, which brought us into a spacious room, supported by great pillars, and flagged (as they term it here) with free stone, with open banisters on each side towards the street; its figure is rather an oblong than a square: this is the place they call the 'Change, where the merchants meet every day, as on the Royal Exchange in London. In a corner, at the south-east part, is a court of judicature, where they keep their public sessions for the city. Having viewed the lower part, we went up a large pair of stairs into a public room, which had a large balcony looking into Skinner Row; and from this balcony I spoke with my friend Mr Geo. Larkin, who was then at Mr Ray's printing house over-against it. He no sooner saw me, but came over to congratulate my safe arrival, expressing himself very joyful to see me; and I was as glad as he, we having a long time had a kindness for each other, and conversed by letter even when I was in America. Having said so much of him, you'll not wonder, Madam, if I send ye an epitome of his character (intending to do it more largely in my *Summer Ramble*): 'He is of a middling stature, somewhat gross, of a sanguine complexion, and a hail constitution both of body and mind; and (which I admire wherever I find it) he is of an even temper, not elated when fortune smiles, nor cast down with her frowns; and though his stars have not been very propitious to him, with respect to his outward circumstances (he having had great losses) yet he has borne all with such a presence of mind, as shewed his losses to be the effect of his misfortunes, and not his faults. His conversation is extremely diverting, and what he says is always to the purpose: he is a particular votary of the Muses; and I have seen some of his poems that can't be equalled. But there is one thing more peculiar to him, which is, whatever he does, is upon the account civil.'

I went up with my friends (Madam) to the top of the Tholsel, and there had a view of the whole city; but a storm that then arose took from us much of the pleasure of the prospect; but of that, and the spacious chambers over the Change, where the *Lord Mayor and aldermen meet, and other curiosities which I saw there, as also of the government of the city (by the Lord Mayor, aldermen, and assemblies) I shall give a more particular account in my *Summer Ramble*. But this I will say here (Madam) that of all the cities in the King's dominions, Dublin (next to London) does justly claim the precedence.

It was at the Tholsel I met Mr Dell,[49] a person 'whose understanding and generous temper set him above the common rate of men, and shew him to be every way a gentleman; I could not but love him for these qualifications, but much more as he was an old acquaintance of my honoured mother-in-law; and, Madam, you can't blame me for this, as she treats me with that tenderness, that I think her my own mother revived, and I find shall love her as much. Mr Dell shewed me a most particular respect at our first meeting, and continued his favours to the last minute I stayed in Ireland, being one of those that were so obliging as to see me a-shipboard.'

From the Tholsel, Mr Dell, Mr Bently and I were going to the tavern, but Mr Larkin, by the way, would have me go into Dick's Coffee-house, where I had been advised by Mr Wilde to keep my auctions: I readily agreed to his motion, and went up, saw it, and liked it, as proper for my purpose; Dick shewing me all the civility I could desire: and I must say this of Dick (notwithstanding our after quarrel), 'That he is a witty and ingenious man, makes the best coffee in Dublin; and is very civil and obliging to all his customers; of an open and generous nature; has a peculiar knack at bantering, and will make rhymes to anything: he's of a cheerful facetious temper, and generally speaking fair in his dealing: and had not Patrick assaulted him with the temptation of a double price, he and I should never have quarrelled and yet, for all that, I must do him the justice to say,

---

* For so the chief Magistrate of the city is styled there, as well as in London.

he carried it civilly to me to the very last; and was so kind as to come (with my friend Mr Dell) to give me a farewell when I left Ireland; thus much for Dick'. As for his wife, I shall say this, 'She's an industrious woman, handsome enough, one that knows her duty to her husband, and how to respect her customers; and in a word, is what a wife ought to be; and I must own, though her husband and I scuffled, she treated me always with much respect.'

From Dick's we went to the tavern, where having drunk a bottle or two (and related the fatigues of my Dublin voyage) we parted, and went each to our several lodgings. In my way home I was attacked by an impudent woman, who desired me to bestow a glass of wine upon her; I made her no other answer than that the house of correction stood not far off; at which she scowered away with all the heels she could make, seeming as much feared as if she had been in the most imminent danger of losing her chastity; when perhaps she could scarce remember the time when she had it. I hope, Madam, you do not esteem anything I have said here, to be designed for the magnifying of my own virtues; it's practicable enough for a man to make his reputation clear and not sin; and assure yourself, I am not insensible that self-praise is a most odious thing in any, and I shall ever account it much more so in myself: however it be, Madam, all my mistakes are entirely submitted to you, who are the best judge of them.

The next day I removed to more convenient quarters, and delivered some letters which I had brought from London. This day Mr Dell gave me a meeting at Dick's; from whence we went to the Castle, the place of residence for the chief governors; by Mr Dell's interest I had here a view of the Lord Galway's[50] bedchamber, and other noble apartments, but I wave them here, designing to speak of them in my *Summer Ramble*: however, I'll here attempt his lordship's character, and hope my honest intention herein will something atone for my great defects; and the rather still, as his lordship's merits are above a Dryden's or a Cowley's pen. I own it is a bold undertaking, to offer at the character of one of the greatest men which our age has produced, especially for one who has not the honour of being personally known to him; however, though I can't perform this great task as it ought to be, yet I'll endeavour at something so like him, that any one at first glance may say it was meant for the Earl of Galway, one of the present Lords Justices for the kingdom of Ireland. Then to proceed (though with a trembling hand) to his lordship's character.

The first thing then which is remarkable in him is, 'He is a person of strict morals, and extraordinary piety. His lordship is advanced to the honours he now enjoys, by his great humility and personal merits. The noble blood that has filled his veins has not swelled his heart: he is as humble as he is great; he seems set by heaven on such a conspicuous place (as is that of being Lord Justice of Ireland) on purpose to guide the people into the paths of love and obedience to their God and King. In a word, he uses such an obliging mien to all, as if he thought the only thing valuable in greatness is the power it gives to oblige.' I would go on with his lordship's character, but (as I said before) I find myself unable for this task; so that (Madam) I shall next proceed (for his lordship's character leads me to it) to give some short account of the present state of the kingdom, according to my best information, though you may wonder that Dunton should trouble his head with politics; but since such is the custom of travellers, why may not I thrust myself into the herd?

The present governors are, their excellencies the Lord Marquess of Winchester, the Earl of Galway, and the Lord Villers, now Earl of Jersey[51] (his lordship has never been here with this character, though he be named in the commission) and the present government is so well administered by those two noble lords, that I have not heard one man repine at them since I came to Dublin. They have officers belonging to the household, such as steward and comptroller, who on state-days carry white rods as the ensigns of their office: when they go to church, the streets, from the Castle-gate to the church-door, as also the great aisle of the church, to the foot of the stairs by which they ascend to the place where they sit, are lined with soldiers; they are preceded by the pursivants[52] of the council-chamber, two maces, (and on state-days) by the king, and pursivant at arms, their chaplains, and gentlemen of the household, with pages and footmen bare-headed: when they alight from their coach (in which commonly the Lord Chancellor and one of the prime nobility sit with them) the Sword of State is delivered to some lord to carry before them; and in the like manner they return back to the Castle, where the several courses at dinner are ushered in by kettle-drums and trumpets. I forgot to tell you (Madam) that in these cavalcades the coach in which they ride is attended by a small squadron of horse; after which follow a long train of coaches that belong to the several lords and gentlemen who attend them.

Having given ye this short account of the chief governors, I shall next proceed to mention something of the estate of the Church, which in all its canons are not the same with that of England; not that they differ from it in any points of religion, but only in some circumstances of government; which by a Convocation which has been sometimes held there, may be altered as the present exigencies require: it consists of two houses, viz. the upper in which the bishops, and the lower where the inferior clergy sit; but they have not thought it needful to call one since his present majesty's accession to the crown. The most reverend the Archbishops are four, viz. Dr Michael Boyle, Lord Archbishop of Armagh, and Primate of all Ireland; Dr Narcissus Marsh, Lord Archbishop of Dublin, Primate of Ireland; Dr William Palliser, Lord Archbishop of Cashel; and Dr John Vesey, Lord Archbishop of Tuam. And the suffragants[53] are eighteen in number; of this number three are of his majesty's Privy-Council, viz. the Bishops of Meath, Kildare, and Clogher, as also the two Primates. To give you a short character of them, take this, what has been told me by some judicious persons, of as well dissenters as others, that they are men of such learning, moderation, and piety, that this church had never a better class of bishops to govern it.

The dissenters in Ireland are a very considerable people, as well for their number as wealth; and all unanimous in a hearty zeal for our present happy government. (And indeed, since my coming hither, I have not heard of any one Jacobite in the whole kingdom.) They have several meeting-houses, large and conveniently ordered within; and these are supplied with sober and pious teachers; among whom I think the Reverend Mr Boyse[54] may justly be named as the chief; one, who by continual and hard study every day, fits himself with new acquisitions towards the happy discharging of his pastoral care; which he expresses with so much meekness and force of persuasion, as make him at once mightily beloved and followed. And one thing this kingdom is extremely happy in, that both persuasions do so well agree, towards promoting the common good, as more cannot well be desired; a great advancer of which union is Mr Weld,[55] a person of sobriety, learning, and solid judgment, and much admired and followed for his preaching.

The Quakers are here in great numbers also, as one might easily perceive that would have considered the mighty throngs of them which crowded about their great speaker and champion, William Penn, when he came hither to hold forth. I cannot hear of any learned men among them, though some of them are very wealthy, and but few of them poor; they can make use of the carnal sword,[56] as well as those who pretend more to it; as you will believe by this story of one among them, whose name I forget; who, in the late war, when the rapparees[57] came towards Edenderry, near the Bog of Allen, in the King's County, he, among others of the militia, went forth to engage them, and put them all to the run, except those who were killed in the action; among them lay one whom the Quaker thought he had killed, and rifled his pockets; but some months after, when a great number of them burnt Colonel Purefoy's house, about three miles from Edenderry, these brisk sparks took the alarm, and making as considerable a body as they could, marched to Purefoy's place, where they found many of the Irish, who had made themselves drunk with the Colonel's strong beer, fast asleep in the ditches; the Quaker, who never was backward in such attempts, finds the same fellow whom he thought he had formerly killed, half tipsy, and in his arms;[58] he called him by his name, saying, 'Verily I thought I had of late slain thee? but now find my mistake; wherefore I purpose to make sure work, and hinder thee from rising any more'; and so immediately knocked him down with a poll-axe[59] which he used always instead of a sword; and then cut off his head. Poor Teig never offered at any resistance, nor endeavoured to save himself by flight, but stood to die like a fool.

Our red lettered gentlemen[60] were never under such circumstances here, as now; for all their bishops and regular clergy are banished by Act of Parliament, which makes it death to find any of them returned again. So that now they are wholly depending on the seculars, and every parish is allowed his priest; but when he dies, there being none to ordain a new one, it must remain without; and this will be the state of the whole kingdom in a little time, when the present set of priests shall be extinct. They have also another law, that no papist shall keep a school, nor any one native of a foreign education be admitted to dwell in the kingdom; so that by these acts I think it will appear plain enough, that the Romish religion is on its last legs in Ireland; and the present Romanists who survive their priests must conform to the Protestant religion, or live and die without the exercise of their own. I do not pretend to make my judgment upon these methods; but I think the next age will have few people inclinable to any more rebellions against England; and some of the papist lords have put their children to be educated in the Protestant faith; and several gentleman have lately abjured the Romish.

These ghostly fathers were to render themselves on the first day of May for transportation at Dublin, Cork, &c. where their names were entered with the magistrate of the town; ye may guess at the lamentations which were made at parting with such precious jewels; and masses were said, and money begged for them, besides what the people voluntarily gave without asking. One old friar, called Father Kereen, who had been a famous exorcist, and excellent good at helping cattle that were overlooked[61] or bewitched (for some of the vulgar are so superstitious to believe this), made sale of good store of holy water, which had helped to cast out devils; and of several other consecrated trinckams, by which it was said he acquired such a sum of money, as might suffice for his support all his days; and such were the tricks played by many of them on going into exile as leaving holy tokens and taking catalogues of their acquaintances' names, to pray for them all the days of their life. Now these kindnesses deserved some returns, which they never failed of; though whether they are as good as their words in remembering them, I leave to their own breasts. Before I leave this account of the state of religion in Ireland, I shall acquaint you with the manner of exorcising their demoniacs (though for my part I think the devil is in the presumptuous priest, rather than the melancholy person) and you may judge how fit such persons are for honest society.

> The exorcist, before he goes to work, ought by way of a preparative, to confess his sins, and receive the eucharist; then he begins the operation with some short prayers, and ties the end of the violet coloured stole that he wears, about the

demoniac's neck; who, if outrageous,[62] must be tied hand and foot; then crossing him, and the bystanders, they go to prayer, and read the 53rd psalm; and after a prayer or two more, he thus speaks to the devil: 'I command thee, thou unclean spirit, whoever thou art, and all thy companions, that do possess this servant of God, that by the mystery of the Incarnation, Passion, Resurrection, and Ascension of our Lord J.C. by the sending the Holy Ghost, and the coming of our Lord to judgment, thou tell me thy name, and the day and hour of thy exit, with some sign; and that thou obey me the unworthy minister of God in all things; and that thou offend not this creature of God, or any of the bystanders in their persons or goods.' Then he crosses himself, and the demoniac on the forehead, mouth, and breast, and reads some gospel, as that of the first of St John, the 16th of Mark, or the 10th of Luke; then falling to prayer, he begs to be enabled to cast forth this cruel devil; then lapping the stole about the possessed party's neck, and fortifying him with the sign of the cross, he lays his right hand on the patient's head, and cries out, 'Behold the cross of the Lord!' (which he shews him), 'fly from it, ye adverse parties: The lion of the tribe of Judah, the root of David hath overcome': then to prayer again he goes, and begins a new exorcism, saying, 'I exorcise thee, most foul spirit, every incursion of the adversary, every phantasm, and every legion, in the name of our Lord J.C. ✕ to fly from, and be eradicated ✕ out of this image of God: He commands thee, who bid thee be plunged from the highest heavens, into the lower parts of the earth: He whom the sea, winds and tempests obey, commands thee.' Then when this does not serve turn, he falls to scold the devil after this manner, 'Hear therefore, and fear, thou Satan, enemy of the faith, and all mankind; thou introducer of death, and destroyer of life, decliner of justice, root of all evils, fomenter of vices, seducer of men, betrayer of nations, promoter of envy, source of avarice, cause of discord, and exciter of sorrow, why dost thou stay? Why dost thou resist, when thou knowest the Lord Christ can destroy all thy power? Fear him who was sacrificed in Isaac, sold in Joseph, slain in the Lamb, crucified in man, and at last triumphed over hell.' Then he makes the following cross in the forehead of the possessed; 'Be gone you in the Name of the Father, ✕ and of the Son, ✕ and of the Holy Ghost ✕. Give way to the Holy Spirit by this ✕ sign of the cross of our Lord J.C.' Then they go to prayers; and after them another excorcism is used like the former, wherein he calls the devil many hard names, and tells him of all the rogueries he has ever committed, and bids him be gone for shame, since all his tricks are discovered.[63]

Madam, I would enlarge in giving a more particular account of the present conditions of the Church and State in this kingdom of Ireland (for as I was a little curious in this matter, so I have met with such ingenious company since I came here, as have been able to satisfy my curiosity in these matters), but my observations on the state of Ireland being more properly a part of my *Summer Ramble* than what relates to my *Conversation* in Dublin, I shall drop it here, and proceed to what is more properly *Conversation*; my design in this letter (as I said at first) being rather to tell ye how I lived in Ireland, than to tell ye what I saw or observed there. And in the account of my *Conversation*, with respect to the occurrences I met with there (for that's the subject I am still upon) I am next to tell ye, that having seen the Castle, and other rarities, I was the next Sunday for going to church (the place where the Lords Justices usually go) and accordingly thither I went in company with Mr Larkin. After we had seen the state in which the government rides to church (which indeed is very splendid, as I hinted before) we crowded into the church, where I endeavoured to compose myself in the most serious manner I could, to attend the service of God performed there. I do not pretend to retain whole sermons by heart, but can have a satisfied conscience in keeping only in my memory a remarkable passage or two that suits best to the edification of my soul; much less then, Madam, shall I offer to describe this place of divine worship, or descant upon the auditory: but as it is most natural for mankind, upon the presenting of fresh objects, to view them at least in a transient manner, I found it so with myself here, notwithstanding the injunctions of God, and my own conscience, to keep close to my devotion; but pardon me,

Madam, if I am necessitated to declare, I did not behold one tolerable face among all those that are distinguished by the name of the fair sex: so that here I can truly say, they were no temptation to me; and that I had no occasion to make a covenant with my eyes: but for myself, I could have been heartily content they had had a certain place of worship from the men, assigned them in the assembly, as the eastern churches have, but for what reason I know not. But this liberty (Madam) that I took to gaze, and make reflections, was only while they were singing an anthem, with vocal and instrumental music, there being two pair of organs in Christ-Church; of which one is a very noble one. But when the minister ascended the pulpit, I heard him with great attention and delight. He was a dignitary of the Church, but his name has slipped my memory. Retiring home from hence with what convenient speed the infirmity of my body would permit me, I dined in my lodging with my landlord H—, a jolly man in his natural temper, but not very serious in matters of religion; I made my repast as short as I could (as is usual with me upon such days) and withdrew into my chamber, where I spent the remainder of the day in such acts of devotion and meditation as were usual with me; but I had some more particular impressions upon my spirits concerning the divine goodness towards me, in respect to the now state of my health, that I had been enabled to go once again to the house of God: and I will own, to the glory of the Divine Name, that some touches in the sermon I had heard that day concerning thankfulness for mercies received, were very helpful to me in the course of this evening's devotion.

The next week I went to see Patrick Campbell, to whom (by his order) I had sent several of Mr Turner's *History*.[64] He treated me well enough the first time I saw him, giving me my morning's draught, and telling me I was welcome to Dublin: but I said nothing then of the books I sent him, nor he to me; which I thought somewhat strange. The second time I went to him, which was the week following, after the usual how-dee's were over, I expected he should have took some notice to me of the books; which he not doing, I took notice of them to him; and then it was I perceived he had a natural aversion to honesty; for he began to shuffle at the very mention of them. However, resolving to be easy with him, I took my leave of him for that time. The third time I saw him, he shuffled about my books at that rate, that a stranger in his shop (to whom I offered to refer my cause) resented it: and from that time forward (only for demanding my own, and telling him how unfairly he dealt by me) he became my enemy. This, Madam, being the person with whom I had the preceding scuffle; if by this you don't sufficiently see his character, give me leave to give it you? which I will do impartially, and without any respect to the controversy I had with him:

> He is of stature, rather tall than otherwise; his hair reddish, his speech very broad, like his country;[65] no scholar, but of good natural parts; very covetous, and extremely proud: he had a very mean beginning (for which no man ought to blame him, for he couldn't help it himself, and consequently it was none of his fault) but his intolerable pride makes it necessary that he be often put in mind on it. I have heard some persons say, that had dealings with him, that they had rather speak to the Lord Mayor about business, than Patrick Campbell; and that he would not look for so much respect. He cares not to part with money, and where he can shuffle he will: he is of Vespasian's mind,[66] and thinks no gain is unsavoury. What good parts he has, he uses ill, employing them for the most part to circumvent his neighbour. (Of which his taking my room over my head is an undeniable instance.) He understands the doctrine of equivocation as well as a Jesuit; and their honesties are much alike, only the Jesuits are the fairer dealers. He pretends extremely to religion, and has got many a penny by the bargain. He'll commonly say grace over a choppin[67] of ale, and at the same time be contriving how to overreach you: candour, and fair dealing are things he often mentions (as a cover for the opposite vices) but never cares to make use of them, unless sometimes to draw in a greater booty.

This, Madam, is a part of his character, which should I draw out at length, it would make a pack too big for a pedlar; but having thus accidentally stumbled upon his original, it will be wisdom to leave him where he was first found. Which yet I am unwilling to do, till I have acquainted you, Madam, that I have enough by me, to confirm every tittle of this character, without referring to anything relating to myself; for I have the history of his life sent me from Dublin since I came over, even from the time he sold thread-laces in Glasgow, by the name of Patrick Ure, to the time that Patrick Campbell begged pardon of the company in Dublin for his pretty experiment of turning Hodder into Cocker, &c.[68] And this attested by several eminent persons in that city, among whom Mr Thornton, the King's Stationer, is one. But having told him I'll be a generous enemy, I intend this history of his life shall be kept secret, unless he shall (hereafter) provoke me to publish it.

From Patrick Campbell I rambled to the ingenious Mr Ray's,[69] who is both printer and bookseller, and the best situated of any man in Dublin; and thence back to honest Ware's, witty Shaw's and grave Mr Foster's; who, as they all deserve an honourable character (which for brevity sake, I here omit), so I shall give it them in my *Summer Ramble*.

Having left Mr Ray, I rambled to Castle-street, where Vulcan[70] with his wooden leg startled me with the creeking of it, for I took it for the *crepitus ossium* which I have heard some of our physicians speak of; however, I was honestly treated by him, and will do him justice in my *Summer Ramble*.

Some time after this, seeing the *Squire of Alsatia*[71] in a play-bill, to be acted, I had a great mind to see it; for there being so many Alsatians in Dublin, I thought it could not choose but be acted to the life: and so having done my business (for I always make recreation wait upon business) I went to the play-house, which place you know, Madam, is free for all comers, and gives enertainment as well to the common man as the greatest peer: therefore having got my ticket, I made a shift to crowd into the pit, where I made my honours to Madam H——y (who I was amazed to find at the play-house) and to two or three other ladies that I happened to know; my next adventure there was, to give a hem to[72] the China orange wench, and to give her her own rate for her oranges; for you know, Madam, it is below a gentleman (and as such I passed in the crowd) to stand haggling like a citizen's wife. I found, Madam, the Dublin play-house to be a place very contrary to its owners; for they on their outsides make the best show: but this is very ordinary in its outward appearance, but looks much better on the inside, with its stage, pit, boxes, two galleries, lattices,[73] and music loft; though I must confess, that even these, like other false beauties, receive a lustre from their lamps and candles: it stands in a dirty street, called Smock Alley;[74] which I think is no unfit name for a place where such great opportunities are given for making of lewd bargains: hither I came dressed (though I say it) tolerably well; though not so much to be seen, as to see the follies of the age; for however the theatre be applauded by a modern gentleman, for the representation of those things which so mightily promote virtue, religion, and monarchical government; for my part, I thought vice, which fundamentally destroys all those things, is here, as well as in other theatres, so charmingly discovered, as to make men rather love than abhor it: like the judge, who, on the bench, discovering the arts of some cow-stealers, to disguise their beasts by altering the figure of their horns, taught a poor fellow the trick, who putting it in practice, was brought to the gallows; however, to give the devil his due, there are some actors here, particularly Mr Ashbury, Mr Husbands, Mr Wilks, Mr Hescot, Mr Norris, Mr Buckly, Mr Longmore, Mrs Smith, Mrs Schooling, are no way inferior to those in London; nor are the spectators, by what I saw, one degree less in vanity and foppery, than those in another place.

For the play, Madam, I need say nothing, it is so well known; it was pretty to see the Squire choused[75] out of so fair an estate with so little ready rino: yet the diversion was not so great, but that the crowd made me more uneasy; a thing I ever abominated, and for the most part made it my business to shun all my days; in a word, no church I was in while at Dublin, could I discern to be half so crowded as this place. I cannot tell indeed how it would have been, had they played on Sunday, as they do in popish countries, and particularly at Rome; where a stranger once observed, all the people suddenly ran out of the play-house into the church, as fast as they could, which made him at first think it was a most religious place; but when he came to hear the friar preach, his words, actions, and other gestures were so comical, that his wonder ceased; for he thought all the actors and players in Christendom were a fool to him.

After spending three or four hours in the play-house, to see a few men and women make fools of themselves, I returned home to my chamber, and could scarce be reconciled to myself, to think how foolishly I had wasted that time which might have been spent to better purpose.

Madam, I should next acquaint you with a prodigious storm which happened in Dublin about the latter end of July; it might indeed be more properly called a hurricane than a storm: it strangely surprised me, though its fury continued not above six hours; there was hardly a house in the city, where it had not left some visible marks of its rage (especially in Christ-Church-lane:) so that it was more safe being in the fields, than in the city at that time; the oldest men alive could never remember anything so terrible as this storm. But to give an account of the mischief it did, would be too great a digression; I shall therefore reserve it for my *Summer Ramble*, as I shall also a comical entertainment made at Kells in the county of Meath, by one Captain Bryan O Brogan, son to Philip O Brogan, Prince of Cavan.

Soon after this great storm, the Duke of Ormond[76] landed at Dublin, and from thence went to his house at Kilkenny, where (in my *Summer Ramble*) I saw His Grace, and had a sight of the castle, and other rarities, by the interest of Dr Wood,[77] whose great civilities I acknowledge in the following pages. About this time the Dublin players, with all their appurtenances, strolled down to Kilkenny; after which it was reported in Dublin, that one Wilks,[78] one of the best actors, had played his last part, being killed in a duel; this report was so far believed, that an igenious person wrote an Elegy* upon him, which was printed, and publicly sold. This news of his death was talked with such assurance, that though Mr Wilks soon after came to Dublin, and shewed himself alive, they would hardly believe him. The ground of this report (as I was told) arose from this, that a countryman seeing a tragedy acted in Kilkenny, wherein Mr Wilks acted the part of one that was to be killed, thought it was real, and so reported it.

I might next mention the sudden deaths of the Dublin sheriffs; the tragical story of a person that was killed by a fall from his horse; and the dismal accident of a child's firing a garret (with himself in it) with gunpowder; but should I relate half the occurrences I met in Dublin, I should swell this letter beyond measure, so I reserved them

* Which elegy I'll insert in my *Summer Ramble*

all for my *Summer Ramble*; and shall next proceed (that I may render the account of my *Conversation* the more complete) to give a particular account of the visits I made in Dublin; for, Madam, as it is an observation, that a man may be known by his company, so I think it is not incongruous to believe that an idea of his conversation may be taken from the persons to whom, and the occasions on which he makes his visits.

And here (Madam) I must first acquaint ye, that soon after my coming to Dublin, Mr Norman,[79] the bookseller, sent one Mr Rogerson to invite me to his house; when I came thither, I found his business was to propose the buying of the venture I had brought over; in which, though we agreed not, he treated me very kindly, shewing me all his house, and therein his picture, done so much to the life, that even Zeuxes or Appelles[80] could scarce exceed it.

From his house he had me to his garden, which though not very large, is to be much admired for the curiousness of the knots,[81] and variety of choice flowers that are in it; he being an excellent florist, and well acquainted with all the variegated tapestry of Nature, in the several seasons of the year. Mr Norman has this peculiar to himself that whatever he has in his garden is the most excellent of its kind: he has a room adjoining to this earthly paradise, to shelter his more tender plants and flowers from the insults of winter storms. From hence he carried me to a large warehouse, where he had a large auction, preparing, as he said, for sale; though I heard nothing more of it while I stayed in Dublin.

Madam, should I give this gentleman's character, I must say, 'He's a little squat man, that loves to live well, and has a spouse who understands preparing good things as well as the best lady in Ireland; he has a hole too much in his nose, which I have heard was occasioned by a brass pin in his nurse's waistcoat; which when he was nuzzling for the diddy,[82] happened to run in it; and for want of a skilful hand to dress it, the hole remains to this day, and yet without disfiguring his face.'

Before I proceed to the next visit, give me leave, Madam, being fallen (a second time) among my brethren, to spend a few lines about them, among the many I trouble you with concerning other people; they are not a corporation of themselves, but mixed with cutlers, and painter-stainers;[83] and their present master is Mr Norman, whose character I here send ye; with this addition, that he never opposed my auction.

Nor must I (Madam) forget the extraordinary civility of the King's Printer, Mr Andrew Crook,[84] 'Who is a worthy and generous gentleman, whose word and meaning never shake hands and part, but always go together: he is one that is as far from doing other men an injury, as he is from desiring to be injured; and though his circumstances are not so great, yet his soul is as large, as if he were a prince, and scorns as much to do an unworthy action. He is a great lover of printing, and has a great report for all that are related to that noble mystery.'

Having paid my respects to the King's Printer, I went next to Mr Thornton, the King's Stationer, of whom I shall say in short, 'He's a very obliging person, has sense enough for a privy-counsellor, and good nature enough for a primitive Christian; he treated me when I came to Dublin, with a bottle of excellent claret; and if I live to publish my *Summer Ramble*, Patrick Campbell shall know (though he was afraid to meet him at the Keys in High-street) there is not a better neighbour, nor an honester man in Dublin.'

As I passed from the King's Stationer, I met with an honest gentleman, with whom I was formerly acquainted in London; it was my worthy friend Dr Smith, of College-green near Dublin; his character is above my pen, yet I may venture to say, he is a man of extraordinary sense; and the only physician I durst commit the care of my health to in the whole country: he invited me to his house, and when I came, gave me a hearty welcome; and for his treat, though it was very genteel,[85] yet nothing seemed so agreeable to me, as the doctor's company.

I went next to Brides-street, to pay my respects to Mr Wallis[86] (a Member of Parliament) and his lady, with whom I had the honour to be acquainted (at Tunbridge) some years ago; I shall ever acknowledge the generous reception I met with here, neither can I forget to characterise his extraordinary kinswoman, 'whose wit and beauty set her above the rest of the fair sex, as having nothing in her but what bears witness to the perfection of her mind and body.'

> Saint-like she looks, a Syren if she sing;
> Her eyes are stars, her mind is everything.[87]

I would say something too of that ingenious gentleman who is tutor to Mr Wallis's children; for I found (in some discourses I had with him) 'That his learning and knowledge had outstripped his years; but he's too modest to bear the character he justly merits; and to speak of him by halves is what I can't approve of; so I'll wave his character with only saying, the conversation I found here, was the most agreeable of any I met in Dublin.'

Durst I here attempt Mr Wallis's character, I might say of him (as was said of the Lord Russel[88]) that he's one of the best of sons, the best of fathers, the best of husbands, the best of masters, the best of friends, and the best of Christians; and his lady is no way inferior to him for virtue, wit, and generosity. And her kinswoman, Madam More (not she that I spoke of before, but one I had the honour to know at Tunbridge) is so like her in these qualities, that were their faces alike too, you could not distinguish one from the other.

In some conferences I had with Mr Wallis about my Welsh travels, I told him I found the following epitaph on a tombstone in Conway-Church, which for the remarkableness of it, I inserted in my journal; it was this, 'Here lies Nicholas Hooks of Conway, Gent. the one and fortieth child of his father, William Hooks, Esq; by his wife Alice; and father of twenty seven children himself,' which was a matchless instance of a fruitful family. To which Mr Wallis replied, he heard there had been a troop in Ireland, wherein one mother had two and twenty of her own children listed. Having taken my leave of Mr Wallis, his lady, and the rest of his family, my next visit was to Sir Henry Ingoldsby,[89] a member of the Privy Council in Ireland, and a gentleman of near ninety years: when I came to his house, I sent up my name, and Sir Henry ordered his gentleman to bring me into a private apartment where he was. When I entered the room, Sir Henry received me in a courteous manner; I told him I presumed to wait upon him, to enquire whether my reverend father, Mr John Dunton, was not once his chaplain and that if he was, it must be forty years ago. Sir Henry did not at first remember it; but sending to his lady, she sent word that she did call to mind such a person; but it was added, my father did not live in the house, but used to come often to it. I then asked Sir Henry, whether one Mrs Mary Hall did not live with him when my father was in Ireland? for that in my father's will, was this expression, 'Item, I bequeath unto Mrs Mary Hall, servant to Sir Henry Ingoldsby when I was in Ireland, five pounds, if ever demanded, or she be not dead, for her friendly offices to me, during a great sickness I had in that kingdom.' I told Sir Henry, I was not put upon this enquiry by the executrix, but that providence having brought me to Ireland (though twenty years after my father's death) I could not be satisfied without enquiring whether this Mary Hall were alive or dead: to which Sir Henry did me the honour to reply, it was a great piece of justice in me, if I had no advantage in it myself: to which I returned, I had not, any farther than to see to the execution of my father's will. But as to this Mary Hall, Sir Henry told me, he supposed she died at Limerick, she marrying thither from his house, to a rich, but ill-natured man, which soon ended her days.

Pardon me (Madam) for the digression of this story: I had some hesitation in my own breast about making this enquiry; I was not satisfied that conscience obliged me to it; but not being satisfied without doing it, I did it; and it yet appearing to me a moot case, because I was none of the executor, I leave it to your determination, whether I could be under any obligation in that case or no? This discourse being ended, I gave Sir Henry an account of the reason of my coming for Ireland; with which he was so well pleased, that he promised to give me and my auction all the encouragement he could; for which I returned him my humble thanks, and so took my leave of Sir Henry for that time.

Madam, I dare not presume to give Sir Henry's character; to describe so great a man would be a theme big enough for my ingenious friend, Mr Charles Wormington (a person of great modesty and worth, and perhaps, the most ingenious poet in all Ireland);[90] but though I shan't presume to characterise this ancient knight, yet I shall say (what everyone does) 'That he has the repute of a person of great honour and probity; and of that great judgment and experience in affairs of state, as renders him worthy of the dignity of a privy-counsellor, which he has been for many years; and though he is now arrived to fourscore ([a]ten more than the age of man) yet he enjoys his

a. Psal. 90:10.

health and strength to admiration; which shews him to have been a person of great temperance, and perhaps (on this account) he has no equal in Ireland, or it may be, in the whole world.'

But to proceed in my rambles: having taken my leave of Sir Henry Ingoldsby, in my way home, I met with Lieutenant Downing, my former fellow traveller to New England. You can hardly imagine, Madam, how agreeable a thing it is to meet with an old friend in a foreign country: it was some thousands of miles off, that we were last together; and we were equally surprised to meet each other here: there was in his company at that time, Captain Annesly, son to the late Earl of Anglesey, to whom I had the honour to be related by my first wife.[91] We stayed not long in the street, but went to drink at the Widow Lisle's in Castle-street; whither I chose to go, out of a principle of gratitude, hers being the first house that received me in Dublin: after a health to the King (and some others of our friends in England) we talked over our New-England[a] ramble: after this I told the lieutenant of my brother Annesley's death; at which he was highly concerned.[92] This discourse being ended, Captain Annesley told me, that the earl, his father, had written an excellent history of Ireland; but it was in such hands as he believed would strip it of some of its choicest remarks; and (Madam) this is likely enough; for there are some men in the world, which are afraid of following truth too close, lest it should dash out their own teeth. I then told Captain Annesley I had printed his father's memoirs[93] (the copy of which I purchased of Sir Peter Pett) and he could not but think them genuine, because of that great amity which was between the earl his father, and Sir Peter Pett.

To give ye (Madam) the captain's character, 'He is a most accomplished gentleman; not (as a wit observes) that thin sort of animal that flutters from tavern to play-house, and back again all his life; made up with wig and cravat, without one dram of thought in his composition; but a person made up of a solid worth, as grave as he is witty; brave and generous, and shews by his humble and courteous carriage, that he is, and was born, a gentleman: and for the lieutenant (my old fellow-traveller) I must say he has much address, and as great

a. This *American Ramble* is now ready for the press.

a presence of mind, as was ever seen; he is most agreeable company, and perhaps the best friend I had in America.'

After three hours spent in this conversation, I went to visit Captain Townley and his lady,[94] as also one Madam Congreve; who were all three my fellow-travellers in the coach from London to Chester: 'The captain is a person of great honour and worth;' and so is his lady; but of these I shall say more in my *Summer Ramble*; but more particularly of Madam Congreve.

In my way home I called upon Mr Kingson,[95] and his wife (styled, the most ingenious) 'who, though she has enemies, perhaps as little deserves them, as any woman in Dublin'; and though I should get hatred by saying this, yet my way is, to do as I'd be done by, and to speak as I find; but having characterized the most ingenious, it is fit next, that I speak of her lord and master: 'He's a very honest sober man, and one of that great modesty, that I heard he went forty miles to demand a debt, which yet he was so civil and courteous as not to ask for when he came there.' But it grew late, so leaving this loving couple at their fine embroidery, I went next to pay a visit to Mr Lum[96] in Castle-street (a Member of Parliament) and one of the chief bankers in Dublin, whom I made use of, to remit my moneys to London: 'He is a person of great integrity, has a good estate, and is punctually just and honest in his dealings. And to complete his character, he's a gentleman of extraordinary sense, which he has the happiness of being able to express in words, as manly and apposite as the sense included under them. He treated me with much candour and respect, as long as I stayed in Ireland. His chief manager of his business, Mr Purefoy, was also very obliging, and ready to serve me upon all occasions.

'Captain Davis,[97] who was also a Member of the House of Commons, gave me a most obliging welcome to Dublin, at the Garter-Tavern in Castle-street: if I should attempt this gentleman's character, it would be to his prejudice; for all that I can say will come far short of what ought to be said. For sense, wit, and good humour there is but few can equal, and none that exceed him; and all these qualities are accompanied with great humility.' Madam, I had first the honour of being acquainted with this gentleman at Tunbridge Wells (the same year Mr Wallis, his lady, and Madam More, drank these mineral waters) and this occasioned the repeating of what conversation we had formerly had at Tunbridge; from this we fell to discourse of the customs and manners of the Irish; the Captain told me, they were naturally a very generous people, and so kind to strangers, that they would go twenty miles to set a man in the right way; and if he happened to be benighted, they would give him the best entertainment they had, and even lie out of their own beds to accommodate him. To this piece of generosity I might add (what was told me by a another person) that they will likewise offer him the convenience of a bedfellow, in case they have a daughter capable of serving him: but (Madam) I will not be answerable for the truth of this, which I only relate as what has been told me; and should it be true, my opinion is, they carry their generosity a little too far. In my further conversation with Captain Davis, I asked him what eminent writers they had in Ireland, and especially whether any of the fair sex? To which he replied, they had a very celebrated female poet (one Mrs Taylor)[98] who had written her own life to a wonder, when but ten years of age. Madam, I thought these remarkable passages worth noting down in my journal; but nothing did so much affect me as a piece of antiquity that the Captain told me he had seen with his own eyes. He had seen a woman very perfect in all her senses (excepting hearing) who said she was under laundress to Queen Elizabeth's chief laundress, and he told me he believed her to be 130 years old, which for a woman (naturally subject to more infirmities than men) I think to be very extraordinary; and I believe your ladyship will be of my opinion. I had the honour of enjoying the Captain's useful and most pleasant company for about two hours, when night coming on we parted.

The day following (in the afternoon) I went to see my ingenious friend, Mr Thwaits; his person is the very picture of Mr Dangerfield,[99] to whom (Madam) he is so very like, both in person and address (Oh what would I give for such a near resemblance of Iris and D—ne!)[1] that I may well affirm, if you have seen one, you have seen the other: and having said this, I need not tell you what an extraordinary man he is: 'Mr Thwaits is a gentleman of a very obliging temper, and I believe is as generous to strangers as any man in Dublin; he may, without compliment, be called an accomplished person; he can do almost everything, and it is hard to say what he does with the greatest grace. And as to wit, I was really afraid to hold any argument with him, for I found he could say what he would, and prove what he said; and in this too, he resembles the ingenious Dangerfield. In this alone Mr Thwaits has the advantage, that his whole life has been so unblemished, even envy herself can't fix a blot upon him. His lady is an extraordinary person, worthy of such a husband; and they both gave me a very generous welcome, worthy of themselves.' In our conversation, I affirmed, that a good wife generally, if not always, makes a good husband; which is undoubtedly matter of fact: for though we suppose the husband to be the worst of men, and one that abuses his wife in a villainous manner; yet his[2] spouse, if she be a good wife, by her meek and patient suffering under such abuses, cannot but some time or other (as long as he's a man) be overcome by the patience of his wife, and at last be brought to compassionate her wrongs; and in time this compassion may turn him to the ways of virtue: but then she must be as well a good wife, as a good woman; for there are many pious women that are far from being good wives. She must be one that's of a good humour, and always appear so to her husband; and if in time this does not make a husband better, he ought to be herded with the brutes, and not reckoned amongst human creatures. And yet after all (Madam) I am afraid that some such brutes there are in the world; but this will make nothing at all against my assertion, because there is no general rule, but admits of some exceptions.

My next visit was to the Lady Sands (Mr Thwait's sister). I had the honour to meet her first at Mr Shaw's (a bookseller on Corkhill) where she invited me to her house (here I had the good luck to meet my ingenious friend Mr Thwaits a second time). 'My Lady Sands is a person of great piety, and extraordinary sense; and I found in those few minutes, I had the honour to enjoy her company, that her husband is as happy in a tender, discreet and obliging wife, as any gentleman in the kingdom of Ireland.' In this visit I had the favour of some discourse with her eldest daughter, whose beauty, virtue, and good humour is equal to that of the best ladies in Dublin. The Lady Sands' husband is Mr Clarkson, son to Mr David Clarkson, the late Nonconformist, so deservedly famous for his learned works.[3] This gentleman I was formerly acquainted with, and if I don't mistake, he was in New-England in that very year that I rambled thither; but though we had been old acquaintance, I missed him in this visit, and never had the happiness to see him, whilst I was in Ireland. At taking my leave of my Lady Sands, she was pleased to send recommendations by me to her mother-in-law, now in England.

From my Lady Sands' house I went directly to my auction, and in my way thither I met the ingenious Mr Wright, an ensign[4] in the Army, but a person of great perfections, both of body and mind. Madam, this gentleman reconciles the lion and the lamb exactly; for being a commission officer, in the field he seems made only for war, and anywhere else for nothing but love. 'He is naturally brisk and gay, yet one of a very compassionate temper; and I see by him that pity never looks so bright as when it shines in steel: but why do I praise particular virtues, when he excels in all? He does nothing but what looks very handsome, and there is a charm in the meanest, and something most bewitchingly pleasant in the most indefensible of his actions.' He was much surprised to see me in Ireland; for he was brother to one that had been my apprentice, which was the original of our acquaintance: we met again by appointment that night at the tavern, with one Mr Young,[5] a gentleman of the College, and another gentleman to me unknown. The ensign told me, he had that day the honour of dining with her Grace, the Duchess of Ormond, which led us to discourse of the matchless virtues of that noble lady, and other subjects, which I now forget. Mr Young also obliged me so far as to settle a particular friendship with me; and I wish I deserved the honour he did me in that matter; for he's a gentleman of great humility, and I believe (if I may judge by those few minutes I spent in his conversation) never read of a virtue which he did not forthwith put into practice. One part of our conversation related to the ensign, who, though the possessor of so many excellencies, yet continues a single man, which gave us occasion to wonder, that none of the Dublin ladies had engrossed[6] so rich a treasure to themselves. We had appointed another meeting before I went away, to drink my bon voyage; but wind and tide (which stays for no man) hurried me away; so I was disappointed of my intended happiness, and forced to be so rude as to leave Dublin, without taking leave of some other friends.

Having left the ensign (and my new friend Mr Young) I went next to pay my respects to the Reverend Mr John Boyse, whose ingenious answer to Bishop King, and several others of his curious composures, have so justly recommended his learning and piety to the world. Madam, I have already sent you this gentleman's character, and shall speak further of him in my *Summer Ramble*. He gave great encouragement to my auction, as well for my own sake (as he was pleased to tell me) as for my reverend father-in-law, Dr Annesley's. He is now preaching on the four last things: his subject was heaven, when (Mr Larkin and) I heard him; and he preached in such an extraordinary manner on that subject, as if (with St Paul) he had been in the third heaven himself, and was returned to relate what he had seen.

I next visited Mr Sinclare,⁷ another Nonconformist minister, in Dublin. 'He is a most affectionate preacher, and a person of a sweet disposition, and extremely obliging.' He gave me a hearty welcome to his house, having been before acquainted with me at Bristol. Some discourses we had about persecution, occasioned him to tell me, that a Nonconformist meeting was suppressed at Galway by the magistrates there, whilst a popish meeting was suffered to be kept unmolested. He spoke very honourably of my father-in-law, Dr Annesley: and promised me, if I came again, I should have all the encouragement that he could give me. I heard him preach on the 30th of September, on Mark 9. 24. about faith, on which he made an excellent sermon.

Nor was my happiness less in being acquainted with Mr Emlyn,⁸ who is Mr Boyse's assistant. I met this gentleman several times at my auction; so that I find he was one of my benefactors. 'He's a very solid, rational, judicious divine, and lives the doctrine he preaches.' I heard his sermon to the Society for Reformation, at New-Row, on 1 Sam. 2:30. This sermon is since printed, and I wish (Madam) I could send it to ye; for some that have read it, say a better sermon was never published.⁹

As to the Reverend Mr Nathaniel Weld,¹⁰ though I had no personal acquaintance with him, yet I went several times with Mr Larkin to hear him; once more particularly, when he preached on the 130th Psalm, about forgiveness; his whole sermon was very excellent, but I took more particular notice of the following passages: 'We live upon forgiveness every day: what joy would forgiveness make in the

black regions! The devils never had the offer of a Saviour; but we are
still in the land of hope.'

Madam, I have already given you a short character of this pious,
learned, and excellent preacher, and shall say no more of him here,
but in my *Summer Ramble* I shall give his and his brethren's characters
at large; for, Madam, to confess the truth (though I go now and then
to hear a divine of the Church of England, as I told ye before) yet
that I more frequently hear the dissenting ministers: I don't know
how your ladyship will relish this? for I don't remember in any
discourses we had in Dublin (where I had first the honour of being
known to you) that you ever mentioned your going to any meeting;
but whatever your practice or thoughts are in this respect, I must
acquaint you, that I practise nothing that I think unlawful; and am
very willing (when your ladyship has answered those twelve hundred
uncommon diverting subjects that I intend to send ye in so many
distinct letters) to defend my practice in this matter; for (Madam)
there are but Thirty-Nine Articles of the Church of England, and
the Presbyterians (who are a religious and conscientious people) approve
of thirty-six of them, and the rest are (justly) called indifferent; so
that (Madam) if hereafter you'll give me leave to write to ye on this
subject, I shall endeavour to prove (in several letters) that my going now
and then to a meeting is no unnecessary separation, or any departing
from the true Church (for such I esteem the Church of England).

Madam, having visited the Nonconformists, my next ramble was
to Mr Harman, a young gentleman, and son to Colonel Harman[11]
(a Member of the House of Commons). In this visit, my friend Mr
Larkin was with me; where, after mutual salutations, (and sitting
down by a good fire) we fell into a pleasant chat, first of antipathies
in Nature; and here Mr Harman told us a story of a gentleman that
bought a muff; this person had a natural antipathy against cats, and
therefore desired the furrier, who sold him the muff, that it should
not be lined with any cat-skin; which the furrier (who lived in Essex-
street) assured him it was not; upon this the gentleman bought it,
and designed to wear it home, but by that time he came to Crane-
lane (which was not above a bow-shot from the furrier's) the gentleman
fell into a swoon, and was taken up for dead; but upon the taking
away the muff, he came to himself again, but fell into a great rage

against the furrier, threatening to kill him; which he having notice of, got out of the way.

Mr Harman's discourse being ended, I next told the story of my aversion to cheese when I was young; and how my father's causing me to eat it unknown, had like to have killed me; which aversion notwithstanding, I afterwards overcame, and now love cheese as well as any man. We then discoursed of the antipathy that cats have to men; and of their taking away men's breath when asleep, with other things to that purpose: this led us to talk of sympathy, and the wonders thereof; and more particularly of Sir Kenelm Digby's[12] sympathetical powder, and the great cures wrought by it. From hence we fell to talk of a third wonder in Nature, viz. men's walking in their sleep; of which Mr Larkin gave a memorable relation of a house supposed to be haunted, which was only occasioned by one of the gentleman's daughters, who walked in her sleep every night; which was at last discovered by a stranger's having courage enough to lie in the room said to be haunted: this naturally led us, in the fourth place, to talk of apparitions; and here Mr Harman asked me what I thought of a spectrum's assuming a human shape? I assured him they might; and to confirm this, told him the story of one Joseph Chambers, who appeared to Mary[a] Gossam (with whom I was well acquainted) in that very night-cap which she put upon his head when she had laid him out.

This story of Chambers appearing after his death led Mr Larkin to tell another of an apparition he had seen in Staffordshire in his youth, which he thought had been a living woman, till he saw it vanish; adding, that he looked upon the denying of spirits, and their appearing to persons after death, to be the next degree to atheism.

After about two hours spent in such agreeable conversation, we took our leave of Mr Harman, 'Who is a gentleman of a fine presence, and of a most sweet and affable temper. He is now in the bloom and beauty of his youth; and his great ingenuity and close application to his study do justly render him the growing hopes of his father's family, and may in time to come render him an ornament to the College.'

a. This Mary Gossam is still living.

I am afraid, Madam, I shall tire you with this tedious relation of my visits; but I hope your goodness will pardon me; for it is necessary to be thus particular, that I may silence the lying tongue of Patrick Campbell, who has had the impudence to say, that I kept company in Dublin, with none but a kennel of scoundrels: whereas you see (by the visits I made) that I was not acquainted with one scoundrel in Dublin, except himself, and the Brass in Copper-Alley.[13]

This naturally brings me to acquaint your ladyship, that among those I employed to bind up books for my auction, 'I had to do with one that I call Brass, a man poor and proud, unacquainted with honour or good manners; to supply the want of which, he is well furnished with conceit and impudence.' Being thus qualified, he was looked upon by St Patrick[14] as a fit tool for him; and accordingly chosen for his auctioneer, though he knew not how to read the title of a Latin book. But the gentlemen of Dublin, who had been genteelly treated with wit and sense at my auction by Mr Wilde, could not bear with the gross ignorance of a Brass Hammer; so that Patrick was forced to discard him in a week's time, and put a better man[a] in his place. This Brass knowing the necessity I was under of having my books bound in order to sale, resolves to make me pay a rate for binding, not only beyond what was given in London, but even beyond what was given by the booksellers of Dublin: I found, Madam, I was in his hands, and remembered the proverb, that he that's in a boat with the devil, must land where he can. There was a necessity of having my books bound, and I was forced to comply with his unreasonable rates. How this consisted with justice and equity I leave you to judge; but those were things Brass never troubled his head about; for when he brought me in his bill, he overcharged even his own unreasonable agreement, which I refused to pay; but offered to refer it to one Mr Servant (a binder in Golden-lane) with whom I had made the same agreement as I did with him; but Servant being a very honest man, Brass refused to have the thing decided by him, because then he was sure it would go against him; and therefore this fellow (who for his impudence I call the Brass in Copper-Alley) serves me with a token[15] from the Lord Mayor, to appear before him,

a. Mr Shaw of Cork-hill.

which I accordingly did (as I formerly hinted in p. 176 of the *Dublin Scuffle*) and having told his lordship what I had offered, he was pleased to say, it was a very fair proposal I made him, and to dismissed us both, which was all he got by his two-penny token.

Having done with this scoundrel (to use St Patrick's phrase) I will next give you an abstract of Mr Servant's character, who, though of the same function, is the direct antipodes to the Brass of Copper-Alley; this being as eminent for honesty, fair dealing, truth, and justice, as the other is for pride, conceit, and ignorance. But Mr Servant's reputation does not need a foil to set it off: 'For he is well known in Dublin to be all that I here say, but I shall add to the good character he has already, that I never met with a more scrupulous or conscientious man in my whole life; he's punctual to his word in the smallest matters, and one that manages all his affairs with discretion: courteous and affable in his conversation, and ready to do everyone what good he can. In short, his life is the exemplar of a Christian's practice.' But leaving Thomas, &c. hard at work (for he's a very industrious man) my next visit shall be to Mr Fey, an eminent lawyer in Dublin. He was a benefactor to my auction, and my very sincere friend: and to say the truth, whatever the lawyers are in other countries, yet in Ireland they are the best gentlemen and the best Christians.

From hence, to close the evening, I went to take a dish at Pat's, 'who is a fair-conditioned man, and very obliging to all his customers: loving to do business without making a noise on it. It was here I sometimes met with Mr Pitts, an honest and ingenious attorney, a man of good worth, and unblemished in his reputation. Madam, he talks finely (dresses his thoughts in curious language) and has good nature in his very looks; he is a true lover of the present Government, and a brave assertor of English liberties, in opposition to popery and slavery.' I would say more of the ingenious Pitts, but that I shall meet him again in my *Summer Ramble*.

Madam, just as I left Pat's, I met with my worthy and ingenious friend, Dr Wood, physican in Kilkenny, with whom, and Dr Smith, I spent some agreeable hours, of which expect a fuller account in the conclusion of this letter; and also in my *Summer Ramble*, where you'll also meet the discourse I had with a gentleman about the Earl of Meath's hunting pig, which will be very diverting.

And now, Madam, as your several directions to me informed you of the changing of my lodgings,[16] so I think it proper here to give you my reasons for so doing.

My first lodgings was at a counsellor's[17] in Wine Tavern Street, who being in some danger of overtaking the law (for he had out-ran his own practice) left his house, and as it is supposed, the kingdom too. Yet I must say, 'As to his conversation, he's a gentleman' (though under a cloud) and sings ("I'll find[a] out a kinder, a better than she," beyond any man in Christendom) and as for his lady, she deserves the following character: 'She's discreet and witty, the best of wives; and I hear, has the name for being a beauty'; it is true, I never thought her so, but I am no judge, I find; for she's bright and fair; and those that admire a r—d colour, cry, There's no sun but in her eyes; but as famous as she is for beauty, I must own, while I lived with her, I saw nothing but what was modest and honourable; and I shall ever have some kindness for counsellor H— as he was the occasion of my being acquainted with my worthy friend, Mr William Wainwright; 'who, though he lives a bachelor, is a person of strict modesty, and has the symptoms of a good Christian; for he's sincere in what he says, and is as religious in all his actions; and to crown his character, he's a person of great humility, and of a most sweet natural temper; and (Madam) I must say, there's no virtue I'd wish in a friend, but I find it in William Wainwright.' He was the first acquaintance I had in Dublin; and we were so little weary of one another, that he was one of those that saw me a-shipboard (when I left Ireland) though to the hazard of his life, for I sailed in a sort of a storm.

And as I thank H— for bringing me acquainted with this worthy gentlewoman, so I'm obliged to him for the favour he did me in first making me known to the virtuous and ingenious Mrs Edwards, whose character (Madam) I shall here give you: 'She's a country gentlewoman, of admirable perfections of body and mind; modest to the highest degree, and of a most agreeable conversation; with which, for my own part, I was very much delighted; and I am ready to flatter myself, mine was not altogether ungrateful to her; and how can you

a. 'Tis a line in a new song.

blame me (Madam) to think thus, since a lady of your quality has not disdained to grant me the honour of a correspondence with you.'

Apelles, the famous painter of Greece, when he was to draw any curious picture, would have several celebrated beauties before him, that he might draw an eye from this, a mouth from that, and a mien from the other, &c. Had Mrs Edwards lived in the time of Apelles, he need not have hunted about for beauties, for he had found them all in this virtuous person; so I'll descend (for my general character does set her in a full light) to a more particular description of her: 'And I'll begin first, with her face, which is neither oval nor long; her hair is black, or near it (and then I need not tell ye it is charming). As to her eyebrows, they are a great ornament to her face, and look as exact as if the hand of Art and Nature had been at work. Excellently well proportioned is her nose, not sharp nor big; but gives a noble air to her face. Her mouth little and pretty; her lips of a charming red;

> And do like to the Twins of Cupid's Mother,
> Still kiss, because in love with one another.[18]

'Her teeth are even and well set, and look as white as snow. Her eyes (her tempting eyes) full of fire and briskness, and tempered with an attractive languishing. As to her neck and breasts, they are the best sized that ever you saw, and of a dazzling whiteness, as well as her arms and hands. As to her body, it is small, and of a curious shape, and is supported with handsome legs, as I do believe (for I never saw them). As to her stature, she is of a little pitch; and is so neat, so free, so disengaged, that there's few like her (save Rachel Seaton,[19] whose picture she is) and Mr—— who unsuccessfully attempted her chastity, swears at her virtue, and often wishes she had fewer charms. She has a noble air in her walk, and has the dress, looks, and behaviour of a gentlewoman; and wants nothing but a fortune to make her so: in a word, she has something so distinguishing in her whole person, that when she was single (for you'll hear by and by she's married) she more distressed her husband's liberty, than others did with all their art, and more curious dresses; so much for her person.

'As to her mind, which is the charm of charms (you know, Madam, I ever thought so) she's pious, but not a jot reserved; and has more devotion in her heart than eyes. As to her wit and singing, it so strangely surprised me that day she went with the counsellor to Malahide (which adventure you'll have in my *Summer Ramble*) that I am hardly yet come to myself; for I could not conceive how a female could have (in that mean cabin[a] where she dwells) all the politeness and accomplishements of a court. As to her heart I can say say nothing, and it is not fit I should; but (Madam) this I'll say (by being a platonic lover; for I am same in Dublin as I was in London) she allows me all the liberty I ask, or virtue will give, which can't be much; for I have a wife of my own, that's (far) more charming in my eye, and one I love above all the world; besides, I am by nature as cold as ice, and I believe (if I may trust my eyes and ears) that she's chaste, so much as in thought. And as she's very innocent, so of consequence very charitable, and speaks ill of nothing.' Madam, she has other extraordinary qualities I could tell you of (for this is but a hasty draft of this excellent person) but here's enough to shew what Mrs Edwards really is, and what all her sex should be.

And now, Madam, who'd think that a person of such virtue should have any enemies? But as Dryden says, *The butt of envy still is excellence*;[20] and she is not without slander, though (I had almost said) she as little deserves it as virtue itself; but the very reflections she meets with (as well as her real virtues) do but add further to her good character; for it is none but scoundrels (I mean such as would corrupt her virtue and can't) that give her an ill word; she's proof against the blaze of gold: then no wonder if a town bull (such a one as A —— S——) should abuse that virtue he can't debauch; such as these reflect on a woman, not because she's lewd, but because they find her too spiritual (too platonic) for their embraces; it is this, like Aesop's fox, makes them cry, *The grapes are sour*.[21] But the bad word of a lewd person is the best encomium a virtuous woman can have; for it is by the judgment of sober people that a reputation stands or falls; and by all such Mrs Edwards was highly valued. I am told, that no less a person than the Countess of Meath honoured her with a tender friendship: the Lady Davis and Madam Gilbert do the same; and she's as kindly received in Mr Usher's family: Mr Magee and his wife

a. At Bally Many

(persons of great piety) scarce covet any other company. Mrs Brown at the Currow[22] has a particular friendship for her; Mrs Parsons, Mrs Ware, Mrs Ryley, have the like; and wherever she boards, they are scarce a minute without her. Then, Madam, I shan't ask your pardon (or Valeria's either) for my giving this tender character of Mrs Edwards; for as you are both virtuous persons, you'd surely be angry with me, should I forbear praising what so much deserves it. Besides I am mistaken in both of ye, if your great innocence does not set you above suspicion (it is only guilty people are jealous); or if it does not (to tell you the plain truth) my innocence is too great to need my concealing my thoughts of her; and the rather still, as her husband has said (in the presence of Mr Larkin) that had he ever been jealous of her (as he never was in his whole life) yet that he should now believe her virtuous, for my having a good opinion of her; which I don't speak out of ostentation, but to shew her innocence, and my own too. Thus (Madam) you see, by my character of Mrs Edwards, that my virtue is safe enough; for though she's a woman (a thing in petticoats) yet my love is all platonic, to all, except Valeria. (So angels love, and all the rest is dross.) Really, Madam, I am such an enemy to running astray, that I heartily wish adultery were death; and that it were burning in the hand, so much as to kiss another man's wife: but there's no sex in souls; and I think it a duty to admire virtue where ever I find it; then surely none but scoundrels (I mean such as are lewd themselves and so can't help suspecting of others), will censure a friendship, where the body has nothing to do; but if any are so vile as to nibble at this character, they may go about their business; for, Madam, I have not an acquaintance in the whole world (except yourself, and the dear Valeria) but may find enough in his own breast to damp his censuring me, or that virtuous person whose character I here send ye.

You see (Madam) by these words, that I am a great enemy to compliments; nay, I often wish (as Valeria says) that there were no such thing in the world; and when I am dead and gone, I would willingly come again to contradict anyone that reports me otherwise than I am, though he did it to honour me.

Madam, having given ye the true character of Mrs Edwards, perhaps you'll be desirous to know who it is that is blest with so great treasure; which obliges me to give ye the following character of Mr Edwards: 'He is a person of an indifferent stature, neither tall, nor short; and though no pretender to any extraordinary perfections, is far from being contemptible: he has a martial countenance, and a mind like it, and will turn his back to no man in a just cause, nor receive an affront from any. He has not indeed the politeness of a courtier, but an honest bluntness, that better becomes him: his only fault is, he has been formerly unkind to his wife; but he has made her part of amends, both in a just acknowledgment, and by an extraordinary fondness since; upon which she has been so generous to forgive him; and he takes it so very kindly, that they are now as happy a couple as any that live in Ireland.'

Having left the counsellor's house (where I came acquainted with Mr Wainwright, and Mrs Edwards, whose characters I have here sent ye) I retreated for a little air and solitude, to Arbour-hill (a mile from Dublin) to the house of one Mr Thomas Orson, who with his wife (an ancient couple) seem to be like Adam and Eve in Paradise; he employing himself in his garden (where I have a nosegay every morning, my landlady finding I admire flowers) and she within doors in making of milkwater,[23] of which she distills very large quantities. I think myself obliged to let them live as long as this paper holds, in gratitude for those parental tendernesses they shewed me when I languished with the bloody-flux[24] (which seized me in this house). Neither were they less kind in curing a bite given me by a [a]great mastiff, who had one night torn me to pieces, had not the drawing my sword baulked his attempt.

Madam, the reason of my coming to this country seat was my great indisposition of body, and being tired with the hurries of Dublin; I have in my *Dublin Scuffle* given ye my thoughts of a private life, for I am as great an admirer of it as your ladyship is of gardens; and I suppose you won't blame me for it; for the three first men in the world were a gardener, a plowman, and a grazier; even the great Cowley, that had known what cities, universities, and courts could afford, broke through all the entanglements of it; and which was harder, a vast praise; and retired to a solitary cottage near Barn-Elms,

a. One of the beasts I fought at Ephesus.[25]

where his garden was his pleasure, and he his own gardener;[26] whence he gives us this following doctrine of retirement; and may (as William Penn says) serve for an account how well he was pleased in his change. The first work (says he) that a man must do to make himself capable of the good of solitude, is the very eradication of all lusts; for how is it possible for a man to enjoy himself while his affections are tied to things without himself. The First Minister of State has not so much business in public as a wise man has in private; if the one has little leisure to be alone, the other has less leisure to be in company; the one has but part of the affairs of one nation, the other all the works of God and Nature under his consideration. There is no saying shocks me so much, as that which I hear very often, that a man does not know how to pass his time: it would have been but ill spoken by Methusalem in the nine hundred and sixty ninth year of his life;[27] the meaning of all this is no more than that vulgar saying, *Bene qui latuit, bene vixit*;[28] He hath lived well, who hath lain well hidden; which if it be a truth, the world is sufficiently deceived; for my part I think it is; and that the pleasant condition of life is in incognito: what a brave privilege it is to be free from all noise and nonsense; from all envying, or being envied; from receiving and paying all kind of ceremonies: our senses here are feasted with the clear and genuine taste of their objects, which are all sophisticated in courts and cities. Charles V, Emperor of Germany,[29] after conquering four kingdoms, &c. resigned up all his pomp to other hands, and betook himself to his retirement, leaving this testimony behind him concerning the life he spent in that little time of his retreat from the world, that the sincere study of the Christian religion had in it such joys and sweetness as courts were strangers to.

Thus, Madam, have I sent you the true reason for my leaving Counsellor H —, and betaking myself to a private life; wherein, not only antiquity pleads for me, but the example of Cowley, and the best and greatest men of the age.

And, Madam, as I am charmed with a private life, and with every day a green prospect, so there is a dainty one adjoining (Mr Orson's house) my present quarters; where I often wander up and down to think of you, and the dear Valeria. I told you before, it was my fortune to travel; and even in Dublin itself, I am not without my rambles: one I make to represent[30] Draper's Gardens: the other Stepney Fields: another St James's Park: and when I pass through Skinner Row (where the scuffle was) methinks I am in Cheapside, and shall soon be at the Raven in Jewin-street, the only house on earth[a] I love. Pray, Madam, let me know if it stands in the old place; it is a mighty pleasure for us travellers to hear how matters go in England. But as much as I love the Raven, I thought myself very happy at Mr Orson's (I mean as happy as I could be without Valeria). But how uncertain are worldly comforts? For I had not (Madam) sojourned many days at Mr Orson's house, but I fell sick (as I said before) of the bloody flux, the usual distemper of the country, and many times fatal; so that I might have just apprehensions of a speedy dissolution of my earthly frame, I being at best of no strong constitution: to say I had no fear of death at all upon me under these circumstances, would favour more of an hardened insensibility of heart, and pagan ignorance, than the piety and consideration of a Christian; but herein an enumeration of the particulars of my past life was presented to me, and things appeared with very different aspects, but yet not so frightful, but that through the divine goodness, I had hopes left of the remission of all my sins, upon the sole account of my Saviour's merits; but I dare not be so presumptuous as to say my faith amounted to an assurance of my eternal salvation: yet I may say, I began more seriously than ever to consider what I was; whence I came; and whither I was going? For (Madam) as I said before, a near prospect of death makes the world, and all things in it, appear with a quite different face from what it did. The belief I should now die, made me to think why I lived; where I should be buried, and what would become of me after death? I now began to review the whole course of my life; and whether, if time would [b]unweave my life again to the first thread, I would live just as I had done?

Ah! Madam, the fashion of the world passes away; and a sick-bed presently convinces us of the vanity of riches, honours, pleasures; how mean and contemptible do these things appear in the eyes of a dying man? They can't help us to a good conscience, give a minute's ease, or save from the grave: sure I am, whilst my distemper lasted, would

a. As is hinted in the *Dublin Scuffle*.   b. See my Farewell to Dublin.

anyone have given me the whole world, I could have thought of nothing but the terrors of death, the certainty of judgment, the glories of heaven, the torments of hell, the comforts of a good conscience, and what I must do to be saved, with the necessity of a good life; and though through mercy I am now recovered, I hope to the end of my life I shall think of the world just as I did when I thought I was leaving it; and to this end I desire death may be much in my thoughts, and the remaining part of my life a continual preparation for it. We read of one, that every time he heard the clock, cried, Well, now I have one hour less to live. I wish I could imitate this good man; however, I will look upon every day as if it were my last, so that when death comes in earnest, I may be ready and willing to die; and after death I doubt not but my body will rise again; I will therefore no longer spend my hours in pampering of that which will be food for worms. But I will not, Madam, enter upon all the conceptions and ideas I had in this sickness, of the future world; some of them being perhaps more the fancy of my own brain, than any true representation of the thing itself: but it having pleased almighty God to make my illness of a short duration, I shall from the more melancholy scene of death, pass to the more pleasing actions of life; and take the liberty to acquaint ye, that I now began to visit my friends, and to take some innocent diversion abroad: but (Madam) no pleasure is lasting with me (I find); for I had not been long recovered, and able to walk abroad, but I was hurried from my Dublin paradise (I mean Mr Orson's house) for Mr Wilde (who managed my auction) being just now arrived from London, I was forced to remove to Mr Landers's in Capel-street, that I might be nearer my business. 'Mr Landers's character resembles that of old Jacob, being a plain but sincere hearted man; and his wife as good a landlady, and one of the best of nurses for an infirm person,' which was then my condition; nor must I forget honest Kate, their servant, whose readiness and care to please me supplied her want of understanding (point-work).[31]

But that my condition in my absence from Valeria might truly resemble that of a pilgrim, who is continually in motion, I was forced to remove yet nearer my auction, upon the information I received of my porter's being turned thief; so that from Landers's house I removed to Mr Cawley's at the Tennis-Court in Wine-Tavern-street.

'Mr Cawley is a very humble and agreeable person, civil and obliging to all his lodgers; and I must say (to do him right) to me in a very particular manner; and so was his wife also, who is a very ingenious, discreet, and prudent person; and both of them expressed an uncommon concern at my parting with them, which was not until I came[32] for England;' nor must I forget my kinswoman Juggee (as I used to call her) who was their trusty servant.

Thus, Madam, I have briefly given you an account of the reasons and causes I had for my several removes from one lodging to another; and how happy I was in meeting with kind landlords. And were I in England again (and I cast longing looks that way every day) I'd say more in their praise; but, oh, this cruel distance! Well, had I the same advantage of speed to send unto you at this time in this place, as they have from Scandaroon,[33] when, upon the coming in of any ship into harbour, they used to send their letters by pigeons to Aleppo, and other places; I say (Madam) had I such an airy postilion, I'd send ye these occurrences more at large.

Madam, if you should ask me, which I liked best of my four lodgings, my answer is, I looked upon them all as places I must quickly leave, which made them all indifferent to me; but could I have enjoyed Valeria there, I should have given the preference to Mr Orson's, his curious gardens being very delightful, and his house a (private) country seat.

Thus, Madam, I have given you a brief account of my way of living in Dublin; with which (had I had Valeria's company) I should have thought myself very happy; for through the divine goodness (abating my first fit of sickness) I enjoyed a competent measure of health; those other indispositions I sometimes met with, served only as mementoes, to put me in mind of preparing for another world; and even under them, I was cheerful and well contented; having (though not exempt from human infirmities) no guilt of any wilful sin lying on my conscience; so that all troublesome thoughts were banished from my breast, and I passed away my life with great delight.

And now being pretty well, I had a mind to ramble into the country for a little conversation among the Irish (of which more anon) and to view the cabins, manners, and customs, &c. of the Dear Joys;[34] but the company I met in Dublin was so agreeable, I could not presently leave it; and which made it yet the more delightful (after my recovery) I sometimes conversed with Counsellor Kairns, Counsellor Stevens, Mr Bourn, Mr Bosworth, Mr Crawcroft, men eminent for piety, wisdom, learning, and all other virtues; by whose conversation I improved my own understanding; and found that the knowledge of my own ignorance was a great step towards being a good proficient in the school of wisdom.

When I could not have such company, I gave myself to reading some useful book or other (the Bible having always the preference) and afterwards to writing my *American Travels*, and *Summer Ramble*, both which I begun and finished in Ireland.

I enjoyed also (especially when I lay at Mr Orson's) the pleasure of walking in a delightful garden, well furnished with the most curious herbs and flowers; whose various colours delighted my eye, and their fragrancy my smell: besides which, I had the satisfaction of a lovely prospect; southwards, towards the city of Dublin, I had the silent murmurs of the river Liffey in my way; westward I had a full view of Kilmainham Hospital, which at that distance (being seated on the summit of a hill) was a very agreeable prospect. To the northwards (or rather the northwest) I had the pleasant sight of a village called Cabra, which was pretty near; and at a greater distance, the fine town of Finglas, seated on a hill, where I had a noble prospect of the sea, and of all the ships in the harbour of Dublin.

Sometimes I would walk down from my lodging to the river-side, which was not a mile from it, where the pleasant rills of running water were extremely delightful.

At other times I would walk through those green meadows from the end of Stony-batter to the Cabra, which is a village about a mile from my lodging, full of stately trees, which gives a pleasing shade, and delightful prospect. From whence, as I came back, I had the sea and harbour directly in my view.

And sometimes, Madam, I walk to Chapelizod, to visit the Lord Clonuff, who is president of the illustrious house of Cabinteely, and confers honours as freely as a prince, though with more ceremony than those of the round-table: during the time of my last being there, he created no less than four noblemen, of which the Duke of Froom was one; the Marquess of Swan-Castle carrying the sword, and assisting at the cermony; but more of this in my *Summer Ramble*, where you'll have the history of my Lord Clonuff at large, with a merry account of the original of the house of Cabinteely, and the honours the president has conferred; with an exact list of the nobility created by the said president.[35]

Sometimes I would, for my diversion, ride out a few miles, either to Santry, Swords, or Malahide, a place as eminent as Billingsgate for people going to eat oysters there: and that which made these little journeys more delightful was that I had now, though at a distance, the sea within my view, which I like well enough on shore, but not on board, for I am always sick on the ocean.

Sometimes I walk along the strand, up to Clontarf, which, when the tide is in, is very pleasant; and the next day perhaps I take a ramble to Donnybrook, Drumcondra, Rathfarnham, Palmerstown, and whither else my fancy leads me.

And sometimes I went to the Dublin bowling green (perhaps the finest in Europe) either to divert myself by playing, or look on those that did; where I have seen the gentlemen screwing their bodies into more antic postures than Proteus[36] ever knew; as if they thought the bowl would run that way they screwed their bodies; and many times would curse it when it did not. And while I thus looked on, I could not but reflect how like the jack[37] is to the world, which most men covet with the greatest earnestness, but very few obtain. And when sometimes I saw a bowl (played by a skilful hand) lie very near her, it has in one small moment, by the unlucky knock of a succeeding bowl, lain at the greatest distance from it; and others have in the same instance, been laid by[38] the jack, that never thought of it: just so it is with the things of the world; some that with toil and industry have gotten an estate, by one or other unforeseen disaster, have in a moment lost it all; when some perhaps that never expected it, by the same accident that quite undid the other, were made rich. So fickle are riches, which as the wise man tells us, make[a] themselves wings, and fly away.

At other times, I have gone further off, and visited some of the Irish cities; and the first I rambled to was Kilkenny, where I was introduced to the acquaintance of my worthy and ingenious friend,

a. Prov. 23.5

Dr Wood, by the following letter, written by an eminent person in Dublin, and which I'll insert here, not out of vainglory (for the praises he gives me shews that his love had blinded his judgment) but that your ladyship might the better see (by that inquisitive temper which he found in me) what variety you are like to have in my *Summer Ramble*.

The letter I delivered to Dr Wood (from my friend in Dublin) was this following, viz.

> Dear Doctor,
> The bearer hereof, Mr Dunton, is my friend (and as such you will look upon him, as a very good and honest gentleman); he goes to your town to look about him, and see the place for some days; I pray oblige me so far as to let him have your assistance to see the Castle, and such other things as his curiosity leads him to, for he is an inquisitive person, and a man not unfit for travel: all the favours you do him shall be thankfully acknowledged as done to
>
> Your
>
> Dublin, Septemb. 12. 1698.   Humble servant, &c.

This letter had that effect, that Dr Wood and his lady gave me a hearty welcome, and afterwards brought me into the company of several gentlemen of worth and quality. I came to Kilkenny on Friday night; and the next morning the doctor carried me to view the Castle (the noble seat of the Duke of Ormond) of which I shall give a most particular account in my *Summer Ramble*. And indeed the alcove chamber and Duchess's closet, &c. will deserve a large descripton; but leaving these noble apartments, I shall next proceed to tell your ladyship, that adjoining to these lodgings is a great window that gave us a view of a private garden of pleasure, I think finer than the Privy-Garden in Whitehall, or any walk I had ever seen: being hugely pleased with this pleasant prospect, the doctor had me up one pair of stairs, where on the left hand was the room where the Duke of Ormond dines; it was high roofed, very large, and hung all round with gilded leather; the table-cloth was laying as we entered the room; and I do think the curious foldings of the damask napkins, and pretty knick knacks that adorned the table (had I time) were worth a particular description; and the plate for the dinner was not less remarkable; there were three silver tankards embellished with curious figures, and so very large, that I believe, would his Grace have given me one of them, I could scarce have dragged it to my lodgings; there were two silver salvers, as large and noble, and a voider[39] made of silver, big enough to contain all, as I perceived it did. Leaving this noble dining-room (for what's dinner or plate either, to a man that has no right to it) we ascended two pairs of stairs, which brought us into a noble gallery, which, for length, variety of gilded chairs, and the curious pictures that adorn it, has no equal in the three kingdoms, and perhaps not in Europe; so that this castle may properly be called the Elisium[40] of Ireland: and were not the Duke and Duchess better principled than to forget heaven for the sake of a perishing glory, they little think of mansions hereafter, who have such a paradise at present to live in. But to return to the description of this noble gallery: the first thing I saw remarkable in it (and indeed the top-glory of all the rest) was the picture of the Duchess of Ormond; the face was finished, but the other parts wanted more of the painter's art;[41] but I must say of her Grace's picture, that were all the beauties in the world lost, it might be found again in this painted face; though that, too, is as much outdone by the original, as a real flame exceeds that of a painted one. There is also a design[42] of drawing the Duke's picture, and when both are finished, Dr Wood told me they are designed to adorn the Tholsel (a sort of Exchange) to which will be added the pictures of all those that have been Mayors of Kilkenny. The next picture I saw remarkable was the Lord Strafford,[43] frowning (like a mere Nero) on the messenger that brought him ill news from the parliament. By him hung the Duchess of Modena's[44] picture (late Queen of England); and next to her stands the late King James, drawn like a man afrighted; so that I told the doctor, I judged the painter designed to draw him just as he looked when he fled from the Boyne.[45] Near King James's picture hangs the picture of an old usurer, telling money,[46] and a few by him, which (considering the moral of it) is pretty enough to behold.

Here is also the picture of that chaste prince, Charles I who (if you'll take his word on the scaffold) never strayed from his queen, in thought, word, or deed; and next to him (if I don't mistake) hangs H—— that lustful Queen:[47] here is also the picture of Charles the Second, that royal libertine; but the Queen Dowager I did not see. There were great variety of other pictures, but I reserve the rest for my *Summer Ramble*. But (Madam) I can't forbear telling ye at present, that at the west end of the gallery stood the *Several Ages of Man*, perhaps the finest draft that the world has seen. On the left side of the room hangs the picture of Vandyke,[48] as drawn by himself, (and a curious thing it is) and a little below him is a Scotch lord, drawn in that garb he hunts, or goes to visit the clans.[49] And I might not forget to tell ye, that on the south side of the gallery hangs two royal buds, Charles the Second, drawn when he was four years old; (Ah Charles! What innocence didst thou out-live?) and James the Second, in hanging-sleeves; and it had been well for England, and himself too, if he had put off his body with his little coat and so exchanged one heaven for another. I should next proceed to describe the pictures of the Duke of Ormond's family, for in this gallery and in Dunmore House (which I'll describe in my *Summer Ramble*) hang all the progenitors of this noble Duke; but to mention these in that manner I ought, would require an age. So (Madam) I must lead you out of the gallery (though with a sad heart, to leave such a pleasant place) and next describe the bowling green adjoining to this princely seat; it is an exact square, and fine enough for a duke to bowl on; nay, Church and State were here at rub, rub, rub, and a good cast;[50] for when the Dr and I come to the green, the Duke was then flinging the first bowl; next troul'd the Bishop of — Colonel R— with about four inferior clergy; at paying our bows to the Duke, he gave us the honour of his hat in a very obliging manner; and here I'd attempt his Grace's character, had not the ingenious Cibbers[a51] done it before me; but I may venture to add to what he has said in the Duke's praise, that the most he has said of him is the least of what he merits; for the Duke is a man of a truly brave and noble spirit, and lives in the world like one that is much above it.

After making our devoirs[52] to the Duke, the Dr and I left the bowling-green, and went next to see the garden adjoining to the

---

a. In his poem published at the Duke's landing in Ireland.

castle, which (though gone to decay) is now repairing by a young gardener from England, and will in few years be as pleasant as the Spring-Garden near Fox-hall. Having seen what rarities the castle, garden and town afforded, the Dr and I parted over a glass of claret; and in the afternoon, I rambled to Dunmore[53] (another seat of the Duke of Ormond's) and is the finest house in Ireland: on some of the floors of this house, I told twenty-four rooms; the staircase that leads to them is hung with curious landscapes, and is so very large, that twenty men might walk abreast; had the house but another branch it would be a perfect H. But without this additional beauty, perhaps it may boast of more rooms than are to be found in some whole towns. Leaving this noble seat (after Peggy Corkran had shewed me all the rarities in it) I returned that night to Kilkenny; and from thence, the following Monday, took a new ramble to view the Boyne, and the ancient town of Drogheda; and whither I went afterwards, you shall know in my *Summer Ramble*. But, Madam, I ask your pardon, for I was going to leave Kilkenny before I had told ye of the chief rarities said to be in it; which are, that in this town there is

> Fire without smoke,
> Water without mud,
> Air without fogg.

I searched into this report, and found it a real truth; and that the fourth element, of earth, was also as pure.

I would here describe the town of Kilkenny, and give a particular character of Mr Mukins, the present Mayor, of Mr Philips, the Mayor elect, the Recorder, Aldermen, and Common Council-men, and several other remarkable things and persons in this place; I would also mention the odd adventure of a lieutenant that travelled with me to Kilkenny; neither would I omit to give you the heads of a remarkable sermon I heard in St Kenny [Canice] Church, where an eminent prelate told us, that look into all divisions of religion, as those of Rome and Geneva, &c. and you'll find (as they are against monarchy) that they have left the good manners to the poor Church of England. Madam, I humbly conceive this passage will deserve remarks (by a better pen than mine) as will several other notable strokes this good bishop entertained his auditory with; but though they are noted down in my journal, yet I reserve the rest for my *Summer Ramble*, lest they make my letter too voluminous.

So (Madam) at present I take my leave of Kilkenny, with only telling ye that morning I left it, Dr Wood wrote an answer to the letter I brought him from my Dublin friend, which I'll insert here, as it further shews how courteous the Dr is to strangers, and to me in particular.

The Doctor's Answer to the Letter I brought him from Dublin.

Dear Sir,
I received yours by Mr Dunton, whose stay here is so short, that I have not been able to shew him what civility I would, especially being every day hurried with country business. I hope to step to Dublin in a little time, and to have the opportunity of drinking a glass of wine with you and him; meanwhile a letter now and then would be acceptable to me, when your leisure will permit. I wish you all happiness, and am,

Sir,
Your affectionate Servant,
NATH. WOOD.

And so, good Doctor (with thanks for all your favours) I bid you and your ingenious lady, farewell.

Thus (Madam) you see, by taking notice of castles, gardens, antiquities, pictures, public fabrics, the rarities in nature, and the civility I meet in my generous friends, that (wherever I go) I still learn somewhat worthy of my knowledge; neither do I in such rambles omit anything that may instruct or delight me; and am much pleased with beholding the beauty and situation of places. Neither did I (in this country ramble) meet with any allay to my pleasures by the dullness or decay of my senses, for I found them all in their perfect vigour; besides, I found travelling got me a stomach, which made me eat coarser fare with a better appetite, though I saw little of that here, for the Kilkenny claret is the best in Ireland; and the Doctor's treats were still rich and noble.

Madam, having said so much of Dr Wood's civilities to me, perhaps you'll expect I should send you the Doctor's character; which I'll do, and his lady's too, that you may see how happy I was in their conversation: 'Dr Wood, like Luke of Evangelist,[a] is the beloved physician in these parts; and he really merits that great respect which the people give him; he's a complete gentleman; very kind to strangers, and obliging to the last degree: and I do think (if I may believe my eyes) he's the happiest man (except myself) that ever entered into a married state. Madam, I own a kind wife often makes an obliging husband of one that would otherwise be very indifferent; but this is not the Doctor's case; for he's a man of that sweet temper, that the worst of wives would be kind to him; but he had met with one of the best; then how happy is this couple, that seem to rival one another in kindness?' This, Madam, will raise your curiosity to know a little more of his lady, but I dare not attempt her character; but this I'll say, 'She[b] looketh well to the ways of her household, and speaks not a foolish word; and her thoughts are so new, so particular, that they raised my wonder to a great height. In the several visits I made the doctor (of which more in my *Summer Ramble*) I could scarce speak for admiring at everything she said or did. I'm sure, Madam, if you did but know her, you'd love Ireland (though it is a coarse place) purely for her sake.' But, Madam, the coach stays for me; so having left the Doctor and his good lady, suppose me now on the road for Dublin; and in my return thither, I was blessed with extraordinary company; they were these following, viz. a French brigadier, who gave largely to all the poor on the road, and I think had the soul of an emperor; for he treated[54] all the way from Kilkenny to Dublin; and had he spoke a language we had understood, I doubt not but our minds had fared as well as our bodies.

I.

Sure there's some wondrous Joy *in doing good;*[55]
Immortal Joy*! that suffers no allay*[56] *from fears,*
 Nor dreads the Tyranny of Years:

a. Col. 4. 14.   b. Prov. 31. 27.

By none but its Possessors to be understood;
    Else where's the Gain in being great?
Kings would indeed be Victims of the State;
    What can the Poet's humble Praise
    What can the Poets humble Bays
    (We Poets oft our Bays allow
    Transplanted to the Hero's Brow)
    Add to the Victor's Happiness?
    What do the Scepter, Crown, and Ball,
    Rattles for Infant Royalty to play withall,
    But serve to adorn the Baby-dress
    Of one poor Coronation day,
    To make the Pageant gay:
    A three hours Scene of empty Pride,
    And then the Toys are thrown aside.

II.

    But the delight of doing good,
    Is fixt like fate among the Stars,
        And deify'd in Verse;
    'Tis the best Gem in Royalty;
    The great distinguisher of Blood;
    Parent of Valour, and of Fame,
    Which makes a God-head of a Name,
And is Cotemporary to Eternity.
This made the ancient Romans to afford
To Valour, and to Vertue, the same word;
To shew, the paths of both must be together trod,
Before the Hero can commence a God.

Madam, having dedicated this poem to the memory of this generous man (whose bounty we lived upon) I proceed to acquaint ye, we had also in company a French major, a gentleman of good sense, but a little passionate.

Our third companion was Johny Ferguson, a very pleasant fellow, and one that did great feats at the Boyne. These three (with myself) were all the men that were in the coach; but we were not without a she companion, I mean the virtuous Mrs Hawksworth, who may pass for a wit; and if ever I go to Constantinople, it shall be on purpose to visit her ingenious son; and I must say, if he takes after his mother, he'll scarce meet his fellow, though he should girdle the world.

The time in such company flew too fast, and I began to wish the way to Dublin had been much longer. In our way home, we had debates concerning the spider's web, the curious work in a turtle's nest, the government of bees, the love of a spaniel-dog to his master, and upon other subjects; but I wave them here, designing all our disputes in the coach shall be part of my *Summer Ramble*.

I was no sooner come home, and had given some necessary orders about my auction, but I rambled to Drogheda, and paid a visit to the famous Boyne, so memorable for the victory King William there obtained over the Irish, though they were five to one; and that nothing might escape my view, that was worth seeing in Drogheda, Mr Wilde sent (by me) the following letter.

To Mr James Jackson, Son to Alderman Jackson in Drogheda

Mr Jackson
Mr Dunton being willing to see your famous town, and the River Boyne, where King William passed over, I desire you will help him to an horse, and either go with him yourself, or prevail with some friend of yours to go, that knows matters and things; I would also have him go into a currough,[a] that he may carry his boat on his arm afterwards. I am,

Your humble servant,
Richard Wilde.

That morning I rode to Drogheda, the air was sweet and kind, the fields were trim and neat, the sun benign and cherishing, and from

a. This currough is a boat made of such light materials, that a man may pass over the Boyne in it, and then wind up[57] so as to carry it in his hand.

everything I met, I received a civility; and which added still to my
happiness, I went in company with the minister of the Newry: 'He's
a divine of great learning and worth, speaks admirably, and inspired
a soul into all our company;' and in my *Summer Ramble* I'll attempt
his character at large. He treated me that night with a noble supper;
not for anything he found in me, but (as he expressed it) for the sake
of my being the son of a clergyman: when I had taken leave of this
generous person, I went to lodge with one Mr Watson, an apothecary
in Drogheda; I was hugely pleased with my new quarters, for my
landlady (though a Roman Catholic) was a very obliging, generous
woman; and for Mr Watson, I don't think there's an honester man in
Drogheda; I found him excellent company, and a very ingenious
man: 'His wit is ductile and pliable to all inventions (as well as to that
of the glister-pipe)[58] from a pin to a pillar, nothing was so small but
his skill could work; nothing so great, but his industry could achieve.'
After I had conversed a while with my new landlord, I went to
Alderman Jackson's to deliver Mr Wilde's letter; before I came to
Drogheda, Mr Wilde told me what a courteous person Mr Jackson
was; and when I came to his father's house, 'he received me in such
an obliging manner, that his favours did transcend report, as much as
they exceeded my desert. Madam, this gentleman resolves to live a
bachelor, which I could not but wonder at; for doubtless Nature
meant him a conqueror over all hearts, when she gave him such
sense, and such beauty (for he's a very handsome man). His wit
sparkles as well as his eyes; and his discourse charms as well as his
beauty; and I found by a little talking with him, that his mind is none
of those narrow ones, who know one thing, and are ignorant of a
thousand; but on the contrary, it is so very large, that although it
cannot be said Jackson knew everything equally well, yet it is most
certain, he can give an excellent account of all things; but though his
soul is enriched with every virtue, yet I thought the most remarkable
thing in him was his great humility and readiness to serve a stranger
(for I might pass as such, having never seen him, but a minute or two
in London).' Madam, meeting with such a friend as this, you may
well think I could never enough enjoy him; so leaving his father's
house, we went together to a place in Drogheda, where we fell into
company with several gentlemen, and particularly with Mr Singleton:

'He's a young sprigg of divinity, and might have stayed at Jerico[a] till his beard was grown;' but when he speaks, it is offhand (as they call it here) so that Nature seems to have made a present to him, of whatever a long study and meditation gives out by degrees to others: he preached in Drogheda church up on this text, *And Jacob[b] was a plain man, dwelling in tents*; and I think it was the most ingenious sermon I ever heard. But my design here is only to hint at things; so I leave this young divine, that I may come to acknowledge the generous treatment I met in Drogheda from Mr Kelsey (for I don't forget the token he sent by me to his friend, Sir Thomas Montgomery). This gentleman has a great deal of wit, and (which is rare in witty people) is master over himself; walks according to the rules of virtue, as the hours pass by the degrees of the sun; and being made of good humour, his life is a perpetual harmony; and by consequence is a great blessing to his wife and children, if he has any. After Mr Kelsey had given me a particular relation of the Boyne fight, and we had drunk a health to his friend in England, Mr Jackson carried me to visit the famous Walker (the ingenious translator of Epictetus).[59] 'He's an universal scholar; and I do believe, were all the learning in Ireland lost, it might be found again in this worthy person; and he's as pious as he's learned: he prefers conscience before riches, virtue above honour; he desires not to be great, but to do good; and is so very exact in all he says, that his words are decrees of wisdom.' When we came to this gentleman's house, his scholars were acting *Henry IV* and a Latin play out of Terence; they were all ingenious lads, and performed their parts to a wonder; but one Ellwood (who acted Falstaff) bore away the bell from the whole school. But Thieves! Thieves! (but no wonder, for I'm still in Ireland) for I had no sooner left Mr Walker's school, but I lost my cane, and a silver box. But (Madam) as thievish as Drogheda is, I can't but think with pleasure of Ireland, as it was there I had the honour to be first known to your ladyship. But more particularly I love Drogheda; where, for two days, the tears I shed for the matchless D—ne,[60] would not suffer me to walk abroad. Madam, it was here your advice was so very reasonable, and went so far towards drying up

a. 2 Sam 10. 15.   b. Gen. 27. 27.

all my tears. But though I've reason to love Drogheda, as it was the town where I grieved so much for D—ne; and as it was here I was blessed with your kind correction for my weeping more than became me; yet after all, Drogheda is a thievish place; and had I but stayed a week in it (as I could scarce forbear, Jackson and Kelsey were so obliging) I had surely been reduced to primitive innocence; so I left Drogheda in a sort of fright, after I had seen the Mayor (who is so clear in his trust, that his virtues shine to Dublin, and from thence to London), the Aldermen, the Primate's house, and the mount that gave me a sight of the Boyne, that fatal place to the popish army. So, dear Jackson, farewell, till I see thee again in London; where thou shalt be (though not so nobly treated, yet) as welcome to me, as I was to you in Drogheda. And (Madam) the truth is, he that confers on me favours so generous as Mr Jackson did, steals me from myself, and in one and the same act, makes me his vassal, and himself my king. When I receive a favour from any man, till I have repaid it, my mind (as Feltham[61] says) is a prisoner; and till a ransom be paid by a like return, I'm kept in fetters, and constrained to love, to serve, and to be ready, as the conqueror desires it.

Madam, I stayed but three days in Drogheda, and am now returned to Dublin, where I hear from England the sad news of the death of my owl (it is the bird of Athens)[62] and has been peering for mice in my house and garden for three years; so out of mere love to this old servant, I fell to write an *Essay in Praise of an Owl*, and have spent about twenty sheets in telling the virtues of poor Madge. A learned author wrote in praise of barrenness; the great Erasmus wrote in praise of folly, and, a late writer has wasted a great deal of paper in praise of a cow's-tail; and I could not see why I might not follow such examples, and endeavour to praise my owl. I confess, Madam, this subject is not grave enough for your perusal; or if it was, I'd write an elegy on poor Madge, and send that and his character for your reflections; but this is a hint by the by, neither will I presume to be thus merry without your leave. But (Madam) I had scarce finished my owl's character (which would take up a month to transcribe fair) but my old rambling maggot began to crawl, and bite afresh: upon which I immediately grew as fickle and wavering, as if I had drunk liquor distilled from a woman's brain's; and nothing would satisfy me now, till I was on another ramble; and the next I took was to Ballymany,[63] to see the Curragh, and the running for the King's Plate. Madam, by this speedy rambling again, you see the toil of keeping accounts was a labour too tedious for my mercurial brains.

Being now resolved for a new adventure, on Tuesday, September 11, I took a coach to one Gent's,[64] a mile out of town, where my horse waited for me; and here my stars threw me upon good company (one of which they called Climene);[65] we set out for Ballymany with the early sun, yet, we had his company but a little while; for just as we got to the Fox and Geese (it is a house your ladyship has heard me speak of) he withdrew into an apartment behind a cloud, so that the day now grew very unpleasant; but our company was so agreeable, that bad weather was little minded.

As soon as we had left the Fox and Geese, Climene gave us a pleasant account of the silly raving of a certain female, whose character expect in my *Summer Ramble*: this relation occasioned a conference about scolding wives, and ducking-stools, which lasted till we came to Rathcoole, where we treated Climene with a bottle of cider (for we all thought a pot in our pate was a mile in our way);[66] having refreshed ourselves in this little town, on we rambled for Ballymany, diverting ourselves on the road with what we had seen and heard in Dublin; and at last we fell to discourse of innocence, and the great chastity of the brave Lucretia;[67] we had no sooner entered on this discourse, but a sure emblem of chastity (an old man of fourscore) limps out of his little house (which I'm sure he might carry on his back) to beg our charity; not (Madam) but we had charity, but having no pence about us, we dismissed this venerable beggar with a promise of being kind as we came back.

The next spectacle we were entertained with was the sign of a church; I call it so, for it was only a steeple standing like a may-pole, without any prop, but a tall pillar, and which to us (at a great distance) seemed little bigger than the spire it supported; we could not but wonder at the humour of these people, that they should fancy only a steeple without the necessary appurtenances of vestry, pulpit, or chancel? but the next person we met told us, it was not the fault of the parish, but plainly the devil's malice to the preaching of God's word; for as fast as the building went on by day, the devil carried it away by night. I then asked, why the steeple had better luck than the other parts of the church? To this he replied, that the parish formerly had been very wicked; and that heaven permitted the steeple should be left standing, to upbraid the inhabitants. Madam, if what this fellow said was true (for we thought it a piece of banter), this steeple is high enough to be a warning to the neighbouring villages.

Being hugely pleased with this fellow's answer, we jogged on to the Naas; we had here stayed for a dinner, could we have persuaded ourselves to have lost the sight of a diverting passage then in view; it was a brace of Dear Joys, that had tied two loaded horses to an old hedge, whilst they formally unstrip, and without fear, or wit, fall to lousing themselves; Climene, who could be witty when and on whom she pleased, bid them be careful that they did not over-stock the ground.

I could not but laugh at this lousy sight; but these being common in Ireland, we left the consideration of this adventure, to discourse on the prospects then in sight; for now, let us turn to the right, or the left hand, we had a charming view of the country; not but a sight of Climene was beyond all we saw (for she's a perfect beauty;) yet (for variety sake) we would now and then look about us.

Madam, being now come to the Liffey (which all pass that go to the Curragh) that river was swelled so high, that poor Leander (as one in our company called himself) was forced to cross it with his Hero[a] behind him. I don't know what information Climene received from her friend Leander, but she was pleased to tell me, she understood I had a mighty passion for my first wife, and that she was a person deserved it; she then enquired, whether I loved any before her? I told her I did. She then asked, who the person was? I told her it was one Rachel — [68] who was so very beautiful, that a Venus might have been formed out of her person; and yet her wit did far exceed her beauty. Having said so much, Climene asked me a hundred questions about Rachel; as, Whether she was rich? What were her parents? How we came to part? And whether I continued to love her after I married Eliza? I told her I did not; but could not but own I took a mighty pleasure in Rachel's company before I knew Eliza (though after I

a. Climene

knew her, I scarce loved anything else); and because Rachel admired poetry, I made my courtship to the Muses too, that I might be the more grateful to her; and, Madam (can ye believe it), I had the good fortune to write something in Rachel's praise, which met with a kind reception; I first presented them to her (and she being tickled with my commendations) shewed them to her Scotch friends, and others; for Clara now (for so I called her) pretended to outdo me in tenderness. But (Madam) these poetic essays had an effect different from what I intended; for I designed by them, only to make my own addresses to her the more acceptable; but she, by shewing them abroad, got the name of a wit and (having acquired a reputation beyond what she had before) began to value herself at a higher rate, and to treat me with disdain; I was not so blind with gazing on her face, or charmed so much with her witty letters, but I could see with what contempt she treated me; and seeing, could not but resent it to that degree, that I thought it my duty to humble her; and in order to it, I sent her the following lines:

I.

Know Clara, since thou'rt grown so proud,
　　'Twas I that gave thee thy renown;
Thou'dst else in the forgotten crowd
　　Of common beauties liv'd unknown,
Had not my verse exhal'd thy name,
And impt[69] it with the plumes of fame.

II.

That killing power is none of thine:
　　I gave it to thy voice, thy eyes:
Thy sweets, thy graces, all are mine;
　　Thou art my star, shin'st in my skies:
Then dart not from thy borrow'd sphere,
Lightning on him that plac'd thee there.

III.

Treat me then with disdain no more,
　　Lest what I made, I uncreate;
Let fools thy mystick forms adore;
　　I know thee in thy mortal state:
Wise poets that wrapt truth in tales,
Knew her themselves through all her veils.

How Clara resented this poem, I never asked, for her pride had given me enough of her (pride was never yet found in a noble nature, or humility in an unworthy mind), and so I left her; and I appeal to you, Madam, whether I had not reason to slight her? As for Climene (my fellow traveller) she gave her judgment in my favour; and (Madam) I want to know whose part you'll take; for this is the wit I so often mentioned to D—ne; and it is your judgment (alone) that can determine whether I did well or ill.

As we walked along, Leander would now and then put in a word against Clara's inconstancy; but Wells (another of our fellow travellers) could not hear the story without railing at the whole sex; upon which Climene bantered them both. This urged them again to ask Climene, how many whining slaves she had murdered herself (for she was very handsome, and very witty) but (Madam) neither Climene, nor any of the company, would come to confesssion.

In such discourses as these, we passed away the melancholy day, 'till we came to Ballymany (our intended quarters). It is a small village of poor cabins, and an old castle, of which there is abundance in Ireland, built, it is said, by the Danes, long before the coming of the English into it; they are square strong buildings of stone, with a small door, and stone stairs, and windows like spikeholes, purposely for strength; for as the Danes enlarged their frontiers, they built these castles on them as curbs to the neighbouring Irish.

Madam, I have often had occasion in some of my letters, to mention these cabins, or huts, but now take the description of them:[70] 'They build them by putting two forked sticks of such length as they intend the height of the building, and at such distance as they design its length; if they design it large, they place three or four such forks into the ground, and on them they lay other long sticks, which are the ridge timber; then they raise the wall, which they make of clay and straw tempered with water, and this they call mud; when the wall is raised to a sufficient height, which perhaps is four foot, then they lay other small sticks, with one end on the ridge piece, and the other on the wall; these they wattle with small hazels, and then cover them with straw, or coarse grass, without any chimneys; so that when the fire is lighted, the smoke will come through the thatch, so that you would think the cabin were on fire: another sort of their cabins is made by laying one end of the stick upon the bank of a ditch, and the other upon a little bit of a mud wall; and then, when it is wattled, they cover it with heath-straw, or scraws of earth; and into this miserable place will half a dozen poor creatures creep for shelter and lodging; but their beds are upon such a firm foundation, that nothing but an earthquake can move them: instead of feathers or flocks, they use rushes or straw, which serves them without changing. Sheets they never provide, and to tell the naked truth, unless they can purchase a poor cadow,[71] which is not often, they ligg together like Adam and Eve before the Fall, not a rag to cover them, but themselves; which may be one reason why they so multiply; each little hut being full of children. They seldom have any partitions or several rooms; but sleep in common with their swine and poultry; and for second or third storey, you may look long enough e're you find any. But as the buildings of Versailles are so very magnificent, as not capable of such a description that may give a just idea of them; so these, in the other extreme, are so very wretched things, that perhaps the pen of the noblest architect would be very defective in describing them. Behind one of their cabins lies the garden, a piece of ground sometimes of half an acre, or an acre, and in this is the turf-stack, their corn, perhaps two or three hundred sheaves of oats, and as much pease; the rest of the ground is full of their dearly beloved potatoes, and a few cabbages, which the solitary calf of the family, that is here pent from its dam,[72] never suffers to come to perfection.' Madam, I should more exactly have described their dwellings or cabins, if I durst have adventured oftener into them; or could have stayed in them (for lice and smoke) when I was there.

But to proceed in my rambles: next morning early, without regarding any ceremony, we made our visit to a popish Father, who was just up, and wiping his eyes; the weather was very fair, and we stayed at the door (which had a little green field before it) until the room within was swept to receive us; the dew lay in pretty spangles on the grass, made by refraction of the sun beams: I had a mind to try the Father's philosophy, and enquired what the dew was? He told me, It was a wapor that fell upon the ground in the night sheason, and that the sun drawed it up again in the day;[73] but Climene told him it was an old and vulgar notion, and exploded by the newest philosophers, who were of opinion, it might be either the moisture which the horses of the sun shake from off their manes, when they were put into his chariot rising out of the sea; or that it might be Thetis's chambermaids had emptied Phebus's pot as soon as he was up;[74] or lastly, and that more probably, it was the sweat of the grass and herbs condensed by the cold of the evening air. Her notions made us all laugh, and the priest swore by St Patrick's hand, she was as witty as she was pretty; and put some other compliments on her, the best of which were much beneath what she truly deserves. The house was now ready, and the maid came to call us in, where we broke our fast, and prevailed with Father A — to accompany us to Kildare, where we were going to be merry; his palfrey[75] was presently saddled, and we mounted; we soon came to the Curragh, so much noised here. 'It is a very large plain, covered in most places with heath; it is said to be five and twenty miles round; this is the New-Market[76] of Ireland, where the horseraces are run, and also hunting matches made, there being here great store of hares, and more game for hawking,' all which are carefully preserved. They have a tradition (I fancy it was taken from the story of Dido's[77] purchasing so much ground as she could surround with an ox-hide, on which she built Carthage) that St Bridget,[78] the great saint of Kildare, begged as much land from one of the Irish kings, for a common pasture, as she could environ with her frieze mantle; the prince laughed at her, and bid her take it; she cut her mantle into so many small shreds, as when tacked together by their ends, surrounded all this Curragh or downs.

Kildare is an ordinary country-town, not near so good as the Naas, though it gives a name to the county, and is an episcopal see, though but of small revenues; and is now therefore united to the deanery of Christ-Church, which is the king's royal chapel in Dublin, as the bishopric of Rochester is to the deanery of Westminster in England.

It has in it the cathedral church, with two or three inns, and those very sorry ones; it has two fairs yearly, and a weekly market, and sends two burgesses to the Parliament; yet after all, it is but a poor place, not lying in any road, and not having any trade belonging to it; there are some shops with hops, iron, salt, and tobacco, and the merchant not worth forty pound. This county gives the title of earl to one of the family of the Fitzgeralds, formerly called Geraldines, who came over into Ireland among the first adventurers in Henry the II's reign; and is now the first earl here, as Oxford is with you; here we dined on a dish of large trouts, and with some bottles of wine made our selves merry; when we took horse our landlord told us we must accept of a dugh-a-durras[79] from him, which is a drink at the door; he had a bottle of brandy under his arm, and a little wooden cup, with which he presented each of us a dram; from hence we went about two miles backward towards the King's County,[80] to view the Earl of Kildare's chair; it is an old castle built on the side of a hill, which overlooks all the neighbouring country: I was told it was built by some of the earls of Kildare, as a watch tower, for which purpose it was very well placed.

From hence we had a lovely prospect towards the north, of a noble vale, part of which was covered with corn, and part with cattle, with some woods; among which were seen some houses of good bulk and shew, raising their heads; beyond these were hills, on which stood several great houses, a fine river ran through the valley; on another side the greatest part of the Curragh lay open to our view, which indeed is a noble plain.

After we had satisfied our eyes with staring about, we steered our course towards the Bog of Allen; which, though it be the greatest in Ireland, yet never was so famous as in the last rebellion, where the rapparees (who are a loose undisciplined people) had their rendezvous when they designed any mischief on the country, to the number of five or six hundred, and where they easily hid themselves when pursued; for as I am informed, this bog is near fifty miles long, with many woods in it, and some islands of very good and profitable land; as the island of Allen, which they say is worth eight hundred pounds per annum.

Madam, His Majesty, for encouragement to breed large and serviceable horses in this kingdom, has been pleased to give an hundred pounds per annum out of his treasury here, to buy a plate, which they run for at the Curragh in September; the horses that run, are to carry twelve stone each; and therefore there are several fine horses kept hereabouts for the race, in stables built on purpose. There is another race yearly ran here, in March or April, for a plate of an hundred guineas; which are advanced by the subscription of several gentlemen, and the course is four measured miles.

Madam, on Thursday the 13th of September, was the day of the race this year for the King's-Plate. There was a vast concourse of people to see it, from all parts of the kingdom. My Lord Galway (one of the Lords Justices) was present at the race, and other persons of great quality. I met on the Curragh (where the race was run) with my worthy friend, Mr Searl, whose character you have in my Dublin Farewell, and several others that I knew in Dublin; after the race was over, our company rode to Ballymany; at this village is a little thatched house, like one of our English country houses, built by the Earl of Meath. After we had seen all the rooms in this noble man's thatched house (which I design to describe in my *Summer Ramble*) we left Ballymany, and dined that day at the Naas, and reached Dublin about nine in the evening.

But (Madam) if the predictions of astrologers be true, such men as I am are very Mercurial folks, I mean the planet, not the mineral: for (Madam) you that know me will believe I never had any great occasion for it; I had not been long in Dublin before the itch of rambling broke out again upon me, though I once thought the fatigue of my Curragh ramble would have abated the sharpness of it, as effectually as brimstone[81] and butter does that in the skin; but what's bred in the bone, will never out of the flesh; and I among the other sons of Adam am in a literal sense born to great travels; and some people are surely so much delighted with the variety of change, that like other Epicureans,[82] they will purchase the fancied pleasure though thousands of difficulties that attend the acquisition: not impertinent to this, is what I remember to have read in the celebrated Mr Boyle,[83] of one who was born blind, because of the adhesion of her eyelids; and her parents living far in the country, from any physicians or surgeons, thought her malady incurable, until the time she was about eighteen years old; when, being called to London about some business likely to require a long attendance, he brought his blind daughter, with the rest of his family, to town; where the union of her eyelids being separated by a surgeon's lancet, she immediately perceived a thousand pleasing objects; she beheld, every minute, new things with admiration; and not satisfied with seeing, as soon as she could conveniently go abroad, she was every day on the ramble, as if she intended to make up for the losses she suffered by her former darkness; and when she became acquainted with the objects of the town, she begged leave to roam about the country, not without expressions of some inclinations to satisfy her eyes with a view of all the world could afford her. Of this girl's humour my landlord found me; for now (after I had settled the affairs of my auction) I travelled east, west, north and south; and (Madam) should I tell ye what Irish cities, towns and villages I next saw, I should lead you such a wild-goose chase, I should tire ye quite, but not myself, for I am never weary with travelling. But (as much as I love rambling) I have just now received a letter from Valeria (crowded with desires to see me) which will shorten my ramble, some thousand miles. I'll see but Europe, Asia, Africa, America, or so, that is all, and be in London by Plato's year;[84] not but I'm a huge lover of travels, and would gladly view 'the Globe Coelestial too (as I told the ingenious D—ne) before I return; I mean climb so high as to hang my hat upon one horn of the moon, and touch the North Pole with my middle finger.' But (seeing you admire I ramble thus) let me go down from the moon a little, to tell your ladyship, that had you but seen Italy (and those other countries I am bound to) you'd rather envy than pity my rambling fate.

Alas! Madam, to change my bed troubled not me, for I could sleep contentedly in America, Ireland, Wales &c. or in any place; for if I had the hardest lodging, I could dream of my Valeria with as much satisfaction, as if I had been sleeping on a bed of down; and when I awake, I please myself with thinking that in a little time I shall see her again: and wherever I ramble, I'm still content, for there's a wheel within a wheel, and nothing comes to pass by chance.

As to my very auctions, if things went prosperously there, I looked upon it as an effect of divine favour, and returned God the praise; if otherwise, it put me on examining myself, and humbling of my soul before my maker; and I look on all cross accidents as trials of my patience. And indeed, still upon self-reflection, I rather wondered that things went so well, than found myself concerned they went no better.

When Patrick took my auction room over my head, it was for him that I was troubled most; that he should deal so barbarously with one that never gave him any cause for it; I was well satisfied in my own innocence, and thought I was concerned to make the world so, by letting of them know the truth of things; and then to leave the issue to that wise Providence that best knows how to order all things for his glory and my good.

You may suppose perhaps (Madam) there are no beggars in Dublin, since I have all this while been so silent, and said nothing of alms-giving; but assure yourself (Madam) to the contrary; for to the best of my knowledge, I never saw them so thick anywhere else, in the whole course of my life; and how to carry myself in respect to these wretches, has been a matter which often disturbed me; to give unto all, is impossible; for a man then must be richer than Crœsus;[85] and not to give at all, is unchristian; but the main difficulty lies in the right distribution, and to relieve those who are most necessitous; but who can know this? For I have heard Bishop Hall say (he that was Bishop of Oxford) that once walking through Moorfields, a beggar followed him with great importunities, and desired him for Christ's sake to give him something, for he was ready to starve; the bishop (not thinking him a fit object for charity) told him, if he refused to give him anything, he believed he'd curse him; no, said the beggar, indeed Sir I won't; well then, said the bishop, I'll try thee for once; upon which the beggar fell a cursing and swearing at him like a very devil.—Madam, when I meet with such vile beggars as these, I serve them as the bishop did; but I am (Madam) if I don't flatter myself, naturally compassionate, easily affected with the miseries of other men in any kind, but much more when I see old age go a-begging; and it is such that have been the principal objects of my charity; and next to them, the blind. I never conceive the beggarman the more necessitous, by being the more importunate and querulous; and of this sort no man, I believe, has been attended with a much greater train: indeed I have heard your old eleemosynaries,[86] who have been trained up to the trade from their younger years (as I am satisfied many have been, both in England and Ireland) can, by long experience, and constant observation, readily distinguish, even in a crowd of men, a compassionate face; and will single him out, as I may say, to be the object of their importunities. But after all, Madam, in matters of the distributions of charity, the right hand is not to know what the left does.

And now, Madam, having given you some account of my *Conversation in Ireland* (both in city and country) and also given ye some hints of my several rambles in it, and what I observed in them, perhaps you may think by this time, I have seen enough of Ireland, to be able to give your ladyship some general character of it: I confess, Madam, I am very bad at descriptions, but a general character of the Dear Joys being what I formerly promised the ingenious D—ne, I shall now send it to you (her other self) and hope your goodness will be as willing to pardon all my mistakes in it, as hers would have been, had she lived to have read what I here send ye. Then give me leave to tell ye in rhyme,

> Off in the seas, and downfall of the skies
> With water compass'd round, a nation lies;
> Which on the utmost Western Ocean hurl'd,
> Fixes the *Ne plus ultra*[87] of the world.
> Water the bowels of this land does clog,
> Which the weak sun converts into a bog.
>
> The sun, whose great and generous influence
> Does life and warmth to every place dispense,
> O'ercome by th' innate venom of this air,
> Can't draw it out, but leaves the poison there;
> So true is what the natives vainly boast,
> No poisonous thing lives on the Irish coast;
> Because their air is with worse poison fill'd;
> So has a toad been by a spider kill'd.[88]

Perhaps (Madam) you may think I am too poetical, and may expect a more particular account of the country and people where my conversation at present lies; so I shall now proceed to a prose-character of the Dear Joys: and here I shall give ye a glimpse of the country; or, as it were, a general view of my Irish rambles. And, as an

Irishman is a living jest, it will be merry and pleasant; but a little mirth must be forgiven to a traveller, who has little else to keep him alive.—Then to proceed to the prose-character of poor Teague; and here I must first acquaint ye, 'That the gentleman who tripped lately to Ireland, calls it the watering-pot of the planets; and the French have named it, *le pott de chambre du diable*, the devil's piss-pot, seldom dry, but often running over, as if the heavens were a wounded eye, perpetually weeping over it.' It is said there is but one good thing in Ireland, and that is, the wind, as it is generally westerly, and sits fair to carry one out of it; which makes good the old saying, It is an ill wind blows no good.

Some of their chief cities are tolerably good, but most of them more populous than rich (Dublin excepted) for though they are thronged like hives, yet being for the most part thieves and drones,[89] they rather diminish than increase their stock;[90] and were it not for the honest English, and strangers amongst them, I am persuaded in process of time, they'd be all starved; so that of all the places I have yet seen, give me Ireland to wonder at; for my part, I think it is a sort of White Friars at large, and Dublin the Mint to it;[91] here's nothing but roguery; in every street you pass, you'll either meet with some highway tailor, or some errant unsatisfied pug, that drinks nothing but wicked sack.[92] But at Dublin they have a Recorder (who at present is Mr Handcock) 'who, besides the reputation that he has for his knowledge of the laws, has also acquired that of a courageous and just magistrate, impartially putting them in execution against lewd and wicked people, without regard to any degree of quality or riches; instances of which are frequently seen in his punishing swearers with two shillings for each oath, according to a new Act of Parliament; and setting insolvent persons in the stocks; and many of the strolling courteous ladies of the town have, by his orders, been forced to expose their lilly-white skins down to the waist at a cart's tail;[93] by which he is become, at once, the fear and hatred of the lewd, and love and satisfaction of sober persons.' Both Church-men and dissenters are joined in this noble work of exposing vice, and all little enough; for though whores are whipt every session (I saw seven but yesterday capering before the beadle) yet the prostitutes here are such very prostitutes, that I heard Mr T— say (an old fornicator in this city) that though he had spent his estate on a whore in Dublin, that his rival no sooner appeared, but she clung to the best chapman.[94] In this case (to use a term in my auction catalogue) he that bids most is the buyer; and if any difference arise, which the gallants cannot decide, miss lies with both, rather than lose a customer. So that you see, Madam, such things as chastity, wit, and good nature are only heard of here; such virtues as temperance, modesty, and strict justice (which your ladyship possesses in so high a degree) have the same credit with the beaus of Ireland, which the travels of Mandeville[95] find with us. I do not hereby design[96] anything of the true gentry, or nobility, amongst whom there are persons of as great valour, as fair estates, as good literature and breeding, and as eminent virtues, as in any of the most polite countries. But really, Madam, if you go into the country (as far as Galway) they are as bad, if not ten times worse, than I relate them; for the men here even steal into the world (lying hickle-de pickle-dey, they are half bastards) and ever after thieving is as natural to them as eating; and for this reason there's scarce a town without a pillory in it; Ballymany has one or two; Carlow has two or three (I think the strongest I saw in Ireland), Kilkenny I think as many; it was here I lost my ring, my gloves, and my very comb; and when I charge them with it, they cry, The devil burn them, if they are thieves; and swear by Chreest and Shaint Patrick, that they never saw it. Madam, I suppose you have heard of Irish evidence?[97] and I must say, a carted bawd[98] is a saint to them. I lay at Kilkenny but four nights, but here is such a den of pickpockets, that I think the thieves in Drogheda are saints to them.

I saw in my ramble to Kilkenny, that enclosures are very rare amongst them; much of their land is reserved for grazing and pasturage; and there, indeed, the grass being very sweet, and holding 'a constant verdure, it is (as a late author observes) indented in many places so with purling brooks and streams, that their meadows look like a new green-carpet bordered or fringed with the purest silver; yet hay is a rarity amongst them, and would cost them more pains than they can well afford, towards the making of it; therefore they seldom or never trouble their heads or hands about it. And then for their arable ground (as the same author observes) it lies most commonly as much neglected and unmanured as the sandy deserts of Arabia, or a ranting young gallant's old bed-rid spouse.'

JOHN DUNTON

Their women generally are very little beholding to nature for their beauty, and less to art; one may safely swear, they use no painting, or such like auxiliary aids of fucusses,[99] being so averse to that kind of curiosity (though they have as much need thereof as any I ever yet beheld) that one would think they never had their faces washed in their whole lives.

As to their misshapen legs (as a witty gentleman expressed it) I'll lay them aside, and next talk of their courtships.

Amorous they are as doves, but not altogether so chaste as turtles, desiring as much to be billing, and very frequently bringing forth twins, as the others hatch young ones by pairs. There needs no great ceremony or courtship, for they generally yield at first summons.

The men, as birds of the same nest and feather, differ only in the sex, not in their good humour and conditions.

Bonny Clabber and Mulahaan, alias sour milk, and choak cheese, with a dish of potatoes boiled, is their general entertainment;[1] to which add an oatcake, and it completes their bill of fare, unless they intend to shew their excessive prodigality, and tempt your appetite with an egg extraordinary.

Thus, Madam, have I given you a brief, but general character of Ireland, which I have intermixed with what I found by the Dear Joys, and what I say of these, I send to you as the character of the better sort of Teagues; for as for the wild Irish, what are they, but a generation of vermin? they have impudence enough to louse in the highway. I have seen six men at it together, and a mile farther, as many women at the same sport; and what is yet more shameless, the women were half naked. It is true, in the infant age, when the innocency of men did not blush to shew all that nature gave them (indeed because they did no more than that taught them) I should not have wondered at such sights; but considering the removes we are now from Adam, I could not but blush for them. If you peep into forty cabins (they are as spacious as our English hogsties, [a]but not so clean) you'll scarce find a woman with a sm—k[2] to her back, or a petticoat can touch her knee; and of ten children (for they are full of brats, for the reason I formerly hinted) not one has a shoe to his foot;

a. As was hinted before, in p. 225.

234

and when one laughs at their nakedness (as who can forbear that is flesh and blood) they cry, Fye! Fye! English mon, you see nothing but what ish her own. And these Irish parents are as proud as they are naked; and rather than dishonour (as they call it) their sons with a trade, they suffer them to beg for their daily bread; and for themselves, they are so lazy, that those of them that are not thieves (and of that number is scarce one in a thousand) they live by the drudgery of their poor wives.

But however careless they be of the living, they are mightily concerned for the dead, having a custom of howling when they carry any one to burial; and screaming over their graves, not like other Christians, but like people without hope: and sooner than this shall be omitted, they do hire a whole herd of these crocodiles[3] to accompany the corpse; who with their counterfeit tears and sighs, and confused clamour and noise, do seem heartily to bemoan the departed friend; though all this is with no more concern and reality than an actor on the theatre for the feigned death of his dearest in a tragedy. Instead of a funeral oration, they bawl out these or the like querulous lamentations: 'O hone![4] O hone! Dear Joy, why didst thou die and leave us? Hadst thou not pigs and a potato-garden? Hadst thou not some sheep and a cow, oat-cake, and good usquebaugh to comfort thy heart, and put mirth upon thy friends? Then, wherefore wouldst thou leave this good world, and thy poor wife and children? O hone! O hone!' with much more such stuff; to all which, Dear Joy, lending but a deaf ear, sleeps on till Doomsday; while home they go to drink, and drown the present sorrow; till the melancholy fit comes upon them afresh, and then they resort to the grave, and bedew it again with tears; repeating and howling their O hones with as much deep sense and sorrow as before.

They have many other extravagant customs daily practised at their weddings and christenings; but I reserve these for my *Summer Ramble*; so I'll conclude their character with only saying, they are a nest of disarmed, lewd, lousy, lazy rebels, that have a will, though not the power, to cut our throats.

I should next speak of their priests (fit shepherds for such wolves) but you'll meet them often in my Malahide ramble, with my conferences with them; so I'll drop them here; but will send ye a further account of my *Summer Ramble* by the next post: for, Madam, my mind is always with you, and my dear friends in England, though at present I am in the country of wrath and vengeance; but my ink is too clean for a further description. Yet, Madam, if you'd see the picture of poor Teague more at large, I'd refer you to a book called, *The Description of Ireland*, that ingenious author being the person I so often quote in this character of the Dear Joys.[5] Thus (Madam) by what I have said, you see what an excellent country Ireland is for a young traveller to be first seasoned in; for let him but view it as much as I did, and I dare undertake he shall love all the rest of the world much better ever after, except Scotland and France; of which more when I get thither.

If you ask, why I stay in such a vile country? Why, Madam, he that's in a boat with the devil, must land where, and as soon as he can; however, I'll stay till you answer this; and then, Hoa! for Scotland, France, Italy, and next the Hellespont (for my geography is now rectified by my learned friend); and it is very likely the length of my ramble will exceed the size of my hour-glass. However,

——All may have,
If they dare try a glorious life or grave.
Herb. Ch. Porch.[6]

And (if I hear Valeria's [voice] well) I care not whether I meet the sun at his rising, or at his going[a] down. All places are alike distant from heaven; and that a man's country [is] where he can meet a friend. Thus, Madam (when it is my duty) you see I can ramble in earnest.

Madam, having now dispatched the character of the Dear Joys, and troubled you with a thousand other impertinencies (that I may still keep within the bounds of my conversation) I'll proceed in the last place, to give you an account of the parting visits I made when I left Ireland and with those conclude this long and tedious letter.

Madam, in these parting visits, I had the happiness of being accompanied by my two friends, Mr Wilde, and Mr Larkin; I have

a. See more of this in the *Dublin Scuffle*, p. 104.

already given you a brief character of Mr Larkin; and it would be unjust not to give you Mr Wilde's, who has deserved so good a one from me, by his faithful managing my auction. 'Mr Wilde (Madam) was born a gentleman, being descended from an ancient family in Herefordshire, and brought up to learning till he was fit for the university; but his inclination leading him rather to a trade, he was bound an apprentice to George Sawbridge, Esq. the greatest bookseller that has been in England for many years,[7] as may sufficiently appear by the estate he left behind him; for (besides that he was chosen Sheriff of London, and paid his fine[8]) he left behind him four daughters, who had each of them for their portions, ten thousand pound apiece; and you may easily imagine, Madam, that serving a master who drove so great a trade, he could not fail of understanding books, without he was greatly wanting to himself: which he was so far from being, that I need not make any scruple to affirm, that there are very few booksellers in England (if any) that understand books better than Richard Wilde: nor does his diligence and industry come short of his knowledge; for he is indefatigably industrious in the dispatch of business; of which his managing my auction is a sufficient proof. He far exceeded even my expectation, and gave the buyers too, such great content, that had I not seen, I could hardly have believed it. Nor does his talent lie in knowing books only, but he knows men as well too; and has the honour to be personally known to very many of the nobility and gentry of the first rank, both in England and Ireland; and there's scarce a bookseller in Dublin but has a kindness for him. If anything hates him, it is the fair sex, for his living so long a bachelor; but they might excuse him, for he's too busy to think of love, and too honest to marry for money; and I believe scorns to creep (for it is beneath a man to whine like a dog in a halter) to the greatest fortune in Dublin; not but Wilde is of a courteous affable nature, and very obliging to all he has to do withal; and it is visible by his carriage, he was bred (as well as born) a gentleman. He had a good estate to begin the world with, but has met with losses; yet when his stars were the most unkind (as was confessed in my hearing by his raving enemy) he was still as honest as ever; and being always just in his dealings, he now, like the sun (just come from behind a cloud) shines brighter and fairer than ever: some men are only just whilst the world smiles; but when it frowns, they act such little tricks, as render their virtue suspected. But Wilde ever preserved his integrity, and is the same good man under all events; and as he was ever just in his dealings, so I must say his universal knowledge in books renders him a fit companion for the best gentleman; and his great sobriety, a fit companion for the nicest Christian; and to add to his reputation, where's a greater Williamite in the three kingdoms, than Richard Wilde? Madam, he has done such eminent service to the present Government, that he can't in time but meet with an ample reward; and it is but just to think he should be preferred, for he's a true lover of his Majesty and the present government; and a strenuous asserter of the rights and liberties of the people, and the Protestant religion, in opposition to popery and slavery; and this he has been from his youth; insomuch that for shewing his zeal in these things, even while he was an apprentice, the Tories and Jacobites (by way of derision) called him Protestant Dick. And by his management of my auction, he has given, both to myself and others, such a specimen of his judgment and great fidelity, that the Right Reverend the Lord Bishop of Clogher has done him the honour (in his letter to me) to tell me he is extremely satisfied[a] in Mr Wilde's fidelity. I do assure you, Madam, I am so well satisfied in his conduct herein, that were I to keep an auction as far as Rome itself, Mr Wilde should be the sole manager. But though Mr Wilde really merits the character I here give him, yet he being one whom I conversed so much with in Dublin (which my inclination would have led me to, if my business had not) he also is one of St Patrick's kennel of scoundrels; by which you may also know what to think of St Patrick, whose characters run counter to the sentiments of all honest gentlemen. And yet even in this Patrick is true to himself, and hereby declares he hates honesty and ingenuity, wherever he finds it.'[9]

But, Madam, I fear you will think me too long in my character of Mr Wilde; and I fear so too, with respect to your ladyship; though as to himself, I have not yet done him that justice he deserves from me; and therefore must remain in his debt, till I publish my *Summer Ramble.*

a. As may be seen in p. 45. of the *Dublin Scuffle.*

But I'll now proceed to the account of my parting visits; the first of which, was rather an invitation than a visit; to the house of Dr Phoenix, who invited myself and three of my friends, to wit, Mr Wilde, Mr Larkin, and Mr Price, to dinner. He lives in that part of the city which is called St Thomas Court; and is a peculiar liberty[10] belonging to the Earl of Meath: we found the Doctor discoursing with the dean of Killaloe, who dined with us: at our first coming, the Doctor saluted us all in a very obliging manner; but was pleased to pay me a most particular respect, in regard (as he expressed it) 'that I had so much obliged the nation in general, and himself in particular, by bringing so large a collection of valuable books into the kingdom.'

After this first greeting, the Doctor had us into his laboratory, and there shewed us his stills, and several great curiosities. Before dinner we had some conversation with the dean about the power of imagination; and the dean told us he knew a man at Barnet, near London, about forty years ago, that professed to have a constant converse with the dead; affirming, that while he was discoursing with others, he was at the same time conversing with the dead. This man would utter many strange expressions of his discourses with dead people, and pretended, by this converse, to tell things done at that moment a vast distance off, which afterwards, upon enquiry, proved true. But dinner then coming up, put an end to our conversation, and found us other business to do, than to talk to melancholy people.

After dinner, the Doctor's lady told us this remarkable story: that some years since, having been delivered of a fine girl, two ladies that were then the Doctor's patients, desired the baptising of the child might be deferred till they were able to go abroad,[11] because they had a mind to stand gossips to it. But the two ladies not being well enough to go abroad, so soon as they thought at first, a month's time was passed since the birth of the child, all which time it remained unchristened. But one day, as the Doctor's lady was in her chamber, looking for something which she wanted in a press, on a sudden she cast her eyes back, and saw sitting down in a chair, an uncle of hers, which had been dead several years; at which being somewhat surprised, she asked him how he did? And he, on the contrary, asked her what was the reason she did not christen the child? She told him it was because her husband promised two ladies should be gossips to it, and they were both yet indisposed, and could not come. The spectrum then called her to come to him, which she accordingly did, and he embraced her in his arms, and kissed her naked bosom, which she said she felt extremely cold. He then asked her where her husband was? And she told him where. After which, he charged her to let the child be christened the next day at three a clock in the afternoon; and then went away (she knew not how). When the Doctor came home, his lady told him what she had seen, and desired the child might be christened, according to the charge given by the spectrum; but the Doctor was unbelieving, and still resolved to defer it till the two ladies could come to be gossips. But the time prefixed by the spectrum being past, and the child not christened, that night the bed clothes were attempted to be pulled off, she crying out to the Doctor for help, who pulled the clothes up with all his strength, and had much ado to keep them on, his wife in the mean time crying out greviously that somebody pinched her; and the next morning, viewing of her body, they found she was pinched black and blue in several places. This did not yet prevail with the Doctor to have his child christened till the two ladies could come to be gossips. But a day or two after, when the Doctor was again abroad, and his lady alone in her chamber, there appeared to her another spectrum in the likeness of her aunt (who had been dead near 20 years before) with a coffin in her hand, and a bloody child in the coffin, asking her in a threatening manner, why the child was not christened? She replied (as she had done to her uncle before) that her husband delayed it on the account of two gossips which could not yet come. Whereto the spectrum (with a stern countenance) said, Let there be no more such idle excuses, but christen the child to-morrow, or it shall be worse for you, and so disappeared. The lady all in tears tells the Doctor of the threatening of this she-spectrum, and prevails with him to have it christened the next day; and in three days after, the child was overlaid[12] by the nurse, and brought home in a coffin all bloody, exactly like that which was shewn her by the last spectrum. The Doctor confirmed that part of the story which related to him; and as to the spectrums, his lady averred before myself, Mr Wilde,[a] Mr Larkin,

a. Mr Larkin, who was present at these relations, is now living in Hand-Ally in Bishops-gate-street.

and Mr Price, that what she related was nothing but truth. The Doctor (after the story was ended) made this inference from it, that the baptizing of infants was an ordinance of God, or else it had not been so much inculcated by two persons or spirits risen from the dead. But my friend Mr Larkin replied to the Doctor, that he was of a quite contrary opinion, and said it was a great argument against infant baptism, that the devil was so earnest to have it done. And when they both referred the matter to the Dean, he put it off, by saying we had some discourse before dinner of the power of imagination, and this seems to be some of the effects of it.

After this discourse was ended, Dr Phoenix caused a robin-red-breast (which he had in a cage) to be brought into the dining-room; where it entertained us whilst at dinner, with singing and talking many pleasant things; as 'Sweet lady, is the packet come? What news from England?' and several such expressions which the Doctor's lady had taught it. The smallness of this bird renders its talking the more remarkable; and perhaps, Madam, this robin-redbreast is one of the greatest rarities in Ireland, if not in the whole world; and I believe Dr Phoenix thinks so; for (as small as this bird is) he told me he'd not sell it for 20 guineas; and I do think, were it sold to the worth of its pleasant chat, it would yield a thousand.

After I had stayed the utmost limits that my time would allow me, I took my leave of the Dean, and then returning the Doctor and his lady thanks for their kindness (both to myself and my friends) we took our leave, the Doctor wishing me a *bon voyage* to England, and a good journey to London. But the Doctor is a worthy person, and I can't leave his house till I have given a character of him; besides, his civilities to me were so many and great, that not to acknowledge them (in a just character of him) would be very ungrateful; for he was a great encourager of my auction, and a very generous bidder. But to proceed to his character: 'Dr Phoenix is a little jolly black[13] man, but so very conscientious, that he's as ready to serve the poor for nothing, as the rich for money. His great skill in physic has made him famous; and which render him the more eminent, his prescriptions are generally successful, and his *aurum potabile* never fails. His wise advice has rescued more languishing patients from the jaws of death, than quacks have sent to those dark regions; and on that score death declares himself a mortal enemy to Dr Phoenix; whereas death claims a relation to mere pretenders to physic, as being both of one occupation, viz. that of killing men. But though his great success makes patients throng to him, yet is he a modest, humble, and very good man, as appears by this: at his first coming to a sick man, he persuades him to put his trust in God, the fountain of health. The want of such seriousness has caused the bad success of many physicians; for they that won't acknowledge God in their applications, God won't acknowledge them in that success which they might otherwise expect.' I would be larger in the Doctor's character, but after all, must come short of it; so will add no more about him, but shall now attempt his lady's character, of whom I might say many pretty things; but (Madam) I fear I shall tire you; however, I say all in little, by only telling your ladyship, that the person I'd here describe is Doctor Phoenix's wife. I say, Madam, it is praise enough to say, she is Dr Phoenix's wife, and that she merits so good a husband. Then let the learned world debate as long as they please about the nonsuch[14] bird, this lady proves (by her great virtues) that in Dublin (if nowhere else) is to be seen a she-phoenix.

Leaving Dr Phoenix's house, our next visit was to the College of Dublin, where several worthy gentlemen (both Fellows and others) had been great benefactors to my auction. When we came to the College, we went first to my friend Mr Young's chamber; but he not being at home, we went to see the library, which is over the scholars' lodgings the length of one of the quadrangles; and contains a great many choice books of great value, particularly one, the largest I ever saw for breadth; it was an herbal, containing the lively portraitures of all sorts of trees, plants, herbs, and flowers: by this herbal lay a small book, containing about 64 pages in a sheet, to make it look like the giant and the dwarf. There also (since I have mentioned a giant) we saw lying on a table, the thighbone of a giant, or at least, of some monstrous over-grown man, for the thighbone was as long as my leg and thigh; which is kept there as a convincing demonstration of the vast bigness which some human bodies have in former times arrived to. We were next shewed by Mr Griffith, a Master of Art (for he it was that shewed us these curiosities), the skin of one Ridley, a notorious tory, which had been long ago executed; he had been begged for an anatomy,[15] and being flayed, his skin was tanned, and stuffed with straw; in this passive state he was assaulted by some mice and rats, not sneakingly behind his back, but boldly before his face, which they so much further mortified, even after death, as to eat it up; which loss has since been supplied by tanning the face of one Geoghagan, a popish priest, executed about six years ago, for stealing; which said face is put in the place of Ridley's.

At the east end of this Library, on the right hand, is a chamber called the Countess of Bath's Library, filled with many handsome folios, and other books, in dutch binding, gilt, with the Earl's arms impressed upon them;[16] for he had been sometime of this house; on the left hand, opposite to this room, is another chamber, in which I saw a great many manuscripts, medals and other curiosities.

At the west end of the Library, there is a division made by a kind of wooden lattice-work, containing about thirty paces, full of choice and curious books, which was the library of that great man, Archbishop Ussher, Primate of Armagh, whose learning and exemplary piety have justly made him the ornament not only of that College (of which he was the first Scholar that ever was entered in it, and the first who took degrees) but of the whole Hibernian nation. At the upper end of this part of the Library, hangs at full length, the picture of Dr Chaloner,[17] who was the first provost of the College, and a person eminent for learning and virtue. His picture is likewise at the entrance into the Library; and his body lies in a stately tomb made of alabaster. At the west end of the chapel, near Dr Chaloner's picture (if I don't mistake) hangs a new skeleton of a man, made up and given by Dr Gwither, a physician of careful and happy practice, of great integrity, learning, and sound judgment, as may be seen by those treatises of his that are inserted in some late philosophical transactions.[18] Thus (Madam) have I given ye a brief account of the Library, which at present is but an ordinary pile of building, and can't be distinguished on the outside; but I hear they design the building of a new library: and I am told, the House of Commons in Ireland have voted 3000*l.* towards carrying it on.

After having seen the Library, we went to visit Mr Minshul (whose father I knew in Chester).[19] 'Mr Minshul has been student in the College for some time, and is a very sober, ingenious youth; and I do think is descended from one of the most courteous men in Europe. (I mean Mr John Minshul, bookseller in Chester.)' After a short stay in this gentleman's chamber, we were led by one Theophilus (a good natured sensible fellow) to see the new-house, now building for the Provost; which, when finished, will be very noble and magnificent.[20]

After this, Theophilus shewed us the gardens belonging to the College, which were very pleasant and entertaining. Here was a sun-dial, on which might be seen what a clock it was in most parts of the world. This dial was placed upon the top of a stone, representing a pile of books and not far from this was another sun-dial set in box[21] of a very large compass, the gnomon of it being very near as big as a barber's poll. Leaving this pleasant garden, we ascended several steps, which brought us into a curious walk, where we had a prospect to the west of the city, and to the east of the sea and harbour: on the south we could see the mountains of Wicklow, and on the north, the river of Liffey, which runs by the side of the College. Madam, having now (and at other times) thoroughly surveyed the College, I shall here attempt to give your Ladyship a very particular account of it; it is called Trinity College, and is the sole University of Ireland; it consists of three squares, the outward being as large as both the inner; one of which, of modern building, has not chambers on every side, the other has; on the south side of which stands the Library, the whole length of the square; I shall say nothing of the Library here (having already said something of it) so I proceed to tell ye, Madam, that the Hall and Butteries run the same range with the Library, and separates the two inner squares; it is an old building, as also the Regent house, which from a gallery looks into the Chapel, which has been of late years enlarged, being before too little for the number of Scholars, which are now, with the Fellows, &c. reckoned about 340. They have a garden for the Fellows, and another for the Provost, both neatly kept; as also a bowling-green, and large parks for the students to walk and exercise in. The foundation consists of a Provost (who at present is the Reverend Dr George Brown,[22] a gentleman bred in this house since a youth, when he was first entered, and one in whom they all count themselves very happy; for he's an excellent governor, and a person of great piety, learning, and moderation), seven Senior Fellows, of whom two are doctors in divinity; eight Juniors, to which one is

Conversation in Ireland. 413

in this Gentleman's Chamber, we were led by one *Theophilus*, (a good natur'd sensible Fellow) to see the *New-house*, now building for the *Provost* ; which when finish'd, will be very noble and magnificent.

After this, *Theophilus* shew'd us the *Gardens* belonging to the College, which were very pleasant and entertaining. Here was a *Sun-Dyal*, on which might be seen what a Clock it was in most parts of the World. This Dyal was plac'd upon the top of a Stone, representing a *Pile of Books*. And not far from this was another *Sun-Dyal set in Box*, of a very large compass, the Gnomon of it being very near as big as a *Barber's Poll*. Leaving this *pleasant Garden*, we ascended several steps, which bfought us into a *curious Walk*, where we had a Prospect to the *West* of the City, and to the *East* of the Sea and Harbour : On the *South* we cou'd see the Mountains of *Wicklow*, and on the *North*, the River *Liffee*, which runs by the side of the College. Madam, having now (and at other times) throughly survey'd the Colledge, I shall here attempt to give your Ladyship a very particular Account of it : 'tis call'd *Trinity College*, and is the sole University of *Ireland* ; it consists of three Squares, the outward being as large as both the inner ; one of which, of modern building, has not Chambers on every side, the other has ; on the *South* side of which stands the Library, the whole length of the Square. I shall say nothing of the Library here (having already said something of it) so I proceed to tell ye, Madam, that the *Hall and Butteries* run the same range with the Library, and separates the two inner squares ; it is an old building, as also the Regent-house, which from a Gallery looks into the *Chappel*, which has been of late years enlarged, being before too little for the number of Scholars, which are now, with the Fellows, *&c.* reckoned about 340 ; they have a *Garden for the Fellows, and another for the Provost*, both neatly kept ; as also a *Bowling-green, and large Parks* for the Students to walk and exercise in. The Foundation consists of

H h h   a Pro-

lately added by —— and seventy Scholars; their public commence-
ments are at Shrovetide, and the first Tuesday after the eighth of July.
Their Chancellor is his Grace the Duke of Ormond; since the death
of the Right Reverend the late Bishop of Meath, they have had no
Vice-Chancellor, only *pro re nata*.[23] The University was founded by
Queen Elizabeth, and by her and her successors largely endowed, and
many munificent gifts and legacies since made by several other well-
disposed persons; all whose names, together with their gifts, are read
publicly in the Chapel every Trinity Sunday in the afternoon, as a
grateful acknowledgement to the memory of their benefactors; and
on the 9th of January, 1693 (which completed a century from the
foundation of the College) they celebrated their first secular day,
when the Provost,[a] Dr Ash, now Bishop of Clogher, preached, and
made a notable entertainment for the Lords Justices, Privy Council,
Lord Mayor and Aldermen of Dublin. The sermon preached by the
Provost, was on the subject of the foundation of the college, and his
text was, Mat. xxvi. xiii. *Verily I say unto you, wheresoever this Gospel
shall be preached in the whole world, there shall also this that this woman
hath done, be told for a memorial of her;* which in this sermon the
Provost applied to Queen Elizabeth, the foundress of the College.
The sermon was learned and ingenious, and afterwards printed by
Mr Ray, and dedicated to the Lords Justices, who at that time were,
the Lord Henry Capel, Sir Cyril Wiche, and William Duncomb,
Esq; in the afternoon, there were several orations in Latin spoken by
the Scholars, in praise of Queen Elizabeth, and the succeeding
princes: and an ode made by Mr Tate[24] (the Poet Laureate) who was
bred up in this College. Part of the Ode was this following:

I.

Great Parent, hail! all hail to thee;
Who hast the last distress surviv'd,
To see this joyful day arriv'd;
The Muses' second jubilee.

a. See his character in my Farewell to Dublin.

II.

Another century commencing,
      No decay in thee can trace,
Time, with his own law dispensing,
      Adds new charms to every grace,
That adorn'd thy youthful face.

III.

After wars alarms repeated,
And a circling age compleated,
      Numerous off-spring thou do'st raise,
      Such as to Juverna's praise,
Shall Liffee make as proud a name,
As that of Isis or of Cham.[25]

IV.

Awful Matron, take thy seat
To celebrate this festival;
      The learn'd assembly well to treat,
Blest Eliza's[26] days re-call:
      The wonders of her reign recount,
      In strains that Phoebus may surmount,
Songs for Phoebus to repeat,
      She 'twas that did at first inspire,
      And tune the mute Hibernian lyre.

V.

Succeeding princes next recite,
With never-dying verse requite
      Those favours they did show'r:
'Tis this alone can do 'em right;
To save 'em from oblivion's night,
      Is only in the Muses' power.

VI.

But chiefly recommend to fame.
Maria, and Great William's name,[27]
    Whose Isle to him her freedom owes:
And surely no Hibernian Muse
Can her restorers' praise refuse,
    While Boyne and Shannon flows.

After this ode had been sung by the principal gentlemen of the kingdom, there was a very diverting speech made in English by the *Terra Filius*:[28] the night concluded with illuminations, not only in the College, but in other places. Madam, this day being to be observed but once in a hundred years, was the reason why I troubled your Ladyship with this account.

Having rewarded Theophilus for his readiness to shew us the gardens, &c. we took our leave of the College; and from thence I went (Mr Wilde and Mr Larkin being still with me) to take my leave of the Honourable Colonel Butler of St Stephen's Green, to whom I was greatly obliged, both as he was a great encourager of my auction, and as I had all along his countenance and favour in it, especially when there was some persons that had a mind to disturb and banter my auction; but by this worthy gentleman's appearing against them, and resenting the affront as done to himself, they quickly cried *Pecavi*.[29] Madam, it would be too great presumption in me to attempt this gentleman's character, for I should but dim the lustre of his brighter virtues, by all that I could write. But the noble favours I received from Colonel Butler oblige me to a public acknowledgement; though all I can say of him will be like lesser maps of the large world (where every prick sets down some ample shire, and every point's a city)[30]: 'His brave and generous soul is so well known, that it is but wasting of time to tell it; then where can I begin, or where shall I end? Should I speak of his learning, I might call him the Mecœnas[31] of Ireland; for the books he buys do by their number sufficiently declare his love to learning; and by their value and intrinsic worth, the vastness of his judgment: neither is he less remarkable for his affable carriage, his sweet and obliging disposition, his large charity, his singular humility, justice, temperance, and moderation; and I do believe his noble attainments in the art of painting have no parallel in the kingdom of Ireland. Madam, I would proceed in the Colonel's character, but I fear his great modesty will make him think I say too much, though I am very sure all that know him will think I say too little.'

When we came to the Colonel's house, he received me (and my two friends) in a most obliging manner; after our first salutations, he had us into his dining-room, hung round with curious pictures, all of his own drawing; some of which were King Edward the VIth, the Lady Jane Grey,[32] the two Charles's, King William and Queen Mary, with others which I now forget. When we were all seated, the Colonel told me he took my coming to see him very kindly, and that if he came to London, he would do himself the honour of repaying my visit. We next fell to discourse of the auctions I made in Dublin, and here the Colonel was pleased to say, I had been a great benefactor to the kingdom of Ireland, by bringing into it so large a quantity of good books. I thanked him for the honour he did me by that expression; and further added, that if all my buyers had been so generous as himself, my venture had been very fortunate. This discourse about my auction, naturally led us to talk of Patrick Campbell (the grand enemy to it) and after I had told the Colonel what treatment I had from Campbell, he said I had just reason to vindicate myself; and that he believed there never was a fairer auction than mine, or a better auctioneer than Mr Wilde; and therefore, Madam, I dedicate the *Dublin-Scuffle* to Colonel Butler, as a generous protector of an injured stranger. Upon the taking my leave of the Colonel, he expressed himself very sorry that I was leaving the country, and said, if ever I returned with a second venture, he would encourage it all he could; for this I returned him my humble thanks, confessing my unworthiness of those many favours I had received from him. Then taking my final leave, he gave me that endearing salutation, which is the great expression of kindness among the gentlemen of Ireland;[33] after this tender favour, he honoured me so far, as to say, he should be wishing for westerly winds (for my sake) 'till he heard I was landed; and so with wishing (Mr Larkin and myself) a good voyage, we parted well satisfied in the honour done us by the noble Colonel.

Madam, I told ye that Colonel Butler was very remarkable for his great humility, and generous temper; and you see by his obliging expressions to persons so much below him, how much he merits that noble character of being humble; I call it so, as pride lessens (or rather disgraces) men of the highest rank, as much or more than it does others; and therefore it is, though Colonel Butler is very eminent for every virtue, yet if he excels in one more than another, it is in his great humility; which further appears by his inviting me often to see him, and (if I may be so proud to use his own expression) in being pleased with my conversation.

Having left the Colonel's house, we all three returned to our several lodgings. In our way thither, we went to take our leaves of the Reverend Mr Searl (at his house in Bride's Alley[34]) and of my worthy friend Mr Jones (at his house in Great Ship-street) but neither of them were at home; however, I had the happiness of seeing Mr Jones's sister (a person eminent for her great piety) with whom I left a million of thanks for all the favours I received from him. And here I parted with my two friends (Mr Wilde and Mr Larkin) and the next day (it being the last for taking of farewells) everyone went as his humour and fancy led him. And the first ramble I took this morning, was to take my farewell of Rings-End (where I had two or three good friends). It is about a mile from Dublin, and is a little harbour like your Graves-End in England; I had very agreeable company to Rings End, and was nobly treated at the King's Head; after an hour's stay in this dear place (as all port-towns generally are) I took my leave of Trench, Welsted, and two or three more friends, and now looked towards Dublin: but how to come at it, we no more knew than the fox at the grapes;[35] for though we saw a large strand, yet it was not to be walked over, because of a pretty rapid stream, which must be crossed. We enquired for a coach, and found no such thing was to be had here, unless by accident; but were informed that we might have a Rings-End car, which upon my desire was called, and we got upon it, not into it. It is a perfect car[36] with two wheels, and towards the back of it, a seat is raised cross ways, long enough to hold three people; the cushion we had was made of patch-work, but of such coarse kind of stuff, that we fancied the boy had stolen some poor beggar's coat for a covering; between me and the horse, upon the cross bars of the car, stood our charioteer, who presently set his horse into a gallop, which so jolted our sides, though upon a smooth strand, that we were in Purgatory until we got off at Lazy-hill,[37] where I paid 4*d.* for our fare of a mile's riding, and almost as pleased as the young gentleman that drove the chariot of the sun would have been, to be rid of his seat; however, they are a great convenience, and a man may go to Rings-End from Dublin, or from hence thither, with a load of goods, for a groat;[38] and we were told, there are a hundred and more plying hereabouts, that one can hardly be disappointed.

I parted with my fellow traveller in Essex-street, and from thence I went to take my leave of my honest barber, Mat Read upon Cork-hill; and because I found him a generous lad, I won't leave him without a character: 'He is a man willing to please, and the most genteel barber I saw in Dublin, and therefore I became his quarterly customer;[39] but as ready as he is to humour his friends, yet is he brisk and gay, and the worst made for a dissembler of any man in the world; he's generous and frank, and speaks whatever he thinks, which made me have a kindness for him; and it was not lost, for he treated me every quarterly payment, and was obliging to the last, being one of those dozen men that feasted me in Essex-street, the Friday before I left Dublin; and that witnessed to the attestation concerning my conversation. He has wit enough, a great deal of good humour, and (though a barber) owner of as much generosity as any man in Ireland. And if ever I visit Dublin again, Mat. Read (or in case of his death) his heir and successor, is the only barber for me. And as for his spouse, though her face is full of pock-holes, yet she's a pretty little humoured creature, and smiles at every word.'

Having shook hands with honest Mat., I went next through Copper Alley to Skinner-Row, for a parting glimpse of Brass and Patrick Campbell; for though they had treated me ill (and that's the reason why none but they, and the old usurer, have a black character in the *Dublin Scuffle*) yet I had good nature enough (though not to discourse, yet) just to see them when I left Dublin. From paying this silent farewell, I went to the Tholsel, where I saw [a]Mr Quin, the present Lord Mayor for the City of Dublin.

a. An apothecary in Skinner Row.

Perhaps Madam, you'll wonder that I should send ye so many characters, and have yet omitted to send the character of a person in such an eminent station; but the reason was, I stayed to be thoroughly informed, before I attempted the character of my Lord Mayor: but Madam, I am now able to give ye his true character; and the least I can say of his Lordship is, 'He's a person of great justice and integrity (as I found in the ᵃhearing I had before him), a courageous magistrate, and a true lover of his king and country; and has the love of all good men. But there's no need of anymore than reading the *Flying Post* of Feb. 16, 1699. to know him as well as if he stood before you; for there it is said, Dublin Feb. 7, *Our citizens are mightily pleased with the Lord Mayor, on the account of the proceedings against the bakers, and relieving the poor from their oppressions; a congratulatory poem hath been lately printed and presented to him, on this occasion.* Thus far the *Flying Post*, in which you see that courage and justice I told ye was so eminent in him. But this faithful discharge of his great trust, is what the citizens of Dublin might expect from him; for prudence and piety have visibly shone through all the actions of his life; and it is not honour or power alters the temper of a good man; and therefore it is, since he has been chosen Lord Mayor of the City of Dublin, that his conduct is such that he is not only a pattern fit to be imitated by all that shall hereafter succeed him, but in many things it will be difficult for any to resemble him; and therefore no wonder the citizens of Dublin have fixed him in so large a sphere of doing good; a private post was not large enough for the service heaven designed by this active magistrate; nor a ᵇ*hill high enough for the notice of one so exemplary*; and to render him the more complete, this brave soul of his has the happiness to live in a very beautiful tenement;⁴⁰ and it had been pity it should have lived in any other.' But I shall stop here, for I had not the honour to be personally known to his lordship; so I shall leave the Tholsel without any other farewell than what I have given in this character; and from hence shall step to the Bull in Nicholas-Street, to take my leave of one who is called (what she really is) the Flower of Dublin: 'no citizen's wife is demurer than this

a. See more of this in the *Dublin Scuffle*.
b. As was said of my Reverend father-in-law, Dr Annesly.

person, as I found at the first greeting; nor draws in her mouth with a chaster simper, and yet a virtuous good woman, and very obliging to all her customers'; and I left her, with some regret. And next rambled to Cow-lane,[41] to take my leave of the Lady Swancastle, who is deservedly famous for her great love to her husband. Madam, a good wife is a good thing, and rarely to be found, said the wisest of mere men; and we have reason to believe him the rather, because (as[a] Mr Turner says) 'the first man, Adam, the strong Sampson, the philosopher Socrates, and many others, have been either over-reached, or afflicted with women': but as many bad wives as there are in the world, I do assure ye, Madam, my Lady Swancastle is none of them; 'for she's an honour to her sex, and a comfort and crown to her husband; and perhaps the most generous person to her friends in the world; of which, the noble cordial she gave me that hour I left Dublin (and many other favours I received from her) do abundantly testify; and though her lord and she are ancient, yet they

> Live as they've liv'd; still to each other new;
> And use those names they did when they first knew.
> Still the same smiles within their cheeks be read,
> —— —— —— As were at first.
> And may the day ne'er come to see a change;
> Let neither time nor age e'er make them strange:
> And as you first met, may you ever be,
> George a young man, and Chrit. a girl to thee.
> What George, tho' you shou'd seem like Nestor, old?
> And Chrit, more years had, than Cumana told;
> Time's snow you must not see, though it appears:
> 'Tis good to know your age, not count your years.'[42]

Madam, leaving this good lady under much grief (for her lord is going to sea with me) my next visit was to Mr Hamer, who (as well as my Lord Swancastle) has met with a suitable wife, and both being of a sweet temper, they live as loving as two turtles; they lately gave

a. In his *History of Providence*.[43]

me a splendid treat, and with them I eat my Christmas[a] dinner; and therefore it was when I gave my [b]farewell supper, I thought it proper to invite Mr Hamer and his wife, as a slender acknowledgement of the favours I received from them.

From Mr Hamer's house I walked into Church-street, to take my leave of [c]Mr Constantine, but had not the happiness to see him (perhaps he was not returned from England); however, Madam, I shall here give you his[d] character; and seeing I did not see him, I desire it may pass as my farewell to him; and the least I can say of Mr Constantine is, 'that he's a very conscientious man; I speak this from my own experience; for when I sent for the bill of the physic I had of him, I found it the most reasonable I ever met with (except [e]Mr Crows, an apothecary in Leaden-hall-street;) and just such a fair dealer is Mr Constantine; and which adds further to his reputation, he's a man that thoroughly understands his trade; he is as intimate with Willis and Harvey[44] (at least with their works) as ever I was with Richard Wilde; and is as well acquainted with the *London Dispensatory*, as I am with my own name. He is so conversant with the great variety of Nature, that not a drug or simple[45] escapes his knowledge; their power and virtues are known so well to Mr Constantine, that he need not practise new experiments upon his patients, except it be in desperate cases, when death must be expelled by death. This also is praiseworthy in him, that to the poor he always prescribes cheap, but wholesome medicines; not curing them of a consumption in their bodies, and sending it into their purses; nor yet directing them to the East-Indies to look for drugs, when they may have far better out of their gardens. And which is admirable in him, when he visits a patient, his presence is a sort of cordial, for he's one of a cheerful temper; and sure I am, that man is actually dying, that is not revived to hear him talk; he never speaks but it is to the purpose; and no man

a. It was then my Lord Swancastle gave me a noble apple, if I could have kept it; of which I have a pleasant story to tell in my *Summer Ramble*.   b. To Mr Bourn, Mr Gee, Mr Dobbs, Mr Servant, Mr Dell, Mr Penny, Mr Tracy (alias Pat), Mr Wilde, Mr Larkin, Mr Price, and Mr Robinson.   c. The only apothecary I made use of in Dublin.   d. In return for the visits he made me, during my illness.   e. Who in his bill of 50*l.* (for physic given to my first wife) used me so very honestly, that I could not desire him to abate[46] a farthing.

ever clothed his words in sweeter epithets. The estate he has got by his great practice has already preferred him to be Sheriff of Dublin; and I don't doubt but a few years will prefer him to the honour of Lord Mayor; and why not, since one of the same profession now fills the chair?'

Madam, I might enlarge on this gentleman's character, but this is my last visiting day, and the farewells I've yet to make won't allow it; but they that would know Mr Constantine further, may see a living picture of him every day in the person of Mr Chambers; who, as he is his brother by trade, so equals him (if any man ever did) in all the virtues of an accomplished apothecary. But the sun had now strode the horizon, so I stayed but a minute in Crane lane, and next posted to Mr Sudal's in Fishamble-street. I was often invited to come hither, but could not do it till this day; when I came to Sudal's, I found his wife was a kinswoman of Mr Doolittle's,[a] and one that I knew in London. 'Mr Sudal is but a little man in his person, but I see (by the treat he gave me) that a great and generous soul may dwell in a little tenement. And the least I can say of Mrs Sudal is, she's an excellent housewife, has a great deal of ready wit; and though taller than her spouse by the head and shoulders, is otherwise a suitable wife; but I think Mr Sudal deserves her, for he's a mighty obliging husband, and very remarkable for the punctual performance of his promise. It is true, his trade and customers oblige him more to time than other dealers; but he is punctual more from a principle of conscience than interest; and indeed Sudal, if I belie ye here, I should scarce think you a Christian.' For as the author of the *Duty of Man*[47] says, p. 227, 'That sort of debt which is brought upon a man by his own voluntary promise, cannot without great injustice be withholden; and he that dies in such an act of injustice (if this author be in the right) dies in a state of damnation: 'For', continues this author, 'when a promise is made, it is now the man's right; and then it is no matter by what means it came to be so.' Therefore we see David makes it part of the description of a just man, Psal. 15.4, that he keeps his promise; yea, though they were made to this own disadvantage. And surely he is utterly unfit to ascend to that holy hill there spoken of, either as that

---

a. A Nonconformist minister in London.

signifies the Church here, or heaven hereafter, that does not punctually observe this part of justice,' thus far the *Duty of Man*. And I find Mr Sudal's life is conformable to the notions of that great man. And Madam, this part of justice (I mean that of keeping of promises) being likewise agreeable to my own sentiments, I could not but have an esteem for him; I stayed with him five hours, much of which time was spent in talking of Madam D —— and the haughty Rachel (that Rachel I mentioned before)[48] but at five I bid them adieu; and next went to High-street, to take my leave of an old usurer. I wish I could say any good of him, but I profess I can't; so I think it proper to conceal his name. When I came to his house, I told Scrape-all, I came to bid him farewell; but this Rich-poor-Man[a] had not the soul to ask me to eat or drink; so that I must say (at parting) Mr L—— is a beggar of a fair estate. I may say of his wealth, as of other men's prodigality, 'that it has brought him to this; another that knows the right use of 200*l*. shall live (creditably, and) to better purpose than he with his 10000*l*. Every accession of a fresh 100*l*. bates him so much of his allowance, and brings him a degree nearer starving. Nay, Madam, I am told (by Mr Larkin that has known him long) that he's so very covetous, that he had been starved long since, had it not been for the free use of other men's tables. It is said covetousness is the only sin that grows young as men grow old; and I found it verified in this wretch; who, though worth 10000*l*., the clothes he had on when I came to see him were never young in the memory of any; and he has been known by them longer than his face. Madam, for my part I am heartily concerned for the poor heir which will have the estate; for the old miser never gave alms in his whole life, or did a generous action; and everyone thinks it will never prosper, but be rather as great a curse to the heir, as it is to the present possessor. Yet, to give the devil his due, he is as charitable to his neighbour, as he is to himself; and rather than go to a doctor (Mr Larkin says he's sure) he'd die to save charges. He has but one kinsman, who was forced to wander to London to get bread. He might have married a great fortune, would this miser have drawn his purse strings; but he'd do

a. As Cowley calls the miser.

nothing for him while he lived, though 500*l.* given or lent him in his lifetime would have done his cousin more service then ten thousand after his death.' But I should starve should I stay here, so I leave Sir Miser, to take my leave of a more generous friend; I mean the ingenious Dr Whaley (a great benefactor to my three auctions). When I came to the Doctor's house, I found he was gone out, perhaps in search after Patrick Campbell, for putting of his title to *Cumpsty's Almanack*;[49] but if Campbell would ask pardon, I believe the Doctor would soon forgive him, for Doctor Whaley is a man of a noble spirit, and justly merits the esteem he has with ingenious men. His Almanack bears the bell from all the rest in Ireland. I was very desirous to have seen the Doctor at leaving Dublin (to thank him for all his favours) but missing of him, I next rambled to Mr Carter's in Fishamble-street;[50] I had but just time to bid Carter adieu, but will say at parting, 'He's a genteel honest printer, is like to marry a beauty, I heartily wish him courage, for faint heart never won fair lady; and he can't but conquer, for he's a witty man, and charms a thousand ways.' Having shook hands with Mr Carter, I went next to visit my friend Sparlin in Dames-street, he's a very ingenious man, and blest with an excellent wife. He was gone to the Custom-house, so I missed taking my leave of him, for which I was heartily sorry, for he was my fellow traveller to Malahide, and I wanted to thank him for old favours, but it was not my luck to meet him at home; so I rambled next to the Keys in High-street, where I met (by appointment) with Jacob Milner,[51] and his man Shepherd. As to Jacob, he's a well-set handsome man, and I shall treat him civilly in my *Summer Ramble*, provided he grows humble, is very respectful to Mr Wilde, and tells Campbell of his great sin in printing *Hodder's Arithmetick* with Cocker's title, and so exit Jacob to make way for his man Shepherd, of whom I shall only say, Trim Tram; for he bought books at my auction, and I found him an honest fellow, and there's an end on it. Having taken my leave of Mr Shepherd, and his good master, I went to spend half an hour with Mr Corbury and his good wife, who are very obliging persons, and I shall ever love them (and one day requite them) for their great tenderness to one of my best friends. But the day spends, and I have other farewells to make, so my next business was to take my leave of my three landlords, Mr Orson, Mr Landers, and Mr Cawley. As I went along, I happened to meet with Mrs Maxfield (a very sensible good woman) she was going (perhaps) to the Four-Courts to hear a trial she had there depending; she hurried so fast after her lawyer, that I had but just time to bid her adieu, and to send a tender farewell to her virtuous daughter.

Having left Mother Maxfield, I stopped nowhere, 'till I came to my three landlords; I have already sent their characters, and shall only add, that after a little wringing of hands, and some tears at parting, I took my final leave of each; and in my way home I (unexpectedly) met with the ingenious Climene, my fellow-traveller to Ballymany; we walked together to Mr Larkin's, and there parted. As we went along, we had a glimpse of a remarkable black[52] man; she told me it was Dr Proby; she gave him a mighty character for his great success in curing the stone, for his skill in surgery, and readiness to serve the poor. But I had not the happiness to be known to him, so I prevented her speaking to him, being here met by my servant Robinson (as true a hearted man as lives) and by his dear spouse, who has brought me a pigeon pie (I had almost said) large enough to victual a single cabin to the East-Indies. Having taken my leave of this happy couple, I should next enquire for the gentleman with a red face, honest Doctor Robinson (I mean him who makes so noted a figure in the Dublin Custom-house). He's a very agreeable friend, punctual to his great trust, yet very obliging; had I a minute to spare, we'd shake hands over a glass of claret; and from him I should step to the Post-house, to take my leave of Mr Shepherd. He's a very generous good man, and I should in justice give him a farewell bottle; but I am tired with my day's ramble, and the sun has got on his nightcap, and if I don't hasten, will be gone to his bed before I am got to my chamber. But I engaged Mr Wilde to make an apology to Dr Robinson, and Mr Shepherd, and to present them in my name, with a farewell-token. This Saturday night concluded my Dublin-farewells, and if the wind be fair on Monday, I shall embark with owner Pickance, and then farewell to the kingdom in general (farewell[a] for ever) and when I get to London, I'll fall to printing this *Account of my Conversation*, and

a. As is hinted in the *Dublin Scuffle*.

also my *Scuffle* with Patrick Campbell, for it is expected in Dublin, as appears by a letter directed to Mr Larkin, which begins thus; viz.

> Sir,
>
> We, or many of us here, would be glad *The Dublin Scuffle* was out, which Dick Pue says he will buy one of, and chain to his table, that the sale may be spoiled by everybody's reading it for a penny a piece, and that he shall get. I am sorry therefore, he is not like to have a severer lash than I am afraid he will, without it be subjoined in a postscript; for Dick and I now are two, and for want of yours, made a *Dublin Scuffle* of our own the other night.

Thus far the letter to Mr Larkin: and an hour ago, I received myself, a letter from Sir Hackney (I call him so as he's Campbell's tool) wondering the *Dublin Scuffle* is not yet out; but withal, threatening I know not what, if I omit the inserting some of his own maggots:[53] it is true, Madam, such a scoundrel as this is scarce worth my notice; yet I would tell ye his name, but that he's ashamed of it himself, and has turned it into a bog-house;[54] but to shew this hectoring tool how much I defy him, and all his abettors, I'll here insert the character of Robin Bog-house (for so he calls himself).

The Character of Robin Bog-house

'His face is full of a certain briskness, though mixed with an air a little malicious and unpleasant; he has a large stock of ill-nature, pride, and wit, in which lies his chiefest excellency, though a very unenvied one. His face is made of brass, and his tongue tipped with lies (for there was not a true word in all his letter); yet as lewd as that and his tongue are, they are the two best accomplishments he has; I find in his letter he has not a dram of tenderness for his best-friends (I mean those that pay him for scribbling); for I guess by his letter, he's going to expose one of them for buying and selling a whore, a second for having a bastard; a third, for being shamefully hen-pecked; a fourth, for being a town-bull,[55] and a fifth, [a]for putting a

---

a. All these I'll prove in a second part of the *Dublin Scuffle*, if I hear any more of him.

cheat on the world. But no wonder he abuses the men, for he's so unmannerly, as to revile even the fair sex; he lately called a lady whore, for no other reason (as it is supposed) but because she'd not give him a night's lodging: then where shall a man find him, for he slanders everybody; and, Proteus-like, appears in all manner of shapes; sometimes he calls himself a student of Trinity College near Dublin; at other times a kt. errant, and fights everything; and the next moment owns himself a poor labourer, and desires his wife would make him a c———d[56] in mere charity to his hungry belly; for he, good man! is willing to hold the door (even to his own flesh and blood), invent lies, slander innocent virgins, swear through an inch board,[57] and do anything rather than starve; so that if two Irish justices and myself be not mistaken, Robin[a] Bog-house will die looking through an hempen casement;[58] or, if he'll kneel low enough for it, perhaps he may come off (for I'll stand his friend when I see him penitent) with being only whipped at the cart's a ——— .[59] And as to his wife, though she's a virtuous woman, yet I'd advise the honest cits[60] of Dublin never to go to Rathfarnham with her, for Robin is so lewd (himself) that he thinks no man travels with her, but makes him a c———d.'

Now if Bog-house is not the person I here describe, yet if he that is will answer this character fairly, I mean to put his name to it (as I shall do in my reply to him, for I hate a coward) I'll answer his letters every post; and if Patrick Campbell will petition for it, he shall be my bookseller, and his opposite neighbour the printer of this skirmish.

Thus Madam, having sent ye the history of my *Conversation in Ireland*, and some hints of my *Summer Ramble* (from the time I landed, to the Sunday I left it); and having also as truly related how I came to be engaged in a *Dublin Scuffle*, and why the said *Scuffle* is so much desired by Dick Pue, and his cousin Bog-house, perhaps you'll expect my remarks on the impatience of these two, till my *Scuffle* arrives in Dublin.

Then first as to Dick Pue; I can't find by the letter sent Mr Larkin, whether he so impatiently desires my *Scuffle*, that he may spoil the sale of it, by chaining one to his table, or that (to use the word in Mr Larkin's letter) he may get a penny by people's reading it; but I rather

a. Alias T. D.

incline to this last opinion, for Dick hopes by the many pence he shall get by it, that he might reimburse himself of that money he paid (for somebody) for secret service, and I know to whom, and what sum, and so shall the world too, except he'll bring Boghouse to light, that the world may know the man that begets Actæon's;[61] and that's all I shall say at present concerning Dick, or his dear cousin.

And now (Madam) having in this letter sent ye the characters of almost everything I conversed with in Ireland, I hope you'll pardon me if (in the last place) I allow myself a character amongst the rest: it is true, Cowley says, the voyage life is longest made at home; however, from that small acquaintance I have with myself, I may venture to say, as to my birth, I account it no small honour that I descended from the tribe of Levi;[62] and, I find an ingenious author of this opinion, who says, I reckon[a] it amongst the felicities of my life, to have been a prophet's son, nor would I leave a pulpit for a throne: to be ambassadors of Jesus is matter of glory, and if you have faith to believe a poet, their children

[b]Do all breathe something more than common air.[63]

And Mr Robinson is of this opinion, or would scarce have set on the great [c]pot for the sons of the prophets. Then I'm honoured as much (to use the words of the same author) in having a minister for my father, as if he had been a lord; and this happiness was continued to me a great while, for my [d]reverend father was rector of [e]Aston Clinton for twenty years; and those principles he instilled into me in that town, do (as my Lord Russel says in the like case) still hang about me, and I hope will (as they did him) give me comfort in my dying moments. My father designed me at first for an Oxford scholar, but afterwards changing his mind, in my fifteenth year he placed me out with an eminent citizen in London, whose kind instructions and great care of my welfare, I shall ever acknowledge. From this account of my birth and education I proceed (for I consider I am not writing my life, but character) to a description of my person, which is So, So; however, two of the fair sex have been tempted to take it for better for worse (a

a. See the *Character of a Good Woman*, p. 125. Printed for John Harris.   b. See the poem dedicated to the Sons of the Clergy.   c. See the sermon he printed on 2 Kings 4. 38.   d. Mr John Dunton.   e. In the County of Bucks.

black man is a pearl in a fair woman's eye) and if you'll believe the dying words of the first, and living testimony of my present wife, never repented their bargain.

Having given ye an odd account of my person, I shall next tell ye with what soul it is acted.[64] Truly, Madam, this house of mine is filled with a rambling tenant (I mean a spirit that would break[a] the vessel, had it nothing to work upon) and being born to travel, I am ever pursuing my destiny; so that you may truly call me a citizen of London, and of all the world (for I've seen America, and design to see Europe, Asia, and Africa); yet wherever I come, I love to be guessed at, not known, and to see the world unseen; and for this very reason am projecting a correspondence with your ladyship, which I'll call the *Art of living Incognito*; and another I'll call the *Character of my living Acquaintance* (perhaps 5000 in number) wherein I'll spare neither saint nor sinner that I ever talked with; no, though (like a rich criminal) he'd buy off his name with a purse of guineas. It is true, it is common to write the character of those that are dead, but the writing the history of living men is a project never attempted before; but if every man would attempt something of this nature (I mean write the history[b] of his life, comprehending as well his vices as virtues) we should begin to know one another a little: but whether they will or not, I have here led the way, and will pursue it till I have characterized all my acquaintance. So that you see, Madam, though rambling is part of my character, yet, that both my eyes are never at once from home, but that one keeps house, and observes the actions of men, while the other roams abroad for intelligence. But rambling having an ill name, perhaps your ladyship would willingly know something more about my religion. Madam, it is the very same you find in the *Account of my Conversation*; and let my enemies say what they please, I'll never alter it, for I never matter[65] abuses (when I can't avoid them); and therefore it is in the midst of reflections my countenance never changes, for I know whom I have trusted, and whither death can lead me; and being not so sure I shall die, as that I shall be restored, I outface death with the thoughts of my resurrection: if I am found dead upon the spot, what matters it? For not

a. See my Preface to the spectators of the *Dublin Scuffle*.   b. As is hinted in my Preface to the *Dublin Scuffle*.

being able to govern events, I endeavour to govern myself (and sure I am, it is the greatest of dominions to rule one's self, and passions); I am advanced already so far in this rare art, that I hope I may say, just censures I deserve not; unjust I contemn[66] (and notwithstanding the sneaking treatment I had from Campbell) I never judge any man unheard, nor never will. I'm amazed to find the pretenders to religion so much guilty of this sin; but I thank God censoriousness has ever been my aversion; for I observe not one report in fifty is[a] true, and therefore believe every man honest till I find him otherwise: most men are led by either prejudice, interest, or some by-end,[67] and therefore in matters of slander, I believe no man's eyes nor ears, but my own: neither do I listen to backbiters, but esteem them worse than the men they'd blacken; or if I find any man as bad as described, if I see him penitent, I never divulge his crime; and that was the reason I took such pains to bring Campbell to a sense of his error; which had I effected, the *Dublin Scuffle* had never appeared. And as I take a pleasure to cover the faults of my worst enemies (when I see them penitent), so I take as much delight to blazon their virtues; and that's the reason so many in Ireland have my good character. Virtue is so charming a thing, that the ancients were wont to say, could men see it with bodily eyes, they'd fall down and worship it; I can't tell what fine notions our forefathers had of virtue, yet sure I am, virtue is a sort of prodigy[68] in our times; so that wherever I find it I can't refrain from admiring it, and to write a character of the person who I think possesses it; and though I design a service to others by so doing, yet if I lose my end, I shall rest content; for I have this peculiar to myself, that I was never much concerned (except for the deaths of Eliza and D—ne) for the things that I can't help, for I do all I can to prevent a grievance, and then I acquiesce in the divine pleasure. Yet does not my pretence to religion make me a jot precise (and this I learnt from the dear Eliza). I value no man for his starched looks, or supercilious gravity; or for being a Church-man, Presbyterian, Independant, &c. provided he's sound in the main points wherein all good men are agreed; and therefore it is I have little charity for

a. This is evident by the harsh reflections (I lately found in the *London-Spy*) on three eminent traders, who are as much noted for their just and honourable dealings, as they are for that great estate and trade God has blessed them with.[69]

censorious men, be they of what party they will. But, Madam, though I'm thus easy in my conversation, yet if justly provoked, I can be angry enough, but it is over in half a minute; and I am not sooner in a flame, than I am reconciled; yet I never flatter any man, but value myself for being a blunt fellow. It is true, your ladyship once satirized me with the name of a poet (for it is the same thing as if you'd call me beggar; even famous Butler[a][70] was forced to die, and be interred on tick) and say all my tender expressions proceed more from the brain and fancy, than my heart. But (Madam) as much as I love rhyming, yet there's four or five in the world (of which your ladyship is one, and the ingenious Hamlen[b][71] another) that I respect without the least mixture of poetry; and I appeal to yourselves for the truth of this part of my character, for you both know I have but one heart, and that lies open to sight; and were it not for discretion, I never think ought whereof I'd avoid a witness;[72] and therefore it is strange I've one friend in the world, for folks don't love to hear of their faults; and I'se[73] downright, and call a spade a spade: I also own I'm very rash in my actions, and scarce ever did anything (save taking two women for better for worse) but I repented of one time or other. I have a great deal of mercury in my natural temper, for which I must have allowance (or shall appear but an odd Christian) but the best men are the most charitable, and no man (if he considers himself) will blame that in me which I can't help; perhaps I shall be blamed for this open confession, but having an honest design in everything I do, I publish that to the world, which others would keep as a secret; and for this reason I creep to nobody, but by daring to tell the truth, do often lose a friend for the sake of a jest; but bating but this fault,[74] though I say it myself, I'm as fit to make a friend as any man I know, for my bosom is my friend's closet, where he may safely lock up all his complaints, his doubts, and cares, and look how he leaves, so he finds them. The dead, the absent, the innocent, and he that trusts me, I never deceive or slander (to these I owe a nobler justice) and am so sensible of another's injuries that when my friend is stricken, I cry out. I was never forward in contracting of friendships, but where I once love, I never hate, no not for a crime, any longer

a. As Oldham[75] tells us in his *Poems*.   b. Now living at Frome in Somersetshire.

than till pardon is asked; and if my friend falls to decay, I'm even ready to rejoice (I ask his pardon) that I have an opportunity to convince him I loved in earnest; and though it were impossible he should ever requite me, while I have anything, my friend shalt have all; nay, I have this peculiar to myself, that I love a friend better for being poor, miserable, or despised; true friendship, like the rose, flourishes best amongst thorns; and my hopes are so strong, that they can insult over the greatest discouragement that lies in the way of serving my friend: and therefore I'd rather serve my[a] friend than barely pretend to it, for I hate a noise where there's no performance. I never do that to my friend, that I can't be content he should do to me; and therefore loving at this warm rate, it is but just I slight what loves not so much as myself.

So much for my birth, education, person, temper of mind, religion, and friendship. As to my dealings with men, my word is my parchment, and my Yea my oath, which I will not violate for fear or gain; and this is one reason why I never eat my promise,[76] or say, *This I saw not, but this I said*. In 600 books I have printed, I never swerved from the price agreed on, or made any printer call twice for his money (which practice I learnt from my honoured master) nor did I ever print any man's copy,[77] or purchase his author by out-bidding; and my way of traffic is all above board, for I betray the faults of what I sell. I have twenty times in Dublin restored the over-seen gain of a mistaken reckoning; and (being haunted with a scrupulous mind) have often paid a sum over twice, for fear of doing wrong; and this even Dick Pue will own, if he has any justice left. But what justice can I expect, when the malice of some men is so deep, and their capacities so shallow as to believe a criminal in his own case, to the prejudice of an innocent man? But they that will judge me by the malicious tongues of my prejudiced enemies, are fitter for a place in Bedlam, than to live amongst honest people, for honest men there are in the world; and therefore I appeal to Mr Wilde in Dublin, to Mr Wilkins in New-England, to Mr Darker in London, and all that have traded with me, for the truth of this scrupulous justice. But as

---

a. The several hundred pounds I've paid for others, sufficiently proves this.

scrupulous as I am in trade, I was never wanting to my belly, nor a wretch to my back; and am the same enemy to prodigality as I am to a sneaking temper; and I think I am right (in this part of my character); for Solomon says, Eccles. 2.24, there is nothing better for a man, than that he should eat and drink, and that he should make his soul enjoy good in his labour. But though I pity the man, Eccles. 6.2, to whom God hath given riches, and not the power to eat thereof, but a stranger eateth it; yet of the two extremes, I think it much better to live beneath than above my estate; for I had rather want than borrow, and beg than not pay. And though I have printed 600 books,[a] I never printed a new title to an old book, nor never undervalued a copy, because I did not print it myself; and I ever thought it as base injustice to run upon another's project; neither did I ever murder any man's name, with saying, *He printed this or that*, the more cunningly to praise myself; and I as little like underselling others, to get chapmen.[78] To sum up my character in few words: *I love rambling, don't love fighting; love Valeria, don't love money; love my friend, don't fear nor hate my enemy: love fair-dealing; had rather be called fool than knave. Let people laugh, while I win. Can be secret if trusted. Am owed more than I owe; and can pay more than that; make my word as good as my bond. Won't do a foul thing, and bid the world go whistle.*[79] Now whatever your ladyship thinks (or my enemies may say against me) all that know me will own this is the true character of John Dunton; or at least, it is the character of what I should[b] be. I write not this out of vainglory, but as a necessary vindication of my life and actions, against the abuses of Patrick Campbell. But perhaps your ladyship will say, I live by ill neighbours, that I praise myself: to this I answer, I see little in this character that adds much to my praise; or if I did, I should spoil it, with telling your ladyship that my faults are so many to my few virtues (if I have any) that I'm ready to own myself the worst of men; and do often cry out with the publican, Luke 18.13, God be merciful to me a sinner. However (Madam), if I have been too kind to myself in this present character, if your ladyship (in your remarks on it) will honour me so far as to take your

a. Of which see a further account in my Farewell Letter to the City of Dublin.
b. As was hinted concerning some other characters in this book.

pencil, and draw me just as I am (for this *Conversation* sets me in a true light), I'll print the character you give me, though it were a satire upon my whole life; for I know you're just, and will write nothing but what you think; and I so little value the praises of others, that I'll print it just as you send it; and if the exposing of my faults will make others avoid them, I shall reckon the publishing of them amongst the chief blessings of my life: and if, when your hand's in at characters, you'll send me your own, it would direct my pen in writing to ye, and be the best rule (next the Bible) that I could live by. But, Madam, if I find (by your character) you're as fallible as other ladies, I'll be as severe upon it (in our future correspondence) as I desire you'd now be upon mine; which (if I know anything of myself) is so far from being romantic, that I appeal to my own conscience for the truth of my whole character; and here conscience will stand my friend: nay, in some sense, a man's conscience is the only friend or enemy he has in the world, for a man can't fly from himself (as I hinted in the *Dublin Scuffle*) and therefore must be as great a fool as knave, if he turns Argus (alias traitor) to his own person;[80] but I am so little guilty of this madness, that I think Argus a base animal to suppress letters, merely to carry on a correspondence of his own with the same persons; for, notwithstanding Bog-land boasts of no venomous thing, such a serpent, there is in Ireland or else I am wrongly informed: but he's a sly invisible tool, and I almost despair of catching him; but that I may do all I can to discover him, I'll fall to write, *A search after Argus*. I hear of him in London by the Bristol packet, again in Dublin (by Dorinda's billet); and perhaps shall see him in Scotland; but shall scarce catch him (except at Rome), in a Jesuit's habit. But if I miss him at Rome, I'll take shipping for St Helena (for he resembles a cousin of mine that was born there) but like was never the same; so I'll leave this island, and rather than search in vain, I'll ramble next to Helicon, to enquire of Madam Laureat (the western nightingale) who justly wears the bays,[81] and has no equal on earth, but your ladyship; and I am apt to think I shall meet him here, for when Herma lays her hands to the spinnet, or charms with her heavenly tongue, the very angels sit and listen to her song; and what can't a lady discover, that can beckon to angels to give her intelligence. But suppose Herma can give no account of Argus, yet this ramble may bless the rest, for she's my friend more than in words; and if I meet her, will wish me a great deal of diversion in my travels; and (being a generous lady) will contribute towards them.

I'll next enquire of Mr Read (the barber I before described) for he'll dine with me tomorrow in Jewin-Street, and then I shall hear of Argus, for Mat. has been viewing Holland, and some say, had a glimpse of Argus in Amsterdam; and not unlikely, for his manners shew him a Dutchman.[82] If I gain no intelligence here, I'll send to Lucas in Crane-lane, for he's a man very inquisitive; and being a grateful person, if he hears of Argus, will let me know it by the first post. But my search is still after Argus and, rather than not find him, I'll next ramble to Simon, for he's a generous good man, and if he knows such a wretch as Argus, I'm sure will bring him out; or at least, direct me to an old gentlewoman (a grave, pious, ingenious lady) who knows Argus by Numb. 3. and is the only person that can discover him: but if I enquire for Argus here, perhaps this old lady will think him a dry subject, and never consent to the favour I ask (no, though I whine like a dog in a halter);[a] but this matron need not fret herself, for it is beneath my [b]spirit to court (a young, much less) an old woman in vain: besides, Rosinante will soon be saddled, and poor Sancho knows the way to the Bath, and if I desire it, will go with me round the world; I mean still, in search after Argus, whom I'll find if possible; but as Scoggin[83] said (when he untiled the ridge of a house to seek for a gold watch), I must as well look where he is not, as where he is; and therefore in my further search after Argus, I'll next step to my friend Ignotus, and from him to the learned Fido, for they are two generous Levites, and would never conceal my enemy. If I miss him here (as I judge I shall) I'll next ramble to a certain Frenchman, and ask if he knows Argus, for Argus says he is intimate with him; but what I get of Monsieur must be by way of petition, for Argus says he's a desperate blade, and I have no fancy to a broken pate. If Monsieur will give no account of Argus, I'll next step to the

a. As was hinted in Mr. Wilde's character, p. 237.   b. As was observed by one that had reason to know.

post-house; for some say this invisible fox gets his bread by sorting (and intercepting) of letters: but if I can have no account of him here, I'll ride post to all the gibbets in Christendom, as the fittest place for a man that betrays his trust; and if I miss of him here, I'll conclude the story of Argus was but a poetical fiction, or that the devil is run away with him.

Madam, I have now finished the *Account of my Conversation in Ireland* (to which I've added my search after Argus, the only serpent thought to be in it), which perhaps your ladyship will think as true as the story of Bevis,[84] or the travels of Tom. Coriat; for how can this hang together, that this letter should be writ at Pat's Coffee-house (as I at first hinted) when part of it seems to be written to your ladyship in Dublin after my arrival at London; and part of it from Dublin, whilst you were in England; and perhaps, Madam, the world will be as much puzzled to find out how I could at the same time mention the last things I did in Ireland, as well as the first, and all this in one letter. How can this come right? except you're a man of art, and can reconcile plain contradictions.

This, Madam, is easily reconciled, if your ladyship pleases to remember, that though it is printed as one continued letter, yet it was sent to you in several (as were also you ladyship's answers); and though this be enough to atone for the seeming contradictions, yet I may further add, it isn't to be thought, that a man that is not quite distracted would quote so many eminent persons (and some of the first rank) to countenance that which they could contradict; and as this alone is enough to prove the truth of part of my *Conversation*: so the additions I made to it since I came to London (upon a further recollection) reconcile all the seeming contradictions in it: for might I not write a great part of it at Pat's Coffee-house in Dublin, and send it to your ladyship at your return to London (with a desire you'd enquire after the state of my house in Jewin-Street;) and is it not equally as probable, that when ever your ladyship went back to Dublin, I should tell ye, upon my arrival in London, of the last things I did in Ireland, with the names of the persons that hazarded their lives to see me a shipboard.

Thus, Madam, though unacquainted with the subtle distinctions of art, yet by the clue of truth, I have led your ladyship out of those labyrinths in which my *Irish Conversation* (printed in one tedious letter) might seem to involve ye.

But (Madam) I fear I have tired you quite, and yet could scarce avoid being thus tedious; for since I was[a] resolved to have my cause tried at your bar, it was necessary to give you a full *Account of my Conversation*; that so, by putting things in the clearest light, you might be the better able to judge me aright. And having done this, I shall conclude with this request to you ladyship, that you'd now read, try, judge, and speak as you find. And whatever your sentence be, you will thereby oblige,

Madam,
Your Ladyship's most humble,
and most obedient servant,
John Dunton

London, April 20, 1699.

---

a. As I said in the beginning of this letter.

REMARKS

ON MY

Conversation

IN

IRELAND.

BY AN

Honourable Lady.

LONDON:

Printed, and are to be Sold by
A. *Baldwin*, near the *Oxford Arms*
in *Warwick lane*, and by the Booksellers in *Dublin*. 1699.

Remarks on my Conversation in Ireland, &c.

Sir,

I should think myself very happy, though much beyond my expectation, could I deserve the great esteem you set upon my correspondence: I confess, as charity and compassion first begun it, finding you overwhelmed with sorrow for the loss of your friend,[1] so your taking it in so good part, obliges me to continue any service I am capable of doing you. I am so great a stranger to you, and all your concerns, I can't so much as judge whether there is any real cause for your taking such pains for the vindicating of your reputation: however, I will take this occasion you offer me, to tell you my thoughts of your opinions and practice.

Your general definition of religion, to my apprehension, is as exact as can be comprehended in so few words; and your universal charity a very commendable virtue; but your care of keeping a conscience void of offence towards God, and towards man, is not so exactly performed: your going to hear the Nonconformists preach, must certainly give offence to the Church of England, and perhaps to God as well. Our Saviour Christ says, Woe to the world, because of offences; and sure, an unnecessary separation from a church that teaches nothing contrary to the true faith, is the highest offence that can be given or taken. I shall not undertake to justify their carriage to the Dissenters, I fear too much the ill effects of it; but whatever personal miscarriage has appeared, it cannot be charged upon the doctrine of the Church of England; it puts no check to our living as pure and conscionably as any Quaker can pretend to do; and must allow them a tender regard to their consciences, if they call that the light within them; but let them remember our Saviour's caveat to have a care that the light within them be not darkness; it has one character of the Prince of Darkness, which is pride, the exalting one's self, and despising others. I think the Pharisee came little short of all the good works the Quakers pretend to; yet the humble sinner was rather justified. All separation casts a blot upon the Church from which we depart, which we ought not to do, be the pretence never too plausible. I know nothing could justify our separation from the Church of Rome, but her defections to idolatry, and making her errors the conditions of her communion. All the faults and miscarriages of the Church-men should be the subject of our humiliation, for they are the tokens of God's displeasure; and we add to our punishment, in making them a means of an uncharitable division amongst Christian brethren; and those that do so, deservedly cut themselves off from the common charity, being instruments of the greatest mischief: I mean the teachers, not the persons misled; those have a title to our pity and commiseration. I am sorry their reputation for preaching prevails with so many to go to hear them; they do not consider what St Paul said to those that were some for Paul, some for Cephas and some for Apollos;[2] nay, some were for Christ, yet in that strife they were all carnal; besides, it gives the greatest advantage to the enemies of the reformed churches to put themselves into the shapes of such teachers to delude us, and keep up those factions and animosities by which they take occasion to scorn and despise our Church and reformation, and strengthen men's prejudices against it.

I am as much persuaded as you, that religion does not consist in names or things; and that Christ's Church is not limited to any nation or party. Our Saviour tells us, we shall all be taught of God, whose infinite and miraculous power extends to all nations in the world, often enlightening them in the midst of darkness; but where he has set lights in his Church, and appointed visible means of salvation, there to despise them, and choose to stray into by-paths, makes us unworthy of the blessing we enjoy, and liable to the judgment of falling into snares and temptations.

I think your arguments against the atheist are as convincing as could be found out; and your abstracted notion of the divine being is very good, and suits exactly with what I have read in a treatise written by Albertus Magnus.[3] Your behaviour at public assemblies, and your care and reverence for the sacrament, are very commendable marks of piety and devotion; and indeed, with that qualification carried with us, no message from God but will be welcome, though from the mouth of very weak or unworthy messengers. I am much pleased with your thoughts of the Communion of Saints, and could wish the world had a freer enjoyment of it.

I highly approve your care for the Sabbath, but am surprised you should refer yourself to me in so great a point. I will tell ye my thoughts, and not lead you out of the way, if I can help it. All the authors I have ever read agree, that the observation of the Sabbath is partly moral, and partly ceremonial, that we should worship and adore that great God that gave us being, at a certain time allotted for it, the light of Nature tells us; and therefore, that a seventh part of our time should be set apart for a solemn and public worship of God, is purely moral; the ceremonial part is the choice of the day. We find God chose the last day of the week for a memorial of the creation finished in six days; but not so strictly confined to the remembrance of the creation, but also of the Israelites' deliverance out of Egypt, a type of our salvation by Christ, as may be seen in the 5th of Deuteronomy; with good reason therefore is it now kept in memory of the last and greatest benefit, the accomplishment of our redemption, and on that account changed to the first day of the week, upon which day our redemption was finished by our Saviour's rising from the dead; this change was made in the Apostles' time, as appears by their so often meeting on the first day of the week recorded in the Scripture, and that they had our Saviour's countenance and authority for it, by his appearing so often to them in their assembly on that day.[4] I think one need not be so scrupulous about the day, but submit to the decision of the Church, who probably fetched it from the practice of the Apostles. Our Saviour tells us the Sabbath was made for man, and not man for the Sabbath; and it is of more moment to observe the duties of the day, than to be able to answer all objections and contentions that ill designing persons can raise against it. That we dedicate a seventh day to God's service, according to his own appointment, and upon the first day of the week, in memory of the great work of our redemption finished upon that day, is satisfactory enough to me; and if I sincerely perform the duties of the day, I make no question of God's acceptance. For the resting from bodily labour so strictly enjoined to the Jews, I take to be partly abolished with the other ceremonies, only retaining so much as is necessary to support the solemnity of the day. I think none can be too strict in consecrating to God that day as totally as our frail natures will permit; and though we can't be all the day (besides the public service) taken up in prayers and meditation, we may do well to keep ourselves out of the way of the world, which will soon quench the flame our divine exercises have kindled; but there were nothing like the conversation of heavenly minded persons, when we can have such; and there are works of mercy and compassion very proper for that day, which may raise our minds to love and praises to God for making us instruments in his hand for the good of anybody. In a word, the best instructor in the duties of the Lord's day is love; which will make us do all with diligence and delight, by which I may suppose you are animated to what you do, or desire to do, on that blessed day.

I agree with you, that the duty of prayer is manifest even by the light of Nature. That supreme being, that made us, can only preserve us, and to him we must apply for our well-being; but Christians, that are dedicated to God in baptism, should take care to sanctify all the actions of their lives by prayer, and never do that thing they dare not beg God's blessing upon: if we did impute to God the happy success of all our labours, we could not be so wanting to ourselves, as to neglect that great favour and privilege of a Christian, of representing all our wants and necessities to God, and engaging his care and providence in our behalf, of begging his Holy Spirit, which he has promised to those that ask it; which will lead us into all truth; teaching us to accuse and condemn our selves for sin and then engage us to the duty of thankfulness; and here I know not where to begin or make an end. Inummerable are the mercies we daily receive, and sufficient to employ all the moments of our life in the contemplation of them; and were our hearts truly thankful, nothing could be wanting to keep us close to our duties, both to God and our neighbour, whatever different ways and modes we find of expressing it. I dare be bold to pronounce that person a true child of God, that in a deep sense of his own unworthiness looks upon all the mercies he enjoys, as the favour and bounty of heaven, for which he can never be sufficiently thankful. And I do not know a stronger foundation to build any person's conversion upon, for if they are born of Christian parents, when they consider that blessing and privilege which thousands want, it must needs engage them in his service who has dealt so lovingly with them; but if an alien from the Church of God should by some great providence meet with the opportunity of being instructed in the faith, how can he choose but look upon this good providence as the effect of God's merciful kindness to him, and work a more kindly obedience, than all the terrors of hell. I confess, the threats of hell is a way I am little acquainted with, yet must own, we cannot know God's mercy in its full extent, without knowing to the full the miseries from which it has redeemed us. But this works naturally upon our love, and turns it into such a fear as works again by love, and makes our obedience cheerful and free, yet I shall not pretend to censure those that perhaps experience teaches to use harsher methods; but I bless God for his more tender dealing with me, for I am persuaded those conflicts and temptations so many find upon their death beds are the effects of those horrors their teachers infuse in them; for I may say with thankfulness, I never saw anyone in that condition, of all my friends that I have buried. And I make no doubt, but the subtlety of the Devil is never wanting to make his advantage of our fears, scruples and superstitions, when he terrifies us with apparitions and spectrums; it is certainly a great happiness to be free from the fears of them, for which you have just cause to bless God; and I can speak it by experience, those ominous presages of persons, deaths, or misfortunes never happened to me, nor any of my relations; who all held a principle against superstition, or any observation of such things.

Your humble and uncommon confession of your own frailties is what we must all own as well as you, if we choose good principles for our conduct; it is all the virtue we can pretend to, the exact performance depends upon many things not in our power.

Your neglect and disregard of dressing, and fine clothes, suits the temper and inclination of the wise, and men of business; it is a weakness even in women, but a great folly in men; and a true conjecture may be often made of the intellects of both sexes by their dress.

You have a strange happiness for a man of business, to have so much leisure for divine contemplation in the fields, and other pleasant places, whereby you furnish your mind with pious ejaculations, which serves you upon occasion to obtain God's direction, blessing and conduct in your affairs; it is then the business goes pleasantly on, when the success is perfectly resigned to God.

It is a pity your great love to your wife should make you so uneasy, that all your philosophy could hardly furnish you with patience enough to support a month's absence. Your excessive loving temper, which I perceive you do not take for a weakness, but a perfection, gives you much reason to applaud your great success in your choice of two wives successively of so much merit.

Though you seem so surprised at the ill company you dined with, I assure myself those men had the model of their conversation from London, with a little addition of their own native vanity, unless they are much altered from what I knew of them: I take them generally to be all acted[5] by a romantic honour, and every man of what rank or quality soever, takes upon him as much as he can, the mien and equipage, living and eating of the nobility, especially of those that come from England: even swearing and profaneness they mistake for great virtues, when observed in men of that rank, without considering that the vice of swearing springs from a base and vulgar education; who, wanting language to express the vehemence of their passions, have contracted an ill habit of supplying the want of truth and eloquence with oaths. If persons of quality ever give so barbarous an example, it is when they are least themselves; either transported with pride, passion, or wine: but whoever they are that do it, they show a very shallow capacity, and weak apprehension of the dreadful majesty of God; and however he may perhaps please himself with his own conceit of his wit and parts, he may be justly branded with the name of fool; which Solomon wisely gives to all that fear not God.

Your often returns from business to retirement was a privilege of being a stranger, and far from your family and relations. I can't be judge of the pleasure you found in Montaign's *Essays*, having never read it. I heard it once commended by a man in reputation for wit, but not so much for virtue, which moved my curiosity the less; and having all I desire in the Port-Royal,[6] I confine myself to a very few books. I envy not your trip to your auction: I have had some of that pleasure of observing bidders for books upon my own account, but, wanting your skill, came far short of your satisfaction.

Your recollection of your actions, how hard soever to others, is very easy to you, who remember so exactly all you say and do: if you as strictly observe the motives from whence they spring, and view your actions in a true light, such a method of examination constantly used, will bring you to all the perfection attainable in this life. The divine contemplation you have so ready upon the sight of every proper object, must needs dispel (as you own) all melancholy vapours;

for the aspiring of the soul to heaven brings heaven to it; and by that light shall best discern its own defects, and God's perfections; and in a manner transform it into joy and love.

You give the characters of several honest men, and one good wife; I suppose you take them for some of the rarities of that city; the places you describe are unknown to me; I never took the pains to see them, and if I had, perhaps my own observation would have come short of your pleasant description. I am little fond of pleasing my sight; wherever I live, my house and garden limit my curiosity; which is the reason I am as much a stranger to Ireland, as those that never were there.

I am much delighted with the account you give of the Church and State; and am perfectly persuaded my Lord Galway justly deserves the high character you give him in every respect; and sure much of the present happiness of that kingdom is owing to his wise conduct, and great example of virtue and piety; to my knowledge there's nothing like it for those people there, who live by no rule but imitation; and the severest laws would have much less effect on them, than his obliging condescension. I wonder what's become of all the Jacobites? There are some for certain, but not so barefaced perhaps in such a government, as to be noted of strangers.

It is also matter of great joy, to hear the bishops and clergy perform their parts with so much charity and condescension to the Dissenters, as gives them occasion to commend their moderation and piety: it were much to be wished, that all our unhappy differences might be consumed in flames of charity; and Ireland, as much as it has been despised, might have the honour to set us that great example; then, as that good prelate, Bishop Hall[7] advised, we should have peace with all but Rome and hell.

It is observable, there are no places where care is so effectually taken to suppress popery, as where they abound most, and are best known; which may be the reason that in Ireland they have in that point outdone us here. It would be a great pleasure to me, to think as you do, that the Romish religion were on its last legs in Ireland; and sure nothing is more likely to produce that effect, than those methods they have taken; or which would better secure the rebellion of that kingdom, beyond all the suppressing laws; for while there are papists to improve every failing or miscarriage in the rulers, and every defect or weakness in the capacities of the people, to the raising such appearances to delude them, as may serve to the promoting their own interest and religion, nothing can be expected but rebellion and mischief; but they who have the art of living incognito,[8] how is it possible to be sure they are rid of them, as hard to know as their great patron, the Devil, when transformed into an angel of light? No, I have not hopes from the rigor of any laws made against them; all my hopes is, that as that adulterous church has lived so long, she is now grown old and ugly, the time is coming, that all her lovers will hate her, tear her flesh, and burn her city with fire; all things seem to be preparing for her execution, notwithstanding the French king's persecution;[9] and who knows but the pope's mournful jubilee may not be a prognostication of it.

That old Father Kereen, I believe I have heard of; there was such an one lived at Athlone, who used to say he could lay a spirit for seven years, and then again for seven more; though I am of opinion they are never wanting to contrive some imposter, when necessary to shew their power, and to delude the people, and keep up their credulity and superstition: yet I believe as well, that they are able to do it, whenever there is any real occasion for it; they are many of them men of much thought and retirement, only designed for the promoting the kingdom of Satan; he can't deny this assistance for the carrying on his own work, and no question teaches them the way he will be dealt with; it is a great happiness for the poor people to be rid of such ghostly Fathers; their superstition once cured may probably secure them from those miseries.

The church you went to where there was music, gives much opportunity of gazing; the mind having the least part in that service of all the rest, it seems to me you should have had more reason to have yielded to the eastern custom of separating the women from the men, had the women appeared more beautiful, since that and soft music might have discomposed your temper for the sermon. For my part, I think women's devotions are as much distracted with gazing at one another, observing how they look, and how they dress, that I could wish some habit were appointed to be worn in religious assemblies, that would give us all the same air, that neither beauty nor quality could be distinguished: I mean only those that sit in pews and galleries; for the ordinary sort, there's less danger, they'll not make it their pride to dress, if quality don't.

I easily credit you, and believe it was more than a fancy that you saw nothing handsome in all the female faces; I have observed in many churches of late years, the same thing; and wonder for what reason all beauty should be fled out of the world, unless it be for the ill treatment it finds here; and truly women make a pretty good shift without it, taking upon them the part that once belonged to men; and obtain by flattery and cajoling, what beauty used to do by conquest; but I confess beauty and charming are two things with me; there is a gracefulness in mien and motion, proceeding from the mind, and makes the whole aspect charming, without the help of complexion and feature; virtue makes the truest beauty and the softest charms for the best and wisest persons.

I am of opinion, as you insinuate, that memory is not the chief qualification for profitable hearing of sermons, as it is a means God has appointed to instruct us as from himself; to observe what touches us in particular is all the concern we have in it; when God speaks to the heart, we can't but remember and take notice of it.

The character of your antagonist has given a very natural description of pride and meanness, two things nearer related than the world imagines, which is often brought to the first, but always takes authority to despise and reproach the latter; but experience shews us pride never prospers and augments so much as in persons of mean quality, or small parts, raised to great honour or riches; and sordidness often comes into the society, but serves only to make pride the more hated, nobody gaining by it; thus loaded with so many ill qualities, he must needs act as he did; it is the part of a generous enemy to conceal his history; and of a good Christian, to let nothing provoke you to expose it, unless the good of the public require it.

It is no surprise to hear so many of the players in Dublin are no way inferior to those in London; it was never the temper of Ireland to let any country outdo them in vanity and idleness, two things that will secure a player from starving; and where they find their interest, their company is never wanted, as appears in their posting to Kilkenny, as it seems they did. That gentleman must needs be very soft and effeminate, that must be taught virtue and religion so charmingly as in the theatre; but for all their constant attendance there, I fear such gentlemen are much strangers to those virtues they pretend to learn there; and have as little use for them as for their time they waste and throw away with so much care and diligence.

I think that gentleman had a great deal of time to spare, that was so curious in his garden; it is a very innocent delight one takes in the products of Nature, but excessive curiosity transforms that pleasure into a vexatious care and labour; and had his visitors been all of the temper of Diogenes, and had disappointed him of applause and admiration, it would have shewed him his mistake in making that an entertainment for the mind, which is more proper for the pleasure and recreation of the body, that takes no less delight in woods and fields, where art is a stranger.

The characters you give your brethren (as you call them) would make one think there were something in that calling inclined men to goodness; you remark so many commendable qualities in them, but nothing is so charming as the idea I have of the lady you have so admirably characterized in distich;[10] one could not wish for greater perfection, or of any other kind than those you have described. I wish the tutor, with all his learning, be not tempted to think his happiness resembles so much the joys of heaven, as may make him too well contented with his earthly tabernacle; and perhaps the lady may owe the last perfection in her character to his conversation; so that the family may well be agreeable to the degree you speak of, the master and mistress being also persons of so much merit.

The remarkable fruitfulness of Mr Hook is considerable, but the two and twenty brothers listed in Ireland as much; many children are not only blessings, but may be observed to be given most commonly to good people that have not repined at them, but been thankful for them; and where they live to men and women's estate, are very often persons of piety and virtue; the necessity they find of yielding and complying with one another in their youth forms in them such a habit of self-denial, as fits them to receive other good impressions in their riper age, if their parents' care is not wanting.

It was a very generous care you took to pay your father's legacy; it could not concern your conscience, not being executor; but shewed a very great and kind respect to your father's memory; but that remorse of conscience so many feel for the wrongs they do in the case of money, is in my opinion a sort of indication that money is generally taken for our chief good; there are injuries we commit against others daily, without regret, which often amount to as great wrongs, for which our conscience never troubles us.

Sir Peter Pett[11] did the world, as well as his friend, a service, in preserving his memoirs; it seems we should otherwise have lost such truths, some persons were afraid of.

That dignified woman, called the most ingenious, must needs have enemies of her own sex, though you think perhaps she does not deserve them; it is crime enough to be distinguished by any good quality; her greatest crime that appears to me, is her suffering her husband to be so much a stranger to his own modesty, that he should take such a journey so ill appointed for his business.

Dublin is very happy in a banker, such a one as you describe, punctual, just, and honest in his dealings; and it may be, he has something of the natural generosity of his country added to it, which made him so ready to serve you as a stranger.

I more admire than envy the celebrated female poet, she must be so much under the dominion of fancy; I can't endure any kind of slavery; and all the fineness of poetry can never make up for the unruliness of fancy, when indulged, which poets must allow; to have one's thoughts sober and regular is a happiness of much value to me.

That aged woman you discoursed of was a great prodigy; if her understanding and judgment had been as strong and lasting as her senses, her experience might have given us much instruction.

I fancy it was a very pleasing surprise, to find a person that perfectly resembled one you thought so accomplished; one of the persons you wished to see, so near a resemblance of, I never saw; but for the other, her beauty was superlative before the smallpox; but after that, she had not many equals; but never expect to find in this age, her sort of beauty, which consisted so much in majesty and grandeur.

Mr Dangerfield I never saw, and can have no notion of the gentleman's perfections from him; but your character makes him very fine; and I suppose his lady's virtues put you in mind of wives making good husbands: I have seen great alteration in men's tempers, from the conversations of their wives, and for the worse, as often as for the better; but to the making a good husband, no doubt meekness and patience are the best ingredients, with the addition of some cunning and flattery, and will go much further in that business than piety and charity, unless prayers and tears are allowed to be of any force.

The gentleman you describe, besides his bravery and courage, his being so full of love and pity, may be the chief reason of his not marrying, in love and compassion to himself, declining a condition of so much toil and trouble, and in pity to the lady, whose share must be more than double to his.

I am very apt to believe the Nonconformists may be in themselves the worthy men you represent them; but wish I could discover what good end they propose to themselves in preaching? If to convince us of the errors of our Church, will not writing do that as well, if it is an error we are ignorant of? But should it be one we know, and for interest, or other reasons, maintain it, there's small hopes then of our conviction; yet it must be a very considerable error that will justify their public preaching, to draw persons off from our Church; but the difference between us is not so great; if the Presbyterians approve 36 of our Articles,[12] the other three had better be made a sacrifice to peace and unity, than give our enemies so much advantage against us by our divisions; but perhaps they design by their excellent preaching, to draw so many to their party as may fright the Church of England into a compliance with them; if such a thing should happen, one can't commend the means they used to accomplish it, so far remote from peace and charity; they seem purely human, and if God should draw from such ways his own glory, yet who knows how their presumption may be chastised? At the same time God has better ways of his own, if we could patiently wait and rely on him; when we go about to mend things, we with our pride and perverseness make them worse; of which the last civil war in England is a great instance. Had we as much humility and charity, as we have the contrary, which every attempt of accommodating has hitherto increased, we would study to find out the means of peace and union, and think no yielding on either side too much for the purchase of such a blessing; which if you know a greater, and can prove in your defence of your practice, any motive more considerable for going to meetings, then I allege for keeping to the Church of England, whatever faults can be imputed to her, I must yield; for then I shall be as much afraid of your arguments, as you were of the gentleman that could say what he pleased, and prove what he said.

I can't but admire at your curing yourself of an antipathy! What can be too strong for such a power? I can't think but you might as well hinder the operation of sympathy, and create in your self an aversion to the fair sex, when you find occasion for it.

If Mary Gossam had pulled off the night-cap, she might have been sure it was the same cap it looked like;[13] but I am apt to think it had as airy a substance as the man that wore it; no doubt the Devil has had that power in all ages, and for his own designs frequently does it, when God permits; taking upon him the persons of all, both good and bad; and for discovery of murders, and such things that seem to cross his general design of doing mischief; but he that can speak truth with intent to deceive, can do what seems good to serve his own ends: and as you threaten to return from the dead to do justice to your reputation, I shall wish you long life, for fear the Devil should take advantage from what you say, and come and vindicate your reputation to me, but I hope I shall die first.

I should have expected from your experience, a more moderate reception of your adversary's slanders; we should not stay till we are informed, but take it for granted, there are persons that belie, and speak ill of us; what is there surprising in that, which is the common treatment the world gives and takes? It had been strange a man of his character should shew any civility, as he thought you his enemy; when he shewed so little at first, when he might hope to make you his friend! That other man you had reason to thank, for giving you the opportunity to clear yourself to my Lord Mayor, which was public enough for the world's notice; and success enough afterwards, to meet with an honest binder in his place.

But it is the greatest wonder to me, you should come off so well with that beautiful country gentlewoman! If she had had no beauty, her agreeable conversation and modesty, with a little compliance for you, had been charm sufficient to engage you; but that you could trust yourself to contemplate every particular beauty, both of body and mind, is daring to astonishment in a man that values himself upon his virtue! But you will say, her virtue abundantly secured you;

how great soever that was, her courage seems no less, in exposing herself to the danger of pleasing.

Though beauty is no great matter in itself, yet the price the world sets upon it, should make it of some value to the owners. What made Solomon find out so contemptible a comparison for a fair woman without discretion, but to shew us that whoever is possessed of such a treasure, should esteem it at the rate others do; which is agreeable to common sense? What could one think of a person that should walk the streets, and go to markets and fairs dressed up in jewels to a great value? Should one not tax her discretion, or think she had some strange design in it, to make a trial how many enemies she should meet? Which would be almost as many as saw her; some designing her mischief to get her jewels, others jeering and exposing her in all places for her folly; for beauty much resembles jewels in this, that though they are the chiefest bravery of nature, they are of the least use; so one may be very happy without beauty; but when one is possessed of such a treasure, it ought to be secured by modesty, and a discreet value of it, and not carelessly exposed to pleasing, but only upon just occasion: but a married woman with such a careless conduct, making no distinction, is as ridiculous as a waiting woman would be, who had her lady's jewels in her keeping, and should lend them to the milk-woman to dress up their pails for dancing.

My design in all this, is to prove there would be no occasion for a man's defending so hotly, either his own, or that lady's virtue, who had a true esteem of her beauty, whether in her own, or her husband's possession; for I am truly moved with compassion for this incomparable person you propose for a pattern to our whole sex, to find she lies under the misfortune of slander and envy; and though she has the support of those sober ladies that honour her with their friendship, it is of little force to take off slander, since there is a charity much in vogue, that forbids distinguishing any but what are notoriously bad, which in this refined age are very few that appear so; her husband had been her best support, had he believed her virtuous upon his own judgment, and not upon the opinion of another; I fear your judgment was not generally prized at that rate.

However, I can't but applaud your happy retreats to the cool country air, after so much heat (though you carried a disease with ye) since there you found a cure; there's none knows the pleasures of gardens and retirement, like those that have lived in the hurry of the world; for that, like other pleasures, must be set off by its contrary.

The very same doctrine Mr Cowley teaches for retirement, I establish for friendship; which never is right, or can be lasting without it; for till we have cast off those restless thoughts of pleasing the world and our vain passions to persons so disposed, the rules of friendship are as severe as school-instructions to boys, with their heads full of play; who are not less blind to all the pleasures and advantages of it. But how must that mind be elevated, that in retirement can be everything to itself? Sure the admonition, instruction, and variety of thoughts a friend would yield us, should infinitely add to the perfection of such a life? And though living *incognito* from being seen and known to the senseless world, is a privilege to be wished; yet to be deprived of the society of the virtuous and religious, is to cut ourselves off from the chief pleasure that gives us a taste of heaven upon earth; with the opportunity of a delightful improvement of every moment of our time spent in their conversation.

Nor can I think that great emperor, Charles the 5th, could have boasted half that sweetness he found in his change of life, had he wholly retired from the conversation of the divine Valdesso;[14] but you must ever be a stranger to the true pleasures of retirement, as much as you pretend to love it, you carry such a busy mind about with you, and crowd your thoughts with fields, gardens, parks, your house, and absent friends. How could you take any thought for a house left in the conduct of such a wife? It is only extravagant and disorderly wives that turn the house out of the windows in their husband's absence.

No question you were as much in Valeria's thoughts, though she might not dream in so much danger. You might well expect death in a distemper so often fatal; and the thoughts you had from that expectation, I believe has taught you experience, and shewed you how much you were deceived in your hopes, that to the end of your life you should think of the world just as you did then when you thought you were leaving it. And did you flatter yourself to think, if time would unweave your life again to the first thread, you would mend your conduct? You are now convinced of the vanity of that presumption, not having had death, and the continual preparations for it, so much in your thoughts, as you then promised yourself. This is judging others by myself; if it is rash and false, I beg your pardon.

I confess I always looked upon sickness as the greatest of all temporal evils; and health the most considerable of earthly blessings; what can discompose the mind like pain and sickness? One may find a remedy for all other misfortunes, by resolving all into the will of God, which orders nothing to befall us but for good; but no resignation ever so great can hinder the sympathy the soul has with the body; that in those occasions our thoughts have little power to entertain any thought but patience per force: if therefore the thoughts of death and judgment, heaven and hell are necessary to reflect on, it is when we are in health; sickness discomposes all serious thoughts; for myself, I would have nothing to do at that time, but to resign myself with all the patience I could muster up, equally accepting release either by death or recovery, which of them God pleases to appoint me; and nothing makes us so ready and willing to die, as a comfortable assurance of our salvation, which will stand us then in more stead than any reflection on our past life, though never so good, or the most serious repetance we can then exercise. Nor can I think it a presumption, because not built on our own performances, but upon the promises of God. If it is possible to judge of the truth of any divine grace, it is possible to know they are his chosen to whom he gives it. How can the Holy Spirit witness with our spirits that we are the children of God, if we are strangers to what he witnesses? All divine graces are the earnest[15] of our eternal inheritance; they are the gifts of God, which he never withdraws, for his gifts are without repentance: nor is assurance a particular favour to some, but to all his chosen, that are careful to try themselves, and their graces; and for those that fear assurance should make them libertines, they would find the contrary if they had it; for it is not the fancy of having, but the real possession of true grace creates assurance, which will be seen and known by its effects, as a tree by its fruits; and no such motive to lead a heavenly life on earth, as a firm assurance in the exercise of divine graces, that we are consigned to a glorious immortality in heaven, so remote from the changes and uncertainties in this life; though perhaps in some sort, a necessary quality for the imperfect pleasures this world affords us.

A little longer enjoyment of your earthly paradise in the country would have put you upon the search of business in town, only upon account of variety; and the idea of it now you are snatched from it has more of pleasure in it, than a longer enjoyment would had given you.

I perceive we are obliged to your inquisitiveness and curiosity (a character you give yourself); for leading you to so many different places, which furnished your table-book with remarks which we shall see in perfection in your *Summer Rambles*; and above all, the fine history of Lord Clonuff,[16] of whom I never heard till now.

You had a very uncommon and particular happiness you had reason to prize, in meeting in your ordinary conversation, five persons eminent for piety, wisdom, learning, and all other virtues; and I agree with you, that the best consolation in the want of such company, is reading, especially the Bible, whatever opinion the generality of the world has of it, if read without pride and curiosity. A humble spirit that reads and lays it up in their minds, finds a time, by God's special favour and blessing, to understand and apply it to themselves, for their comfort and direction in proper times and occasions.

Following your fancy led you to a great deal of variety, but the bowling-green, above all, has charms for me; I think it no improper recreation for ladies; and where men, who are desirous to civilize themselves in ladies' companies, might partake with them there. The only difficulty is, there are very few bowling-greens in private families, they are so chargeable to keep; and all public meetings for diversion soon grow scandalous in this corrupt age.

The pleasures of Kilkenny, so magnificent as you describe, might give one the idea of a paradise, were not one principle, felicity, wanting, of not being able to contain a great mind. You say the owner lives like one that's much above it; so he may say, as a great favourite in the court of Ahasuerus,[17] What does all this avail me?

And truly by the company he had at bowls with him, I am apt to think there were others also as soon satisfied, and had enough of his paradise; they are all pleasures for the eye, which is never satisfied with seeing, but by change of objects is in perpetual search of a felicity, which always comes far short of our expectations. The novelty once over, there's an end of the enjoyment.

Sure the natives of that place where the four elements are so pure must needs have a more refined nature. I shall observe with more exactness, the character of those persons, when I come to them; and indeed you find so many things to admire, in a country where others think everything deserves to be despised; makes me believe the perfection lies in yourself, that knows how to extract out of every subject all the virtues it contains; that temper fits you for a traveller, whose design is observation; and truly, the contemplation of perfection is pleasanter than of faults and defects; that mere self-love is enough to persuade us, while we fix our thoughts upon the first, to overlook the latter.

And that lady, whose full character you reserve for another place, I own would reconcile me to any country and circumstance, that would give me the opportunity of edifying in her conversation.

That great and generous brigadier, who treated all so nobly, shews the largeness of a Frenchman's soul, when out of the slavery of his own country, and under the benign influence of a Lord Galway. Your poem[18] was deservedly dedicated to him, I shall spare my remarks upon it; I don't pretend to judge of wit, but shall leave it to its peers.

One can't but look upon those miserable cabins you describe, as the just desert of sloth and idleness; and by their manner of living in them, one might believe St Paul's injunctions had been observed in the severest sense, that because they did not work they had been denied the food of their souls, as well as bodies. It is a severe reflection upon us, to suffer those that are, or should be Christians, to live just under our noses, in as ill a manner as the worst of heathens.

I can't blame you for leaving those sad objects for Kildare, if you designed mirth, for which that other place was very unfit; the country must needs be fine, whatever the town is. St Bridget did not set herself to cut and sew for what was not worth her pains. I have observed no places so pleasant as those that have been chosen heretofore for abbeys and priories. You were in the right to take the old Father with you; those men serve much to make up a jest. My Lord Kildare had well placed his chair, in respect to the Curraugh; which however pleasant of itself, is much heightened by remembrance of the pleasant rancounters[19] at the horse-races.

I know not whether the predictions of astrologers be true; but I know a man may make them true if he pleases, and too often does so;

if you like to be mercurial, it will be hard to fix you; the girl that upon opening her eyes was saluted with so much novelty, was moderate, in respect to your boundless curiosity; you take in all objects by whole-sale, which you are forced to dress and refine in your fancy, before you can expose them to the view of others less fond of them. I never had, I assure you, so fine an idea of Italy, as to desire to see it; it is a place too full of artifice and cunning for my simple genius. I must own, I rather pity than envy your rambling fate; were I in that distemper, I knew a way to cure it; but there's no prescribing to you, till you are willing.

The satisfaction of your travels not disturbing your sleep, is, in my opinion, no great matter; it were something if you could never sleep nor dream of Valeria, or desire to see her without it; and what great miracle to be content with pleasures of your own choosing? You might better boast of a contented spirit, if you could be content to stay at home, and never travel, but upon just occasion.

You take the right way of reflecting upon your good or bad suc-cesses, that truth once established. That nothing comes to pass by chance, sets us above all difficulties, but excludes not our care and providence for the accomplishment of our designs, only moderates us, and makes us indifferent as to the success: cross accidents may well be looked upon as trials of our patience, especially in small and common things; but the more considerable misfortunes have higher ends, which we should make it our business to find out. I know God's ways are unsearchable to us in themselves, but those that concern us in particular are lessons he sets us to learn, which we must be careful not to overlook; and I think the most general language all afflictions and misfortunes speak, may be interpreted as calls to humility; as pride is the root of all evil, humility must be the proper remedy; but in occasions where no remedy can be found, we may justly say,

Shall we receive from Power Divine
Life's sweets, and at his grief repine?
From both, his tribute let him raise,
From these, our patience; and from that, our praise.[20]

Your trouble for Patrick's fault more than your own injury, was very charitable, but upon a wrong foundation; for his fault had not been less but greater, had it been the resentment of an injury; for then it had been spite, malice, and revenge; whereas it might be now a little heady pride and insolence, to see how far his money or interest would go, and how far he could have his humour; there are many will venture disobliging their neighbours, much less strangers, for as trifling considerations; therefore if you clear your innocence, he must appear less criminal, and by consequence ye do him a kindness with yourself.

It is much to be admired, your courteous gentleman, so full of charms, could resist the glory of conquest, if he found the ladies laid down their arms; but his great humility made him a stranger to such thoughts, and procured him the happiness of living a bachelor, by which he was worthy of honour; if, like the widows St Paul mentions, he was a bachelor indeed, and designed it for a good end; but if his motive was self-love and liberty, he, like the widows that live in pleasure, is dead while he lives;[21] everyone is a debtor to the public, and of that married persons do best discharge themselves, as heads of families, and on that account great benefactors to their country: but those that the providence of God exempts from the toils and troubles of a married state must consider they were not made for themselves; but, as they have opportunity, must sacrifice their time and fortunes to do good, and make themselves sharers in the labour man is condemned to.

I believe the young divine is perfectly the man you represent him, by the text he chose; young men have something extraordinary in them, when they are so remote from the ambition natural to that age and function, who seldom content themselves with less than the deepest points, and highest rhetoric, to shew their learning in; a plain man, so little suits their style or humour, they think it would degrade them, and spoil their preferment, to take notice of such, either in, or out of their sermons.

But of all your friends, who you thought you could never enjoy enough, I prefer the man that carried the decrees of wisdom in his mouth; he might well be a blessing to his wife and children, if he had any; for such a man is a blessing to all that know him; there's no miscarrying in his company: where wise counsel is so ready, I applaud the happiness of his scholars, and wish them better employment than acting plays; which I suppose was but in order to the better and more real sort of acting they would arrive at in time. I wonder what remedy his wisdom prescribed you for your loss? I take it was in his house you cried out Thieves. I am ready to think, the occasion you took to love Drogheda was by his advice; it is only wisdom can make one take pleasure in tears and grief; unless the comfort you took to find you had such strength to recover with such weak remedies, as of my prescribing, might outweigh the rest of your troubles.

I can't imagine what you mean by primitive innocence you were so frighted at; unless it was parting with all your substance (as the primitive Christians did in charity) to requite the kindness of your friends? I perceive he that generously confers favours upon you, loosens the tie you have to yourself by love, and rivals you in the glory of generosity, which is your mistress; and till you have outdone your rival, and regained the victory, you appear to yourself like a slave in fetters; but if, to recover your liberty, you should leave yourself as bare as they in primitive innocence, it would nothing resemble it, proceeding as it does, from another cause, and for another end.

There's nothing extraordinary in a poet, or one of much fancy, who, to shew his art, gives the ornaments of high perfections to very mean objects; but in you it might be also the effect of that gratitude and generosity you so abound with, that occasioned so large a character of your owl. I don't question, but if it should want gravity to recommend it to my reflections, it does not want wit to make it agreeable and proper for diversion; you have my leave to be as merry as you please: I apprehend it necessary to those of your complexion, but you know I am under an obligation not to ———.[22]

Since the maggot[23] takes you so often, your stars are very kind to make you always so happy in conversation with your companions in travel; and above all, with a female wit and beauty, who helped you out so well with your remarks; but sure nothing could be better than the remark the man made upon the steeple that stood when the church could not; we never want divine warnings, were we so wise to make a right use of them.

Your female companion wanted not the curiosity of a perfect woman, no more than the charms of perfect beauty; but if her wit was as perfect as the rest, she might choose that inquisitive way as the most sure to oblige you, and make the conversation the more agreeable between you.

I can't much condemn Clara, if she could find in her heart to outdo you in tenderness; I think it a laudable ambition to outdo you in wit too; and it may be she feared to be defective, if she did not value herself upon it, as wits often do, especially upon the sudden accession of the unexpected honour received by it; and as humbling as your verses were, it is like they rather increased her pride, to find a man of so much sense, so much concerned for her; and if you value my judgment, I think you had as much reason to slight her when she outdid you in tenderness, as when she outdid herself in pride and contempt of you.

I might suppose there were no beggars in Ireland, from your making no remarks of the charity, amongst those persons whose many other virtues you mention, as well as from your saying nothing in particular of the beggars; for I am satisfied, it is the false notion of the charitable, that makes so many beggars, when they think themselves obliged to give to all that ask, from our Saviour's command; they are not so ready to take notice, that he adds, And from him that would borrow of thee, turn thou not away; the world abounds not much with that kind of charity: to my apprehension, our Saviour intended that precept to shew us the charitable disposition a Christian ought to have, both to give or lend, upon occasion; but not to make ourselves and charity a prey to those that make it their trade to cheat and abuse both the one and the other. There is nothing would do charity more right, than a law that should forbid relieving beggars at random, merely to be rid of their noise and clamour; and ways found out to employ the charity of well-disposed persons, to the good and benefit of the town and country where they live, that the truly poor may find persons to apply to for relief, who both knows them and their wants: such a law, and the careful execution of it, would deserve the Parliament's care, as much perhaps, as any other they can pretend to bless the nation with; and thus the public charity secured, there is more liberty for the private, of which the charitable persons themselves take so slight account, their left hand scarce knows what their right hand does, so many and various are the occasions of charity they are engaged in, consisting in many different ways of doing good, as in lending money or goods, and not exacting the payment where the persons are not in a condition to pay; in forgiving wrongs and injuries, concealing and bearing with infirmities; in advice, and admonishing; in a word, in everything in which we can assist one's neighbour, though with some difficulty and hardship to one's self.

Your character of Ireland in verse, is very fine and just, but I shall shorten my reflections upon your prose character; it is not a subject I love to dwell upon; perhaps the moisture of the air may contribute much to their phlegm and sloth; but I suppose it is the contempt in which the government holds them, that is the cause of their brutality; sure if it were thought worth their pains, they are as capable of being civilized as the other barbarous nations who have been brought up to Christianity. You talk of priests for their conductors; sure they must have been priests of Dan,[24] that had so well instructed those people; for I perceive the best among them that live in cities, excell only in fashionable villainies.

I am inclined to think your friend Wilde deserves to the full all the glories of his character, both as to his virtues, and natural endowments, to be as you affirm of him, the same good man in all events, and a fit companion for the nicest Christian; add to this his great love to the present government. These are all virtues of no common size; yet it is very possible he may fail of that reward you expect for him in time, and meet a more ample reward in a place where time shall have nothing to do; nor can he lose by that, even in this world, for virtue is its own reward and end.

It is a surprising character you give of Doctor Phoenix! I know not whether such another will spring out of his ashes? To be modest and humble, ascribing all his success to God, and to impart his skill to the poor for charity, are virtues the generality of our physicians are strangers to; and though they pretend to rail at quacks, they have both one aim; which is more at their patients' purses, and their own fame and reputations, than the health and recovery the sick party gives their money for.

Though I acknowledge the force of imagination to be very great, I can't conceive how two such persons should be so transported, as one to fancy the story, and the other the circumstances to support it; nor is there anything incredible in the whole relation attested by two such persons as you represent them: the lady's courage was the most surprising part of the story; but I confess it would neither confirm nor destroy the doctrine of baptising children with me, as I believe it was the Devil; what he teaches is of little weight, his policies are so refined, it is hard to guess at his designs; but to be sure, his intent is always to deceive; and then most certainly, when he most contradicts his own interest. I wonder at the Dean's so slightly imputing it to the force of imagination, unless he's of the same mind with a minister I once discoursed with; who denied the Devil's power to possess any persons: notwithstanding many instances I alleged out of the New Testament, he affirmed all those were only lunatics. I was much surprised at such audaciousness against such plain scripture! Could I find the like for souls entering into bodies after they have cast them off, I should not generally impute all apparitions to the Devil, as I do. Not that I believe they enter into bodies to appear in, but that we only are deceived with the appearance of a body; for in this case the persons had been dead so long, their bodies must needs be corrupted. I believe as well, in some special occasions, God sends his angels still, as he did formerly, in human shapes, to warn or protect his servants from some dangers; but not to take upon them the persons of the dead, to teach or confirm any point of faith or doctrine; I never found anything in Scripture to countenance such an opinion. If imagination had such a power over the lady as the Dean pretended to think, to save his giving sentence in a case so difficult (though who knows but he did believe so in reality?) that pretty Robin had been a subject proper to delude her, having qualities so much above his kind. I wish, when the bird dies, the Devil don't take its shape and visit the lady again, she gave him so kind an entertainment in the person of her uncle.

Libraries appear much greater in the eyes of the world, in my opinion, than indeed they are; we think we have a great treasure there of the thoughts of men, but the multitude of those thoughts shews the weakness of them. What need so much be said? If they were all agreed upon the truth, one demonstration would reduce all the rest to silence, and bring knowledge to a much narrower compass. I take that to be the curse that belonged to the soul of man; that as his body was condemned to labour, and the earth at the same time to bring forth thorns and thistles, so his mind should have a continual thirst and desire after knowledge, and be constantly deceived with appearances. Yet what can be more proper to humble man for his first presumption, when it brings him at last to see and acknowledge his own weakness and ignorance, and to find, after all his pains in human learning, there's no true knowledge but that which David found in the study of God's law, which made him wiser than the aged?

I hope you will not be startled at this stupendous temerity of a foolish woman; it is my sense, which I have your leave to own upon every occasion you give me; and I find some countenance to this opinion in the first volume of the Port Royal.[25]

But whatever I think of the vast curiosity of books and libraries, I am no enemy to the studious; for I allow fine buildings and gardens can't be better bestowed than on such; the labours of the mind require that pleasure; it goes as far as anything that's human, towards the inspiring great and noble thoughts; the body can't be denied such innocent pleasure, while the hardship of study debars it of so many others.

The dial placed on the pile of books perfectly shews us the boundless curiosity of human knowledge; it was labour in vain; not that he could not do what he proposed; but for what good was it? He did it because he could do it, and that the world should know so much; like those that make it the only end of their study, to be reputed learned.

It must be a great and magnificent jubilee that's celebrated but once in a 100 years: it is remarkable, that there never was a crowned head, that ever had those honours done to their memories, as that blessed Queen[26] has had: no length of time can deface the memory of her good deeds, so strong and lasting above all her ancestors; it shows us plainly, that God accomplishes the greatest things by the weakest means, that to him alone we may ascribe the glory; and no question but so she did in an eminent degree, she had so great success in all her enterprises. Mr Tate's ode, I believe, was very pleasing, when finely sung; he's a little dark in his praise of the succeeding princes; should the world last another age, nothing could deprive the 9th of January of such another joyful jubilee, unless some universal blessing, transcendent to all we have yet enjoyed.

In your character of Colonel Butler, there is nothing wanting to a very accomplished person; and perhaps the innocent recreation he allowed himself, of painting in the intervals of his study, as it contributed a great deal of pleasure, so much of his virtue might be owing to that happy genius that filled up his vacant hours, and gave him neither leisure nor inclination to seek the occasions of diverting in places of vice and idleness.

I perceive the art of painting is affected amongst the gentlemen in that country; your friend D—ne had her picture drawn by a gentleman in Ireland, but he was no great artist then; he may be improved since.

The Colonel's humility you admired so much, is very often the effect of a great and noble education, that, whatever there is within, fails not to appear outwardly humble and obliging; wisely considering, nothing shocks the generality of the world so much as pride; but to you it might be a particular mark of respect, you having obliged his learned temper in so many circumstances.

I wish the Lord Mayors of England would emulate those in Ireland, and by their good deeds furnish matter to the news letters of applause, and our poets would not be outdone by the Irish in congratulatory poems. I confess, I think it strange, that as they are generally rich men, and have so great opportunity of doing good, and whatever trouble it gives them, it is but for one year, that they should not use all their effort to reform, as much as possible, all the abuses in the city, of which they themselves might reap the benefit so many years after; with the prayers, applause, and blessings of all the persons concerned. And why they should not every one exceed his successor, by the experience he might get from the others' failings, no reason can be given; unless, because they are rich men, who have been so used to draw all fish to their own nets, they can think of nothing else but mere Lord Mayors, and Justices of the Peace. Such in their offices as they ought, they have it much in their power to give this kingdom a very different face from what it now has.

I perceive you are much taken up with the observation of the men's wives you took your leave of, never failing, whatever haste you had, to inform yourself of all their good qualities. I wonder what could you think of reckoning up the bad ones, when you met with

536 *REMARKS on my*

laſt another Age, nothing could deprive the *9th* of *January* of ſuch another joyful *Jubilee*, unleſs ſome *univerſal Bleſſing*, tranſcendent to all we have yet enjoy'd.

In your Character of Collonel *Butler*, there is nothing wanting to a very accompliſh'd Perſon; and perhaps the *innocent Recreation* he allow'd him-ſelf, of *Painting* in the intervals of his Study, as it contributed a great deal of Pleaſure, ſo much of his Vertue might be owing to that *happy Genius* that fill'd up his vacant Hours, and gave him neither Leiſure nor Inclination to ſeek the occaſions of di-verting in Places of *Vice and Idleneſs*.

I perceive the *Art of Painting* is affected amongſt the Gentlemen in that Country; *your Friend D——ne bad her Picture* drawn by a Gentleman in *Ireland*, but he was no great Artiſt then, he may be im-prov'd ſince.

The Collonel's *Humility* you admir'd ſo much, is very often the effect of a *Great and Noble Education*, that, whatever there is within, fails not to appear outwardly humble and obliging; wiſely conſider-ing, nothing ſhocks the generality of the World, ſo much as *Pride*; but to you it might *be a parti-cular mark of Respect*, you having obliged his learned Temper in ſo many Circumſtances.

I wiſh the *Lord Mayors of England* would emu-late thoſe in *Ireland*, and by their good Deeds furniſh matter to the *News Letters* of Applauſe, and our Poets would not be out-done by the *Iriſh in Congratulatory Poems*. I confeſs, I think it ſtrange, that as they are generally rich Men, and have ſo great opportunity of doing good, and whatever trouble it gives 'em, *'tis but for one year*, that they ſhould not uſe all their effort to reform, as much as poſſible, all the Abuſes in the City, of which they themſelves might reap the benefit ſo many years after; with the Prayers, Applauſe, and

none but good? You might from your own experience and observation, almost believe there was no such thing as a bad wife in the
world.

I think you are a little singular in your love and esteem of apothe-
caries; there's few has your inclination or reason for it; they are to
most persons, like their physic, more toothsome than wholesome.

You lay great stress, and not without reason, upon performing of
promises; but I see no reason why that should be more damnable
than other sins as mischievous; if the person promised with a design
to deceive, never intending to perform it, it is a great and presumptuous sin; but repentance is the remedy for that, as well as the least sin,
which is no less dangerous without it; as also when a person promises,
and for their interest forbears performance, because it is to their own
injury, it is not safe to live or die in such a sin of self-love and injustice;
nothing can secure them but repentance, and only such a one as repairs
the injury. But it is possible to make a promise with a full intent to
perform, yet afterwards want the power; or the promise may be of such
a nature, that not performing may be rather an advantage than injury to
the person engaged to; both these cases lessen the crime, and make it
rather a misfortune to have promised, than a sin not to perform; which
would make one almost afraid to engage in any promise.

Sure no persons deserve one's pity like the poor misers; there is
much of constitution in it, and which improves much by a long habit
of scraping; though they see and know their fault, they can no more
cure it, than an old inveterate disease, when one goes the wrong way
about it: for this is their case, they think all the world envies them,
because they wish to have their bags;[27] without considering, they as
much despise them for their way of living. Nobody would be condemned to riches upon such terms, but those of their own temper:
but sure it is not impossible for the heir to enjoy those riches with
comfort, if he uses them as all riches ought to be used, taking no
other portion of them to himself than his condition requires, and
makes himself steward to the poor for all the rest; this will sanctify
one part to himself, and give him the blessed opportunity of doing
with the other part a great deal of good.

You were well advised, not to discompose your temper with the
thoughts of your enemies, till you had taken leave of your friends;

and if you had left them out of your thoughts still, it had been no great harm: but you think their crimes deserve chastisement; and the justice you owe to your reputation obliges to the exposing such men.

What need you ask pardon for your own character amongst the rest? It had been an unpardonable fault, to pretend to know everyone you conversed with a few moments, and not know yourself, with whom you have conversed so long: besides, it is using them as you use yourself; and, that you did not remark their faults, as you have your own, is, that they concealed them from you.

There's great reason for laying the foundation of your chief perfection upon your descent from the tribe of Levi; for according to St Paul, they are, or should be, the men that rule their own houses well, having their children in subjection with all gravity; for though grace comes not by descent, yet by a sober and virtuous education, the enemies of grace are so far disarmed, that when it pleases God to send it, it must needs have the better reception; a long habit of submission and self-denial will qualify them to act more readily to God's glory, than those that are over-loaded with the evil customs and corruptions of the world.

I can't think but it is the happy success of being so agreeable to both your wives, makes you so in love with the state of marriage, so inconsistent with your great love and fancied destiny to travel; of which I think with you, that the chief pleasure is of seeing the world unseen; not being known, but guessed at. I fancy therefore, the project you design to call *The Art of Living Incognito*, will be very pleasant; but to publish the characters of your living acquaintance will be a great and difficult task, especially for you that are so very scrupulous of doing the least injustice; many person's words, looks, and actions belie their hearts; and without an infallible rule, of which I know nothing, you will at least be thought to err, there being no means to prove the contrary; though you should incline to the most charitable side. Truth is the same in both, and there's the same injustice to commend as discommend, where they don't deserve it; besides the danger of creating amongst your acquaintance much envy and uncharitableness, there must appear in all your words and actions, an excessive charity, and exact justice, to take off any suspicion of your being acted by prejudice or partiality: if anything can secure you, it must be the persons being all living, to whom you must answer for any wrong you do them; and from those you commend, your pardon is secured against all accusers, but only truth, which condemns if injured: but sure the characters of the living are much to be preferred before those of the dead; we see plainly how little truth their characters contain. How are all the good deeds of the virtuous heightened, one would think there were nothing of sin or infirmity in them? And for the vicious, their crimes are exaggerated; they scarce allow them the least degree of human virtues: but if the world were as much in love with truth, as it were to be wished, there might be good use of such characters; and persons would as willingly see the pictures of their minds, as of their faces, and be as fond of making them worth the drawing.

But to find persons willing themselves to publish and expose their own faults and infirmities, we may expect in the next age, if it brings the reign of charity according to Monsieur Jurieu;[28] and hardly till then, though you set the example; but for vices, they are too monstrous and deformed, to dare the exposing themselves in a full light; for which I thank them, for I hate the sight of them.

I perceive you think you have many enemies upon account of religion, because you favour no particular party; it is certain, in any place where there are many factions and divisions, none are so generally hated as those that carry fair with all, and take part with none; and that's all the many names and distinctions in religion are good for, to make feuds and animosities, and by that means one knows from whence they come, having none of the effect and power of that religion that comes from above, which is first pure, and then peaceable. Sincerity and charity is the surest mark of Christian religion. It were much to be wished, all the reformed churches were united in the spirit of charity; then, we may expect the enlargement of Christ's kingdom; while at this day so many fall from us to atheism, seeing so much of self-interest, and the spirit of the world, in the strictest and most formal professors amongst us; and it is to them a temptation to believe there is nothing but secular interest in that which we call religion, in which there is so much contention to raise themselves one above another in riches and honour; this is what many see and lament, and wish they themselves may see before it is too late.

They can be but mere pretenders to religion, that allow themselves lightly to censure or judge anyone; for both charity and humility forbid such a practice; we see our own depraved nature in everybody's faults, which ought to humble us with sorrow for them, as if they were our own; and that will prevent, if we have the least charitable concern for others, our being pleased or desirous to see faults, and divulge those we can't choose but see; for no faults can in charity be exposed, that have the least pretence to infirmity: your carriage therefore to your adversary was exceeding Christian and charitable, and made his faults such as deserved to be exposed as a foil to virtue, if it needed any, which I scorn to think; for I am an equal rival with you in the love of virtue, as it appears only to my mind; but were it to be seen with bodily eyes, I fear I should come far behind you. It is a very laudable design you carry on, of recommending virtue, by giving such noble and pleasant ideas of it in the characters you make; and sure it cannot want success in all respects; there must certainly be some persons it will prevail upon; as in St Cicelie's Ode,

> See what Glory can persuade
> Those that are for Glory made,[29]

may be here applied to virtue; but whatever is the fate, you are always happy, while so resigned to the divine pleasure: an easy and contented temper is a great blessing. But why should you value yourself for being a blunt fellow? Can't everyone be master of that virtue, if they like it? And why disdain ye the name of a poet, only for being poor? Is there such virtue in being rich? What reason can be assigned for such an inevitable fate, unless it is the effect of fancy; which, as it raises their thoughts and expressions far above the truth, so it raises themselves in imagination, to the condition of angels, that need nothing; which makes them take care for nothing, till it is too late? Or, perhaps divine providence will not trust such men with a talent of riches, who so idly throw away their talent of time, which is far more precious.

Yet after all, you seem to own you treat your friends with distinction, some from the brain, and others from the heart; but it is not easy to judge of this part of your character, though I dare affirm you never deceive others, till you have first deceived yourself. I believe it is very hard, and must be the work of time, exactly to determine this distinction; yet one would think a heart that lies open, could not fail to be known, both to itself, and others; but according to the Italian proverb, He that builds his house in the street, it is either too high, or too low. So a man that should have no better means of knowing himself, than what he may get from the light and testimony of others, may be as much a stranger to what he truly is, as the men in great power and riches that feed upon flattery, as well of their own, as others, must needs frame an idea of themselves, very different from what they really are.

Though it is nothing strange the generality of the world should not court your friendship, in respect to your love to truth, and speaking freely of persons' faults; but it would be very strange, if that person should not have one friend in the world, that has one of the best qualifications for it. To have one's faults truly and sincerely told one by one's friend in charity, is an advantage nothing in this world can equal; and of great value to those that understand it, and is what you have the most reason, of anyone, to prize; for if anything fix your mercury, cure your rashness, and save your repenting of every thing you do, it must be the light and counsel of a friend. I can't hinder myself from thinking, that your never repenting of taking two women for better for worse, was the effect of a very good and wise friend's counsel; what else could make you do a thing so extraordinary, when so contrary to your natural practice? But to take a little from this great miracle, perhaps your knowing it was good not to repent, made you fancy you did not.

And yet after all, you must pardon me, if I don't think you as fit to make a friend as any man; for he that is a single man, and chooses to be so, is fitter; for what must your wife do, when you give all to your friend? And a man more moderately qualified, is fitter; for he may be suited in the temper of a friend; but where can you be matched in fidelity compassion, and generosity? You may expect that return of love and gratitude (for who can choose but love such qualities?). But yet the love that you describe, which crimes can't deface, is as transcendent as all the rest; and if you think it just to slight what loves not as much as yourself, I wish you may, it is pity you should not; but I fear you never will be suited with a friend. I cannot blame your not being forward in contracting friendships, it is so uncertain how they may prove; but to a long and tried fidelity, I own all to be due that you propose in your friendship.

The exactness of your rules in traffic and dealings[30] is of very good example; there are few lay that stress upon it they ought; there's more of religion in it than is generally considered, while their thoughts are taken up with the love of gain. You have a great happiness in sitting so loose from the love of money, and yet retain so just a value for it, as to make the proper use of it.

I don't see you have commended yourself so much in your character as needs either apology or pardon; the glory you assume in point of friendship, you have only in speculation, not practice; it is not what you are, but what you should be, whenever you engage with a friend deserves it. Nor shall I make any apology for disappointing you of the satyr[31] you expected; though I think I have in many particulars drawn you just as you appear to me in this light; and since I thus far endeavoured to serve you, I hope I may be excused from writing my own character; the publishing one's own faults, is not a common virtue; it is the fate of novelty to please or displease extremely; let me see the event therefore, before I take the example. I leave you in pursuit of Argus,[32] supposing him a common enemy, which justifies the pains you take to find him; and upon the whole matter, as far as I am informed by this account of your *Conversation*, if my sentence is of any value, I judge it must be a very malignant temper, or a great interest and self-love, could make any man your enemy. And thus concludes

Your, &c.

Notes

The Dedication (pp. 1–5)

1   There is some uncertainty about the identity of Colonel Butler. At this time, the only Butler in the Irish parliament who did not have a knighthood was Francis Butler, member for Belturbet, Co. Cavan. His family owned a house on St Stephen's Green (as did Dunton's Colonel Butler), but he was not entitled to be styled 'the Honourable', unless this title (like the appellation 'Colonel') was an informal rather than a legal one. Francis Butler is not known to have had any military connection except, perhaps, with the Cavan militia. (Both his son and his grandson were colonels of a Co. Cavan troop of horse, but a connection between Francis Butler and the militia can not be proved as the relevant records do not go back before 1708.) An outside possibility (raised by Professor James Woolley) is that the two titles 'Colonel' and 'the Honourable' might have been applied to him if he were the commander of the ceremonial guards at Dublin Castle, the Battle-Axe Guard. But little is known of this corps in the 1690s, and no connection can be proved. A completely different 'Colonel Butler' was John Butler (d.1714) of Westcourt, Co. Kilkenny, a career soldier who became a colonel in the Irish army. As a nephew of the first duke of Ormonde, this Colonel Butler was certainly from a noble family (which the other Butler was not) and could well have been known as 'the Honourable'. But this Butler was not a member of the Irish parliament, nor do we know that he had a house on St Stephen's Green. On balance therefore, Francis Butler of Co. Cavan is the more likely contender for the dubious honour of being the dedicatee of this book. Francis Butler's son, Theophilus (later first Lord Newtown Butler), was a keen collector of contemporary verse and his manuscript verse collection 'The Whimsical Medley', now in the library of Trinity College, Dublin is one of the most significant sources for English and Irish verse of the period, including that of Swift. Dunton gives a 'character' of Colonel Butler at pp. 248–50 below. (I am very grateful to Professor James Woolley for suggesting that Francis rather than John Butler was probably Dunton's patron and for providing the details given above about Francis Butler.)

2   Patrick Campbell, the bookseller with whom Dunton quarrelled. Dunton gives a 'character' of him on p. 181 below.

3   According to Dunton, Butler was a skilled artist.

4   i.e. Judas come back to life.

5   skilful.

6   erase.

To the Spectators of the Dublin Scuffle (pp. 7–10)

1   Dunton claimed to have published six hundred books of which he was only ashamed to own six. The most significant of these was his 1693 edition of *The Second Spira, being a fearful example of an Atheist who had apostatized from the Christian religion, and died in despair at Westminster, Dec 8, 1692*. The manuscript for this work was given to Dunton by Richard Sault (d.1702), a mathematician and editor who collaborated with Dunton in the publication of the *Athenian Mercury*. The story on which the book was modelled was of an Italian lawyer named Francis Spira, a Catholic who turned Protestant and later recanted but who, by denying Christ, was commonly labelled an atheist. His biography, first issued in 1548, was frequently reprinted in Italian, French and English during the seventeenth century. Although Sault claimed to know the anonymous author of *The Second Spira*—a tale of a modern atheist modelled closely on the original—Dunton and others suspected that Sault had written or 'methodised' the text himself, or even that he was the 'Second Spira' himself. The book, which recounts vividly the horrible sufferings of a dying atheist, was published as a moral tract and immediately reprinted several times. According to Dunton, thirty thousand copies of the book were sold in six weeks. It caused the furore to which Dunton refers in this passage. He returns to the matter in detail on pp. 89–93 below. For a modern account of the affair, see McEwen, pp. 67–77.

2   i.e. the Dublin citizen's wife.

3   i.e. printings. *Some Account of my Conversation in Ireland in a Letter to an Honourable Lady, with her Answer to it* forms the third part of this book. 'Conversation' here means 'method of living among others', so that the title could be rendered as 'Some account of the time I spent in Ireland'.

4   Dunton's 'summer ramble' consists of six (or, by some counts, seven) letters in which he describes his wide-ranging rambles through Ireland; he intended to publish them when he got back to London and gave them the title 'Teague Land, or a Merry Ramble to the Wild Irish'. However, for some reason the book remained in manuscript and eventually became part of the Rawlinson collection in the Bodleian Library, Oxford (Rawlinson D.71). Charles McNeill reported on it in *Analecta Hibernica* 3, and Edward MacLysaght printed the bulk of it, though in an expurgated and partly modernised version, as Appendix B to the third edition of his *Irish Life in the Seventeenth Century*, Shannon, 1969 (see pp. 320–90). However, MacLysaght considered Dunton 'an old hypocrite' who could be 'boring as well as obscene', and chose to omit anything which he considered 'bawdy'; as a result, MacLysaght's edition is untrustworthy and the text as a whole clearly needs to be re-edited. Working in the 1970s, Professor Alan Bliss rescued an important passage which MacLysaght had considered to be 'of no interest' and used it as a text for analysis in his book on spoken English in seventeenth-century and early eighteenth-century Ireland (see Bliss pp. 133–7 etc.).

5 Essayist; d.1641.
6 'P.C.' is Patrick Campbell and 'T.F.' is a London bookseller, so far not positively identified. [Ms Mary Pollard has suggested, however, that 'T.F.' might be Thomas Fabian, a London printer who specialised in divinity, and is listed by H.R. Plomer in his *A Dictionary of Printers and Booksellers who were at work in England, Scotland and Ireland 1668–1725* (Bibliographical Society, 1922).] 'Phil[aret]' is Dunton's name for himself. 'Stuff' in this context means 'rubbish'.
7 Dunton's London address.

A Poem on the Dublin Scuffle (pp. 11–15)

1 This first letter and the poem which follows it, though ostensibly written by 'T.B.', are almost certainly substantially if not wholly the work of Dunton himself. However, if 'T.B.' was a real person, he might be Thomas Bennet, at one time a rival, at another time a partner of Dunton in the London booktrade. In this case, Bennet would also be the nominal author of the series of 'Remarks' on Dunton's first twelve letters.
2 i.e. Patrick Campbell.
3 Richard Pue (d.1722), owner of Dick's coffee house in Skinner Row, the back room of which was the Dublin venue for Dunton's original auctions. By reneging on his arrangement with Dunton and letting the room to Patrick Campbell for *his* book auction, Dick caused the 'scuffle' between Dunton and Campbell. Pue is remembered today as the founder (in 1703) of *Pue's Occurrences*, the first Irish 'newspaper' in the modern sense, which was published twice a week for seventy years.
4 'T.B.' is suggesting that Campbell had formerly been a pedlar with a pack strapped to his back. The jibe is repeated several times in the verses and in the *Scuffle* itself, e.g. on p. 46.
5 i.e. a tool of Patrick Campbell.
6 A nickname for Patrick Campbell. (See also line 1 of the second poem.) Francis Grose's *Dictionary of the Vulgar Tongue* (1785) defines 'niffnaffy' as 'trifling' while the *Lexicon Balatronicum* (1811) describes a 'niffynaffy fellow' as a trifler.
7 trousers.
8 stomach trouble.
9 Campbell's address was 'at the Bible in Skinner-Row'.
10 Richard Wilde, whom Dunton employed to manage his auctions, and Pat of Pat's Coffee House.
11 'to set one's back up' means 'to be annoyed'.
12 i.e. as when he was a pedlar with his pack strapped to his back. See also line 15 of the poem.
13 i.e. Skinner Row (also spelt 'Skinner's Row', 'Skinners' Row' and 'Skinner-Row'), now Christchurch Place, where Patrick Campbell's shop was situated.
14 For the account of the letting of the auction room, see below p. 27.

15 Printed as 'Dutton' in the 1699 edition—presumably a comic rhyme.
16 trepan, to snare or trap.
17 i.e. this poem. The reference seems to be to the proverb 'The ape hugs her darling till she kills it': see Thomas Fuller, *Gnomologia* (1732), 4396. But see also the story 'An Ape and her two Brats' in *Fables of Æsop*, tr. Sir Roger L'Estrange (London, 1694), p. 223.
18 Though the initials 'S.M.' could conceivably belong to another of Dunton's London booktrade acquaintances—perhaps Samuel Manship with whom he co-published a book in 1692—it seems more likely that this is another pseudonym for Dunton himself, and that the second letter and poem are also from his pen.

THE DUBLIN SCUFFLE ETC.

The First Letter etc. and Remarks on the First Letter (pp. 17–25)

1 'Your counter-scuffle in London' may well be a reference to the very public row between Dunton and Jean de la Crose in 1691–2. See Parks, pp. 109–28.
2 painting or drawing.
3 William Turner, *A Compleat History of the most Remarkable Providences ... which have happened in this present age ...* (London, 1697). Dunton was both printer and publisher of this book. Selections from a spiritual diary kept by Dunton's first wife (who died in 1697) and the text of the sermon preached at her funeral were included in this work.
4 i.e. exposed to ridicule.
5 A Pythagorean philosopher of Crotona who first asserted that the earth turned on its own axis; 'rate' means 'price'.
6 Archbishop James Ussher (1581–1656), provost of Trinity College Dublin and archbishop of Armagh, left his fine library to the College.
7 The Samaritan Pentateuch is a divergent form of the first five books of the Old Testament; the Syriac Bible consists of versions of the Old Testament made for early Syriac-speaking churches.
8 The account of the visit of the queen of Sheba to King Solomon is in I Kings x.
9 Thomas Stanley, *The History of Philosophy* (London, 1655).
10 Edward Leigh, *A Treatise of Religion and Learning* (London, 1656).
11 The remark comes from the section 'Democritus to the Reader' in *The Anatomy of Melancholy* by Robert Burton (1577–1640).
12 i.e. a bargain.
13 A common (often pejorative) phrase used by seventeenth- and eighteenth-century travellers and settlers in Ireland to refer to the native Irish.
14 See below, pp. 209–17.
15 'Wisdom, wonderful to relate, came to the Irish.'
16 The first word in this adaptation from Juvenal 10. 50 should be '*Vervecum*'. The phrase means 'Born in a land of blockheads under a thick climate'. The idea that members of the Roman Catholic church (such as the 'wild Irish'

mentioned in the sentence above) were slaves to its tyranny was a common one in Protestant rhetoric of the time.

17 Richard FitzGilbert de Clare, earl of Pembroke (known as 'Strongbow'), led the forces which began the Anglo-Norman conquest of Ireland in 1169.

18 A 'forestaller' was one who bought up goods before they reached public sale in order to raise the price, and an 'engrosser' was a wholesale merchant.

19 A reference to the generally held belief that there are no snakes in Ireland.

20 The reference is probably to Silenus the satyr in Virgil's sixth Eclogue. The 'northern proverb' is untraced, though Thomas Nashe, *Works* (1593), iv, 240 has the following: 'Is it not a common proverbe amongst us when any man hath cosened or gone beyond us to say "hee hath played the merchant with us"?' and Randle Cotgrave defines the word 'larron' as 'either a merchant or a theefe' in his *French-English Dictionary* of 1611.

21 The mountain in Greece sacred to the muses; it is not clear what place in Ireland is referred to here.

22 Originally a kern (Ir. *ceithearn*) was a light-armed Irish foot soldier but, by the late seventeenth century, the word was also used generally to refer to 'the wild Irish'.

23 The legendary Christian king supposed in medieval times to have reigned over a wonderful country in the heart of Asia.

24 The philosopher's stone was said to turn base metals into gold, the grand elixir was said to prolong life indefinitely, and the *aurum potabile* (drinkable gold) was esteemed as a cordial medicine.

25 to dance in a frisky or fantastic way.

26 i.e. force them to pay excessive prices.

27 the winged horse of the muses.

28 dealers or merchants (i.e. those carrying out Dunton's auctions for him).

29 a coarse, heavy woollen cloth, equivalent to the modern tweed.

30 whiskey; Ir. *uisce beathadh*, 'aqua vitæ'.

31 lest.

32 eaten.

The Second Letter etc. and Remarks on the Second Letter (pp. 25–39)

1 i.e. the type had been set and was ready to be printed.

2 an ale house in Dublin.

3 i.e. Richard Wilde, Dunton's auction manager.

4 An attempt to imitate Campbell's Scottish accent.

5 Dunton claimed that Campbell failed to pay him for some copies of William Turner's *A Compleat History of the most Remarkable Providences ... in this Present Age* which Dunton (the publisher of the book) had sent over from London at Campbell's request.

6 See note 4 above.

7 One common use for waste paper in seventeenth-century Ireland was to line pie dishes.

8 Dunton means that he is not from a family of labourers; his forbears have been clergymen for the last three generations.

9 Dunton suggests that his books would be worth a further £290 if he were to employ 'setters' to raise the bids at the auction and so swindle the purchasers.

10 Elnathan Lum, a member of the Irish House of Commons.

11 was astonished. The 'bill' later in the sentence was a promissory note—the modern cheque.

12 See below, p. 47 and n. 8 to *The Fourth Letter*, p. 313, where the sharp practices of Cumpstey and Whaley in reprinting mathematical texts by Hodder and Cocker are fully explained. A 'sutler' (later in the sentence) was one who followed an army and sold provisions to the soldiers.

13 I Corinthians xv. 32.

14 i.e. the one man of conscience—another attempt to imitate Campbell's Scottish accent.

15 Dunton is implying that Campbell has no religion.

16 The detailed allusions throughout this paragraph are obscure.

17 This history of the fictitious 'Athenian Society', invented by Dunton and Sault as a pretext for the printing of their highly successful *Athenian Mercury*, was written by Charles Gildon and appeared in 1692 with the words 'printed for James Dowley' on the title page: Dunton later admitted that he had had Dowley print it for him. See *Life and Errors* (1818) p. 261.

18 Started in 1665, the *London Gazette* became one of the longest-running London newspapers.

19 See above, notes 4 and 14.

20 See above, notes 4 and 14.

21 St Paul's Church-yard was the centre of printing and bookselling in seventeenth-century London and over 2500 titles were published by booksellers working in or near the churchyard during the century. Thomas Parkhurst, the noted Presbyterian bookseller to whom Dunton had been apprenticed in the 1680s, published from 'The Bible and Three Crowns'.

22 A Dublin newspaper printed by Cornelius Carter which ran from March 1698 until about 1724. Much of its content was reprinted from the London papers.

23 This reference seems to be to one of the punishments prescribed for perjury in seventeenth-century Ireland—the nailing of the ears of the guilty party to the pillory.

24 unidentified.

25 day in, day out.

26 These lines are probably by Dunton himself.

27 See n. 13 in *Notes to pages 191–234* on p. 328, and p. 197 below.

28 i.e. a book bound in the best way.

29 Greek biographer (*c*.46-*c*.119).

30 The works referred to are: Isaac Barrow, *Works*, four volumes (London, 1683–87), one of the many English translations of *The History of the Jewish Wars* by the first-century historian Flavius Josephus; Walter Raleigh, *A History of the World* (London 1614, 1617); and John Milton, *A Complete*

Collection of the Historical, Political and Miscellaneous Works of John Milton … (London, 1698).

31 Richard Pue, the 'Dick' of Dick's coffee-house.

32 with money.

33 Guy Fawkes (1570–1606) was the chief conspirator in the Gunpowder plot, designed to blow up the English Parliament building. Almanzor (from the Arabic *al-mansur,* 'the victorious') was a title adopted by several Muslim rulers, notably Abu Amir al-Mansur (938–1002), famous for his victories over the Christians in Spain.

34 Thomas Brooks (1608–80), *Precious Remedies against Satan's devices* (London, 1669).

35 reveals.

36 lantern.

The Third Letter etc. and Remarks on the Third Letter (pp. 39–44)

1 A sheet of paper of the largest size used by printers at the time, 25 x 20 inches or, since Dunton later says he used a *double* sheet of royal paper (p. 41), 50 x 40 inches.

2 i.e. the boat bringing mail and packets from England.

The Fourth Letter and Remarks on the Fourth Letter (pp. 44–48)

1 St George Ashe (1658?–1718) successively Fellow of Trinity College Dublin (and tutor to Jonathan Swift), provost of TCD, bishop of Cloyne, of Clogher and of Derry.

2 i.e. people employed by the auctioneer to force up prices.

3 Many Scottish churches contained a 'stool of repentance' which those guilty of certain offences (particularly of a sexual nature) had to mount, dressed in a white robe, to make a public statement of repentance.

4 Robert Rochfort MP.

5 more than what is necessary.

6 procurer.

7 his failings deserve to be told in as public a manner …

8 i.e. he deserves to stand in the stocks with the perverted title page nailed up as a sign of his guilt. In 1698, Patrick Campbell and Jacob Milner were found to have prefixed the title and preface of Edward Cocker's *Arithmetic* to the text of James Hodder's *Decimal Arithmetic.* They apologised to the Guild of St Luke the Evangelist (the trade association for the printers and stationers of Dublin) and promised not to re-offend. Dunton implies (p. 28) that two other members of the Dublin bookmaking fraternity, Andrew Cumpstey and John Whalley, were also involved in the deceit. No copies of the book have survived. For the Guild's report on this affair, see Phillips, p. 21.

9 licence of approval or sanction.

The Fifth Letter and Remarks on the Fifth Letter (pp. 48–53)

1 despite.

2 *The French Book of Martyrs* (see below, p. 83) which had obviously appeared in the Dublin retail trade at a price higher than it had reached at one of Dunton's auctions.

3 unless.

4 Since important feast days were shown in red ink in almanacs and calendars, the phrase means that the 'bon-voyage' message should be presented as an important document.

5 A common seventeenth-century proverb, first recorded in 1589.

The Sixth Letter and Remarks on the Sixth Letter (pp. 53–8)

1 financial affairs.

2 A penny (or other tip) given at a parting.

3 Dunton himself was the author (and publisher) of *A Congratulatory Poem to the Ministers Sons, on their splendid feast, Thursday December 7th, 1682* (Parks 6).

4 This probably refers to Patrick Campbell.

5 Proverbs xx, 14.

6 basis.

7 Matthew Gun or Gunne, a bookseller of Essex Street.

8 lawyers.

9 'Those who are born presbyters are rarely wont to be happy.'

The Seventh Letter and Remarks on the Seventh Letter (pp. 58–60)

1 to press me for money I owe you.

2 A proverb that first appears in Chaucer.

3 Hodder. See above n. 8 to *The Fourth Letter*, p. 313.

The Eighth Letter and Remarks on the Eighth Letter (pp. 61–2)

1 counsel.

2 A problematic and obscure passage. The first and second dashes may stand for persons—perhaps 'Dick' and 'Patrick Campbell'?

The Ninth Letter etc. and Remarks on the Ninth Letter (pp. 63–8)

1 John Bently or Bentley, a Dublin bookseller employed by Dunton for bookbinding.

2 skull.

3 Julins Palmer was burnt in 1556 at Newbury in Berkshire for refusing to abandon his Protestant opinions.

4 The proverb is 'Save a thief from the gallows and he'll cut your throat'.

5 Probably one of many stories told of the goodness of St Catherine of Sienna (1347–80).

6 i.e. Thomas Servant, the binder (who was also a bookseller).

7 One of Dunton's employees.

8 The earl of Meath's chaplain was probably Fleetwood Fisher, a graduate of TCD (BA 1691, MA 1693); the king's printer in Dublin at this time was Robert Thornton.

9 perverse.

The Tenth Letter and Remarks on the Tenth Letter (pp. 68–75)

1 John Brent was employed as a printer by both Dunton and Campbell.

2 For Cocker, see above n.8 to *The Fourth Letter*, p. 313. 'Whalely' is John Whalley (1653–1724), described by Gilbert (i, 188) as 'the chief quack and astrologer in the city of Dublin'. He wrote and published his own astrological predictions.

3 Proverbs xxvi, 5. Answer a fool according to his folly.

4 Andrew Cumpstey, 'philomath, compiler of almanacs and astrological obser-vations' (Gilbert ii, 262), was also a schoolmaster. He died 24 November 1713. John Whalley, his inveterate enemy, published an engraving of Cumpstey, his head made to look like that of a sheep and covered by a large wig, 'making astrological observations in the company of two hideous owls' (Gilbert i, 379).

5 i.e. three copies of William Turner's *A Compleat History of the most Remarkable Providences* ... See n. 5 to *The Second Letter*, p. 311.

6 misrepresent, tell lies about.

7 lawyers.

8 See n. 33 to *The Second Letter*, p. 313.

The Eleventh Letter and Remarks on the Eleventh Letter (pp. 75–8)

1 This reference could be to the bookseller (and presumably also bookbinder) John Foster of the 'Dolphin' in Skinner Row—near the premises of Patrick Campbell.

2 Tom Nelson, employed by Dunton.

3 Thomas Servant, the bookseller.

4 See n. 13 in the *Notes to pages 191–234* on p. 328.

5 i.e. cuckold.

6 unidentified.

7 unidentified Irish nobility.

8 Cervantes's novel *Don Quixote* was one of the most widely read books of the seventeenth century. The Hydra was a mythological monster with one hundred heads: whenever one head was cut off, two replaced it.

9 In Greek mythology, the Hekatoncheires were giants who each possessed fifty heads and one hundred arms and hands.

10 The mythological Danae, daughter of Acrisius, the king of Argos, was seduced by Zeus who took the form of a shower of golden rain.

11 children.

The Twelfth Letter and My Last Farewell to my Acquaintance in Dublin (pp. 78–112)

1 i.e. using the devices of rhetoric.

2 Probably a misprint for 'all in volumes' i.e. bound into volumes.

3 Lists of books to be sold on the next day.

4 Details of the works featured in this comprehensive list of the publications current in 1698 can be found in standard bibliographical works such as the *English Short Title Catalogue* (available on-line at www.rlg.org).

5 intend.

6 keeping account of.

7 the Irish Sea.

8 breech, buttocks.

9 the unidentified London bookseller.

10 i.e. from a labouring background.

11 Sir James Hales (d.1549).

12 This paragraph contains a partial list of the works printed or published by Dunton between 1681 and 1698. Parks gives a full checklist of his publications (including some works associated with him), accurately transcribed from the title-pages. See Parks, pp. 215–393; but see also Albert B. Cook, 'Corrigenda to Stephen Parks' Bibliography of John Dunton', *Papers of the Bibliographical Society of America*, (Austin, Texas) 1980, 74, 134–6. (The sentence which begins at the bottom of page 82 is not effectively completed until the third line of the next paragraph.)

13 The references to internecine strife between London booksellers are, as yet, unexplained.

14 Michel de Montaigne (1533–92).

15 Diogenes, the Stoic philosopher, flourished about 150 BC.

16 This refers to the fact that some booksellers were prepared to allow chapmen —who travelled around the country selling the contents of the packs on their backs at fairs etc.—particularly good terms.

17 bills.

18 i.e. those who are always moving but never advancing. In many large kitchens, a small dog was forced to run around the inside of a wheel attached to the spit; this turned the spit slowly and ensured that the meat was roasted evenly over the fire. The next sentence, though it sounds like several passages in the Old Testament, is not a biblical quotation.

19 Abraham Cowley (1618–67), 'The Wish' in *The Mistress or Love Poems*.

20 A quotation from Cowley's imitations of Horace.

21 Dunton had published Stevens's *The Whole Parable of Dives and Lazarus* (Parks 290) in 1697.

22 i.e. kidney stones, from which Dunton also suffered severely.

23 judging.

24 See above, n. 1 to *To the Spectators of the Dublin Scuffle*.

25 i.e. Richard Sault.

26 Edmund Bohun (1645–99), licenser of the press in London in 1693.

27 Dunton printed several works by the New England divines Increase Mather (1639–1723), president of Harvard College, and his son Cotton Mather (1663–1728).

28 John Tillotson (1630–94), archbishop of Canterbury. His works were published in London in 1696.

29 perverse.

30 from *The Temple: Sacred Poems and private Ejaculations* (Cambridge: 1633) by George Herbert (1593–1633). A 'distich' is a two-line stanza of verse, usually making complete sense on its own.

31 Sir Thomas Overbury (1581–1613), poet and writer of 'characters', was imprisoned in the Tower of London and poisoned there.

32 The preface to *The Second Spira* was signed 'I. S.' (for 'J. S.'). According to Richard Sault, these were the initials of a mysterious 'John Sanders' who had given him the text of the book and who was the 'second Spira'. Most readers (including Dunton) did not believe this story and Dunton later asserted that Sault himself had become an atheist and that the experiences in the book were his own. See McEwen, pp. 67–76 and notes.

33 This reference is to a totally different book, spawned by the furore caused by Dunton's *The Second Spira*. Its title is: *A True Second Spira: or, A soul plung'd in his case, but yet recovered. … To which is added an account of Elizabeth Boodger … With a funeral sermon preached by Tho. Sewell …* London: printed for, and sold by Will. Marshall at the Bible in Newgate-Street … MDCXCVII.

34 i.e. I've made an agreement about the whole thing …

35 i.e. to myself and to you

36 Colonel Butler, to whom the book is dedicated.

37 Proverbs xx, 24 (1699)—an error: *recte* Proverbs xx, 14: 'It is naught, it is naught, saith the buyer; but when he is gone his way, then he boasteth.'

38 'A rolling stone gathers no moss', first recorded in this form in 1546.

39 A class mate of Swift at TCD (BA 1686), John Jones later ran a very successful school in Dublin. As an undergraduate, he delivered a Tripos Speech at a graduation ceremony which so insulted the provost and Fellows of the college that he was deprived of his degree. John Barrett, vice-provost of TCD in the early nineteenth century, tried to prove that Swift was the author of the offending speech. See John Barrett, *An Essay on the Earlier Part of the Life of Swift* (London, 1808).

40 Peter Davys (1668–98), a friend of Swift who became master of the school attached to St Patrick's cathedral. His widow, Mary, was an accomplished poet and playwright.

41 'His good deeds live after him.'

42 John Stearne (1660–1745), later dean of St Patrick's cathedral, Dublin, bishop of Dromore and of Clogher. A friend of Swift and benefactor of Trinity College, Dublin.

43 The Reverend John Francis, prebendary of Christ Church cathedral, rector of St Mary's Dublin and (from 1696) dean of Lismore.

44 A lecturer was an assistant preacher. Mr Searle was probably the Reverend Richard Searle, later of Ballytore, Co. Kildare.

45 See above, n. 8 to *The Ninth Letter*, p. 314.

46 See above, n. 1 to *The Dedication*, p. 307.

47 Elnathan Lum, MP for the borough of Carlingford; Robert Grayden, MP for the borough of Harristown, Co. Kildare; and John Reading, MP for the borough of Swords.

48 Probably the Christopher Ussher who was admitted BA at TCD in May 1655.

49 Sir Henry Tichborne, MP for the county of Louth; Robert Stopford, MP for the borough of Inistioge, Co. Kilkenny (who was among those attainted by the Jacobite parliament in 1689 and was probably a brother of Swift's friend James Stopford, bishop of Cloyne); Captain John Aghmooty, MP for the borough of St Johnstown, Co. Longford; the Recorder of Dublin, Sir William Handcock, MP for Athlone and Stephen Ludlow, MP for the borough of Charlemont, whose descendants became earls of Ludlow. 'Mr Justice Coot' was the Hon. Thomas Coote, third son of Lord Coote of Coloony. Coote, who was Recorder for Dublin in 1690 and MP for the city in 1692, was appointed a Justice of the King's Bench in 1693.

50 Henry Echlin, son of Robert Echlin of Ardquin, Co. Down, entered TCD in 1667 at the age of 15. He went on to become a distinguished lawyer and baron of the Irish court of exchequer. He was made a baronet in 1721.

51 A lawyer whom Dunton visited before he left Dublin (p. 198).

52 A list of attorneys and merchants active in late seventeenth-century Dublin, some of whom (Faustine Cuppage and George Osborn, for example) appear in the list of those attainted in 1689.

53 For information on John Brent, Stephen Powell and John Brocas, see the entries in Robert Munter, *A Dictionary of the Print Trade in Ireland 1550–1775* (New York, 1988).

54 very sincere. (Nathaniel, one of the first disciples, was recommended by Jesus for his sincerity.)

55 The source of this quotation is uncertain. A periphrasis is a wordy or roundabout way of speaking, an amplification (as here).

56 One of the printers' signs in Skinner Row.

57 Dunton seems to be asserting that his London bookselling business, carried on 'At the Sign of the Black Raven' in Jewen Street, was doing well enough for him not to need to advertise *The Dublin Scuffle*. Or, (see below, p. 117), the passage means that his new wife has settled in to his house at the sign of the Black Raven. Dunton often uses the word 'Athenians' to mean his friends and associates—members of his fictitious 'Athenian Society'.

58 The Greek poet Musaeus tells how Leander was drowned swimming across the Hellespont (today the Dardanelles) to meet his lover, Hero.

59 The name Dunton gives his second wife, Sarah Nicholas, whom he married in 1697.

60 As noted in the introduction, Dunton did not complete the ambitious writing and publishing plans set out in these two paragraphs. However, it is interesting that he asserts that the 'Remarks' he prints on his various letters were sent to him by different correspondents—something which is highly unlikely to be true.

60 The journal founded by Dunton in 1691; see the introduction.

61 whimsical fancy.

62 Elizabeth Annesley whom Dunton married in 1682; she died in May 1697. She is referred to in his writings either as 'Iris' or as 'Eliza'.

64 The reference is to the Confessions of St Augustine.

65 i.e. 1686.

66 In fact, Dunton and his second wife were to have a stormy and unhappy relationship.

67 Dunton is reminding us that, in becoming his wife, Valeria has vowed to stay with him 'for richer for poorer'—the phrase comes from the marriage service.

68 In early printings of the breviaries, prayer books and catechisms, the capital letter 'N' was used to indicate where the speaker or reader should insert the name of a person; where more than one name was to be inserted, printers should have used the two letters 'NN' but sometimes mistakenly printed a single letter 'M'. Dunton is quoting, again, from the marriage service.

69 from day to day.

70 Though John Harris, who died in 1698, had been a business partner of Dunton in London, the work to which Dunton here refers, *An Essay proving that we shall know our Friends in Heaven, writ by a disconsolate widower on the death of his wife* … (Parks 291), was 'Printed and are to be sold by E. Whitelock near Stationers Hall'.

71 A common seventeenth-century phrase meaning to accuse someone of something.

72 A witness, someone who is on oath in a court of law. The reference later in the sentence is to false witness given at the trial of Anthony Ashley Cooper (1621–83), first earl of Shaftesbury, in 1681.

73 even if.

74 William Sherlock (1641–1707), dean of St Paul's cathedral, London.

75 These two references are unexplained. Buff was a colour used for army uniforms, so this could refer to a military man.

76 signal.

The Answer to my Twelfth Letter (pp. 112–118)

1 thirteen.

2 The reference is to cockfighting, widespread in the seventeenth century.

3 This refers to extispicy or the examination of the entrails of sacrificed beasts and birds as a form of divination, widely practised in the ancient world.

4 Edward Millington, a famous London book auctioneer and a friend of Dunton.

5 Gilbert Burnet (1643–1715), bishop of Salisbury, who came from Scotland.

6 i.e. the Roman Catholic Church—though the phrase 'the whore of Babylon' (Rev. xvii, 1, 5 etc.), with the same meaning, is more common in seventeenth-century English Protestant writing.

7 i.e. something in him which is stinging or hurting him.

8 shield i.e. you have hit him where it hurts, in his reputation.

9 a buffoon or clown.

10 i.e. John Sanders, the clergyman whose initials are printed at the end of the preface to *The Second Spira*.

11 bumbailiffs or (in Ireland) sheriff's assistants.

12 methodicalness.

13 'We love with the liver' — because the liver was, according to traditional thinking, the seat of the affections. This appears to derive from a passage in the Scholia or ancient commentary on Persius 1.12: *Et hoc secundum physicos dicit, qui dicunt homines splene ridere, felle irasci, iecore amare, corde sapere* ... 'He says this following the natural philosophers, who say that men laugh with the spleen, are angry with the bile, love with the liver, are wise with the heart ...'

14 brief summaries of their characters.

15 to do more than is demanded or required.

16 Valeria, Dunton's second wife. See also above, p. 103.

17 Genesis viii, 7.

18 i.e. to be raped, as Lucretia was by Tarquin in Roman legend.

19 'To cry roast meat' means 'to make known one's good luck' so the passage means 'don't both get on well and boast about it'.

20 The last word of this quotation from Horace *Epistles* 1.17.50–51 should be '*individiaeque*'. The passage means: 'But if the crow were able to eat quietly, it would have more food and much less strife and envy.'

THE BILLET DOUX

The Thirteenth Letter &c. (including Dunton's First Letter to the Citizen's Wife and Remarks on the Billet Doux and on the First Letter to the Citizen's Wife) (pp. 121–6)

1 Dunton gives the (probably imaginary) citizen's wife the name Dorinda and her watchful husband the name Argus. He had already used the name 'Philaret' for himself in his 1697 publication *The Challenge* and in his 1698 *An Essay proving we shall know our friends in Heaven*, and he uses it again here. It recurs later in Dunton publications in 1707 and 1714. See Parks's bibliography entries 278, 291, 292, 293, 337 and 371. Since the mythological Argus had many eyes and could see infidelities hidden from others, the phrase 'Argus-eyed' grew to mean 'jealously watchful'. See also the introduction.

2 wait for.

3 See above, note 1.

4 the appearance of my letter.

5 presumably this refers to Captain John Seamore. See above p. 122.

6 cuckold.

7 whore; the terminal 'r' seems to reflect the seventeenth-century pronunciation 'hoor'.

8 reveal.

9 in their proper form.

10 A reference to a band of soldiers commanded by Lieutenant-General Percy Kirke (1646?–91) who was involved in the raising of the siege of Derry in 1689. The complicated military and political alliances in Ireland during the Jacobite war are reflected in the remainder of the sentence. Kirke was famous for his cruelty to captured rebels during Monmouth's Rising in 1685.

11 a female citizen.

12 *The Art of Love* by Ovid (43BC–17AD), was widely available in English translation at this time, and was considered a titillating book. In *Unfit for Modest Ears* (London, 1979), p. 3, Roger Thompson writes: 'For students of the erotic in Stuart England, "the professor of extra-marital seduction" was Ovid.'

13 chlorosis or green sickness was a disease which affected young women.

The Fourteenth Letter &c. (including Dunton's Second Letter to the Citizen's Wife and Remarks on the Second Letter to the Citizen's Wife) (pp. 126–40)

1 Dunton published *A Treatise of Fornication* (Parks 108) in 1690: *God's Judgments against Whoredom* is untraced, but see *The Night-Walker* (Parks 272) of 1696, a monthly account of 'evening rambles in search after lewd women'.

2 A conflated version of Proverb vii, with direct quotation from verse 27; the second quotation is Proverbs xxii, 14.

3 An anonymous tract entitled *Concubinage and poligamy disprov'd: or, The divine institution of marriage betwixt one man and one woman only, asserted …* (London, 1698).

4 Matthew vii, 6.

5 Dunton indicates that he is here quoting from another text for about twenty lines, but the exact source is untraced. 'The George and Garter' is a reference to one of the twenty-five Knights of the Most Noble Order of the Garter, the highest order of knighthood in Great Britain—the 'George' being the jewelled pendant of St George, patron saint of the order, worn by the knights — and 'c———d' in the sixth line is 'cuckold'.

6 Hercules, the supreme hero of Greek mythology, was once sold into slavery; Omphale, queen of Lydia, bought him and made him wear women's clothes and undertake women's tasks.

7 Mark Anthony (*c.*80–30BC), Roman general, loved Cleopatra (69–30 BC), queen of Egypt. See Shakespeare's *Antony and Cleopatra*.

8 'The mouth of strange women is a deep pit'. The word 'discovers' in the next line means 'reveals'.

9 This extended list gives examples of typical punishments for infidelity from a variety of biblical and historical sources. See Genesis chapters xx, xxvi, xxxviii, xl; Thucidides, *History of the War between Athens and Sparta* i, 15 (for the Locratians) and Tacitus, *De origine et situ Germanorum* for the Sermai and the Cumani.

10 Richard Allestree, *The Whole Duty of Man* (London, 1658).

11 cuckold.

12 unrecorded word: perhaps means 'to crush', from the mortar of a pestle and mortar.

13 I Corinthians vi and vii.

14 Genesis xxxix, 12.

15 Genesis xix, 30–38.

16 A poetic name for the Jews or the sons of Israel (Deuteronomy xxxii, 15). 'They were fed horses …' is Jeremiah v, 8.

17 unidentified.

18 Jeremy Taylor (1613–67), bishop of Down and Connor.

19 The fabulous king of serpents, said to be able to kill those on whom it looked.

20 pining for food, starved.

21 Jane Shore (1445?–1527) mistress of Edward IV; Madam Creswell, a famous bawd and procuress in Restoration London; and Nell Gwyn (1650–87), Charles II's most famous mistress.

22 St Jerome.

23 The source of this story is untraced, but a 'stove' was a hot air bath or a sweating room.

24 The story of Paphnutius is untraced, but the term 'a Delilah' was used of any temptress. See Judges xiii–xvi.

25 The celebrated Greek philosopher and mathematician of the sixth century BC to whom is attributed the pre-Copernican view of the universe.

26 The phrases from the *Book of Common Prayer* all refer to the human body.

27 Dunton's first father-in-law, Dr Samuel Annesley, was (like Dunton's own forebears) a clergyman.

28 Something that is the disgrace of doctors (because incurable).

29 A work by Robert Carr, published by Dunton in 1690.

The Fifteenth Letter &c. (including Dunton's Third Letter to the Citizen's Wife and Remarks on that Letter) (pp. 141–8)

1 twists and turns.

2 the right to be superior to her. The passage from Ephesians recommended above begins: 'Wives, submit yourselves unto your own husbands, as unto the Lord.'

3 This seems to be a reference to the *Palatine Anthology* 9.370, a story about a deer which gets caught in a fisherman's net.

4 justifiable, acceptable.

5 Eriphyle betrayed her husband for a golden necklace. *Æneid* 6, v, 445.

6 The friend who, in ancient Greece, accompanied the bridegroom when he went to fetch home the bride—the present-day best man.

7 The exact source of this proverb or fable has not been located.

8 Plutarch, the famous Greek philosopher and biographer, died about the year 120 AD.

9 Gloves were sometimes given as a tip or reward for services.

10 The phrase (which is from Juvenal 1.56) should read: *Doctus spectare lacunar*. It means 'Trained to gaze at the ceiling' and was generally used of a husband turning a blind eye to his wife's infidelities. The other references in this passage are obscure and no fable about a bag of fleas can be found in any seventeenth-century translation of Æsop.

11 One of the most famous relics in the cathedral of Aix-la-Chapelle (now Aachen, Germany) was material said to have been woven by the Virgin Mary.

12 saliva, spit.

13 A proverb first recorded in 1646.

SOME ACCOUNT OF MY CONVERSATION IN IRELAND

Notes to pages 151–91

1 Though the 'Honourable Lady' was probably a real person, the letters which bear her signature have clearly been amended by Dunton himself. The title of this section of the book means: 'Some account of the time I spent in Ireland'.

2 Source untraced—probably by Dunton himself.

3 This close friend or relative, who is mentioned several times by Dunton in this section of the book, is so far unidentified, but the references seem to be to a real person whose death occurred while Dunton was in Ireland. He was clearly deeply affected by the loss.

4 St Paul.

5 the 'promised land' of the Israelites.

6 The list contains names of prominent Church of Ireland clergy and of non-conformist preachers active in Dublin in 1699.

7 William Penn (1644–1718), English Quaker and founder of Pennsylvania.

8 i.e. by sailing westward and passing through the Straits of Magellan or eastward round the southern tip of Africa.

9 William King (1650–1729) successively dean of St Patrick's cathedral, Dublin, bishop of Derry and archbishop of Dublin, the most prominent churchman of his age. Joseph Boyse (1660–1728), Presbyterian minister in Dublin from 1683 until his death. Boyse was a noted preacher and a vigorous defender of Presbyterianism. He and Bishop King carried on a pamphlet dispute in the 1690s.

10 Thomas Randolph (1605–35), poet and dramatist. These lines seem to be a misquotation of lines 19–20 of Randolph's 'On the inestimable content he enjoys in the muses ...' *Poetical and Dramatic Works of Thomas Randolph*, ed. W Carew Hazlitt (London, 1875), p. 520.

11 Probably a reference to a remark made by Clement Ellis (1630–1700), rector of Kirkby, Yorkshire, and author of many popular devotional works.

12 One who observes the Sabbath—here the Jewish Sabbath, Saturday—strictly. Dunton goes on to consider the possible merits of observing both Saturday and Sunday as 'Sabbaths'.

13 See above n. 10 to *The Twelfth Letter*, p. 316.

14 religious ceremonies.

15 i.e. I take off my hat.

16 George Herbert (1593–1633) who was much admired for the saintliness of his life.

17 Metrical versions of the psalms were used in Protestant churches, including those of the Church of Ireland, throughout the seventeenth and eighteenth centuries. The earliest versified psalms were by Thomas Sternholt (d.1549)

and John Hopkins (d.1570). A 'new' version, by two graduates of Trinity College Dublin, Nahum Tate (1652–1715) and Nicholas Brady (1659–1726) first appeared in 1696 and was soon widely adopted.

18 the Eucharist.

19 This passage seems to mean that the Christian ideas in the scripture reading of the morning, though they can be nurtured during the day—one of the attributes of the classical god Apollo was that he was god of the day—must be the subject of religious contemplation in the evening if they are to be of value.

20 The pelican was fabled to revive or feed its young with blood from its own heart.

21 ghosts.

22 In some Greek myths, the youth Endymion, whose beauty had conquered Selene, the moon-goddess, was allowed by Zeus to sleep for ever. In other stories, he awakes.

23 The Cinque Ports are five English ports on the English Channel. Here the phrase refers to the five senses.

24 The first two lines of 'Necessary Observations', *The Poetical and Dramatic Works of Thomas Randolph*, ed. W. Carew Hazlitt, p. 555.

25 Henry Booth, 2nd Baron Delamere (1652–94) whose *Works* include advice to his children and a selection of the prayers used in his household.

26 affectedly fastidious.

27 A reference to a story about King Stephen (1097?–1154); a 'noble' was an English gold coin worth 6*s*. 8*d*.

28 Ballybough Lane, now Ballybough Road and in Dublin city.

29 This quotation is untraced, so the identity of S—— has not been established.

30 Untraced—probably by Dunton himself.

31 The list of books to be sold at Dunton's auction that morning.

32 A public meal regularly provided at a fixed price in an eating-house or tavern.

33 A confused gabble. It was said that Dover Court church in Essex possessed a cross which spoke, and the crowd that gathered to witness the miracle was so great that the doors could not be closed. The confusion and noise of the crowd gave rise to the term.

34 smart young men.

35 Wilde was the manager of Dunton's auctions, Price was the accountant and Nelson, Robinson, James and Bacon were the porters.

36 certificate of execution—here probably an account of the profit after expenses.

37 advertisements for the next auction.

38 The Tholsel or city hall was in Skinner Row (now Christchurch place) near Dick's coffee house.

39 broker.

40 sinful parts of my temperament.

41 'to make a notch on the tally-stick being kept for me in the heavenly treasury' i.e. to add a good mark to my record.

42 The phrase means 'he is quit' so here equals 'the discharge of my account with Heaven'.

43 See n. 3 in *Notes to pages 151–91*, p. 323.

44 A reference to the medieval view of the cosmos in which the outermost of the crystal spheres, the *primum mobile*, revolved once around the stationary earth every 24 hours, taking with it the other spheres (in which were set the sun, moon, planets and stars).

45 alive, ready to be seen.

46 a temporary place to feed. The implication seems to be that Dunton is looking for an (amorous?) adventure.

47 i.e. the friend you once had at the Black Raven (Dunton's London address).

48 When Dunton describes someone he meets, he considers his description a 'character' and puts it into inverted commas. This character contains an early usage of the phrase 'son of a gun', a pejorative term for a man or a fellow. For a list of the Dublin booksellers mentioned in *The Dublin Scuffle*, see Appendix A.

49 unidentified, except as one of those who purchased books at Dunton's auctions.

50 Henri de Massue de Ruvigny, 1st earl of Galway (1648–1720) was one of the three lords justices of Ireland 1697–1700. The other references are to the poets John Dryden (1631–1700) and Abraham Cowley (1618–67).

51 Charles Powlett, 7th marquis of Winchester (d. 1722) who became duke of Bolton on the death of his father in 1699 and was later lord lieutenant of Ireland (1717–19); Edward Villiers, Viscount Villiers (d. 1711) who was created earl of Jersey in October 1697.

52 In this sentence, the word means attendants or heralds. In the next sentence, the king-at-arms is the chief herald (in charge of the granting of armorial bearings) and the pursuivants-at-arms are his assistants.

53 A suffragan bishop is either an assistant bishop or one lower in rank than an archbishop. ('Suffragant' was an acceptable spelling in the seventeenth century).

54 Joseph Boyse (1660–1728), Presbyterian minister in Dublin from 1683 until his death. See n. 9 in *Notes to pages 151–91* on p. 323.

55 Nathaniel Weld (d.1730), the Presbyterian minister in New Row.

56 i.e. a sword used to fight in this world—as opposed to a spiritual sword.

57 Ir. *rapaire*; an Irish foot-soldier or, as defined by G.W. Story in 1691: 'such of the Irish as are not of the Army, but the Country people armed in a kind of an hostile manner with Half-Pikes and Skeins, and some with Sythes, or Musquets' (quoted in Bliss, p. 267.) King's County is now Co. Offaly.

58 It was illegal for a Catholic to carry arms at this time.

59 a battle-axe or, perhaps, a butcher's axe. The use of the term Teig (sometimes 'Teague') (Ir. *Tadhg*) for a native Irishman—see the next sentence—was common among the English in seventeenth-century Ireland.

60 Catholics, referring to the extensive use of red ink in printed Roman breviaries.

61 to look upon with the 'evil eye', to bewitch.

62 violent.

63 This passage is clearly copied from another text, currently unidentified.

64 Dunton had published William Turner's substantial folio *A Complete History of the Most Remarkable Providences, both of Judgment and Mercy, which have hapned in this present Age* … in April 1697. See Parks 282.

65 Scotland.

66 Vespasian (9–79 AD), emperor of Rome, was noted for his avarice.

67 a liquid measure of about two litres.

68 This reference is explained in n. 8 to *The Fourth Letter*, p. 313.

69 The Dublin printers and publishers mentioned in this paragraph are Joseph Ray of Skinner Row, John Ware of High Street, Josias Shaw of Cork Hill and John Foster or Forster of Skinner Row. Robert Thornton the King's Stationer (mentioned in the preceding paragraph) had his shop in Essex Street at this time.

70 Dunton's name for the Presbyterian printer and bookseller Eliphal Dobson (d.1720). *Crepitus ossium* means 'cracking of the bones'.

71 *The Squire of Alsatia* is one of the best plays of Thomas Shadwell (1642?–92). The 'Alsatians' in the play are rogues who dupe the gullible 'squire' using a very funny argot or jargon. William Smith Clark gives a useful summary of the significance of Dunton's account of his visit to Smock Alley in *The Early Irish Stage* (Oxford, 1955), pp. 105–8.

72 i.e. to call over. A 'China orange' was a sweet one—as opposed to a bitter 'Seville' orange; it was believed that sweet oranges came from China.

73 These were small rooms, provided with latticed casement windows, situated over the doors which led onto the actual stage and positioned at the same level as the middle gallery of the auditorium. They were used as upper rooms or balconies in some productions but, when not in use for that purpose, were rented out as boxes to richer members of the audience—particularly to 'ladies of quality' who could adjust the windows so that they could be seen by or hidden from the main audience. The 'lattices', which were unique to the Dublin stage, were often known as 'lettices'. See Clark, *The Early Dublin Stage*, p. 55.

74 now West Essex Street.

75 cheated, tricked. 'rino' was a slang word for money.

76 James Butler, 2nd duke of Ormonde (1665–1745).

77 Dr Nathaniel Wood of Kilkenny, physician. Dunton gives a 'character' of him at p. 215.

78 Robert Wilks, active in Dublin theatres between 1688 and 1699.

79 William Norman of Dame Street.

80 Two famous painters of the classical world.

81 flowerbeds.

82 nipple.

83 The organised body which gave legal status to and provided controls for the stationers (i.e. all those involved in the book trade) of Dublin was the Guild

of St Luke the Evangelist. Two other trades, the cutlers and the painter-stainers, belonged to the same body. See Pollard, pp. 5–6 and Phillips, pp. 3–25. William Norman was Master of the Guild in 1698.

84 Andrew Crook's printing works were in Copper Alley.

85 though the food and drink he provided were very elegant …

86 A member of the English rather than the Irish parliament.

87 Dunton probably wrote this couplet himself.

88 William, Lord Russell (1639–1683), known as 'the patriot', was beheaded in 1683 for his part in the Rye House plot.

89 Sir Henry Ingoldsby (or Engoldesby) had been governor of Limerick in the 1650s. He was at this time MP for Co. Clare in the Irish parliament.

90 A poet who does not seem to have published anything nor to have left any manuscripts.

91 Samuel Annesley, Dunton's first father-in-law, was a nephew of the 1st earl of Anglesea.

92 The reference must be to Dunton's father-in-law, the Reverend Samuel Annesley who died in December 1696. The term 'brother' seems to refer to the idea that any two practising Christians are 'brothers-in-Christ'.

93 *Memoirs of the Right Honourable Arthur Earl of Anglesea, late Lord Privy Seal* (London, 1693), Parks 182.

94 Captain and Mrs Townley and Madam Congreve are untraced.

95 Untraced.

96 Elnathan Lum, member in the Irish parliament for the borough of Carlingford.

97 Henry Davis the young MP for Carrickfergus or John Davis, member for Kildare.

98 No published poetry by Mrs Taylor has survived.

99 Mr Thwaits and Mr Dangerfield are untraced.

Notes to pages 191–234

1 See n. 3 in *Notes to pages 151–191*, p. 323.

2 'his' is clearly a misprint for 'her': Dunton means to say that the husband will be overcome by the patience of his wife.

3 David Clarkson (1622–86), Congregational minister in London, who published many works condemning episcopacy and Roman Catholicism.

4 the lowest rank of commissioned officer.

5 Probably Caleb Young, who entered TCD in 1690 at the age of 16: he became a scholar in 1693, BA in 1695 and MA (which entitled him to be called 'Mr') in 1698.

6 monopolised.

7 Mr Alexander Sinclare, minister to the Scottish Presbyterian congregation in Bull Alley.

8 Thomas Emlyn (1663–1741), minister to the English Presbyterian congregation in Wood Street, later famous as the first Unitarian minister in England.

9 *A Sermon preach'd before the societies for reformation of manners in Dublin, October the 4th, 1698 by Tho. Emlyn* (Dublin, 1698).

10 Nathaniel Weld, minister to the congregation in New Row.

11 Wentworth Harman, member of the Irish parliament for Co. Longford.

12 Sir Kenelm Digby (1603–1665) author, naval commander and diplomat who claimed to have discovered a sympathetic powder for the cure of wounds.

13 The man Dunton called 'Brass' and referred to several times throughout this book as 'the Brass in Copper Alley' was probably Samuel Adey or Edy, the only bookbinder known to have been active in Copper Alley at the time of Dunton's Irish visit.

14 Patrick Campbell.

15 a cheap warrant.

16 as you have had to address letters to me at several different lodgings …

17 lawyer.

18 These lines are probably by Dunton himself.

19 Dunton's first love.

20 *The Poems and Fables of John Dryden* ed. James Kinsey (Oxford, 1958).

21 Many editions of *Æsop's Fables*—though, surprisingly, not the 1692 translation by Sir Roger L'Estrange, contain versions of the well-known story of the fox who wanted grapes but could not reach them.

22 the Curragh (racecourse).

23 a cordial distilled from milk and herbs.

24 dysentery.

25 I Corinthians xv. 32.

26 Cowley's retreat was near Chertsey, west of London. He retired there in 1665.

27 The Old Testament patriarch who is said to have been 969 when he died (Genesis v. 27).

28 An exact translation is: 'He who has hidden well [i.e. lived a quiet life] has lived well.'

29 The fourth member of the house of Habsburg to hold the title of Holy Roman Emperor, Charles V (1500–58) was famous not only as a great warrior but also because, in old age, he abdicated and retired to a humble house in the south of Spain.

30 i.e. one I pretend is like Draper's Gardens [in London] … etc.

31 a kind of thread lace made wholly with a needle.

32 left.

33 The name given by the Turks to the port which served the city of Aleppo, about sixty miles (thirty leagues) inland. It was also known as Alexandretta and is now the city of Iskenderun in southern Turkey.

34 native Irish men and women. The phrase was particularly common in the late seventeenth century. Laurence Eachard wrote in 1691 that: The Irish 'are vulgarly called by the names of *Teague* and *Dear-Joy*' (quoted in Bliss p. 265).

35 This passage has puzzled commentators. Elrington Ball's conjecture (*A History of the County of Dublin*, six vols., Dublin 1906, iv, 173) that 'the house of Cabinteele' was 'a favourite house of entertainment' where mock

investitures took place is probably correct. Certainly there was no real-life Lord Clonuff. Dunton's later reference to Lady Swancastle of Cow-Lane (p. 253) seems to confirm that the whole thing was an elaborate joke.

36 Proteus, son the Poseidon, god of the sea in Greek mythology, could change shape at will.

37 the small bowl at which the large bowls are aimed.

38 beside.

39 A tray into which dirty dishes and fragments of broken food are placed during the meal or when the table is being cleared.

40 paradise.

41 It was not uncommon in the seventeenth century for a portrait painter to complete merely the head of the sitter, the remainder of the painting being filled in later by others.

42 A sketch from which the duke's picture would be painted.

43 Thomas Wentworth, 1st earl of Strafford (1593–1641) Charles I's lord deputy and lord lieutenant in Ireland. Caught up in the struggle between the king and parliament, Strafford was executed 1641.

44 Mary of Modena (1658–1718), second wife to James II.

45 The dukes of Ormonde were related to the Stuarts—and so to the reigning Queen Mary and her sister the future Queen Anne—through James II's first wife Anne Hyde. The display of royal portraits, including those of the deposed James II and his queen was, thus, not inappropriate.

46 This picture still hangs in Kilkenny castle.

47 Henrietta Maria (1609–1669), queen of England and wife of Charles I seems to be the queen referred to here. She had a reputation as a devout and fervent Catholic which may well have been what sparked this unworthy comment from the prejudiced, Protestant Dunton. The 'Queen Dowager' in the next line is Catherine of Braganza (1638–1705) who outlived her husband, Charles II, by twenty years.

48 Sir Anthony Van Dyck (1599–1641), employed as portrait painter by both James I and Charles I.

49 The 'scotch lord' in this painting is Lord Mungo Murray, younger son of the earl of Atholl. See Jane Fenlon, 'John Michael Wright's "Highland Laird" identified', *Burlington Magazine*, October 1988, 767–9.

50 These seem to be the words Dunton hears being used by those playing bowls: a 'rub' is an impediment which hinders or diverts a bowl from its proper course and to 'cast' can be used of the action of bowling the ball.

51 Colley Cibber (1671–1757), poet, actor and playwright.

52 bows.

53 Dunmore House, a large house four miles from Kilkenny, was owned by successive countesses of Ormonde. It had been extensively refurbished shortly before Dunton's visit. Dr Thomas Molyneux, visiting Kilkenny in 1709, reported that the main part of the house had, at that stage, been demolished (TCD MS 883/2,92) but other accounts state that the house merely fell into decay later in that century. (This information kindly supplied by Dr Jane Fenlon.)

54 entertained [us] to food and drink.

55 Though they are quite irrelevant in this context, Dunton here quotes two stanzas from one of Swift's early pindaric odes, 'To the King on his Irish expedition'. He also seems to lay claim to authorship of the lines since he dedicates them to the memory of the French brigadier immediately after the quotation, and since they are referred to as Dunton's in the final *Letter from an Honourable Lady* (p. 290). There is little doubt, however, that the lines are by Swift. Until recently (June 2000), it was thought that, apart from this appearance of the first two stanzas, the earliest printing of the poem was in the rare fourth volume of Samuel Fairbrother's Dublin 1735 *Miscellanies begun by Jonathan Swift D.D. and Alexander Pope, Esq... to which are added several other poems...* (Teerink/Scouten 4). However, Professor James Woolley has unearthed a probably unique copy of a 1691 printing of the poem in the Derry and Raphoe Diocesan Library—G.II.b. 14 (8)—an article on which is forthcoming in the *Proceedings of the Fourth Münster Symposium on Jonathan Swift*. The poem was printed by the Dublin printer, John Brent. This discovery renders invalid the extensive earlier speculation on how Dunton knew of this text, particularly comments by Harold Williams and Pat Rogers in their editions of Swift's poetry (Oxford, 1958, i, 6–7 and London, 1983, p. 601 respectively) and articles by Irvin Ehrenpreis in *Modern Language Review* xlix (1954), 210–11 and Mackie L. Jarrell in *Texas Studies in Literature and Language* 7 (1965), 145–59.

56 abatement.

57 get up on his feet in such a way.

58 a clyster-pipe, used for giving an enema.

59 Ellis Walker (b. 1671, BA TCD 1682) whose verse translation of the works of the Greek stoic philosopher Epictetus was first published in 1692.

60 See n. 3 in *Notes to pages 151–191*, on p. 323.

61 Owen Felltham (1602?–1668) author of a series of moral essays called *Resolves*.

62 Since the owl was the emblem of Athens, it was appropriate that Dunton, as founder of the Athenian Society, should keep one as a pet. The references in the following lines are to *Maggots: or Poems on several Subjects ...* by Samuel Wesley which Dunton had printed in 1685. The volume includes a poem 'On a Cow's Tail'.

63 A village near the Curragh, Co. Kildare, which, in the seventeenth century —as now—was an important venue for horse-racing in Ireland.

64 a livery stable.

65 As usual, Dunton gives his companion an obscure classical name.

66 i.e. if they had a few drinks, the journey would pass more quickly.

67 who stabbed herself, according to legend, after being dishonoured.

68 Seaton.

69 To 'imp' is to graft feathers onto a bird's wing in order to improve its flight.

70 Parts of the descriptions of Irish life which are contained in the next few pages are taken from *A Brief Character of Ireland* (London, 1692); other

passages are repeated in the manuscript of Dunton's 'A Summer Ramble'. See the introduction.

71 Ir. *cadódh*, a rough woollen or frieze covering or cloak. to 'ligg' means to lie.

72 shut up away from its mother.

73 For an extended passage of Hiberno-English in Dunton's work, with a full linguistic analysis, see Dunton's 'Report of a Sermon' in Bliss, pp. 133–7 and notes.

74 In Greek mythology, Thesis was one of the sea deities and Apollo was one of the names of the sun-god, Phoebus.

75 horse.

76 the centre of horseracing in seventeenth-century England.

77 founder and queen of Carthage in North Africa.

78 One of the patrons of Ireland, who lived in the fifth and sixth centuries.

79 Ir. *deoch an dorais* means a stirrup-cup or parting drink.

80 now Co. Offaly.

81. sulphur.

82 Those who delight in sensual pleasures—though this meaning derives from a misunderstanding of the teachings of the Greek philosopher, Epicurus.

83 Robert Boyle (1627–91), one of the greatest natural philosophers and scientists of the age.

84 i.e. in about 25,000 years—the time it would take the stars and constellations to go through all their movements once, according to the pre-Copernican theory of the universe.

85 King of Lydia in the sixth century BC, said to be the richest man on earth.

86 those dependent on charity.

87 point beyond which it is not possible to go.

88 These verses are probably the work of Dunton himself.

89 i.e. yet being for the most part [inhabited by] thieves and idlers … Again, many passages in the descriptions printed over the next few pages are taken, without acknowledgement, from *A Brief Character of Ireland*. See introduction.

90 wealth.

91 i.e. Ireland as a whole is a White Friars (properly a church served by friars of the Carmelite order but here used to mean a place where one is cheated) and Dublin the centre where the thievery is hatched.

92 i.e. someone sitting on the roadway, or some wandering, unsatisfied harlot who drinks nothing but terrible, cheap white wine …

93 A common punishment for prostitutes was to be whipped at the cart's tail—i.e. tied, half-naked, to the back of a cart and whipped as the cart went through the streets.

94 in this context, a chapman is a customer.

95 i.e. an account of something fantastic. The *Travels* of Sir John Mandeville (1371) describe the marvels he saw in the east, many of which were clearly too fantastic to be genuine.

96 describe.

97 false evidence.

98 See above, n.70.
99 cosmetics.

Notes to pages 234–70

1 Ir. *bainne clabair* (milk ready to be churned) and Ir. *mulchán*. Bliss (pp. 271–3) discusses these words, their meanings and their derivations at some length. Briefly, bonny-clabber was soured, clotted milk and mulahaan, mullagham or mallabanne was a kind of cheese made from buttermilk. 'Choak cheese' is a variant of the English dialect word 'choke-daw', a kind of hard cheese. This passage is copied verbatim from the anonymous *A Brief Character of Ireland* (1692) (Sweeney 702). See introduction.
2 smock, undergarment.
3 hypocrites.
4 Ir. *ochón*, alas.
5 In fact, as explained in the introduction, the book from which Dunton lifts much of the material in this section is *A Brief Character of Ireland* (London, 1692).
6 George Herbert, 'The Church Porch' (1633).
7 This famous London bookseller had connections with the Dublin book trade. See Pollard, p. 93.
8 Money paid by those who declined to take up public office.
9 'St Patrick' seems to stand for Ireland in this passage and 'Patrick' for an Irishman—not, as usually with Dunton, for Patrick Campbell. The passage as a whole is very surprising as it seems to contradict all Dunton's other references to Richard Wilde.
10 The Liberties are small areas of Dublin city which, in medieval times, enjoyed self-government. Though the Reformation brought about changes in their relationship with both church and city government, the Dublin Liberties were still 'governed', in a sense, by those whose names they bore in the late seventeenth century. The most important liberties at that time were those of the dean and chapter of St Patrick's—which Swift was to 'rule' over with some pleasure some years later—and that belonging to the earl of Meath.
11 i.e. to leave the house where they were confined during their illness. 'Gossips' were godmothers.
12 smothered. (Babies often slept in the same beds as their wet-nurses and this form of death was not uncommon in the seventeenth century.)
13 of a swarthy complexion.
14 which has no equal.
15 i.e. the anatomists had asked for his body for dissection.
16 Henry Bouchier (d.1654), one of the early fellows of Trinity College Dublin, became 5th earl of Bath in 1627. His widow, Rachel, spent £200 on books for the college library as a memorial to him (John William Stubbs, *The History of the University of Dublin*, Dublin, 1889, p. 110). The books remain in the Trinity College collection, complete with 'the Earl's arms impressed on

them'; a catalogue of the Bath collection (produced in *c*.1720) is in the manuscript room of the TCD library. [My thanks to Charles Benson, Keeper of Printed Books at Trinity College, for information for this note.]

17 Luke Challoner (1550–1613), not the first provost of Trinity College, but vice-chancellor from 1612.

18 Charles Gwithers MD, a medical colleague of the famous William Molyneux and a member of the Dublin Philosophical Society. According to Theo Hoppen (who quotes from it in *The Common Scientist in the Seventeenth Century* (London, 1970), pp. 180–1), Gwithers published an extraordinary paper on physiognomy in *Philosophical Transactions*—a paper so bizarre that it attracted the attention of John Evelyn.

19 John Minshull, who had been at school in Chester, was admitted to TCD in July 1695 at the age of seventeen. He became a scholar of the college in 1697.

20 In almost every case, the university buildings which Dunton saw were replaced by new ones during the eighteenth century.

21 i.e. a box hedge. A 'gnomon' is the rod in the centre of the sundial, the shadow of which shows the time.

22 George Browne (b.1660), provost of Trinity College, 1695–9.

23 'In the circumstances'—a phrase used by Cicero in his *Letters to Atticus* 7.8.2, and elsewhere.

24 Nahum Teate (afterwards Tate) (1652–1714), later poet laureate. The Ode was issued as a separately-printed broadside in Dublin in January 1694. (Sweeney 4938). [The date given for the centenary festivities a few lines earlier is the 'Old Style' date.]

25 the rivers in Oxford and Cambridge.

26 Trinity College was founded by Queen Elizabeth I.

27 i.e. William and Mary, on the throne jointly at the time of this centenary celebration.

28 A student chosen as orator, one of whose duties was to deliver a satirical speech, in a mixture of English and dog-Latin, at conferring ceremonies.

29 'I have sinned'. For details on Colonel Butler, see n. 1 to *The Dedication*.

30 'prick' means (here) a small point. The phrase means that, on maps of the world, a county takes up only a small space and a city is no more than a dot.

31 A celebrated patron of the arts in classical Rome.

32 Lady Jane Grey (1537–54), declared queen of England on the death of Edward VI, but only 'reigned' for nine days. Executed by order of her successor, Mary I.

33 Dunton claims here (and elsewhere in the book) that Irish gentlemen greeted and parted from each other with a kiss on the cheek as a sign of affection.

34 now Bride Street.

35 Another reference to the fable told in some editions of Æsop's fables of the fox who wanted grapes but could not reach them.

36 a general term for any wheeled vehicle.

37 now Townsend Street.

38 a coin worth 4*d*.

39 i.e. Dunton paid Read every three months.

40 (rented) house.

41 A lane which ran from Castle street to Fishamble Street. For 'Lady Swancastle', see above, n. 35 in *Notes to pages 191–234*, on p. 328.

42 The source of this verse has not been traced, and it is probably by Dunton himself. The lines are addressed to George Larkin who sailed to England with Dunton (p. 103) and his wife, called here by the name 'Chrit'. The classical references, to Nestor and to the Sibyl of Cumae, are to two figures famed for being very old.

43 William Turner, *A Compleat History of the Most Remarkable Providences …* published by Dunton in London in 1697.

44 The standard medical textbooks of the seventeenth century were by Dr Thomas Willis (1621–75) and Dr William Harvey (1578–1657).

45 medicinal herb.

46 reduce.

47 Richard Allestree, *The Whole Duty of Man* (London, 1658).

48 See above, n. 19 in *Notes to pages 191–234*, on p. 324.

49 See above, n. 4 to *The Tenth Letter*', on p. 315.

50 Cornelius Carter (d.1734). As Munter says (*Dictionary of the Print Trade in Dublin* p. 51), Dunton was taken in by Carter, a notorious rogue who printed false news and an error-ridden New Testament, and who forged imprints of other printers.

51 Jacob Milner (d.1701). He was involved in the Hodder and Cocker affair with Patrick Campbell in 1698. See above, n. 8 to *The Fourth Letter*. 'His man Shepherd' was probably Thomas Sheppard who set up as a bookseller in Dublin in 1704.

52 swarthy.

53 whimsical fancies.

54 A 'low' seventeenth-century word for a privy.

55 defined in a seventeenth-century word-list as 'a wencher'.

56 cuckold.

57 A board of wood one inch in thickness.

58 looking through a noose.

59 arse. i.e. he will be whipped at the cart's tail (see above, n. 93 in *Notes to pages 191–234*), p. 327.

60 citizens.

61 Actæon was the mythological huntsman changed into a stag when he saw the goddess Diana naked, and subsequently eaten by his dogs—but the reference here is obscure. A word may have been omitted after 'Actæon's'.

62 i.e. priests. Dunton's father, grandfather and great-grandfather (all bearing the name John Dunton) had been clergymen in the Church of England.

63 Dunton himself was author of this line which is in *A Congratulatory Poem to the Ministers' Sons* which he printed in 1682 (Parks 6).

64 animated.

65 care about.

66 condemn.

67 secret purpose.

68 something abnormal.

69 The *London Spy* was a short-lived periodical by Edward Ward (1667–1731). The first issue appeared in November 1698.

70 Samuel Butler (1612–80), author of one of the most celebrated satires of the seventeenth century, *Hudibras,* died in poverty; 'tick' means credit.

71 This poet appears to have left no publications.

72 i.e. I would not mind anyone knowing what is in my thoughts.

73 This seems to be an imitation of a rustic (a 'downright person') saying 'I is' for 'I am'.

74 leaving this fault out of account …

75 John Oldham (1653–83), poet and friend of Dryden.

76 This remark seems to be linked to the saying 'Eaten bread is forgotten'.

77 written material purchased by a publisher and ready for printing.

78 customers.

79 go off and call for it but not get it.

80 i.e. jealously watchful of himself (and so a traitor to himself). The next two pages are an elaborate 'poetical fiction' (p. 269) in which Dunton allows himself an extended and elaborate whimsical fantasy. He personifies one side of his character (the treacherous side which will 'suppress letters, merely to carry on a correspondence of his own with the same persons' etc.) as 'Argus'; this side of him (attached to the rest of his character as it indubitably is) has clearly been in Ireland and Dublin and plans to go to Scotland and to Rome. Dunton could 'despair of catching' this treacherous side of himself but he could 'search after' it by writing a pamphlet or by writing poems (which would explain the references to Helicon—the haunt of the muses).

81 This seems to be an amalgamation of 'to wear the bays' meaning to be the victor in a competition and 'to wear the laurels', meaning to have poetic skill.

82 In this long paragraph, Dunton engages in a frantic search for the 'Argus' side of his character (see above, n. 80). He imagines himself asking if any of those he has met in his travels—Read, Lucas, Simon, the old gentleman, a certain Frenchman etc.—can help him find 'Argus' and ends up searching 'all the gibbets in Christendom' for the side of himself which 'betrays his trust' (p. 269). The picture of the fantasy world is heightened by references to *Don Quixote* and by the introduction of 'my friend Ignotus (unknown)'. This is the most inventive, energetic and original passage in the book.

83 *The First and Best Part of Scoggin's Jests*, a well-known joke-book attributed —without any real evidence—to Andrew Boorde (?1490–1549), physician and cleric who wrote the first handbook of Europe and gave the first account of the language of the gypsies. *Scoggin's Jests* was first printed in London in the early seventeenth century and frequently reprinted.

84 *Sir Bevis of Hamton* was a medieval chivalric romance and the *Travels of Tom Coriat,* though untraced, is probably another such tale.

Remarks on my Conversation in Ireland by an Honourable Lady (pp. 273–305)

1 Dunton's female friend, identified only as 'D—ne'.

2 I Corinthians i, 12.

3 Albertus Magnus (1206-80), scholastic philosopher and churchman: Thomas Aquinas was his pupil.

4 According to church calendars, Sunday is the first day of the week.

5 activated.

6 Since Port-Royal, a convent near Versailles, was famous as a centre of Jansenism, and since the 'Honourable Lady' was as fervent a Protestant as Dunton himself, this must be a private (possibly jocose) nickname for the place where the lady lived.

7 Joseph Hall (1547–1656), bishop of Exeter and of Norwich.

8 i.e. but since the popish priests have developed the art of living in secret …

9 A reference to Louis XIV's revocation of the Edict of Nantes (1685).

10 See above, p. 200.

11 Sir Peter Pett (1630–99), a Fellow of the Royal Society and a patron of Dunton.

12 The central tenets of the Church of England (and of the Church of Ireland) are the Thirty-Nine Articles of Faith to which all ordained clergy must subscribe.

13 There was enormous interest in stories of witches and apparitions in the late seventeenth century. The most popular book on the subject was Joseph Glanvil's *Saducismus Triumphatus: or Full and plain Evidence concerning Witches and Apparitions* (London, 1681). Some of the accounts of supernatural events included in the second part of that book, particularly the section 'Proof of Apparitions, Spirits, and Witches, from a choice Collection on Modern Relations' (and its extensive continuation) come from Ireland. The 'Honourable Lady' here offers an explanation of the ghostly experience of Mary Gossom which had been mentioned by Dunton on p. 196.

14 For Charles V, see above, n. 29 in *Notes to pages 191–234*, p. 328. 'Valdesso' was the Italian form of the name of Juan de Valdes (*c.*1500–41), an influential Spanish religious writer who is said to have been appointed secretary to the viceroy of Naples by Charles V in the 1530s. He certainly lived in Naples and was known to Charles V through his twin brother Alphonso de Valdes (*c.*1500– 32), a senior figure in the emperor's court.

15 pledge, foretaste.

16 See above, n. 35 in *Notes to pages 191–234*, p. 328.

17 Ahasuerus was king of the Medes and Persians. The quotation comes from Esther v, 13.

18 i.e. the poem by Swift at pp. 215-16 above.

19 encounters

20 source unknown.

21 I Timothy v, 5–6.

22 meaning unclear.

23 whimsy.

24 The priests of the city of Dan made graven images. See Judges xviii.

25 The religious community at Port-Royal, near Paris, was a famous centre of
Jansenist thought during the seventeenth century. The reference here seems
to be to an English translation of a book by Pierre Nicole (1625–95). The
book was printed in London in 1696 by Samuel Manship, a stationer with
whom Dunton sometimes co-published books (see Parks 157), and was
entitled: *Moral Essays, contain'd in several treatises on many important duties:
Written in French by Messieurs du Port Royal. Done into English by a person of
quality. First Volume.*

26 Elizabeth I. See above p. 246.

27 i.e. bags of money.

28 Petrus Jurieu (1639–1713), French Protestant divine.

29 During the 1690s, an annual musical festival was held in the London
Stationers' Hall to celebrate the feast day of St Cecilia, the patron saint of
music. Dunton, as a liveryman of the Stationers' Company, would have
attended these events. The lines quoted here, which are presumably from one
of the many odes composed for this occasion at this time, are so far untraced.

30 trade, business.

31 satire, criticism of your character.

32 See nn. 80 and 82 in *Notes to pages 234–270*, p. 335.

Appendix

Checklist of Dublin Booksellers, Stationers and Binders mentioned in the text, with the addresses from which they operated in 1698

Adey (or Edy), Samuel, Copper Alley (probably the bookbinder Dunton called 'the Brass of Copper Alley').

Bentley, John, at the corner of St Nicholas Street, over against the Tholsel.

Brent, John, at the back of Dick's Coffee House, Skinner Row.

Brocas, John, at the back of Dick's Coffee House, Skinner Row.

Campbell, Patrick, at the Blue Bible, Skinner Row.

Carter, Cornelius, at the back of Dick's Coffee House, Skinner Row.

Crook, Andrew, Copper Alley.

Cumpstey or Cumpsty, Andrew, at the sign of the Royal Exchange, on the Wood Key.

Dobson, Eliphal, at the Stationers' Arms, Castle Street.

Forster (or Foster), John, at the King's Arms, Skinner Row.

Gun, Matthew, at the Bible and Crown, near Essex Street Gate.

Gun, Nathaniel, at the Bible, Essex Street, Essex Gate.

Milner (or Miller), Jacob, Essex Street over against Essex Bridge.

Norman, William, at the Rose and Crown, Dame Street.

Powell, Stephen, at the back of Dick's Coffee House, Skinner Row.

Pue, Richard, at the back of Dick's Coffee House, Skinner Row.

Ray, Joseph, Skinner Row, opposite the Tholsel.

Servant, Thomas, Golden Lane.

Shaw, Josias, Russel's Coffee House, Cork Hill.

Sheppard, Thomas, apprentice. Later bookseller near the Horse Guard, Dame Street.

Thornton, Robert, Capel Street or Essex Street.

Ware, John, over against St Michael's Church, High Street.

Whalley, John, at the Blew Posts, next door to the Wheel of Fortune, on the west side of St Stephen's Green (and also at premises) next door to the Fleece, St Nicholas Street.

Index

Absalom, 137

Abimelech, 131

Abu Amir al-Mansur, 313n

Actaeon, 261

Adey (or, Edy), Samuel, Dublin bookbinder, 328n; *see also* Brass in Copper Alley.

Aesop, 147, 201, 310n, 322n, 333n

Ahaseurus, 289, 336n

Albert the Great, St (Albert Magnus), 274, 336n

Aleppo, 207

Allestree, Richard, author of *The Whole Duty of Man*, 321n, 334

Almanzor, 35, 74, 313n

Anabaptist preacher in Francis Street, 153

Annesley, Capt., son of earl of Anglesey, 189

Annesley, Dr Samuel, Dunton's father-in-law, 194, 252, 322n, 327n

Annion, Capt., 101

Apelles, 200

Argus, husband of the Citizen's Wife, 7, 122ff.

Argus, Dunton's name for a side of his character, xiv, 267ff., 305

Art of Living Incognito, The by J. Dunton, xxv

Ashbury, Joseph, actor, 183

Ashe, St George, bishop of Clogher, 44ff., 96, 175, 238, 246, 313n

Aspin, Mr, 98

Aston Clinton, Bucks., 261

Athenian Mercury, ixff., xvii, 105, 308n, 312n

Athenian Society, ixff., 318n, 330n

Athlone, 280

Aughmuty, Capt. John, 100, 318n

Augustine, St, 105, 319n

Bacon, a porter, 167, 324n

Baldwin, A., London printer and bookseller, 119, 149, 271

Baldwin, Mr, Fellow of TCD, 97

Ball, Elrington, 328

Ballybaugh Lane, Dublin, 164, 324n

Ballymany, 201, 221, 224, 233, 258

Barn-Elms, Surrey, 203

Barnet, nr. London, 239

Barrett, John, vice-provost of TCD, 317n

Barrow, Dr Isaac, 33, 312n

Bath, Rachel countess of, 243, 332n

Bathsheba, 134

Battle-Axe Guard, 307n

Bennet, Thomas, London bookseller, 309n

Bentl(e)y, John Dublin bookseller employed by Dunton for bookbinding, 64, 65, 171, 172

Bible and Three Crowns, London, 32, 312n

Bible in Skinner Row, Dublin, Patrick Campbell's address, 31, 105

Bible, Syriac, 18, 310n

Billet Doux etc., The, xiii, 7, 8, 32, 117, 119–148, 267

Billingsgate, London, 209

Bishops Gate Street, 240

Black Raven in Jewen Street (Dunton's London address), 170, 318n, 325n

Bliss, Professor Alan, xxix, 308n

Blount, Sir Thomas Pope, x

'Bog-house', Robin, 259ff.

Bohun, Edmund, licenser of the press in London, 90, 316n

Bolingbroke, Viscount, xxvi

Bolton, Dr, 98

Bonny, Mr, attorney, 101

booksellers, list of Dublin 325n, 338n

Boorde, Andrew, 335n

Booth, Henry, 2nd Baron Delamere, 162, 324n

Boston, New England, viii

Bosworth, Mr, 208

Bourn, Mr, 208, 254

Lucas, Samuel, 42, 51
Lucretia, 118, 221
Ludlow, Stephen, MP, 318n
Lum, Elnathan, Irish MP and banker,
    28, 100, 190, 312n, 317n, 327n
Luttrell, Narcissus, xxvi

McEwen, Gilbert D., xxix, 317n
MacLysaght, Edward, xiii, 308n
McNeill, Charles, 308n
Magee, Mr, 201
Malahide, Co. Dublin, xxii, 201, 209,
    257
Mandeville, 233, 331n
Manship, Samuel, 310n, 337n
Mark Antony, 131, 321n
Marsh, Mr, 98
Marsh, Narcissus, archbishop of
    Dublin, 175
Martin, Samuel, attorney, 101
Mary of Modena, queen of England,
    211, 329n
Mary Stuart, queen of England, 248
Mather, Increase, president of Harvard
    College or his son Cotton, 91, 316n
Maxfield, Mr, 258
Meath, bishop of, 175, 246
Meath, countess of, 201
Meath, earl of, 99, 198, 228, 239, 332n
Mecaenas, 248
Millington, Edward, London book
    auctioneer, 113, 319n
Milner, (or Miller), Jacob, Dublin
    bookseller, 257, 313n, 334n
Milton, John, 33, 312n
Minshull, John, bookseller in Chester,
    244
Minshull, John, student at TCD, 243f.,
    333n
Molyneux, Dr Thomas, 329
Monmouth, duke of, viii, 320n
Montaigne, Michel de, 9, 85, 167, 278,
    316n
Montgomery, Sir Thomas, 219
More, Madam, 187, 190
Moss, Mr, attorney, 101
Moulins, Mr, 98
Mrs Ware, 202
Mulkins, Mr R., mayor of Kilkenny,
    213
Munter, Robert, 318n
Murray, Lord Mungo, 329n

Naas, Co. Kildare, 222, 226, 228
Nantes, edict of, 336n
Nashe, Thomas, 311n
Neck or Nothing by J. Dunton (1714),
    xxvi
Nelson, Thomas, employee of Dunton,
    167, 315n
New England, viii, 18, 104, 105, 171, 189,
    193, 262
New Voyage around the World, A, xxiii
Newmarket, 226
Newry, Co Down, 218
Nicole, Pierre, 337n
'Niff-Naff', nickname of Patrick
    Campbell, 11, 13, 29, 32, 309n
Nonconformists, 273, 284
Norman, William, bookseller in Dame
    St, Dublin, 185f., 326n, 327n
Norris, Henry, actor, 183

O'Brogan, Capt. Bryan, 184
O'Brogan, Philip, prince of Cavan, 184
Oldham, John, poet, xiv, 264n, 335n
Ormond, 2nd duchess of, 193, 326n
Ormond, duke of: *see* Butler, James
Ophir, 24
Orson, Thomas, D.'s landlord in
    Dublin, 203ff., 257
Osborn, George, attorney, 101
Overbury, Sir Thomas, xix, 92, 317n
Ovid, 125, 321n
Oxford Arms in Warwick Lane,
    London, 119, 149, 271

'Packing Penny', a Dunton
    advertisement, 53ff.
Palliser, William, archbishop of Cashel,
    175
Palmer, Julins, 64, 214n
Palmerstown, Co. Dublin, 209
Paphnutius, 137, 322n
Parkhurst, Thomas, London bookseller,
    viii, 312n
Parks, Stephen, introduction *passim*,
    xxixff., 316n
Parnassus, 23, 311n
Parsons, Mrs, 202
Pat's coffee house in High Street, 26,
    27, 39, 40, 151
Paul, St, apostle, 132, 135, 274, 290, 292,
    301
Pegasus, 24

INDEX

Sherlock, William, dean of St Paul's, 111

Sholdham, Mr, 101

Shore, Jane, 135, 322n

Silenus the satyr, 311n

Sinclare, Alexander, Scottish Presbyterian minister in Bull Alley, Dublin 194, 327n

Singleton, a young divine, 219

Skinner Row, xv, 12, 29, 251, 309n, 324n: *see also* Dick's coffee house

Smith, Dr, of College Green, 186, 198

Smith, John, attorney, 101

Smith, Mrs, actress, 183

Smock Alley, Dublin, xxii, 183, 326n

Solomon, 18, 23, 24, 25, 71, 127, 136, 266, 310n

Sparlin, Mr, in Dames Street, 257

Spira and *Second Spira*, ix, xii, xvii, 69, 89ff., 114, 115, 308n, 317n

Spira, Francis, 93, 308n

Spring-Gardens near Fox-hall, 213

Squire of Alsatia, 182, 326n

St Canice's cathedral, Kilkenny, 213

St Lawrence's coffee house on Cork Hill, 8, 122

St Luke the Evangelist, Guild of, 327n

St Michael's church, High Street, Dublin, 27, 98

St Patrick, Order of, 11

St Paul's Church-yard, London, centre of printing and bookselling, 32, 312n

St Stephen's Green, xxii, 248

Stanley, Thomas, 18n, 310n

Stationers' Hall, xx

Stearne, John, minister of St Nicholas' church and later bishop of Dromore and of Clogher, 97, 153, 317n

Stephen, King, 162, 324n

Stepney Fields, 205

Sterne, Lawrence, xxiv

Sternhold, Thomas, 158, 323n

Stevens, counsellor, 208

Stevens, Revd Mr, 87, 316n

Stonybatter, Dublin, 208

Stopford, Robert, 100

Story, G.W., 325n

Strafford, Lord: *see* Wentworth, Thomas

Strongbow, 21, 77, 311n

Sudal, Mr, 255f.

Summer Ramble, viii, xiii, xxiii, 19, 23, 33, 49, 53, 76, 104, 170, 171, 173, 179, 182, 184, 198, 201, 212, 213, 218, 221, 235, 238, 257, 289

'Swancastle, Lord', 253, 254

'Swancastle, Lady', 253, 329n, 334n

Sweeney, Tony, xxix

Swift, Jonathan, x, xi, xv, xx, xxiv, xxvi, 307n, 313n, 317n, 330n, 336n

Swords, Co. Dublin, 208

Synge, Dean, 98

T.B. (?Thomas Bennet, q.v.), 11, 13

T.F., unidentified London bookseller, 10, 82, 84, 85, 86, 108, 114, 115, 309n

T.W., 32

Tacitus, 131, 321n

Tarlaquin, 137

Tarquin, 118

Tate, Nahum, poet laureate, 158, 246, 297, 324n, 333n

Taylor, Jeremy, bishop of Down and Connor, 134, 321n

Taylor, Mrs, 191, 327n

'Teague Land' by John Dunton, 308n

Teague (Irishman), 232, 234, 325n, 328n

Temple, Sir William, x, xi

Tennis Court in Winetavern Street, 206ff

Terence, 219

Thamar, 131

Thetis, 225

Tholsel, Dublin, 167, 171, 172, 211, 251, 252, 324n

Thompson, Robert, 321n

Thornton, Robert, the King's stationer, 28, 42, 66, 182, 315n, 326n

Thucidides, 131, 321n

Thwaits, Mr, 191f., 327n

Tichbourn, Sir Henry, 100, 318n

Tillotson, John, archbishop of Canterbury, 91, 92, 316n

Townley, Capt., 190, 327n

Tracy, Patrick, 42, 254

Treatise on Fornication, 127

Trench, Dean, 98

Trench, Mr, 250

Trinity College, Dublin, 96ff., 167, 242ff., 260, 333n

Tunbridge Wells, 186, 187, 190f

Turner, William, author of *History of … Remarkable Providences*, 17, 28, 71, 180, 252, 310n, 311n, 315n, 326n, 334n

349